Ottoman Passports

Modern Intellectual and Political History of the Middle East
Fred H. Lawson, *Series Editor*

Select Titles in Modern Intellectual and Political History of the Middle East

Ottoman Passports

Passports

Security and Geographic Mobility, 1876–1908

İlkay Yılmaz

Syracuse University Press

CALOUSTE
GULBENKIAN
FOUNDATION

The translation of this work was supported by the Calouste Gulbenkian Foundation.

First Edition 2023

23 24 25 26 27 28   6 5 4 3 2 1

For a listing of books published and distributed by Syracuse University Press,
visit https://press.syr.edu.

ISBN: 978-0-8156-3818-6 (hardcover)
978-0-8156-3811-7 (paperback)
978-0-8156-5693-7 (e-book)

Library of Congress Cataloging-in-Publication Data

Names: Yılmaz, İlkay, 1981- author.
Title: Ottoman passports : security and geographic mobility (1876–1908) / İlkay Yılmaz.
Description: Syracuse : Syracuse University Press, 2023. | Series: Modern intellectual
and political history in the Middle East | Includes bibliographical references and index.
Identifiers: LCCN 2023006432 (print) | LCCN 2023006433 (ebook) |
ISBN 9780815638186 (hardcover) | ISBN 9780815638117 (paperback) |
ISBN 9780815656937 (ebook)
Subjects: LCSH: Passports—Turkey—History. | National security—Law and legislation—
Turkey—History. | Migration, Internal—Law and legislation—Turkey—History. |
Residential mobility—Turkey—History. | Turkey—Politics and government—1878–1909—
Sources. | Turkey—Foreign relations—Sources. | Abdülhamid II, Sultan of the Turks, 1842–1918.
Classification: LCC KKX3022.7 .Y55 2023 (print) | LCC KKX3022.7 (ebook) |
DDC 342.56108/2—dc23/eng/20230608
LC record available at https://lccn.loc.gov/2023006432
LC ebook record available at https://lccn.loc.gov/2023006433

Manufactured in the United States of America

Contents

Illustrations

Acknowledgments

I have written this book with the help of several institutions, colleagues, and fellowships. During my doctoral research, I had the opportunity to spend one year at Leiden University and benefited from Erik Jan Zürcher's advice and critiques. My adviser, Adalet B. Alada, always supported me with great patience. I had the privilege to get a Calouste Gulbenkian Foundation translation grant to translate my book, which was first published in Turkish in 2014 as *Serseri, Anarşist ve Fesadın Peşinde, II. Abdülhamid Döneminde Güvenlik Politikaları Ekseninde Pasaport, Mürür Tezkeresi ve Otel Kayıtları* (Istanbul: Tarih Vakfı Yurt) and translated into English by John William Day. Special thanks to Day for his careful translation of a difficult text.

I have revised the translated text and rewritten some of the sections by means of fellowships from Alexander von Humboldt Stiftung and the Einstein Foundation. I am grateful to Leibniz-Zentrum Moderner Orient not only for hosting me during this period but also for creating a safe space for my work during my exile in Berlin. I'm grateful for the discussions on my work, particularly to Ulrike Freitag, Malte Fuhrmann, Paolo Gaibazzi, Leonidas Karakatsanis, and Antia Mato Bouzas. I also thank the Friedrich Meinecke Institute and Oliver Janz at Freie Universität Berlin for hosting me during the last months of this work.

I am indebted to the administration of the Başbakanlık (now Cumhurbaşkanlığı) Osmanlı Arşivi (Prime Ministry Ottoman Archives), the İslam Araştırmaları Merkezi (Center for Islamic Studies), the Leiden University Library, and the Staatsbibliothek Berlin.

I thank two anonymous reviewers for their insightful comments on my manuscript. I am also grateful to the editors of Syracuse University

Press. Fatima Raja, with her extremely professional work, did the copy-editing of the revised version of my manuscript. I am indebted to her; she was always very careful about the details of my work and exceeded my expectations as a copy editor.

I was lucky to be showered with the love, friendship, and support of Özgün Basmaz, Yelda Kaya, Rita Ender, Çiçek İlengiz, Nicola Verderame, and Owen Miller.

My greatest gratitude goes to my family, Huriye, Zeki, and İlbay. I'm so lucky to have them. I thank them for supporting me even under extremely difficult political conditions and for teaching me to live an honorable life.

A Note on Transliteration
and Translation

Throughout the book, I have used the anglicized versions of some common Ottoman Turkish and Arabic words. Hence, I use the spellings *bey,* "Sharia," and *vizier,* but *paşa* instead of *pasha* and *kadı* instead of *qadi.* I chose to use the term *fesad* instead of its English translations "sedition," "seditious," "mischief," and "conspirator."

Transliterations are based on a modified version of the system used in the *International Journal of Middle East Studies.* However, I omitted the underdots on consonants and macrons on vowels.

As noted in the acknowledgments, John William Day translated the Turkish version of this book into English, and I revised parts of the translation. Thus, unless otherwise indicated in the notes and bibliography, all translations of Turkish text into English are Day's and mine.

Ottoman Passports

Introduction

In 2016, I was one of the signatories to a peace petition in Turkey titled "We Will Not Be Party to This Crime." It was a reaction to the state violence and securitization of the Kurdish issue. The petition demanded a return to the policies of the peace process that had aimed at ending the conflict between Turkey and the Kurdish armed guerilla movement (the Partiya Karkerên Kurdistanê [Kurdistan Workers Party]) but had been stopped in 2015. After we signed and submitted the petition, and while mobbing and disciplinary investigations were targeted against signatories from Istanbul University (seventy-two scholars), I received a phone call from the Istanbul Police Department informing me that a judicial investigation had been opened against me and my fellow signatories by the Terror and Organized Crime Section of the Chief Prosecutor's Office (İstanbul Cumhuriyet Başsavcılığı Terör Ve Örgütlü Suçlar Soruşturma Bürosu) in Istanbul. Instead of to the Istanbul Court (İstanbul Adliyesi), as is usual practice, my colleagues and I had to go to the Anti-Terror Section of the Istanbul Police Department to give our first statements. Beginning in March 2016, the first round of signatories (1,128 academics) was called in as "suspects" to give our initial testimonies against the charge of engaging in "propaganda in support of a terrorist organization."

Over the course of six months, from January 11 to July 15, 2016 (the date of the failed coup d'état), signatories of the petition also faced informal practices of "blacklisting." After the failed coup d'état, the government declared a "state of emergency" in Turkey, which lasted for two years. Over this period, 406 signatories of the peace petition, among other academics, were expelled through State of Emergency Decrees (Kanun Hükmünde Kararname), which could not be appealed in a court of law. Their passports were canceled indefinitely, and they were denied for life the right to work in any academic institution or the public sector in Turkey.

I was lucky enough to get a research grant at Leibniz Zentrum Moderner Orient. Just after arriving in Berlin, I learned from the Turkish consulate that my passport had been tagged as "suspect" in the Turkish police digital databases. For that reason, I did not return to Turkey for a year for fear of possible imprisonment and confiscation of my passport.

The trials against "Academics for Peace" started in December 2017. I was in the first group of fifteen people tried, and soon after the indictment the label *suspect* on my passport register was removed from the police databases. As with the trial itself, what was happening in my digital passport register was also arbitrary. Prepared by the Chief Prosecutor's Office (İstanbul Başsavcılığı) in Istanbul, the indictment charged the signatories with "making propaganda for a terrorist organization" (Antiterror Law [Terörle Mücade Kanunu], Art. 7/2). According to the decision of the 33. Heavy Criminal Court of Istanbul (İstanbul 33. Ağır Ceza Mahkemesi), eleven colleagues and I showed no regret for signing the petition. We were sentenced to twenty-seven months imprisonment under the Turkish Antiterror Law. Because this sentence was far more than two years, it could not be suspended (*sursis*). I was convicted on February 21, 2019. This arbitrary sentence was a violation not only of freedom of speech but also of academic freedom because my own statement at the court hearing was based on my academic work in the field of Ottoman–Turkish security history. I won my case in the Higher Court, and my sentence was canceled one year later.

Even though the Turkish police database labeled me "suspect," I was invited to give a talk in the United States. After the events of July 15, 2016, hundreds of thousands of Turkish passports were canceled based on the official reason that they were lost or damaged, although their bearers were never informed. With the declaration of the State of Emergency, the Turkish government performed this cancelation using the new technology of digital databases in the passport system.

Turkey is a member of Interpol (International Criminal Police Organization), and the cancelation of Turkish passports had international implications. The new security concept of "war on terror" that followed the attacks on the United States on September 11, 2001 (9/11), was utilized as a legitimization tool for new global passport technologies (such as digital biometric passports) and entry regulations. I could easily become a victim of these technologies while trying to travel for an academic talk because they were used as part of daily border controls, particularly at airports, and as part of larger discriminatory migration policies. These passport cancelations and labels in the databases were not the result of a judicial process but an administrative act in which the Turkish government entered these passports into the digital databases as being lost or damaged. The surveillance apparatus thus criminalized those who were marked by the political regime as "unwanted elements." With the passport cancelations, the Turkish government divided and separated its own citizens, and passports were used to exclude unwanted elements deemed a "threat to national security."

I arrived at the airport in the United States and waited for my passport check. As usual, a US border officer asked the reason for my visit and my occupation. When he learned that I was an historian working on passport history, he smiled and said: "You know better than me, this is all arbitrary. Right?" I answered: "I know, I know. But I guess we should play our parts. It's a theater at the end." We laughed, and he gave me the permission to pass.

Passports as Global Technologies

Nearly 115 years ago, a thirty-three-year-old Armenian woman named Margirid, the wife of Hachik, who was the son of Arvan, and her twelve-year-old daughter, Aznif, from the town of Çardak, Karahisar-ı Şarki, in Sivas, were given permission to leave for North America on the condition of no return to the Ottoman Empire. Their internal passports—which were required for travel within the empire and could also be used as identity documents in practice—were confiscated, and their international passports were inscribed with the sentence "No return to the Ottoman Empire henceforth." They were registered for immigration to America, which also meant the deprivation of their citizenship according to a decree aimed at Armenians. Their photographs were filed at the local police station and circulated to the Ministry of Interior (Dâhiliye Nezareti) and

Ministry of Foreign Affairs (Hariciye Nezareti) (figure 1).[1] The main reason for those bureaucratic regulations was that the Ottoman government suspected every Armenian who migrated to North America as a potential revolutionary, a conspirator against the Ottoman Empire. At the same time that the Ottoman government deprived Armenians who migrated to North America after 1896 of their citizenship rights, Armenians with US passports were not allowed to reenter the Ottoman Empire.[2] Margirid and Aznif were also the target of those regulations.

Unlikely though it seems, Margirid and Aznif's file was closely related to an event that shook another empire: the assassination of Empress Elizabeth of Austria-Hungary on September 10, 1898. In the wake of this assassination by the Italian anarchist Luigi Lucheni, the Italian government hosted the International Conference of Rome for the Social Defense against Anarchists (1898). This conference was one of the first interimperial collaborations that led to the founding of today's Interpol. The conference discussed how to define anarchists and anarchist acts as well as contemporary methods of policing, surveillance, and extradition. Passport technologies and practices were important for knowledge exchange on controlling geographical mobility and for interimperial information sharing as part of gathering intelligence on "suspects." The bureaucratic infrastructure of passport practices was later standardized internationally. This historical turn also affected Ottoman passport practices. The Ottoman Empire was one of the first states to actively use the new technologies of filing, registering, and circulating intelligence, which also involved the use of photographs, even before the conference.

In the nineteenth century, the intensity of migration and political developments of the time brought about new definitions of identification for states.[3] In particular, in the new system that emerged after the French Revolution, individuals became known in terms of their citizenship ties. As of September 20, 1792, the individual began to take on an existence solely in terms of the place where their identity was registered and according to their citizenship.[4] It became increasingly important for states to determine who their own citizens were. This determination occurred in one sense by demonstrating the uniqueness of every individual using

1. Margirid and Aznif, 1907. BOA, DH.TMIK.M, 255/26, 22 Şaban 1325
(Aug. 10, 1907), Başbakanlık Osmanlı Arşivi (Prime Ministry Ottoman
Archives), Istanbul. Courtesy of Devlet Arşivleri Başkanlığı—Cumhur-
başkanlığı Osmanlı Arşivi (Presidency of State Archives—Presidential
Ottoman Archives), Istanbul.

identity documents and in another by standardizing individual identity, reducing individuality to an impersonal unit within the classification systems created by the state.[5] Not only did these documents render the individual legible to the state, but the state also became visible through these types of documents: residence registries, travel permits, and work permits.

Passports were used as an intelligence resource of sorts and allowed for different restrictions or interventions for people belonging to different groups. Particularly in Europe, changes in passport practices during periods of revolution were significant.[6] Numerous examples show people being subjected to different practices according to their class position or ethnic origin.[7] In France's revolutionary period, controls that we might describe as passport practices were focused entirely on security and public order and were carried out in particular with the aim of preventing those groups defined as "vagrants" from freely changing places of residence.[8] The Regulation of 1791 in France, considered to be the beginning of the passport system in Europe, was based entirely on politics: it was created to be able to track nobles or counterrevolutionaries who wished to cross the border.[9] The Chinese in America,[10] Catholics and Poles in Germany,[11] the Irish in England,[12] and Roma peoples and other migrant poor populations nearly everywhere in Europe were perceived as suspicious individuals and were treated accordingly, including being subjected to deportation.[13] With the Revolutions of 1848 and the rise of socialism throughout Europe, many governments issued antisocialist laws.

In 1878, based on a claim that the public order was under threat, passport requirements for those arriving from elsewhere and permission to transit were reintroduced. In addition, particularly during times of political transformation, foreigners were seen as potentially dangerous elements in nearly every country. In France, although in theory the state recognized freedom of travel for its own citizens, in practice foreigners were kept under tight control through the Constitution of 1791, for which new methods were developed. Indeed, one might reasonably have the impression that the very word *foreigner* was understood to mean a person whose credibility was doubted.[14] On the basis of geopolitics, state elites defined threats to the survival of the state and, based on this definition, constructed a discourse of threat related to those coming from elsewhere.

This problematization of foreignness was directly related to the international system of states and is important in that it points to a period in which the structural basis of the state was transforming.

The Ottoman Empire and the Use of Passports

In the Ottoman Empire, instead of adopting a brand-new system, the state used traditional social control techniques along with the new administrative technologies to monitor and restrict geographical mobility. Such control was needed, it was felt, because of the clear limits to the state's infrastructural power. Borders were quite porous, and the central state's administrative apparatuses grew weaker the farther they stretched from the capital. The central state benefited from local traditions of registration[15] as the basic administrative level of its passport system from the 1840s on.

This book offers a fresh take on travel regulations and mobility restrictions in the late Ottoman Empire during the reign of Sultan Abdülhamid II, a period known as the Hamidian Era (1876–1908). It reconsiders the history of two political issues, the Armenian Question and the Macedonian Question, and investigates how the Hamidian government tried to govern these political problems by controlling geographical mobility. One of the significant questions in my research concerns how the Ottoman government concentrated on improving the state's capacity to create knowledge of the Ottoman population and implement political decisions throughout the realm using its administrative infrastructure. Unlike existing works, which have focused on these two political problems separately, I analyze them together, which has allowed me to draw on the history of both mobility restrictions and state control—for instance, regulations on passports and internal—travel permit systems within the context of a rapidly expanding Ottoman police state.

This book provides a global institutional history of mobility restrictions and state documentation, analyzing travel regulations and other security practices within the tumultuous political climate of the late Ottoman period. It explores the Ottoman government's mobility restrictions as part of its attempt to collaborate with joint European security efforts to form an interimperial criminal justice network against anarchism. At the Conference of Rome (1898) and at a later conference in St. Petersburg (1904), significant issues were raised, including record keeping, the setting up of institutions for the surveillance of suspected individuals, and the use of passports, travel permits, and hotel registrations. The Ottoman Empire was one of the governments participating in these conferences, which were themselves the first attempts to create international police cooperation. The new constellations of Ottoman passport practices were part of the everyday politics of security and can be examined only by placing them in the context of the Armenian and Macedonian Questions, both of which were centered in the frontier regions of the empire, as well as in the context of antianarchism during the late Ottoman Empire. This book explores how mobility restrictions became critical to targeting groups such as Armenians, Bulgarians, seasonal and foreign workers, and revolutionaries.

My work has three aims. First, it investigates the international and internal-security aspects of the Armenian and Macedonian Questions in the late Ottoman period. It analyzes how these two important political topics became issues of security for the Ottoman government. In doing so, this book discusses the different political demands not only of the political elites in Bulgarian and Armenian communities but also of revolutionaries, who were mobile both bodily and intellectually in the interimperial sphere. It further examines how international political conflicts affected the Ottoman government's approach to these issues. Macedonia and Eastern Anatolia were marked by interstate competition, paramilitary violence, and extralegal (state) violence. Instead of analyzing the two frontier regions as regional exceptions, this book examines them as part of the overall debates on state formation and addresses mobility controls in the discussions of control over territory and people. Second, it explores the violent tactics of revolutionaries and anarchists as well as the international police cooperation that emerged against such violence. Acts of terror became potent propaganda tools, and the Ottoman government responded with coercion, drawing on old and new security concepts to legitimize its newly oppressive tactics. The Ottoman government also joined in international security collaborations against anarchism as it sought to crack down on the overlapping categories of working-class foreigners, Armenians, and Bulgarians who were suspected of working against the regime. Third, the book takes up the official discourse surrounding mobility restrictions and how those restrictions played out in practice, comparing them to those being enacted in rival empires across Europe. In this way, the book situates the Ottomans within global debates on migration, border control, and police collaboration in the late nineteenth century. Taking up these new policies on surveillance, mobility, and control offers a timely look at the origins of contemporary immigration debates and the historical development of terrorism and counterterrorism.

Amid the radical currents that emerged in opposition during Sultan Abdülhamid II's reign (1876–1909), questions of mobility haunted Ottoman elites, who searched for new security tools to exert state control. As was the case elsewhere in the world, in the geography of empire, too, there was a great deal of geographical mobility. People changed places for a variety of reasons, not only to change homes. Thus, the concept of geographical mobility seems more apt than spatial mobility because the former includes smaller journeys, seasonal labor migration, and even constant relocation shaped by political mobilization. Thus, in this book the term *mobility* refers not only to emigration or immigration but also to all kinds of movement, whether voluntary travel or forced displacement.

In Russia and Europe, anarchists were deploying "propaganda by the deed," such as assassinations and bomb attacks, sparking antianarchist regulations. As the increasingly radical political opposition turned to violence that threatened the status quo, the Ottoman government grew more and more suspicious of particular classes of Bulgarians and Armenians, in particular those who were seasonal and transimperial workers. It deemed them and other imperial subjects as threats, potential revolutionaries, and members of secret societies. The government also became suspicious of the Armenian poor and Bulgarians who *might* join revolutionary circles. This book investigates Ottoman methods of control during this period and asks the following questions: First, what was the political context that shaped Ottoman security policies on geographical mobility? Second, which discursive traditions did the authorities draw on to define suspects, and how did they craft discourses to cast these groups as serious threats?

Finally, which mobility restrictions were enacted, and how did these measures play out in practice? To answer these questions, this book investigates not a specific region but a certain set of practices.

This work puts forward two main arguments. First, the regime's attempts at controlling mobility were directly connected to the central government's legitimacy crises, rising radical opposition, the increasing use of violence as revolutionary propaganda, and the loss of territories during the age of high imperialism. Second, mobility restrictions provide a useful indicator of the regime's power and a means for tracing long-term changes in Ottoman administrative practices. During the nineteenth century, the Ottoman Empire came under the influence of its imperial rivals, the European Great Powers. After the Treaty of Berlin (1878)—in which European diplomacy aimed to define and regulate notions of population (e.g., majority/minority) and state boundaries—the Ottoman government started to conceptualize its own internal problems with reference to European and Russian colonial expansion. As a result, it targeted internal threats to the regime with new security policies that created new categories of suspects. This process also produced a new regime of internal passports aimed at controlling the state's newly defined "internal enemies." Sovereignty, modern power, and security created new kinds of marginalities and helped the state define new classes of subjects. These marginalities were usually attached to an ethnic and/or class identity, which can be traced in emerging Ottoman passport practices. Challenges to sovereignty gave rise to new attempts to restrict mobility. Building on these concepts, this book argues that the intersections of sovereignty, modern power, and security can be discussed via passport policies during the Hamidian Era, based on voluminous correspondence and other documents in the Ottoman archives.

My own work began as an attempt to give meaning to state–society relations in the late nineteenth century. To narrow the scope of such a broad subject, and as a way of focusing on dominant understandings of public order during this period, I carefully studied the files of the Ottoman Ministry of Police (Zaptiye Nezareti), a unit of analysis that offered the most promise for this study. These files contain a large collection of documents related to multiple areas of everyday life, particularly for Istanbul. Yet the existence of a great many documents related to comings and goings in Istanbul and, in particular, the frequent use of the concepts of *fesad* (sedition, seditious, agitator) and *serseri* (vagrant) in these documents helped to give shape to my basic questions, which looked increasingly at the reasons for attempting to control geographical mobility in the reign of Abdülhamid II and at the apparatuses used for such controls. Archival work, which began with the files of the Ministry of Police, continued with a focus particularly on the files of the Commission for Expediting Initiatives and Reforms under the Ministry of Interior (Dâhiliye Nezâreti Tesri-i Muamelât ve Islâhat Komisyonu), which was founded after the Treaty of Berlin. As the archival documents made clear, state efforts to control geographical mobility through documents, records, and civil servants had opened a space for discussing the political order of the Hamidian Era. This study attempts to answer the following question: How, after the Congress of Berlin in 1878, did the state refashion the definition of "threat" in relation to the Macedonian and Armenian Questions (rooted in the Tanzimat era)? To this end and with an eye to bridging global history and sociopolitical history, I evaluate regulations and practices related to passports and travel in terms of everyday security issues and situate such practices in the context of the Armenian and Macedonian Questions.

Finding an answer to the questions I have laid out here amounts basically to interpreting certain key administrative transformations within the state. I have therefore drawn on one of the most fruitful conceptual and theoretical debates on such matters—namely, Charles Tilly's, Anthony Giddens's, and Michael Mann's contributions to the sociology of the modern state. In attempting to make sense of the modern state's complex relations to surveillance and administration, Michel Foucault's writings on surveillance, discipline, governmentality, and security led me to debates on raison d'état. This debate offered a means to understand state elites' mindset during the Hamidian period. To analyze the ways in which the state intervenes in everyday life, I examined literature on social control. Setting out along these three main axes, I have, through an eclectic assemblage, tried to interpret the historical backstory shaping understandings of threat and security during the reign of Abdülhamid II. These axes also constitute the first two chapters, which detail the study's conceptual and historical framework.

The search for an answer to the question of what state elites had to say about elements they perceived as threats forms the third and fourth chapters of this book. This search pushed me to research two international events attended by the Ottoman government on the concepts of anarchists and anarchist actions, the Conference of Rome (1898) and the St. Petersburg Protocol (1904). In addition to evincing international cooperation on the matter of security, these conferences also exposed what states had to say about groups they characterized as threats and the similar practices they adopted with respect to these groups. Again, the concept of anarchist taken up at these conferences was a new concept for the Ottoman government, as it was, indeed, for all states at the time. That said, the question of how to evaluate the fact that such terms as *anarşist* (anarchist), *serseri* (vagrant), and *fesad* (agitator, seditious, sedition) are used side by side in archival documents was crucial to my being able to make sense of the state's official administrative discourse. To my mind, the links between these concepts both signal a continuity in the discursive field that the state constructed related to groups it perceived as a threat to security and set in motion a process of securitized criminalization and marginalization of these groups.

Finally, in chapters 5, 6, and 7 I address what the state precisely did to control geographical mobility. In doing so, I tried to find a point of connection with past experiences, from the perspective of the Ottoman government, as in the concepts of agitator and vagrant. It seems to me that traditional mechanisms of social control to an important degree laid the groundwork for modern practices around passports. (The same can be said for the formation of identity in the modern sense.) While trying to conceptualize information gathering and the limits of bureaucratic knowledge, I approached surveillance, which is based on a system of permanent registration, according to Foucault. The modern system of registration is based on the recognition of individual identity and alienated administrative representation, both of which were ironically used with traditional social control mechanisms in the Ottoman case. Registration or administrative filing practices also paved the way for discrimination. Ottoman passport practices show the political effects of categories of identities in civil registration. The state benefited from these registers or identity markers to track migrants, criminals, and so-called suspects.

It is worth underscoring that these developments were not particular to the Ottoman case. The period examined was one in which geographical mobility was widespread and thorough, to a degree that I did not initially expect. And, of course, both the apparatuses for controlling geographical mobility and the interpretation of mobility through certain categories of identity are related to forms of intervention in ways appropriate to internal conditions as well as to new administrative strategies deemed necessary by the logic of governing.

Chapters 6 and 7 aim to reveal the nature of administrative orders and their practice in daily life. Though the incidents in this part of the study reflect the state's stance and actions, the latter are not the focus here; rather, I look at the difficulties encountered by people subjected to these practices and how they evaded the difficulties the practices caused. Aiming to examine the construction of state power through the mediation of modern state apparatuses, this study ultimately seeks to render visible the forms of discrimination that took shape around the strategies of administration transformed by this reconstruction of power.

My research on Ottoman passport practices reveals a state network of administrative offices, correspondences between these offices, both high-level bureaucrats—including ministers—and lower-level public officials, registers and personal identity documents, international passports, internal passports, photographs in administrative files, and identity documents. Not only the political decisions in high politics or law but also everyday administrative decisions and regulations in daily life and basic paperwork created an administrative network that hung like a black cloud over the heads of the "labeled." This administrative network consisted not only of administrative structure as offices but of bureaucrats, bureaucratic correspondence, offices, documents, photographs, traditional social control mechanisms and their actors. These labels were also created on the ground of securitization of political issues and used through the administrative network.

Ironically, while I was searching for what happened to Margirid and Aznif's passports as part of the securitization of the Armenian Question, my own digital passport register was marked as part of the securitization of the Kurdish issue. Although the techniques today are more technologized—instead of ink, paper, stamps, and old photographs, we now have digital databases, passport chips, and biometric information—the general political problems and the mentality behind the labeling process remain the same. This unfortunate continuity reveals the long-term effects of the dark side of the modern state.

I

Theoretical Framework

The Modern State, Power, and Security

The period of Ottoman reform in the mid–nineteenth century, known as the Tanzimat (1839–76), was the main shift in the means of establishing modern state administration in the empire. The Hamidian Era that followed (1876–1909) has been discussed both as part of the modernization process of state structures and as a period of regression. State-sponsored reforms to the economy, administration, and society undeniably continued in this period, while constitutionalism faced a rupture, and the reign of Abdülhamid II was defined as an autocratic political regime. Sociological discussions on modern state structure give us an opportunity to understand the changes in the Ottoman government's administration and governing strategies and to analyze the institutional changes, new regulations, and even correspondence between administrative offices during the Hamidian Era. This ongoing change in how the state was organized was not just a matter of administration: it deeply affected the everyday lives of ordinary Ottoman subjects.

Discussions of the Modern State and Power

A wide literature exists on the modern state and modern techniques and uses of power. Charles Tilly, in describing the modern state, draws a distinction between *direct rule* and *indirect rule*.[1] A state that intervenes minimally in the daily life of subjects through the use of local intermediaries and institutions pursues indirect rule. Such a state, rather than entering into the lives of each individual or gaining their dependency, establishes domination over local communities thanks to alliances established with powerful go-betweens. In this manner, the state assures a continuous flow of resources from local people to the center and interferes minimally in everyday practices. Yet when the need for resources increases, particularly owing to war, the state resorts to the direct transfer of resources from subjects through the elimination of intermediaries, which amounts to the establishment of direct domination. This shift leads to the emergence of new apparatuses to strengthen central administration, paving the way for direct rule. According to Tilly, the use of such means (beyond taxation and census taking) as general conscription and systems of policing enabled the modern state to gain entry into the microspaces of social life and to access resources that are otherwise under the local control of such spaces. This intensification of administrative systems is a key indicator of the transition to direct rule. The process also exposes dynamics that constitute spaces of intervention and negotiation in the determination of citizenship rights. From such practices emerge the contemporary all-powerful state, the civil service created to administer and control it, as well as the administrative structure created for such a system, which generates new forms of political organization.

Two features of the regulations related to practices of policing are relevant to this study and require us to distinguish the sources of the relational existence of disciplinary power and the modern state: observable public spaces and policing.[2] The modern state took shape alongside both the administrative structure required by the system of capitalist economic production and a new understanding of the law. One of its distinguishing features was the coming together of direct and indirect surveillance. Debates on the issue of surveillance are, for Tilly, directly related to citizenship rights, which he breaks into three categories: civil rights (surveillance as policing), political rights (surveillance as reactive monitoring by state administrative power), and economic rights (surveillance of the modes of production).

Anthony Giddens, an important name in sociological perspectives on the making of the modern state, pursues a line of inquiry similar to Tilly's. Giddens clarifies how the forms of administrative rule of traditional states differ significantly from modern acts of governance. In traditional states, ruling takes place in a space surrounded by borderlands rather than within specific borders. Administration should here be understood as the management of fragmented social structures through relations established with local power groups—in other words, through the use of local intermediaries. We encounter the administrative concentration accomplished through the expansion of administrative regulations and intensified surveillance along borders in a distinct sense only with the construction of the modern state and, finally, at the point at which the state transforms into the structure of the nation-state.[3]

Giddens mentions four institutional aggregations by which modernity is identified: concentrated surveillance, capitalist enterprise, industrial production, and the adoption of a centralized control of the means of violence. Considering these clusters alongside two forms of power resources—allocative and authoritative—Giddens presents a formula for the forms of rule used by the modern state. In characterizing certain resources as *allocative*, he refers to those employed in material production, whereas *authoritative* resources are related to people's means of control over their own activities. The degree of concentration and the form of these two types of resources reveal important details about techniques of power. The analysis of social systems with an eye to temporal and spatial variables makes possible an analysis of how the relations of autonomy and dependency, systems of power, or forms of domination between different actors or groups of actors have been established. The durability of social systems within social life has to do with how innate they are to institutions of domination as well to the mediation of institutions. As such, durability also points to the ways in which social systems have a hold on power's institutional mediation.[4] All manners of domination should be interpreted within this framework, particularly by attending to relatively stable forms of control.

One should also attend carefully to the difference between the scope and intensity of governing or administration. The relation between the space or spaces of the exercise of discipline (which is to say, punishments applied to ensure obedience) and the intensity of discipline yield for us a map of meaning related to governance. In traditional state structures, the space of the sovereign's rule is quite broad, and punishments are more violent. Yet the degree to which the sovereign is able to enter into the daily life of subjects is limited. In traditional state structures, it is possible to speak of a form of governance without entering into (that is, without governing) daily life. As long as there is no rebellion, and taxes are paid, the state does not interfere in the daily lives of subjects. Ruling or governing rests on the institutional mediation of power and is conducted through disciplinary strategies made up of the forms of rule. Doubtless, this structure leads to the emergence of subaltern counterstrategies and gives rise to the "dialectic of control" that Giddens considers alongside human action.[5]

The main factors of the modern state's uses of power relate to sources of authority. According to Giddens, all systems of power rest on the predictability of the everyday—that is, of what is brought about through regulation. The key method here is surveillance, in two senses. The first involves the encoding and storage of information related to the deployment of forms of power for the regulation and coordination of human behavior. The second sense refers to the exercise of authority by a certain class over individual actions. In practice, for modern states these two senses often overlap.

The relation between *surveillance* and *administrative power* extends from the traditional state to the modern state. The use of writing as an administrative means of note-taking for the purpose of keeping records holds undeniable importance as an act of surveillance, particularly in nonmodern states. Writing allows for both the encoding and the storing of information. Both functions make possible states' standardization and effective coordination of certain phenomena and certain fields of action. In the modern state, the practice of record keeping leads to the expansion of statistics, which are kept with the aim of building a strategy of administration, as well to the elaboration of such statistics. Surveillance by means of the encoding of information aids in the regulation and coordination of human behaviors.[6] As a consequence, surveillance is for the modern state one of the most important elements of the foundation of administrative rule.

Within debates on the modern state, absolutism can be interpreted not only as bringing about the supremacy of the ruler and the monopolization of sovereign rule but also as constituting a system to ensure the coordination of administrative rule.[7] Three basic elements ensure the authority of the absolutist state: the centralization and expansion of administrative power, the development of new legal mechanisms, and changes in the means of financial administration. These elements carry with them certain regulations and implementations in the centralization and coordination of the state. In nation-states, at issue is a form of administration whereby geographical borders also specify the scope of administration. We thus encounter administrative rule as the most basic element of the modern nation-state.[8] This process should be considered through the coming together of direct surveillance and indirect surveillance, in terms of which we should also interpret the functions of customs officials and border guards, the storing and coordination of passport information, and the sharing of information across different administrative units. Developments in information technologies as well as the proliferation and categorization of the information that states collect for administrative purposes present important opportunities for the *internal pacification of administrative power*.[9]

Michael Mann has expanded Anthony Giddens's debate on modern nation-states and power both historically and theoretically.[10] Mann argues that social power is formed along four basic lines—ideological,[11] economic, military, and political—and he looks into the relations between these four sources of power. He seeks to answer whether one or more of these sources is more decisive at the point of society's formation.[12] In particular, at stake in the problem of modernity is a shift in power from ideological power to military and economic power as the source of social power.[13] According to Mann, societies are established at multiple convergences of different networks of power.[14] In this framework, societies are not singular and should not be seen as either closed or open social systems. Mann, in analyzing these networks of power, also attempts to define different types of power. According to him, organizational power should be analyzed through six different ideal types, formed along three main axes: the collective–distributive power axis, the extensive–intensive power axis, and the authoritative–diffused power axis.

In the first axis, *distributive power* manifests as a zero-sum game between two or more actors. One actor's possession of power means a loss of power for another, which represents a vertical relation of power, describing domination over others. The power of the bourgeoisie over the proletariat, the power of an occupying army over the local people, and the power of a monarch over subjects are all examples of distributive power. Through this concept, Mann points to the unequal distribution of such values as dignity, authority, and welfare.[15] *Collective power* is the establishment of domination by multiple actors working together over a third actor or over nature. Here, different actors share power. As such, collective power possesses a positive content.[16] It is among the elements that make distributive power more powerful. One can thus say that Mann's concept of distributive power is born on the hierarchical grounds, created by observation and surveillance and by coordination and control, that are inherent to the distribution of labor within networks of power. In this framework, vertical distributive power is at least as functional as horizontal collective power.[17] Mann notes that it is through institutionalized laws and norms that a few people at the pinnacle of power are able to peacefully contain the masses below them. Yet because institutionalization is necessary to achieve collective aims, social stratification constituted by collective power comes to characterize social life.[18] The acquisition of legitimacy by distributive power thus occurs precisely in the process of legitimizing collective power because distributive power is possible only with the establishment and consolidation of collective power.[19]

In the second axis, *extensive power* organizes many people within broad borders and is capable of creating a stable, minimal cooperation. Yet its social efficacy is of a lower level. *Intensive power* points to the capacity for strictly organizing people by assuring a high degree of mobilization and managing loyalties, regardless of geographical extent or numbers.[20] Examples of intensive power are generally seen in limited geographical spaces. Whereas networks of extensive power establish power within large borders through a low level of social mobilization, intensive power networks control a small-scale space through a high level of social mobilization.[21]

Finally, in the third axis *authoritative power* is made up of certain orders and deliberate obedience. *Diffused power* is meanwhile less deliberate and is defined as similar social practices established on the basis of similarities between spontaneously occurring habits and practices, embodying decentralized power relations yet not explicitly regulated. Diffused power is constituted not from administration and obedience but as a result of the natural, ethical, or self-evident general interests of these practices.[22] Even if Mann does not clearly distinguish between these two forms of power, the basic difference between them can be understood as related to differences between degrees of hierarchy and centralization. Another difference is the degree of awareness that social actors have of the relations of power.[23]

All these types of power may overlap or be transitive. For instance, capitalism's productive capacity (which contains a systemic or organizational capacity), the administrative capacity of patrimonial states, and the logistic range of a warring power may together constitute examples of both extensive and intensive power. An important reason why this overlapping of power is also described as collective power is that it suggests a capability of changing or controlling the sociospatial plane of a specific collectivity's capacity. These different types of power are not mutually exclusive; on the contrary, they usually occur within the same networks of power. Mann's conceptualization makes possible the theorization of dozens of subtypes of power (such as extensive, authoritative, and military power). Thus, one can compare the absolutist states of the early-modern period and their various networks of power (which can be described as the articulation of extensive, authoritative, and political power) with the contemporary United States, an example of articulated networks of intensive, diffused, and ideological power. This conceptualization also allows for the emergence of new questions about the forms of relations between distributive and collective power within any network of power.[24]

Michael Mann—like Anthony Giddens in his discussion of the modern state via Max Weber—also distinguishes between two forms of power: the *despotic* and the *infrastructural*. The first has to do with the establishment of power over society by state elites. The second is established within society through the state's own instrumental structures. Despotic power is formed over civil society in premodern imperial and absolutist states, but it holds little infrastructural power to penetrate society. Infrastructural power points to the state's capacity to enter into civil society and implement political decisions through the forms of power it establishes within society: it relates to the institutional capacity that a centralized state, whether despotic or not, employs to penetrate in its own borders. Alongside this concept, we should also consider the concept of collective power discussed earlier, which is established within society by coordinating it through the state's infrastructural apparatuses. Infrastructural power defines the state as a set that penetrates its own borders through its center and its institutions, spanning center and periphery. Weber put forward the idea that the state's despotic power increases in proportion to the multiplication of apparatuses that Mann later defined as infrastructural power. Yet, for Mann, this outcome is not a natural one. Infrastructural power simultaneously gives rise to civil society's penetration of the state. Infrastructural power, through its effective structure, strengthens collective power. The ordering of social life by state institutions gives rise to the centralization and naturalization of social life. As such, infrastructurally powerful states are able to more effectively "encage" society.[25]

Considering that bureaucratization[26] goes hand in hand with absolutism, patrimonialism, and constitutionalism, it makes little sense to discuss regime and administration as separate matters. Yet revisionist studies see this claim as baseless. Mann defines infrastructural power as a power that coordinates civil society. This is important especially for constitutional regimes with representative assemblies.[27] According to Mann, infrastructural power can be said to be more effective compared to despotic power. Even if he does not explicitly discuss the origins of infrastructural power or which networks it contains or constructs, it nevertheless constitutes a useful concept for the analysis of modern states.[28] Mann generally uses *infrastructural power* and *despotic power* as antonyms. And, to be sure, administrative and political centralization is not the sole distinguishing factor of state power. These factors by themselves are thus not enough to understand the power of the state. But the issue here is how to determine which organizational networks should be seen as important for understanding the state's power.[29]

At the end of the nineteenth century, bureaucracy in modern states acquired the features that make it possible to strengthen states' infrastructural power. Revolutions played an important part in this development.

The civil administrative structure is the most important means for state elites to enter into civil society. Bureaucratization should be thought of alongside the expansion of the state's material and symbolic fields of communication. Some states become their own producers to meet the demands on public-transport, communication, education, and other systems. This same period also coincided with the rise of philanthropic activities organized as part of broader welfare programs.[30] For Mann, all these features point to society's encagement by the state. In a sense, this encagement in class and nation continues. In this framework, we can say that Mann's concept of *normative pacification* is synonymous with the disciplining of society.[31]

In the eighteenth century, the state's infrastructural apparatuses functioned at different levels and in different manners, and that infrastructural power functioned within a more confined field. The unity and integrity of the state weakened in two ways. First, there was a need for the existence of an elite located in the center and for networks to carry the elite's policies to civil society—networks that Mann defines using Weber's conceptualization of "party." Second, party networks crystallized in diverse ways in the state's internal and external institutions. These networks within the state's polymorphous structure had to be mobilized to affect state institutions and policies. As parties multiplied, the state's fields of activity widened, and the diversity of such activities increased, the state's polymorphous character expanded.[32] And on account of party networks, the state was able to penetrate society within its borders and mobilize resources.

The phenomenon that Mann sought to explain through the term *polymorphous* was the expansion of both the scope and the function of the state.[33] This polymorphicity also points to the fact that the state is not to be understood as a monolithic whole. State power crystallized in certain circumstances and at certain times. State power must be analyzed with an awareness of the circumstances of this crystallization as well as of the fact that power functioned in different capacities in each circumstance. State–society relations that grew denser and began to supplant the despotic state power established over society amounted to the crystallization of different groups within civil society. In this manner, the polymorphous state functioned both downward and upward. Thus, power was established within society. In this period, when the state was still gathering its strength, it underwent various transformations and lost consistency because by assuming new and different functions it was no longer under the control of a single autonomous regime. This conceptualization of the polymorphous state was, then, an evolutionary analysis of the state and of political power. The state, while gaining power, lost its autonomous form and became enmeshed with other sources of social power.

In the nineteenth century, while the state's reach receded relative to civil society, its fields of activity expanded. Mann takes up the combinations he establishes between various forms of power (authoritarian and diffused, intensive, and inclusive) as the organizational expansion of networks. He describes this stance as *organizational materialism*. According to Ralph Schroeder, Mann supports the idea that power always requires an organizational form and has no amorphous structure.[34] Until 1820, geopolitical diplomacy and military power (in the hands of an elite group) were determinative. As political power subsequently increased its fields of activity and infrastructural power, the citizen assumed a central role in the institutionalization of class relations.[35] The state, while holding infrastructural power, was democratized as a result of cooperation with citizens and classes. This transformation was a result of political, not economic, power and should be conceptualized as a shift toward infrastructural power—that is, a structure of power established directly from within society. Just as such a perspective rescues Mann from a political reductionism condensed to economic or elite theory, it also opens space for demonstrating the materialization, through plural analysis, of the state's different forms or its different forms and conditions, crystallizing along the paths of infrastructural and collective power and of democratization processes that can be conceptualized as popular modernity.[36]

Although the modern state succeeds through its laws and administrative structure in entering into relations with a population inside its own borders (which also points to a style of administration that Weber described as legal rational authority), such a structure also makes it possible for citizens or parties to enter into the modern state. One can thus talk about an expansion in the state's fields of activity more so than in its size in the process wherein the modern state is constructed. This expansion should be read not as growth in the autonomous or despotic power of state elites but as a politicization of social life and, in a Weberian sense, the strengthening of parties more than elites. Articulations between networks of power brought about the encagement of social life through new identities and in this way propelled the modern state's crystallization in the form of the nation-state.[37] The state can be conceived of as both a political actor and a space where politics occur. Its various divisions as a body politic were, through differentiation across state institutions, open to penetration by multiple power networks.[38] Different forms of power created different structures, and existing structures continued to function in the same manner. Thus, Mann renders Weber's analysis more fluid and dynamic. Each fraction, composed of the different articulations of ideological, military, political, and economic power, is perceived as a social network, or a chain of connections binding people together.[39] Mann notes that the growth of capitalism in the nineteenth century, particularly through military revolutions, transformed western Europe, leading to a recession in authoritarian power and an expansion of diffused power. At the same time, he defends the arguments that ideological power loses its grip and that modern ideologies take a more immanent than transcendent shape and are formed as modern political actors in terms of classes and people.[40]

To explain the rise of the modern state, Mann proposes the autonomy of *military power*, which, for him, includes the police and policing practices. In particular, he states that a more profound and widespread transformation of routine police work must be interpreted as pacification through civil society's routine practices of policing and internalized discipline. Explaining this argument, he cites, first, Foucault's description of a shift in punishment from a form that is authoritarian, open, punitive, characterized by spectacle, and involving violence to a form that is penetrative, diffuse, hidden, routinized, disciplinary, and internalized, and, second, Giddens's views on routinization and surveillance as the sources of disciplinary power. In the nineteenth century, controlling the lower classes was attempted through the discourse of moral and public order. Because capitalization and urbanization weakened forms of local-regional-segmental control over the lower classes, regimes faced a problem of social control that was more widespread than before. At the time, dispossessed members of the lower classes migrated not just from the countryside to cities but to many different places to find work, and they also occasionally rebelled. As such, they became elements that needed to be controlled. However, the means of control had to be planned and implemented on a wider scale. One of the results was the articulation of welfare practices with policing practices to ensure and perpetuate the regime's order.[41] This articulation of welfare practices with policing practices bears the traces of a new type of understanding of public order.

Mann links the rapid development of police administration to cities formed by capitalism, to the migrants who came to those cities (and who were difficult to control, with their traditional ties now severed), and to the potential of revolt among these migrants. He emphasizes in particular the importance of mechanisms of policing for the management and subjugation of uprisings. Giddens gives importance to the development of administrative and communicative power and notes that this process has an authoritative—rather than diffused—character, though it is useful enough to be applied in both ways.

At this point, the three basic elements of the absolutist state according to Giddens (the centralization and development of administrative power, the development of new legal mechanisms, and changes in the manner of financial administration) are important in terms of management through the penetration of society or, per Mann, in terms of the observation of structural changes at the point where power is established from within society. This type of construct further introduces the potential for an expansion of the state's knowledge of society and each individual. For the nation-state in particular, one of the factors leading to the emergence of such a possibility is an increase (in both quantitative and qualitative terms) in official statistics—especially those related to taxation and population. While population statistics are in one sense directly related to taxation, they are in another sense tied to centralized states' struggles to protect an internal order from uprisings, banditry, and crime.[42]

Tilly, Mann, and Giddens can be said to come together in identifying a state apparatus with a technological and administrative structure capable of *penetrating society*. The most basic features of such a state apparatus are surveillance and an impersonal power structure that extols rationality. The modern state has several characteristics that enable it to possess these features and distinguish it from other state forms. Foremost among these characteristics are that the modern state is an aggregate of institutions and that it possesses a bureaucracy: administrative personnel able to ensure the institutions' functioning. Organized as a functionally centralized power within certain borders, the modern state has a monopoly on making laws that determine the lives of the population living within those borders and a monopoly over the use of violence.[43] These features are undeniably important in terms of the ability of the state's regulatory power to penetrate the population.

The modern state, when employing or forming regulatory power, is affected by social classes, ethnic identities, and constructions of gender relations. Owing to its institutional features, it should not be seen as the tool of any one class or as a subject possessing absolute autonomy. Indeed, most of the time, the modern state is shaped by social and political conditions and processes.[44] Thus, the state's monopoly on legitimate violence cannot be understood solely as a link established between class relations and security practices. Ethnic identities within a society and social relations such as gender also affect the state's deployment of the monopoly of violence.

Foucault's analyses add another dimension to debates on the modern state through his understanding of power as immanent to social relations and of that power as giving rise to a multiplicity of micropowers and specific relations of power. This type of multiplicity leads to the diversification of power. Yet such diversification and dispersion are tied to the more general mechanisms of different forms of power or are tied to one another through their articulation in different forms of power. In Foucault's understanding of modern power, the articulability of state power to both institutions and discourses brings about a condition where the state is immanent to all social relations and precisely for this reason is polyvalent: it is able to draw together different strategies.[45] Foucault's analysis of power has set in motion a wide-ranging and continuing discussion about technologies of power, programs of normalization, and the deficiencies of state strategies.[46]

In what Foucault characterizes as a "double movement" in a period that saw the beginning of the dissolution of feudalism, the formation of a centralized state, and the determinative separation of religious ideas following the Reformation of the sixteenth century, the concept of administration was problematized through such questions as who should rule, how, and by what means or instruments. From this perspective, the nineteenth century is a period in which a series of administrative regulations, which can be interpreted within the triad of capitalism, liberal democracy, and modernization, were finally institutionalized and penetrated the practices of everyday life through the construction of a new mentality and understanding of morality. This century is one in which power properly crystallized in a form where the aforementioned allocative and authoritative resources coexisted.[47]

What Foucault conceptualizes as *governmentality*[48] occupies an important place in discussions of power. Governmentality is concerned with the administration of "things," in particular populations. Government, differently from sovereignty, is concerned with such matters as the welfare and longevity of society.[49] First, governmentality can be interpreted as the governing of a population along the axis of political economy. This form of administration aims to govern both society and individuals. For this reason, governmentality should be analyzed through the consideration of an administrative understanding that aims for the continuity of an economic system, assuring that policies of health, welfare, wealth, and well-being penetrate society. Second, the concept of governmentality includes relations between the state and other forms of power, in particular sovereignty and discipline. Governmentality both sustains and reconstitutes the techniques, rationalities, and institutions of discipline and sovereignty (which can be seen as their characteristic features).[50] Third, governmentality involves the enframing of a population through security apparatuses such as the army, police, diplomatic structures, and spies. On the axis of the national economy, this structure further affects the administration of the systems and mechanisms of health, education, and social welfare. Power, as sovereignty/discipline/government, characterizes the foundation of authority's modern form. The governmentality of the state, as an administrative apparatus, aims to optimize health, welfare, and, indeed, as Foucault says, life itself. All forms of power related to the state are thus *biopolitical* in nature.[51]

According to Foucault, biopolitics is the intersection where the human itself becomes a resource for political power and is coincident with developments in capitalism. There are ever-greater attempts to incorporate human bodies into controlled forms of production in line with the needs of capitalism and a calibration of matters related to the population according to economic processes. Since the seventeenth century, this calibration has engendered the formation of biopower, aiming at the administration of life.

Biopower functions at two levels. The first assures an increase in the body's capacity and potential, and its main aim is the conjoining of the body, through disciplining it, with the system of economic surveillance and control. This first level thus constitutes an anatomopolitics of the body. The second level, meanwhile, is biopower's control of the biological characteristics of the human. Foucault defines this control as a biopolitics of population or a paradigm of security. At this second level, power aims at controlling all individuals in the field of government by incorporating them into power's political strategies. It does so based on existing spaces rather than through the constitution of such new ones as disciplinary mechanisms. Its basic aim is not to reduce risk to nothing.[52]

Security and Raison d'État

According to Foucault, when a government's traditional pastoral techniques (inspired by the model of shepherd and flock) reach a crisis point, the protection of the state and thus the problem of the security of the population under its administration become constituent of government. These developments rest on a new understanding, inspired by a reading of Newtonian physics, of administration by states as forces. The security paradigm takes shape through an understanding of force against force. This understanding is employed in arenas beyond foreign policy. For instance, applying techniques of vaccination instead of isolation in the fight against pandemic illness relies on a similar logic; or in a situation where child mortality rates are on the rise, trying to lower the mortality rates of other age groups would decrease the overall effects of child mortality on the population growth curve. In both situations, a similar strategy is applied. Illness is not entirely eliminated, and child mortality is not entirely prevented. Each situation is instead brought to a "tolerable" level. The strategy of balancing force with force requires an ability or willingness to discard or write off a certain part of the population. The security paradigm does not try to eliminate risk entirely. Rather, by calculating temporal and variable factors, it attempts to regulate risk based on existing conditions.

In the Foucauldian perspective, security should be considered as a problematic rather than as a concept, value, or process of valuation, an understanding that expands the field of discussion about security. Different problematizations of security emerge alongside different discourses of danger or threat. Such discourses give rise to the foundation of security over different objects of reference and the creation of different techniques of administration and political rationalities for these reference points. These types of problematizations derive from specific knowledge–power structures.[53]

In modern times, one can point to two basic problematics of security: the first is geopolitics; the second is biopolitics. Geopolitics is based on the establishment of the European state system through the Treaty of Westphalia of 1648, whereby the militaristic discourse of international relations dominated the modern discourse of security and rendered its own particular system of values within individual and collective life as the universal value. In this discussion, politics emerged in the form of a social contract established by a hierarchy of needs with security at the top. By taking the form of a security shield of sorts, this discourse assured allegiance to the state through the threat of insecurity caused by the state's vulnerability. As the primary provider of security in this logic, the state had to secure a monopoly over the legitimate use of force. And, precisely for this reason, the definition of threat had to be monopolized on the grounds that it also monopolized the legitimate use of violence.[54]

Discussing the concept of raison d'état necessarily involves discussion of the problematic of security, one of the concept's constituent elements. The transition to the modern state caused sovereignty to become independent of traditional values, wherein states had to justify their actions in different ways. First noted in the sixteenth century, raison d'état remains to this day among the most fundamental elements affecting the politics of modern states. Raison d'état tells a statesperson what must be done to protect the state's health and power. Every state has its ideal action and ideal raison d'état according to different moments, and a statesperson's job is to be able to discern such moments.[55] The framework of raison d'état—the well-being of the state, its continuity and interests—becomes among the most important justifications of the state.[56] In this understanding, the state's interests are its basic point of reference. There emerges an abstraction of the state: an understanding of the state as abstracted from civil society; it has its own interests, disconnected from society. Thus, the state as an entity unto itself is constructed as a subject with its own reasons for its actions. The basic reference point in state actions goes beyond maintaining morality to ensuring the continuity of the state. More than the precedence of law, ensuring that continuity, along with state security, is considered a law above all others.[57]

This logic is not specific to absolutist forms of government. Carl Schmidt's discussion of sovereignty in relation to parliamentary structures is significant in terms of its problematizing of the distinction between friend and enemy. An enemy is determined not purely for religious, moral, legal, or economic reasons but through politically determined distinctions between friends and enemies. Sovereignty is made clear by who makes decisions in times of crisis—that is, by who makes the political decision of who the enemy is.[58]

The interrelated concepts of raison d'état, the state's interests, state security, and national security point to the problem of what happens when the security and continuity of the state are (perceived to be) at stake. From the perspective of raison d'état, threats related to foreign policy, internal disarray, uprisings, and internal threats pave the way for the state to legitimize any action on the grounds of security. In this way, the state is able to regulate the social order from within, however it sees fit.[59] The state not only constructs the social order but also occupies an epistemological space. As such, the state imposes its power of knowing and judgment on society such that it is able to legitimize its power over civil society.[60] It is thus possible to imagine the state as an institution of both knowledge and obtaining knowledge.

Furthermore, through the link of knowledge and power, the state is able to legitimize its practices over and within civil society.[61] Certainly, the basic factor that makes all this possible is the collection of information related to society by the state. Security intelligence is, at this point, the first instrument applied to obtain knowledge about civil society. Through this application, the work of policing (or control) becomes possible. For the state to collect the information it desires, it must first construct the channels for collecting this information. This process of construction points precisely to the formation of the apparatuses of infrastructural power, which depends on the ability to encode and store the information collected. Encoding information means not only classification but also the construction of reality by renaming according to the state's perspective and for the state's own sake.

The Modern State, Administration, and Policing

The remaking of power in its modern sense involved the replacement of punishment through the use of force (or punishment as a spectacle of torment) with punishment as a corrective project.[62] In this process, power became both more effective and more diffuse than it had been, not through practices of punishment but through the repetition of institutionalized practices.[63] In place of traditional forms and notions of justice, the state began to assemble new judicial institutions, a new theory of crime, new laws, and new institutions and mechanisms, such as a police force and prisons to facilitate the implementation of new laws. We encounter these new institutions within the framework of reforms such as the legitimization of the right to punish from a legal and moral perspective, the nullification of previous legal decisions, the abrogation of customary laws, and the activation of modern legal systems.[64] As a result, though, what were once considered ordinary, peasant forms of behavior could, following these systemic reforms, constitute a crime.

Most of these changes introduced a novel understanding of discipline and work tied to new modes of production.[65] The modern system of punishment attempted to regulate illegalities rather than eradicate them. In order to do so, according to Pasquale Pasquino, the police had a broad field of authority, more so than the other state institutions. Here, it is instructive to attend to the shifting meaning, across time, of the term *police*. The term was defined in western European settings in the eighteenth century as the proper ordering of public affairs: "to police." Yet with the separation of public and private yet to take form, one can view practices of policing at this time as attempts to collect information about the population, create statistics, and reshape society. In the eighteenth century, practices of policing (led by a police force and increasingly approached as criminology) were more and more linked with the proper order of society. Administration or government became the ability to efficiently exercise police regulation of society. Pasquino emphasizes the need to use concepts such as government and administration rather than bureaucracy in discussing such practices. As such, the social totality is constituted not so much by a group or a class but by a network or by continuous, conjoined activities.[66] In this framework, we encounter the immanent relations that various forms of domination established, with modern forms of power as a reference point that determined who had which rights and what differentiated the basic categories of rights. Daily life was thus shaped along these lines.

The work of policing was carried out not only by police organizations; other administrative mechanisms were also important sources of intelligence. Social services, social security, and the police themselves were the basic administrative apparatuses for obtaining information. For the state to administer society, passports, licenses, ID cards, and residence documents were also instruments to gather intelligence about a population.[67] In a strongly organized state, such instruments worked in conjunction with its capacity for infrastructural power. Only when information was standardized did such documents point to an accumulation of information registered and arranged by the state. Statistics and censuses can thus be seen as important methods for establishing the state's regulatory technology. They point to how elements within society are classified by the state and transformed into categories.

The functioning of modern law was formed on this basis. In this sense, regulations to coordinate administrative rule and the penetration of all individuals within a state also brought about the encoding and classification of information obtained by direct or indirect surveillance. This process, as James C. Scott discusses, served to render society "legible," with the aim of regulating populations so that the state might more easily carry out functions such as military conscription, taxation, and the prevention of uprisings. Through these means, the state came to possess a detailed map of its subjects. A complex and obscure community was rendered legible for the state and was standardized and rationalized for the purposes of administration.[68] This attempt to simplify society also increased the state's field of intervention and power. Yet this simplified depiction of society by the state showed not so much what society actually was but rather what the state attached importance to. Such a depiction was based on the categories the state itself constructed.[69]

This need to categorize and construct society brought about a transition to a system of policing for internal security, collecting information through reactive methods, and prioritizing preventive functions.[70] To be sure, when observation and policing were linked with such aims as regulating what was considered perversion, this raised the problem of how to define perversion. Here, the modern state's police work became—beyond a technical problem of administration—a moral project as policing was tasked with categorizing perversion.[71] Yet the state did not always confine itself to this moral project; it also attempted to carry out the work of cleansing society of elements it deemed harmful through the apparatuses at its disposal. In this way, it defined acceptable and unacceptable forms of life, which, in turn, rested on the thesis that for the general welfare and happiness of society parts of society must be excised or suppressed. The basic component of biopolitics can be thought of as how, considering the general functions of the population, practices determined to be harmful might be brought under control or neutralized, thus sidestepping the need for prevention.

The state's problematic of ensuring centralized control within its borders is in its clearest form immanent in its mechanisms of surveillance, intervention, and punishment. As such, to penetrate within borders, to control the behavioral codes of individuals, to monitor, and to punish should be interpreted as the deployment of new methods to control rather than eliminate what the new, punitive system sees as illegalities.[72] Yet different practices may occur in the center and in the periphery, as

Stein Rokkan asserts.[73] The infrastructural power may not have the same power everywhere within its borders: it may be stronger in the capital or in urban centers but weaker in the provinces. Within a certain geography, therefore, and for certain agents, a more powerful infrastructural capacity may be at work.

The increase in urban populations and changing work discipline gave rise to new norms and practices related to public order, with new codes deployed to determine crimes against public order. These newly defined crimes included a whole range of public behaviors, such as street fighting, drunkenness, prostitution, spitting, publicly eating in the presence of those fasting, and so on. Patrolling, considered a part of preventive policing,[74] was carried out in certain regions with a certain intensity and routine[75] and was done largely to prevent or punish crimes against public order. The police possessed broad discretionary powers related to such behaviors encountered while on patrol.[76] And, to be sure, constant surveillance, which includes patrolling and was routinized particularly in working-class neighborhoods, seemed preferable to open repression.[77]

Policing in line with the protection of public order was aimed largely at controlling the urban poor.[78] Recalling that the urban poor were seen, particularly by the police, as potential criminals, it is possible to say that the practices of policing produced certain popular stereotypes of criminality.[79] The modern police became an indispensable tool for protecting the public order from these threats and for subjecting the poor to social discipline—though how effectively is a matter of debate.

Beyond the fear of the working class itself emerged an international fear of socialist, anarchist, and nationalist movements in the nineteenth century. Different types of social divisions and disorders were organized, particularly along these ideological axes. The new political demands and social movements underscored both the state's inability to bring about the unity and integrity it so often emphasized and its insatiable longing for order.[80] As a consequence, when the social order imagined by state elites and the upper classes could not be brought to fruition, this imagination was translated into exclusionary and discriminatory policies for the rest of society, which sparked social reactions, and those reactions in turn triggered important transformations in the practices and mentality of government. In an administrative sense, new definitions emerged related to an internal enemy, and new techniques were increasingly used in the struggle against these internal enemies in the name of the state's survival. All of these transformations, definitions, and techniques should be considered alongside the modern state's administrative mentality, the technologies of power it employs, and the understanding of raison d'état undergirding this structure.

Conclusion

This theoretical discussion of the modern state, surveillance, and raison d'état paves the way to an examination of Ottoman security policies, interimperial discussions on security practices, and Ottoman passport practices during the Hamidian Era. The discussion of modern state structure, based on the literature of historical sociology and Foucault's work on raison d'état, is a reference point for understanding routine practices of surveillance as modern power and the knowledge–power structures within it. The concept of infrastructural power is significant not only because it enables us to explore administrative structures as infrastructures of the modern state apparatus but also because it points out ideological structures as legitimization tools that, along with the definition of what constitutes a threat, can be discussed through the framework of raison d'état.

2

The Modern State, Power, and Security Policies in the Hamidian Era

A Historical Framework

Through its security policies and practices during the Hamidian Era (1876–1909), the Ottoman state demonstrated the ways it positioned itself vis-à-vis different social groups. This period of more than thirty years, encompassing all the complexities and dynamics of the nineteenth century, was a historical frame wherein significant bureaucratic reforms were undertaken related to the formation of the Ottoman Empire's modern state apparatus. It was at this time that the integration of the empire—as a semiperipheral country in the interimperial competition—into global capitalism was largely materialized. In other words, during this period important transformations occurred in both the apparatuses of infrastructural power and the foundations of collective power. Worldly authority, through state policies of centralization, took shape in the differentiation of political institutions. As a consequence, when considering the problem of internal security in this period, marked by the beginning of the process of the *encagement* of society and the struggles for power in the lead-up to the First World War, one must understand the links between contemporary dynamics and administrative, legal, and political transformations.

Security policies and practices present many possibilities for us to discuss high politics alongside the materialization of these policies and practices in daily life. With respect to elite politics during the Hamidian Era—keeping in mind that the boundary between internal and external politics was ambiguous and that politics was indeed constructed on this ambiguity—one can more easily understand the social and political power struggles that are the subject of security practices. This perspective presents a way of thinking about administrative changes that helps us to understand the political and social grounds upon which they rest rather than just seeing them as progressive modernization reforms. In its administrative regulations of the nineteenth century, the Ottoman Empire had two specific aims: to hold the empire together from within and to make sustainable its existence through diplomatic policies of balance by positioning itself as one of the Great Powers. Administrative reforms should thus be understood not simply through the modernization paradigm but in terms of the nineteenth century's contemporary political practices. These practices render visible the transformations of and transitions between different types of power. The two basic aims of the empire's administrative regulations also point to two basic processes through which it perceived itself in danger. From the perspective of political elites, the situation of the "Exalted State" should be considered the object of, first, a power struggle among the Great Powers and directed at the Ottoman Empire through debates on the "Eastern Question"; second, the reforms through which state elites continued Tanzimat reforms; and, third, the particular internal dynamics of the period: the new politics of order formulated in response to irredentist Balkan nationalisms and the Armenian revolutionary movement.

The Ottoman Empire and the State of Politics in the Hamidian Era

In the nineteenth century, the Ottoman Empire was unable to control armed and disobedient groups, particularly after the Janissary Revolt of 1806, thus showing vulnerability in its ability to ensure law and order. Alongside this vulnerability, the state's usual inability to sanction *paşas*— or state-appointed individuals whose mercenary soldiers could be put into the service of the Ottoman government but who in return had the right to collect taxes and enjoy a great deal of political autonomy—when they employed force against the people and thus negatively affected peasants' trust in the state and even led uprisings.[1] Here, one of the most critical problems was that the articulation between collective and extensive power began to damage the legitimacy of the state's despotic power. As the foundations of collective power were shaken, extensive power lost its stability, and distributive power consequently began to weaken. These dynamics led to Balkan peasants organizing for their own self-defense.[2]

Problems began to emerge in alliances established by the Ottoman state with local power groups as required by despotic power. With a weak central state, local power groups came to dominate in their regions, but landowners' efforts to guard against abuses failed owing to the weakness of infrastructural power. Nor was the central state able to prevent infractions by local power groups on matters of tax collection. In addition, as villagers' conditions remained unchanged, regardless of whether they were able to communicate their complaints to the center or not, the number of village revolts rose after the Serbian Revolution of 1804–35.[3] Most importantly, because of the inadequacy of infrastructural power apparatuses to bring about a transition from indirect to direct rule—because the state's intervention in these types of situations might result in localized revolts—the center usually opted not to intervene directly, and, in time, peasant uprisings could not be prevented.

The Macedonian Question

The Macedonian Question emerged from three basic causes: transformations in urban and agricultural structures; the Ottoman government's policies against local autonomies based on political representation; and, finally, the Great Powers' policies with respect to the Ottoman Empire, shaped by their own imperialist interests.

First, change in agricultural productivity and tensions between a productive system ill-suited to the economic opportunities available in the region and to local landholding patterns pointed to the weakness of collective power, paving the way to social unrest. In this conjuncture, Slavic intellectuals in the region's important urban centers found rich grounds for setting into motion a serious ideological struggle to get Macedonia out from under Ottoman rule. This group, which struggled to position itself between the Macedonian provincial elite and the Ottoman government, was an important driving force for the spread of nationalism. In addition, local-level revolutionaries, teachers, and priests promoted these ideas and transformed them in local settings. The use of violence also transformed nationalist ideas by creating borders between perpetrators and victims that strengthened identities and belonging. Even if the rural population and the elites did not share aspirations or methods, nationalist ideas traveled across the region and became a central part of the political mobilization of the peasant masses.[4]

Second, with the establishment of the Bulgarian Exarchate in 1872, an actor was recognized not on religious grounds but on ethnic grounds for the first time within the Ottoman system of government. This was an important turning point—as much as the ethnic conflicts in Macedonia were—in the organization of revolts against Ottoman rule.

Third, the Macedonian Question, which had both social and ethnoreligious origins, created a space for the Great Powers to increase their influence in the region, and alliances and conflicts among the Great Powers directly affected the formation of the Macedonian Question.[5]

Following the economic crisis of 1873, heavy tax burdens sparked peasant revolts in the Balkans, and severe repression only exacerbated the tensions. The Herzegovina Uprising spread to other districts in Bosnia Province, which created conflicts in Montenegro, Serbia, and Bulgaria.[6] In 1875, the Ottoman state, unable to suppress the Herzegovina Uprising, was compelled to appeal to the League of the Three Emperors, an alliance between the German, Russian, and Austro-Hungarian Empires (1873–87), which internationalized the problem. In the end, the Ottoman state accepted the religious reform proposed by the league in the Andrássy Note, but those in revolt did not. The league then proposed in 1876 the Berlin Memorandum, which built on the reforms proposed in the Andrássy Note, but it was rejected by the Ottoman government. Meanwhile, the Bulgarian Uprising (also known as the April Uprising) occurred that year. With this multiplying crisis in government in Istanbul, Sultan Abdülaziz was dethroned and succeeded (after the three-month reign of Murat V) by Abdülhamid II. The Hamidian Era began.

In this situation, the League of the Three Emperors agreed on two strategies. If the Ottomans were successful in quelling the revolt in Bulgaria as well as the Serbian–Ottoman and Montenegrin–Ottoman wars, the status quo was to be maintained. But if the Balkan states succeeded, the Ottoman territories would be reconfigured. Rather than a Greater Balkan state, Serbia and Montenegro's holdings would expand, Bulgaria would add territory from Rumelia and Albania, Greece from Thessaly and Crete, while Istanbul would remain a free city. Moreover, Russia would expand as far as the Caucasus by retaking Bessarabia, and Austria-Hungary would gain certain privileges in Bosnia-Herzegovina. The latter two decisions were eventually to result in disagreement.

In Europe, the Ottoman state's strong response to rebellion also gave rise to anti-Ottoman public sentiment, and Balkan nationalism became an important turning point in the so-called Eastern Question. In Great Britain, as it became clear that the Ottomans would emerge as victors against Montenegro and Serbia, a public campaign was initiated around the violent suppression of the Bulgarian Uprising. William Gladstone, then in the opposition, wrote an anti-Ottoman pamphlet titled *Bulgarian Horrors and the Question of the East*, which attacked the Disraeli government for its support for the Ottoman Empire in interimperial diplomacy. The pamphlet was widely supported in the British press, turning public opinion against the Ottoman Empire and affecting discussions in the British Parliament.[7]

Austria-Hungary, even while supporting the Ottoman Empire's policy of cohesion, sought to bring the Balkan provinces into its own sphere of influence. Russia tended to support Balkan nationalist efforts in line with its support for pan-Slavism. In this context, a series of developments at the heart of the Ottoman Empire brought a reformist wing to the forefront and would eventually lead to the dethroning of Abdülhamid II in 1909 on the grounds that he violated the Constitution. After the Serbs declared war against the Ottomans, the Bulgarians, with Russian support, demanded autonomy. At this point, Great Britain, wishing to avoid an escalation of the crisis, called for an international conference, which led to the Constantinople Conference in December 1876. At precisely this time, Ottoman elites announced a new constitution (Kanun-i Esasi) and rejected the reforms recommended by the Great Powers, asserting that the new constitution already assured rights that met all their recommendations.

In March 1877, the London Protocol was signed, under which the Ottoman state was to cede a small region to Montenegro, reduce its army, and be responsible for necessary reforms in Bosnia, Herzegovina, and Bulgaria. If peace in the East were disrupted in the future, the Great Powers had the right to express their opinion on the matter. The Ottoman Assembly (Meclis-i Mebusan) rejected the London Protocol, which led to a Russian declaration of war on the Ottomans. The Ottoman–Russian (or Russo-Ottoman) War concluded with the Treaty of San Stefano (1878); however, the treaty's regulations related to Bulgaria upset the Great Powers. Under its terms, the Ottoman state was to establish a Bulgarian princedom whose borders were to span from the Danube to the Aegean and from Thrace to Albania. Russia would participate in the affairs of the Bulgarian government, and Russian soldiers would occupy Bulgaria for two years.[8] These stipulations were contrary to the interests of Great Britain and Austria-Hungary, and the British Royal Navy sailed to the Bosphorus with the aim of convincing Russia to accept a new, postwar regulatory order.[9] Later in 1878, the Berlin Congress was convened to decide on the situation.[10]

The Berlin Congress and the Treaty of Berlin affected virtually every aspect of the Hamidian Era for the next thirty years. Greater Bulgaria, established by the Treaty of San Stefano, was divided into three states. The borders of the Ottoman Empire grew narrower, and reforms were on the horizon both in Macedonia and in the Eastern Provinces of the Ottoman Empire, where there was a substantial Armenian population.[11]

In the 1880s, Bulgarian nationalism was organized along two main evolutionary and revolutionary trends. To bring about the Greater Bulgaria envisaged in the Treaty of San Stefano, the revolutionary movement sought in the short term to add Eastern Rumelia to Bulgaria and in the long term to add Macedonia by fomenting a popular revolt there. This second aim led to the opening in Bulgaria of many agencies to provide aid to Macedonia. Bulgarian political elites requested the Great Powers to implement Article 23 of the Berlin Treaty, which concerned reforms to be carried out in Crete, Epirus, Thessaly, Macedonia, and other territories. Marches were held in Sofia in 1885, and telegraphs were sent abroad. In the same year, a memorandum was sent to the Ottoman government requesting that Article 23 be implemented, warning that otherwise there would be revolt in Macedonia. Secret organizations formed to this end gained support in Macedonia, as did banditry.[12]

In Thessaloniki in 1893, the Internal Macedonian Revolutionary Organization (IMRO) was established. This organization envisioned an autonomous Macedonia within a Balkan Federation. However, as Duncan Perry writes, its leadership was more focused on the revolutionary process than on a possible post-Ottoman political body.[13] Following the founding of IMRO, a Bulgaria-based organization known as the Supreme Committee or the External Macedonian Revolutionary Organization also joined the Macedonian struggle to promote Bulgarian participation. It designed press campaigns, conducted propaganda in other Balkan countries, held political demonstrations, supported candidates who adopted the Macedonian cause in the Bulgarian Assembly elections, and sent delegations to European courts and assemblies. In 1895, the External Organization and the Bulgarian government undertook a large-scale pressure campaign with the aim of setting off an uprising in Macedonia. To this end, Bulgaria was armed on all sides, but the Ottoman state's preparedness and a lack of cooperation among Bulgarian peasants made the uprising unsuccessful.[14] However, international affairs now became a major determining factor of politics in Macedonia and other spaces under Ottoman rule. In effect, of the four bases of social power identified by Mann (ideological, military, economic, and political), military power was now foremost. Furthermore, shifts in local power groups gradually began to negatively affect the alliances that had been established to ensure indirect rule. And as the old forms of production and domination changed, so did social demands and strategies.

IMRO largely comprised urban intellectuals, which hampered its ability to reach out to peasants and farmers. This weakness was eventually overcome through the organization's charter, prepared in the summer of 1896, which set out a new organizational schema that prioritized provincial and village committees. The organization was renamed the Bulgarian Macedonia-Adrianople Revolutionary Committee; the central committee in Thessaloniki was to be its highest decision-making organ, even in some cases having the right to appoint people to serve in provincial committees.

Under Article 10 of the organization's charter, each committee had its own secret police force to punish anyone who impeded the cause of revolution.[15] It remains a point of debate whether the organization was able to remain secret until 1897 by employing clandestine techniques of communication and harsh punishment. According to Perry, earlier arrests of IMRO members suggest that the Ottoman authorities were not completely ignorant of its existence.[16] Certainly, in 1897, according to Pancho Dorev's edition of the archival documents on the matter, after a Muslim was robbed and killed in the village of Vinica, the Ottoman police (*zabtiye*) carried out raids on homes, discovering arms and ammunition. Thus, almost coincidentally, the Ottoman government became aware of the existence of the Bulgarian Macedonia-Adrianople Revolutionary Committee. At this point, it realized that regional unrest did not stem solely from Bulgarian agitation and that there was definitely a local political organization behind it. It was clear that new entities wished to enter the field of legitimate politics—indeed, wished to transform this field. This realization led to widespread raids on homes and arrests across the region. Yet soldiers were commanded not to raid every armed household but to search for bombs and dynamite, not just rifles, specifically among the Christian population.[17] The command made such a distinction for two reasons. First, nearly all villagers in the area were armed.[18] As such, it would be illogical to search every household for weapons. Second, this period had seen a rise in bombings and a related rise in antianarchist sentiment, and conspiracy theories abounded, so the primary weapons searched for were bombs and dynamite.[19]

Prince Ferdinand of Bulgaria, the region's ruler under Ottoman sovereignty, pursued the ambition of a Greater Bulgaria and gained support from one of the Great Powers to organize an uprising in Macedonia to this end. The state that supported these plans had committed to intervene on behalf of the rebels. However, there were various perspectives on this matter within IMRO. IMRO attempted to increase its influence in Bulgaria while at the time increasing violent activities in nearby countries, in particular political violence, assassinations, and unrest. Terror was at the time viewed by those outside the so-called Generals group within IMRO as a legitimate means in the struggle for liberation.[20] Such activities carried out to spread fear were not to be limited to the countryside but were to bleed into cities as well.

One of IMRO's most important figures, Gotse Delchev, approached Mihali Gerdzhikov, the leader of the Macedonian Secret Revolutionary Committee, later a member of IMRO, and an expert on terror methods who had grown close to Armenian organizations while studying in Geneva. Further, a French anarchist brochure was translated into Bulgarian and printed to instruct organization members on methods of terror.[21] On February 10, 1903, the decision was taken at a meeting of the Serez revolutionary cadre to systematically carry out acts of political violence in lieu of uprisings. Continuous terror activities, it was thought, would require the continuous presence of a large number of soldiers in Ottoman regions, which would be an economic drain on the empire and would pave the way for the Great Powers' intervention on the side of the Macedonians. With this decision, organization members began to learn to use dynamite.

The Thessaloniki Assassinations

Delchev and his band held a meeting with an anarchist group named Gemidzhi, which planned to dynamite a railway bridge in Angista, outside Drama, on April 1, 1903, and later to carry out assassinations in Thessaloniki. This group had been founded in Switzerland in 1898 by Bulgarian and Macedonian students[22] who were working for Macedonian independence and who, in establishing relations with Russian émigré circles, had grown close to adherents of the Russian revolutionary and anarchist Mikhail Bakunin. In 1899, they prepared plans of action aimed at European cities within the Ottoman Empire. One of these plans was to assassinate the sultan himself. When the Supreme Committee/External Macedonian Organization—a Bulgarian paramilitary organization that had close ties with IMRO in the 1890s—decided to support these activities financially, the anarchist circle expanded to include Thessaloniki and Istanbul. The group also kept up its communication with other anarchist circles via Geneva.

In 1900, Gemidzhi rented a shop across from the Ottoman Bank in Thessaloniki and dug a tunnel to the bank, which was completed in 1903.

On April 28, activities in Thessaloniki began.[23] Pavel Shatev, a ticketed passenger aboard a French passenger boat named *Guadalquivir* departing from the port of Thessaloniki, set off some ten to twelve kilograms of dynamite that he had managed to hide in his luggage, tearing into the boat. On that same evening, there were explosions on the rail lines between the city's old and new train stations. The target was a train from Istanbul, but the explosion occurred ahead of schedule, and only a small locomotive was damaged. On the evening of April 29, explosions rocked Thessaloniki's electric and water supply. Then a bomb exploded at the upmarket café El Hambra. Cvetko Traikov, who was apprehended after an assassination attempt on the governor, blew himself up.[24] On the night of April 29, the Ottoman Bank was blown up. The German Bowling Club, the French Hospital, and the Colombo Hotel, which stood on the same street, were also damaged. Explosives were thrown at the German School; bombs, handmade incendiary weapons, and dynamite were directed at cafés, clubs, hotels, and the Eden Theater in the European quarter.[25] On May 2, an attack was organized against the military garrison but failed. The next day, an activist was shot dead on his way to blow up the telegraph headquarters.[26] These events, which came to be known as the Thessaloniki Assassinations, were condemned in Europe[27] and proved damaging to the Macedonian cause. On April 19, 1904, the Italian general De Giorgis was appointed as chief of police in Thessaloniki by an international commission.[28]

Following the Thessaloniki Assassinations, the Ottoman government oversaw efforts to prevent possible violent retaliation by Muslims who were gathering in mosques to plan counteractivities. To avert a possible massacre, Austria-Hungary and Italy sent fleets to Thessaloniki. On May 6, rumors spread in Manastir that Bulgarians had bombed mosques, and Muslims set out to kill Bulgarians. By the time the gendarmerie quickly cut off the streets in the city center, several people had already lost their lives.[29]

In response to the Thessaloniki Assassinations, the Ottoman government adopted a policy of arresting all agents proven to have ties with IMRO,[30] dealing it a significant blow. The incidents led to the government's growing perception of threat related to Bulgarians as well as to its ratcheting up of precautions and the emergence of new security practices. Sometime after the attacks, intelligence was received that Bulgarian revolutionary groups were organizing a similar event in Istanbul.[31] Orders were given to the Bulgarian Exarchate to turn over the names of suspect Bulgarians in Istanbul.[32] News was subsequently received that Bulgarian secret society members were planning the assassination of the Russian envoy, and security precautions were scaled up.[33] They included making frequent patrols in Galata and Beyoğlu in Istanbul; checking up on and analyzing information related to the identity of all shops, shopkeepers, and tenants in the area, particularly by means of their municipal tax records; as well as collecting information about and notification of foreigners in the area and anyone else considered suspicious.[34]

The ensuing inquiry found no basis for information received on planned dynamite attacks against the Sublime Porte (Bab-ı Ali) and Yıldız Palace (the Imperial Palace) by anarchists associated with Bulgarian revolutionary organizations,[35] but state elites' biggest fear came true when a similar incident occurred in Istanbul, leading to an increase in security measures for the capital.[36] An inquiry began into the possibility of an attack by Bulgarian and Armenian revolutionaries against the Ottoman Bank in Istanbul. Working together, the municipality and the police began to map out all the residents of the area surrounding the bank in the Galata neighborhood. Police, gendarmerie, and military guards surrounded the building. In the event that any bank employees were taken in any incident involving the bank, the responsibility would lie entirely with the bank. Bank administrators were advised to move to a system of joint liability for officers and to keep a record of their comings and goings. Similar measures were considered for the Crédit Lyonnais Bank.[37]

The intelligence reports kept coming, and paranoia about attacks by revolutionaries grew. The Ottoman government received information about an assassination plot targeting a foreign civil servant who was to be transferred to work alongside the inspector general of Rumelia.[38] Rumors spread in Istanbul that Bulgarians had poisoned Thessaloniki's drinking water.[39] Intelligence was received that Terkos Lake, one of Istanbul's sources of water, would be poisoned by Bulgarian and Armenian secret-society members and that Küçükçekmece Lake was also in danger.[40] All of these rumors turned out to be baseless. Flour sent from Plovdiv to the military was held up for days for inspection by Bulgarian customs administrators, leading Ottoman officers to consider the possibility that the flour was poisoned.[41] Bombing activities and guerrilla warfare throughout the period stoked perceptions of threat and conspiracy theories. Ottoman bureaucrats acted in line with a raison d'état based on this perception, which increasingly encompassed the field of politics.

The Railway Bombing and Its Aftermath

On March 7, 1903, the same year as the incidents described earlier, the gendarmerie found 110 pieces of dynamite, totaling some twenty-six kilograms, on the railway line between Anbardere and Yıkıkhan, near Çatalca in Thrace.[42] Linc Mayer noticed the dynamite and informed the gendarmerie. According to the investigation report, the fuse connected to the dynamite was joined to an iron rod and covered with rocks. The blasting caps were placed on an iron rod meant to catch a spark through contact with the passing train. Yet the rod became delinked from the unit and was found on the ground. The approaching train was stopped, and the dynamite was taken to the police station. According to the Ottoman investigation report, the only clues found were the footsteps of forty people around where the dynamite was placed. The central administration was notified of the incident by telegraph, and the Ministry of Interior notified the lieutenant governor of its investigation into the communal and religious affiliations of the surrounding villages' inhabitants. Because the dynamite was spotted by the gendarmerie twenty minutes after the watchman for the train line, Teodor Kiriov, had already passed by it twice without seeing it, the investigation then shifted to Kiriov. He claimed under interrogation to have seen nothing and to have no knowledge of the affair and was sent to a military court.[43] The fact that the dynamite, placed close to the Anbardere police station, was not spotted by passersby raised suspicions. According to the lieutenant governor of Çatalca, Cevad Bey, an outsider could not have carried out the plan. Because it was considered highly likely that Bulgarians or members of the Macedonian committees were behind the incident, it was seen as unsuitable for Bulgarians to work on the line as long as the investigation by the Ministry of Interior continued. Instead, people with clean police records from other communities were to be employed in their place, and this directive was to be communicated to the company and to the Ministry of Public Works and Trade (Ticaret ve Nafia Nezareti).[44] As part of the investigation, the dynamite and caps were sent to Edirne. At the same spot two nights earlier, a certain Mahmut, a switchman at Çerkesköy, was notified by the train stoker, Tatar İbrahim, of two handguns thrown onto the train to Vienna. To ensure the security of the railways, the order came from Edirne that gendarmerie detachments were to carry out repeated patrols.

It was revealed that a few days before the incident the guard at Kurtdere, Istıranca Sakstandi, had gone to the security booth near to Yıkıkhan and asked another guard, Lütfi, which signal would stop a train and whether the trains departed alone or were accompanied by the gendarmerie. Sakstandi now became the subject of the investigation. When his account did not match what Lütfi said, Sakstandi was taken into custody and transferred to the military court in Edirne.[45] On the grounds that Bulgarian and Armenian civil servants and laborers had information on such matters as dynamite and fuses, the Ottoman government subsequently recommended to the Eastern Railways Company and the companies of the Dersaadet—Thessaloniki and the Manastir lines that "treacherous people [eşhâs-ı muzırran]" were not to be employed on the railways. Because railway guards were responsible for the security of the rails through their constant supervision and inspection, and because outsiders could not take on such tasks, the companies were required to avoid employing any guards or laborers under suspicion. The Ottoman Assembly also issued a decision to this effect. Any "seditious sorts [erbab-ı mefsedet]" among employees were to be replaced, and in the event that they were not, the Ottoman government would accept no responsibility for any damages incurred as a result of the companies' inability to ensure the security and safety of Europeans.[46]

In the ensuing investigation, it was discovered that of the twenty-seven workers stationed between kilometer points 97 and 101 in Kabakça and Sinekli, there were eleven Bulgarians and only one Muslim. The Eastern Railways Company was served notice to dismiss the Bulgarians.[47]

Its director sent notification that, alongside an increase in the number of guards, care would be taken in the employment of officers and workers and that all manner of precautions were in place. The director further requested that to ensure that trains proceeded safely, night patrols be carried out, and bridges like those in Thessaloniki be brought under close protection.[48] A request was made for the construction of a security booth near each of the bridges at Bahşayış and Gökçeli, at the cost of one thousand kuruş per booth. A reduction in the size of the gendarmerie the previous year had led to thirty-four privates being dismissed from the infantry, but now its size was insufficient in the face of the Bulgarian attacks. Because only nine privates of the gendarmerie infantry remained in the center, the Çatalca lieutenant governor, Cevad Bey, requested that thirty-four gendarmerie privates be immediately registered and employed or that thirty-four soldiers or police privates be sent from the Dersaadet infantry to serve as gendarmerie officers.[49]

In an appendix to his memorandum, Cevad Bey reported that armed people had been sighted three nights earlier between Kabakça and Sinekli and the previous evening between Sinekli and Türbedere. The people in question were two villagers suspected of aiding and harboring members of the Bulgarian Committee. They were immediately arrested. As Cevad Bey had anticipated, there was an attack by the Bulgarian gang in Tırnova, connected to Kırkkilise, and information was received that the gang was found to possess a thousand kilograms of dynamite. There was no gendarmerie on guard on the train line from Ispartakule to Küçükçekmece. It was thus thought that Bulgarian revolutionaries would blow up these rail lines and bridges. Cevad Bey renewed his request for gendarmerie assistance several times but did not receive a positive reply for some time.[50]

Through an official memorandum, number 298 (dated April 6, 1903), soldiers and gendarmerie officers were stationed in the areas deemed necessary to ensure the safety of train lines. Because the people selected to live in these locales were responsible for the protection of the lines, measures were taken to restructure liability through an Ottoman Assembly decision sent to the Ministry of War (Harbiye Nezareti) and the public inspector and from there to the lieutenant governor of Çatalca.[51] Yet through this process it was discovered that the company had not hired Muslim or

Greek (Rum) workers to replace its Bulgarian workers.[52] However, with information in hand regarding which railways the Bulgarians planned to blow up, protecting those lines by quickly relocating sufficient personnel there became one of the most pressing issues. It was possible to protect the line between Çerkesköy and Çatalca, but the ten gendarmerie privates on hand were not enough to protect the line from Çatalca to Küçükçekmece. Another fifty gendarmerie officers were needed.[53] Such observations sped up the employment of gendarmerie officers. And, indeed, after the director of Eastern Railways approached the military command on the matter and noted that sufficient precautions were not being taken with the necessary speed and seriousness, the process gathered even more speed.[54]

Amid all this correspondence, one Dimitri, son of Tanash of Istıranca, was kidnapped by five people in Terkos, near the Saray road. According to Dimitri's statement, he was asked whether there were soldiers in Istıranca along the road to Istanbul, and this group, which grew to seven in the forest, wore kalpak hats and bullet belts.[55] Because the station engineer, Linc Mayer, had previously served as a military captain in Austria, he was seen as among those responsible for the incident on the grounds that he had knowledge of using explosives.[56] Following this incident, shots were fired on the Skopje train as it passed by Ahmetova, and a bomb was found on one of the bridges on the line.[57]

On August 2, 1903, the long-planned and widespread uprising began in Macedonia. Known as the Ilinden (Preobrazhenie) Uprising, it spilled over from Manastır to villages in Edirne and into Thessaloniki. Some two thousand people died, and nearly sixteen thousand were made homeless.[58] The Ottoman government brought in units from Anatolia to suppress the uprising. Albanian militia units were employed as supporting forces, and special courts were created to try anyone thought to be related to the uprising. On August 9, IMRO sent a memorandum to representatives of the Great Powers in Sofia describing the destruction that regular and irregular government forces had carried out in Macedonia, and so the security techniques employed by the Ottomans again began to attract the Great Powers' attention. The Ottoman government had earlier declared a reform decree about reorganization of gendarmerie and administration of the region as a response to pressure from Great Britain, France, and Russia in 1902. The Vienna Program of reforms in Macedonia began, the same reforms as those in the Ottoman decree in 1903. It was decided that the Vienna Program would be drawn up again, resulting in the reform package known as the Mürzsteg Reforms.[59] These reforms were eventually, though not immediately, approved by the Ottomans. At the heart of the Mürzsteg Reforms was the rehabilitation of the Ottoman gendarmerie.[60]

Though the Mürzsteg Reforms led to some immediate improvements in Macedonia, in the long run they paved the way for an increase, not a decrease, in unrest. At this time, the Russo-Japanese War of 1904–5 and the Entente Cordiale were also underway, both of which deeply affected the Great Powers' diplomatic relations. Russia's war with Japan meant a weaker Russian political activity in the Balkans. European diplomacy projected different political scenarios in the Balkans according to the possible results of the war. With the signing of the Anglo-Russian Entente in 1907, the conflict in the Balkans eventually grew to uncontrollable dimensions in the region, in part because the governments that signed the reform program sacrificed it in favor of other diplomatic priorities.

The Armenian Question and the
Armenian Revolutionary Movement

The Armenian Question was another significant political issue in Ottoman politics at the time. Twice it was made an international matter. Through the Treaty of San Stefano in 1878, the Armenian issue was discussed at the Berlin Congress with the participation of a delegation sent by Ottoman Armenians. To the document that emerged from the congress was added Article 61, regarding reforms to be carried out in regions where Armenians lived in significant numbers. It included a number of demands from Ottoman Armenians. Thus, the Macedonian and the Anatolian reforms, which introduced new security measures, came to the fore in the Berlin Treaty as a result of the collision of a number of local and international events.

Though the Armenian community in the Eastern Provinces was the target of violence and double taxation by Kurdish warlords, the Ottoman government did not solve these problems and framed them as public-order issues. After the appearance of the Armenian Question in the Treaty of San Stefano, it grew into an international problem in the Cyprus Convention of June 4, 1878, and in the Berlin Treaty of July 31. In response, Ottoman political elites' approach to the matter increasingly took shape within a politics of territorial integrity. Territories lost—first the Balkans, then Lebanon, and finally through the Ottoman–Russian War (1877–78)[61]— intensified paranoia around security matters among the elites. Article 61 of the Berlin Treaty led to the formation of the Ottoman government's attitude toward the Armenian community within this framework of paranoia and to continued tension and insecurity between the government and the Armenian population.[62]

Political developments in the Balkans since 1875 also had a direct impact on the Armenian Question. After the issue was raised in the London Protocol on 1877, in Article 16 of the Treaty of San Stefano it was held that reforms were to be carried out according to local needs in places where Armenians lived and that their security against Kurds and Circassians would be guaranteed. According to this treaty, the guarantor of this article was Russia.[63]

The gradual rise in the use of violence in the mid-1890s occurred alongside the internationalization of the Armenian issue.[64] The administrative reforms introduced through the Berlin Treaty involved the reorganization of the military police, the creation of townships (nahiye), the strengthening and expansion of judicial institutions, the reorganization of tax collection, the use of the police and the gendarmerie in tax collection, and Armenian representation in the institution of tax collection proportionate to their population.[65] These four basic matters were in accordance with the Ottoman government's changes to administrative structure under the Tanzimat reforms.[66] Yet because the Armenian reforms were the subject of an international treaty, the Armenian people found themselves in the middle of an international power struggle.[67] Ottoman state elites approached the reform program as an intervention by the Great Powers into the empire's internal affairs and so placed the Armenian people in the category of suspect people. The reform program caused state elites to attempt to spread administrative reforms across the empire, with the aim of keeping European intervention into Ottoman internal affairs to a minimum.[68]

Rural Armenians living in Anatolia's Eastern Provinces not only regularly paid taxes to the state after the Tanzimat reforms but also paid traditional taxes to the local power holders, the aghas and beys. This double taxation as well as attacks by nomadic Kurdish groups made Armenians among the most aggrieved groups amid a power vacuum in the Eastern Provinces, especially after 1840. The Armenian community's appeals to the Ottoman government about the attacks and violence directed at them yielded no results. In the early 1870s, the Armenian community submitted a report to the Sublime Porte explaining the situation of Armenians in eastern Anatolia—that they lacked basic security of life and property in the face of the tribes and that the only way to address this issue was to strengthen Ottoman administrative authority. This plea went unanswered.[69] In 1902, another appeal to the vizierate through the Armenian Patriarchate conveyed the complaints of local people, including that the police took food and fodder from villagers without compensation and that the latter were frequently subjected to violence and pressure in state tax collection.[70] Beyond the state's inability (and lack of desire) to intervene in this situation, it was mandatory for local people to assist the police forces in tax collection, which caused the Armenians to fear the state and feel even more insecure.[71]

Between 1879 and 1880, famine led to local uprisings, particularly in eastern Anatolia. Regional stability was overturned entirely as pillaging became the rule of the economy. That the Ottoman state was unable to sufficiently intervene in this situation, together with the fact that security reforms on the agenda for years had simply not been carried out, resulted in increased violence in the region.[72] These factors triggered the formation of the *fedayi*—Armenian armed bands established as self-defense groups against Kurdish warlords and Ottoman bureaucrats in the 1880s—which eventually turned into revolutionary movements. Although the Armenian revolutionary movement followed a road similar to that taken by the IMRO in the Balkans, it did not receive the same international support and was met with a strict policy of suppression because of the state's fears of division. This policy of suppression, even of simple village uprisings against taxation, grew to become massacres as the state made a strategic change to favor Kurds over local elements in parallel with clashes between

Kurds and Armenians. This strategic change is evident in, for example, the formation of the Hamidiye Cavalry with Hanefi Kurdish tribes, following the example of Cossack units in Russia.[73] State elites also associated peasant uprisings in the region with sedition (*fesad*), as discussed in later chapters. In addition, we must not forget the established tradition of resistance by local people, particularly in mountainous regions such as Sasun and Zeitun, in the form of revolts against taxation.[74]

This background explains why Armenian guerrilla movements began to surface, especially in the 1880s, and why the Armenian revolutionary movement arose in the 1890s. After 1878, Armenian revolutionaries began to organize, particularly in Zeitun, Van, and Erzurum.[75] In 1889, three members of the Armenakan Party, an Armenian organization, were captured in Van and found to have documents with information on political activities. This discovery stoked the Ottoman government's worries that a major secret Armenian organization had been formed.[76] It subsequently began to monitor all Armenian organizations, including aid organizations, and countless Armenians were labeled suspects or criminals. Thereafter, the Armenakan Party carried on with agitation and political violence, including attacks on Kurds, assassinations, and the killing of Nuri Efendi, a police agent in Van.[77]

Members of the Hunchakian (Social Democrat) Party (founded in Geneva in 1887), known as Hunchaks, argued that Ottoman Armenians could achieve socialism only through independence, which in turn would be achieved by training people through propaganda toward two goals: agitation and terror. Because the effects of propaganda were limited, actions such as demonstrations against the government and agitation campaigns directed at groups tied to the government through shared interests were seen to be crucial. Violence was aimed not only at the government but also at those working on behalf of the government. Efforts to foment a general uprising in the Ottoman Empire was considered one of the most important activities in service of this aim.[78] In the struggle against the Ottoman government, the Hunchaks also advocated for alliances with local non-Armenians. All of these programs demonstrated the impact of the revolutionary movement in Russia on the Hunchaks, in particular the movement arm known as Narodnaya Volya (People's Will).[79] In 1896, the

Hunchakian Party split not by debates within socialism (as in Europe) but between those favoring socialism and those who wished to depart entirely from the socialist project. The second group argued that Armenian liberation should come about through nationalism and that the party's socialist program had led to a decrease in European support.[80]

The Dashnaktsutyun (Armenian Revolutionary Federation, ARF) was established in 1890 in Tiflis to bring socialism to and liberate Armenians in the Ottoman Empire.[81] The ARF emerged from a desire to bring together all Armenian organizations in Russia under a single umbrella. Its organization, methods, and aims thus differed slightly from those of the Hunchaks, who wished to unite Armenians in the Ottoman Empire, Iran, and Russia into a socialist state. The ARF was made up of different groups: some defended the use of peaceful methods, but others advocated for the use of violence; some considered socialist ideas the basis of Armenian nationalism, whereas others operated on an understanding of nationalism that entirely excluded socialism.

ARF's manifesto of its program began with a long preamble on the principles of socialism.[82] The Ottoman Armenians' situation was likened to that of Spartan slaves. The manifesto emphasized the aim that Ottoman Armenians would one day possess political and economic freedom and laid out its basic elements: a democratic government based on equal voting rights; equality before the law for all people; freedom of expression and publication; land for the landless; the reorganization of taxation according to what one could pay; the doing away of all forms of unpaid and coerced labor; military conscription instead of military taxes; mandatory education; the speeding up of industrialization; and the creation of communal structures in society. The manifesto specified the following methods to achieve these goals: spreading propaganda about the party's values; creating guerrilla forces prepared for combat; establishing party intelligence units; organizing financial regions; terrorizing and carrying out war against the government, government informants, traitors, and all sorts of colonizers; as well as protecting innocent people and local people against attacks.[83]

In its manifesto, ARF explained that it would not wait for European support for the liberation of Ottoman Armenians. Some of the socialist elements within ARF maintained close ties to the Russian revolutionary movement. Some were also members of various revolutionary organizations in Russia, notably Narodnaya Volya. For the nonsocialist revolutionary groups within the party, the priority was to assure the independence of Armenians living in the Ottoman Empire. Meanwhile, the socialist revolutionary groups presented two main goals: to prioritize the destruction of the czarist regime in Russia in alliance with Russian and Georgian revolutionaries and, like their nonsocialist peers, to defend Ottoman Armenians' struggle for independence.[84]

Actions in Istanbul

As these groups organized, they introduced the parallel use of uprisings (which had become characteristic of the period), public actions, and methods of terror to achieve their goals. Alongside uprisings in different geographies of the empire, the actions in Istanbul in particular reveal how the strategies they used created fear among state elites. The first major action in Istanbul was the Kumkapı Demonstration in 1890, which was organized in response to the Musa Bey trial. Musa Bey was a Kurdish chief who had kidnapped and raped a young Armenian girl, Gülizar.[85] The case became a symbol of the oppression of Armenians in the provinces, and after Musa Bey was acquitted of the charge, a protest was organized in Kumkapı, the Istanbul district in which the Armenian Patriarchate was located. On July 27, 1890, the Ministry of Police received information regarding an action planned in the church next to the Armenian Patriarchate's headquarters.[86] On July 29, a manifesto was read out in the patriarchate's church, detailing the poor conditions of Armenians in the empire and impugning the patriarchate, the sultan, and the government.[87] When a priest attempted to oppose this statement, a gun was fired at him. The patriarch himself was attacked while trying to leave the church, and his beard was pulled.[88] The Hunchaks then compelled the patriarch to march straight to Yıldız Palace as a representative of the community to meet the sultan. Soldiers blocked the marchers, and clashes ensued.

Though unsuccessful, the protest created a public stir, and the Hunchaks were able to show that they could organize a mass action in the capital. An important reason for the action's scale was that the Hunchaks had ensured the participation of seasonal Armenian laborers from Muş and Van.[89] Despite the mass arrests that followed, the Hunchaks continued to organize actions, particularly in the countryside. In 1891, they joined the Eastern Federation, made up of Macedonian, Albanian, Cretan, and Greek revolutionaries. Actions continued in 1892 and 1893, and many Armenians who were suspected of participating in them began to be arrested and tried.[90]

As local clashes and massacres continued in the East, in 1895 the Hunchaks organized their second major action in Istanbul: the Sublime Porte Demonstration (Bab-ı Ali Nümayişi). On September 28, they sent a telegraph to consulates informing them of their intent to carry out a peaceful petition action. The petition voiced their complaints and demands on five basic subjects, which can be paraphrased as follows:

> Alongside complaints related to the Ottoman government's continuous massacres against Armenians, against unjust arrests, cruel punishments against detainees, the injustices carried out by Kurds, corruption in tax collection, and complaints related to the Sasun massacre, a call is made here for equality before the law, freedom of press and expression, freedom to organize, the recognition of habeas corpus rights for detainees,[91] the right of Armenians to carry weapons so long as Kurds are not disarmed, the redrawing of the political borders of the six Armenian provinces, the appointment of a European administration to these six provinces, and the carrying out of financial and land reforms.

The petition also specified that these reforms were necessary not only for Armenians but for all Ottoman subjects.[92]

The Ministry of Police received information about the petition, with five hundred signatures, and about a demonstration that was to take place.[93] On September 16, a document signed by the Armenians of the provinces (taşralı Ermeniler)[94] was sent to the Chairmanship of the Criminal Court of Appeals (Mahkeme-i İstinaf Cinayet Riyaseti), stating that a peaceful petition would take place and warning that if government forces used violence, the responsibility would be theirs alone. Upon receiving this document, the Ottoman government requested that the Ministry of Police investigate whether the participants were in fact rural Armenians. The decision was taken to look into the identities of those who brought the letter and its signatories, and all government bodies, in particular the Ministry of Interior, the Ministry of Foreign Affairs, and the Ministry of Justice (Adliye Nezâreti), were tasked with taking exceptional precautions.[95] The government also decided that the action in question would lead to clashes and that this "insolence" was to be prevented.[96] It believed that this petitioning action was, like the Kumkapı Demonstration, intended to attract the attention of European governments. To prevent any European intervention, it decided that officers were not to open fire on the crowd and that no blood was to be spilled. To ensure security, it was ordered that the crowd be dispersed by the police and cavalry units.[97] The environs of administrative buildings were taken under military protection. Cavalrymen were positioned along the road to the Sublime Porte, and police patrols were stepped up, aiming to prevent the crowd from nearing the Sublime Porte.[98]

The police prevented the demonstrators from entering the Sublime Porte, but clashes broke out and continued on Istanbul's back streets.[99] The chief of police in Istanbul, Hüsnü Bey, interpreted the news that an armed group had collected at the patriarchate church in Kumkapı in the previous days and had placed in the middle of the church a black cross made of silver as indication that the patriarchate supported the crowd.[100] In fact, the day of the demonstration was the Armenian religious feast of Khachverats, for which four thousand people had gathered in the Kumkapı church and in churches in Galata and Beyoğlu. The Hunchaks had chosen this day for the demonstration to ensure a better turnout; indeed, in the second half of the nineteenth century, mass actions and massacres alike generally coincided with religious holidays. The Hunchaks requested that the patriarch take their petition to the Sublime Porte, but he declined, stating that such a demonstration would result in violence. He argued it would be better if a group presented the petition. As the crowd began marching, conflict broke out in the city.[101] Louise Nalbandian notes that there was disagreement among the Hunchaks whether the action should be carried out peacefully or violently. It is clear from the ensuing incidents that even if it was decided to demonstrate peacefully, some demonstrators did not abide by the decision.[102]

When the crowd arrived at the Sublime Porte, they were prevented from entering. Minister of Police Hüseyin Nazım Paşa later claimed that in the resulting clashes Major Servet Bey, a gendarmerie assembly member, was stabbed by a group of Armenians; however, according to the *New York Times* he was shot and killed as the clashes intensified.[103] The violence soon spread to the districts of Kadıköy and Üsküdar. The government decided to stand in the way of Muslim attacks on Armenians to prevent ethnic conflict in Istanbul.[104] Yet as far as can be ascertained from Hüseyin Nazım Paşa's correspondence, lower-class Muslims in a number of the city's neighborhoods began to carry out attacks against Armenians.[105] Various sources mention armed groups of Muslims.[106] The police were supposedly charged with the responsibility for placating Muslims, but the Sublime Porte Demonstration nevertheless resulted in a pogrom against Armenians.[107]

One of the precautions that the Police Ministry took was to bar all Armenians from leaving the shores of Istanbul on September 30, 1895, based on intelligence that many were intending to travel to such neighborhoods as Üsküdar, Tophane, Beyoğlu, and Fındıklı. Yet as incidents occurred around Sultanahmet, information passed to Hüseyin Nazım Paşa from cavalrymen indicated that many Armenians had taken small boats from Galata, Tophane, and Fındıklı toward the pier in Sirkeci, the main port of Sultanahmet. Most of them were coal heavers, pole porters, and other seasonal workers. Again, according to Hüseyin Nazım Paşa's memoirs, the crowd grew large enough to break through the police barricade.[108] According to Ottoman reports, most of the clashes, which went on for days in the streets of Istanbul, were not between the police and Armenians but between Muslims and Armenians.[109] Armenians took shelter in churches, upon which the Ottoman government ordered that any armed Armenians gathered there be prevented from leaving.[110] Churches were blockaded by the police, and the weapons inside were collected by foreign embassies and handed over to the police.[111]

In these protests and the Sasun Rebellion (or Resistance) (1894), which resulted in a massacre of Armenians, several developments occurred. In May 1895, Great Britain sent a memorandum to the Ottoman government about the reforms planned for the Eastern Provinces under Article 61 of the Berlin Treaty. In response, the sultan publicized his own reform package in June 1895. Said Paşa, who was made grand vizier in place of Cevad Paşa, called for military intervention into the Sublime Porte Demonstration. Abdülhamid II rejected this request, and on October 2 Kamil Paşa, known for his closeness to Great Britain, took Said Paşa's place, and Said Paşa was transferred to the Foreign Affairs Ministry.[112] On October 6, the Great Powers delivered a verbal note on the unrest during the demonstration and the massacre of Armenians that had followed it.[113] After the announcement of the sultan's reform, ethnic conflict broke out in Zeitun, Trabzon, Erzurum, Bitlis, Van, Kharput, Diyarbakır, Sivas, and Kilikia (Çukurova). Every clash led to a pogrom against Armenians.[114]

On August 26, 1896, twenty-six Dashnak (ARF) militants dressed as porters took customers and employees hostage in the central building of the Ottoman Bank in Istanbul. Armed ARF militants placed explosives at various points in the building. Alongside the occupation of the bank, a great deal of commotion was raised in the city with explosions and gunshots from militants stationed throughout the city.[115]

The police and the military quickly blockaded the bank building. A document laying out the militants' demands was sent to foreign ambassadors: the resignation of the Armenian patriarch, reforms in the provinces they called "Armenia," a guarantee of security of life and property, judicial reform, and a general pardon. The government was not prepared to meet these demands, but through the mediation of Maximov (first name not known), the chief interpreter of the Russian embassy, the sultan permitted the perpetrators to freely leave the bank and subsequently the country. By morning, these individuals were taken to the port under military supervision and boarded the yacht of the bank's general director, Sir Edgar Vincent. They passed on to a French ship, the *Gironde*, and proceeded to Marseilles.[116]

This chain of events led to severe unrest in Istanbul. Lower-class Muslims with clubs in hand began attacking and killing Armenians on the streets. The target of the attacks were the Armenian lower-class porters in particular.[117] To save themselves from the massacre that began on August 26, 1896, and lasted for a full three days, some Armenians tried to hide.[118] Although there is disagreement between sources as to how many

Armenians were killed at this time, it is safe to say that the number was in the thousands.[119] Although the bank raid set the events into motion, the responsibility for the massacres did not lie with the Dashnaks. An urban Muslim mob attacked Armenians with the aim of eradicating them. The European diplomats in Istanbul suspected that the Ottoman government had encouraged and even instructed the mob to kill Armenians in the city.[120] According to the police report, just as the government did not stand in the way of these attacks, it did not apprehend most of the assailants. The death toll given in the memorandum presented to the Ministry of Interior also suggests there was a massacre of Armenians in the city.[121] In interpreting these figures, Edhem Eldem notes in particular a near-eight-fold difference between the figures that former minister of police Nazım Paşa gives and the figures in foreign sources. Yet even in Nazım Paşa figures, the ratio of deaths to injuries among Muslims was two and a half to one, whereas for Armenians it was close to nine to one. Nearly thirty-five times more Armenians died than Muslims. These ratios suggest that the Armenians who died, most of them unarmed aside from a small minority, were killed by large and likely armed groups.[122] Even Nazım Paşa's report, however else one may construct his narrative, gives an account of a massacre of Armenians. The massacre stopped rather suddenly, which also created the suspicion that the kill order had been given by the sultan himself. Following three days of violence, the Armenian porters in the city were driven away, and Kurds came to take their place.[123]

On July 21, 1905, during the Friday service and after prayers there was a great blast as a bomb exploded next to the mosque that the sultan was leaving. Abdülhamid II was left unscathed, but twenty-six people died, and fifty-eight were injured, most of them soldiers and stable hands. This assassination attempt was carried out with explosives placed in a special compartment made in a Victoria-type car imported from Austria. The duration of the sultan's walk to his waiting vehicle had been taken into account, and the bomb was set to explode in one minute and forty-two seconds. On this occasion, however, the sultan lingered in a conversation with the *sheyhülislam*, and so the assassination attempt failed.

In the investigation following the incident, the inquiry commission employed new techniques of policing, such as cross-examinations, chemical analysis, autopsy, and the analysis of hotel, passport, and customs records.[124] The commission quickly arrived at the name of a Belgian anarchist, Edward Jorris, and determined that the assassination had been planned by a members of the Armenian resistance movement. From the inquiry report, it is understood that the assassination plot was organized such that after the killing of the sultan, bombings across the city would create further disorder and, it was hoped, lead to intervention by the Great Powers.[125]

Just as these three incidents in the Ottoman capital, Istanbul, are important for understanding the perception of danger among political elites at the time, they are also critical in showing the grounds on which state security policies took shape. There were also many assassination attempts directed at Armenian civil servants or those seen as close to the Ottoman government. Perhaps the most important attempt was on the life of the Armenian patriarch but was prevented thanks to information received beforehand.[126] To prevent revolutionary violence, it was important for the Ottoman government to investigate the producers of explosive materials or those stockpiling such materials.[127]

While the Armenian revolutionary movement had its own particularities, like other revolutionary movements across the world it made use of propaganda, guerrilla struggle, journalism, and education as means of mass mobilization. What made the movement dangerous to the state, according to the Ottoman government, was not just nationalism or the demands for reform but that Armenian organizations in locations where Armenians predominated were becoming political actors. Revolutionary organizations took the stage as new political actors who, unlike the patriarch and the traditional Armenian elite, the *amira*, were not under the central government's control and who demanded radical changes to the political structure. According to the Ottoman government, these groups were capable of mobilizing the Armenian people. Another dimension of the situation was the Ottoman state's fear of the empire being divvied up by the Great Powers, whose influence was expanding in the last half of the nineteenth century. This political fear also influenced security policies through the prejudiced assumption that Armenians were being provoked by foreign powers.

Particularly after the 1880s, there was a gradual increase in oppressive state practices in line with security policies,[128] pointing to a profound crisis in legitimacy. The alternative of having one's own state, instead of living under the Ottoman government, had given rise to armed struggles such as those seen first in the Balkans and later in the Armenian movement. The existing political system was both unwilling and unable to meet these emerging demands.

One might ask, however, why policies of control grew at such an accelerated rate. If one recalls the place of the empire in the international system since its first major defeat to Russia in 1774, the trend toward new security regulations against the threat of the internationalization of security vulnerabilities within the empire, particularly after the Berlin Treaty and the raising of the "Eastern Question," is less surprising. The Eastern Question meant that political problems related to the Ottoman Empire had become the subject of international politics. It also meant that the empire's internal problems often resulted in communities' demands or interventions shaped by alliances with one or more of the Great Powers. The Eastern Question and the politics of whether to hold the Ottoman Empire together or divide it were of undeniable importance in the formation of international alliances. The changing international balances caused the Ottoman Empire to practice a form of diplomatic acrobatics. For the Ottoman political elite, this situation created a sort of siege mentality; as Said Paşa said, "We find ourselves stuck among European states and principalities. . . . The Sublime State has been a member of the European family of nations for some fifty years."[129]

The Crisis of Legitimacy and the Perception of Threat

One of the important changes that strikes one regarding the situation after the Berlin Congress is the loss of the Ottoman Empire's control over regions where Christians lived in great numbers, such as Bosnia, Herzegovina, Bulgaria, Kars, and Ardahan. In the years before the conference, many Muslim refugees fleeing Russia's hardening pan-Slavism had sought shelter in the Ottoman Empire. They were followed by an influx of Muslim refugees from the Balkans. Thus, demographic changes within the empire were of undeniable importance.

Before the Berlin Congress, census practices were carried out that, with the aim of enforcing tax and military obligations, targeted the male population and registered only religious differences.[130] The number of immigrants is thus unclear from these censuses.[131] Following the Berlin Treaty, not only did the Ottoman Empire lose territory, but it also lost nearly 4.5 million people, most of them Christians. With Muslim migration after the Ottoman–Russian War of 1877–78, the proportion of Muslims in the empire increased further. The empire needed new governance strategies for this new demographic situation and to counter separatist nationalist movements. As discussions on the so-called Eastern Question continued, the Ottoman government felt a need for reforms to ensure the empire's survival. For this reason, Abdülhamid II's administrative reforms were seen by the Ottoman political elites and state actors less as interventions to deceive Europe and more as practical interventions to ameliorate the situation, with an eye to the empire's survival. In such a situation, the government aimed first and foremost to gain information related to human and natural resources. The 1881 census should be evaluated within this context.[132] At the same time, gaining better understanding of the population became critical to resisting European powers who interfered in the empire by using the situation of its Christian subjects as an excuse.[133]

In the nineteen years between 1877 and 1896, official records show that around a million Muslims from Crimea, the Caucasus, and the Balkans immigrated to the Ottoman Empire. By 1908, the number had exceeded two million. The arrival of Muslim immigrants increased the overall proportion of Muslims in Anatolia, and Islam was deployed as a method of assimilating immigrants.[134] There was doubtless a direct link between the empire's new population structure and its attempt to employ pan-Islamism.

Not only did the demographic distribution change throughout this process, but internal power balances also shifted. In 1876, Abdülhamid II dissolved the Parliament.[135] While on the one hand he continued to carry out administrative reforms, on the other he shifted political power from the Sublime Porte to Yıldız Palace and tried to legitimatize this shift by using pan-Islamism as the basis for a new politics of legitimacy. Pan-Islamism thus emerged in this context as a defensive ideology of resistance to the West.[136]

According to Selim Deringil, the application of pan-Islamism as a means of legitimation had two basic levels. The first comprised propaganda and education directed at Muslims within the empire so as to incorporate them as much as possible and to position the sultan as holder of the caliphate. In this way, an imagined community of Islam was created and expanded. Second, the framework for Muslims who were subjects was situated along a narrow and exclusionary political axis by standardizing and spreading the Hanafi school of Islam, while Muslims who were not subjects were excluded through travel restrictions.[137] This distinction also created the exclusion of non-Hanafi Muslims. This period is one in which the symbols of power in the Ottoman Empire were reinvented and redesigned through pan-Islamism and rendered broadly visible.[138]

At this significant point, the government began collecting statistical data. Gathering more detailed population statistics points to a long-term change in techniques of governing. Even after all its territorial losses, the Ottoman Empire was geographically expansive and in population terms remarkably heterogeneous. In this context, there was a clear wish to craft government strategies in accordance with information gathered about the population living in the empire's territories. Indeed, the knowledge gathered through both old and new techniques of surveillance was used to govern people more than to learn about their inclinations. Governing and administering the population became more important than ruling over the population within the borders of the empire through traditional apparatuses.

The Hamidian Era saw attempts to improve the efficacy of the census system. A trained cadre was developed, and audits by inspectors were put in place to prevent negligence in record keeping. In 1900, the Population Registry Charter (Sicill-i Nüfus Nizamnamesi) was renewed and, with minor changes, went into effect in 1902. The rules around population registers and identity documents grew stricter, and the records on those registered through the census grew more detailed.[139] New administrative units were established to make use of these new technologies and aimed to penetrate the population through health and welfare policies.[140] Reforms were devised, and the state was governmentalized as an administrative apparatus. The state aimed to render society legible. New techniques of surveillance suited to this end were put into practice, and policies were developed based on the data obtained. The state then waited for people to act according to anticipated codes of behavior. Rather than entering into people's behaviors as part of a governmental project, the government during the Hamidian Era developed coarse methods of interventions intended to delimit behaviors. These methods rested on the distinction between acceptable and unacceptable behaviors and included everything from the censorship of printed materials and theater plays to house searches and mass arrests. The underlying reason for the creation of such methods was the problem of legitimacy, pointing to a broader hegemonic crisis. In this condition of crisis, the government was eager to find new mechanisms to ensure social control and to develop strategies related to the repressive apparatus until the hegemony of new policies of legitimacy was achieved.

In the Hamidian Era, limited surveillance techniques were developed, and priority was given to policing practices organized such that the individual's ties to the existing social order (or to the order imagined by the center) would not be broken and anyone's opposition to this social order would be prevented. Yet although the transformation of the techniques of government was notable, it was limited in nature. Even if the political will existed, the empire lacked the apparatus for implementation. The limited nature of infrastructural power shows that at the scale of the empire, power was still exerted through indirect rule in most regions.

In addition, a parallelism was established between the security of the sultan and that of the regime and the empire. As in czarist Russia, even if political policing and everyday policing were carried out in tandem, the emperor was at the center. He held the monopoly on power and on the security of the state, with which he was identified.[141] This was demonstrated when, following an attempted coup by Ali Suavi in 1878, Abdülhamid shut himself in the palace and by the fact that the problem of security (both his own and that of the empire) became one of the major problems of the day. This shift should be understood not as a sign of paranoia but as the basis of the new politics of legitimacy.[142] In accord with the concept of raison d'état, the government attempted to establish a tight link between the security of Abdülhamid and his regime and the security of the state. This link can also be traced in the link between forms of public assistance by the sultan and the politics of legitimacy. As discussed in the previous chapter, these connections show how welfare practices and policies of policing became articulated in Mann's sense.

The censorship policy pursued throughout the Hamidian Era[143] left its traces in security measures, such as the strict passport regime and particularly in the control of comings and goings in Istanbul, the tracking of suspicious characters, and the fear of anarchist activities in Europe. The Hamidian Era was for the Ottoman Empire a period when the category of the internal enemy in the modern sense was constructed, and the borders of politics were formed through this basic reference. The security precautions put in place after the Armenian revolutionary movement began were particularly of incontrovertible importance for the capital. That situation opened a broad space for state security activities on the pretext of an internal threat.

Political Elites and Security Policies

This conjuncture gave rise to the foregrounding of the security problem for the Ottoman government and to the political formations that emerged in tandem. Modern legitimacy policies were invented to secure subjects' loyalty, and attempts were made to eliminate through policies of repression anything thought to constitute a threat to security. The dissolution of the Constitution, censorship practices, practices of exile, a ban on assembling, and surveillance mechanisms were individual components of the policies of repression. Alongside such visible and severe methods, forms of record keeping, initiatives to control geographical mobility, and methods to suppress or incite ethnic conflict and lynching after certain political events were established as the state's more subtle repressive strategies. Weber's definition of the modern state in terms of its monopoly on legitimate violence is of central importance here. However, as Alf Lüdtke discusses in his critique of Weber,[144] the central point is to guarantee the legitimacy not of the state itself but of the state's actions as an apparatus.

In particular, one must consider the forms of violence immanent to the state though often unseen. Thus, the need to consider a matter that Weber did not discuss: the practices of domination and the conditions for the possibility of state domination. Domination and violence are most often possible in terms of social mechanisms and strategies crafted by administrators.[145] In this sense, the symbolic practices that rested on pan-Islamism and that portrayed the sultan as a protective father should be considered alongside policies of oppression and domination. As Jeff Goodwin notes, one cannot say that in the presence of powerful revolutionary movements, a wide spectrum of society has accepted the state's monopoly over legitimate violence.[146] What distinguishes the Hamidian Era is the state's awareness of and intervention in the crisis of legitimacy. Precisely because the state was in the middle of such a crisis, one should not be surprised by its use of oppressive policies. This crisis situation for the Ottoman political elites revealed that the security and survival of the state were in danger. Such a condition brought the implementation of strategies developed in accordance with the Ottoman government's definitions of a legitimate threat and the state's interests. This intervention amounted to a reconstruction of the social order. Yet in this condition of crisis, the state also gained a new space to organize the social order as it deemed fit.[147] Another matter that must be discussed here is the nature of the law in terms of Weber's monolithic legal system and the application of standard rules in the same way to all agents. In conditions of crisis and above all when security and legitimacy are at stake, it is difficult to speak of a legal system functioning in this fair manner. As will be seen in the later discussions of passport practices, the government in fact developed different practices and rules for different agents in accordance with its perception of threat.

What is surprising is that because the empire's infrastructural power apparatus was insufficient to ensure intensive power, its security implementations created insecurity for certain subjects, especially Armenians, and so what was meant by "security" was in fact generally the regime's security, not the people's. This is a natural consequence when raison d'état is applied only with an eye to the survival of the state.

Moreover, Ottoman political elites' perceptions of nationalism often derived from reactions to central-state practices and the Great Powers' economic expansionism. However much the Ottoman government might have prioritized local demands in the early stages of security implementation, its place within both the world economic system and the international order of states introduced certain limits to how it met these demands. Yet more than these effects, the government's way of perceiving its own subjects complicated the resolution of many problems. That political elites at times perceived the economic field and the political field as entirely separate and at other times as entirely the same further complicated matters. The perception of the state's subjects and the political field was rooted in the fact that the ideological notion of the circle of justice (*daire-i adalet*), so foundational to Ottoman political thought, appeared to have left behind Western ideas but in fact rested on an understanding of modernization based on Western notions and internalized by political elites. The idea of the circle of justice is that any power wishing to govern securely and to ensure public safety and security must be able to collect taxes and cultivate military power. Nor is autocratic rule confined to ensuring public safety: it also assures the fertility of agricultural production. In this way, it symbolizes and legitimizes the hierarchical social order. Those at the bottom of the hierarchy must ensure the continuity of production, meeting the needs of the upper rungs.[148]

These ideas and practices bring about a politics constituted on the belief that the government or political elites know what is best for citizens and a politics that prioritizes loyalty to the state rather than an understanding of citizenship that prioritizes the individual.[149] In the Hamidian Era, such a politics brought about both new legitimacy policies in a rapidly changing world and oppressive policies, particularly from the 1880s on.

In the port cities of the Balkans, the Aegean, and the Marmara, which were undergoing integration with European capitalism, there emerged such changes as the rise of a new middle class, new forms of labor, and ethnic divisions of labor. That is, even while there were structural changes to collective power, the spread of nationalist movements and territorial losses brought about the search for a new understanding of administration. Such a search was manifest in the early implementation in the Hamidian Era of techniques and attempts to render traditional institutions more visible through new forms of representation. Through this implementation, the Ottoman government attempted to exercise its sovereignty over the population within its borders, which became the space of state activity in a range of matters, from obtaining statistical information to organizing interrelations, controlling codes of behavior, as well as monitoring and controlling such situations along with disease and famine.[150] If such a broadly defined space of activity had legally specified borders, at its foundation was the assumption that the Ottoman government knew what constituted the common good for the people. This search for modern techniques of power should be considered in terms of Foucauldian debates on governmentality. Yet what distinguishes the Hamidian Era is that even while the Ottoman state was attempting to penetrate the population, it almost never honored the distinction between public and private space in matters related to security. The broad authority granted to the police to carry out searches, to control practices in hotels, apartments, and inns, as well as to conduct raids on homes, associations, and churches clearly demonstrates how state elites approached this subject.

Alongside such practices, one should not forget that aid organizations and other institutions formed by non-Muslims in particular were subject to constant police monitoring. New administrative regulations and institutions traced a wide network of authority related to administrative practices carried out on the population and tied to security. In most analyses of Ottoman governments in the nineteenth century, the effectiveness of civil or military bureaucracy, as a group or class, is central. The structure that emerged through the types of legal regulations and practices described here should be considered as underscoring the social totality brought about by administration, as an aggregate not of bureaucracy but of a network or functions.[151] As such, the discussion of security will reveal how the state and political elites imagined society. Decisions taken in relation to security both rendered politics a technical matter and increased state intervention in daily life. The administrative network emerged as a pattern, a mentality, whose form can be traced in laws, regulations,

Council of State (Şûrâ-yı Devlet Tanzimat) decisions, and the like. This network also reveals how implementation extended from the very top of the bureaucracy to its lowest levels and how spatial and temporal differences and contradictions functioned within this network.

Migrant Laborers, Europeans, Suspicious Characters, Internal Enemies

The Armenian revolutionary movement and nationalist struggles in the Balkans brought the concept of *fesad*—"agitator," "sedition," "villain"—to the fore in the discourse of security. Although a distinction was observed at the discursive level between *fesad rüesası* (lead agitator or the one leading sedition) and the ignorant popular classes, the severity of the measures taken was at times risible—for instance, when the German emperor visited Istanbul, nearly half of the city's people were sent away, and another part of the population was held in prisons until the emperor left—or else completely disregarded the security of certain groups of people, as in the Armenian pogroms following the Ottoman Bank takeover.

Without a doubt, the administrative elites' discourse on the ignorance of the people is an indication of the elites' perception that only they were capable of making the correct decisions about and of ruling on everything, whereas the people, like children in need of direction, were incapable of recognizing what was needed for their own good. Other political dimensions included the facts that the traditional strategies of governance no longer functioned as a result of modernization reforms and socioeconomic changes in big port cities such as Istanbul and that the state's capacity to make independent decisions on a range of economic issues had faded.[152] Such a situation amounted to a powerlessness for the Ottoman government, which was lacking the ability to directly enter into the lives of its subjects because it had yet to constitute a modern apparatus of power. It was precisely on account of such powerlessness that administrative regulations and practices related to the problem of security were so severe. The Hamidian Era thus proceeded through the government's struggles to regain legitimacy with both consent and coercion in the face of an empire-wide crisis in legitimacy. We encounter a Janus face: searches for legitimacy to be gained at the symbolic level on one side and oppressive policies ready to be deployed at any moment on the other.[153]

Precautions related to the problem of security should also be understood in this manner. Seasonal migration laborers, generally considered in the literature in the context of public order, were seen in the Hamidian Era much as they had been since the time of Selim III (r. 1761–1808): along the lines of both public order and security.[154] Yet the beginning of the use of political violence—and more precisely anarchist terror—by the Macedonian and Armenian revolutionary movements, particularly after 1890, was among the reasons for the introduction of stricter controls on seasonal laborers. This situation also introduced in the Ottoman context the implementation of antianarchist precautions already seen in Europe. The Ottoman government, which was already closely following developments in Europe on this matter, not only increased its precautionary measures but also introduced new practices aimed in particular toward laborers who migrated to Istanbul for work. Although it is not known whether these practices were applied to everyone, the police records show that they were certainly carried out with respect to Armenians. The state viewed Armenians, especially those belonging to the lower classes, as potential threats. Certainly, such precautionary measures were not limited to Armenian migrants; the same security inquiries were conducted on foreign laborers working in different sites across the empire, with Austrian and Italian laborers garnering the most attention. Yet we must not overlook Abdülhamid II's frequent use of exile not just to control the elite, as is commonly thought, but also to threaten the lower classes. For example, some members of the Ottoman Labor Union (Osmanlı Amele Cemiyeti), organized between 1894 and 1895 at the Tophane factory, were exiled for doing nothing more than holding a meeting.

It is crucial to note that the era's understanding of security contained certain class distinctions, though it would be incorrect to claim that these distinctions were particular to the Ottoman Empire. In Prussia, France, and Austro-Hungary, too, links were drawn between vagrancy, anarchism, and seasonal laborers.

Moreover, all foreign nationals arriving in the empire were seen as potential threats. What we might call high-degree security practices became commonplace, particularly toward Europeans, and, apart from passport controls and customs practices, included the close monitoring of foreign nationals and searches of their hotel rooms. These practices were a reflection of the state's concern regarding its position within the international arena. This period, when the Eastern Question was still very much on the agenda and the empire was attempting to win a seat among the Great Powers, was characterized by insecurity and distrust. A curious and contradictory picture emerges of the empire: on the one hand pampering arriving Europeans, assuring their safety and security, wishing to portray the empire positively, but on the other shoring up the empire against Europeans by means of security measures.

The problem of censorship should also be considered alongside perceptions of threat to security. Censorship of the press, publications, and the theater was widespread. It included prohibitions on informing state officers overseas of news related to assassination attempts; on printing materials with what was considered seditious content or bringing such materials into the empire; and on depicting in the theater anything that might incite people or portray the death of the leader of any country.[155] It also included attempts to ensure that the state's ideology was the sole ideology in speech and print. Using censorship in this way, the state aimed to prevent the import of seditious ideas from outside into the empire, eliminate competing ideologies, and create an empty space for a new political hegemony.

Conclusion

The Hamidian Era was characterized by the government's attempts to advance policies of both oppression and consent, though the former were more visible, because the state was unable to truly respond to the rising forms of nationalism. As important as who or what state elites viewed to be a threat, in line with discussions of raison d'état, was the matter of how they classified and named these people. Such a process of classification and identification brought with it new administrative apparatuses and regulations to obtain information about the populace. The new forms of population regulation worked to render the population legible with such aims as conscription, taxation, the prevention of uprisings, security, and public order. Thus, in the Hamidian Era the beginning of the institution-alization of social services, social security, the police; the use of identity cards, passports, and residence documents; and the keeping of records on such matters increased the state's infrastructural capacity and cre-ated a space for the administration of society. The government built up a standardized pool of information about society and set about categoriz-ing various elements within it. This process also brought about a range of regulations and practices related to subjects or situations seen as threaten-ing. Largely taking shape in line with raison d'état, this process opened up a broad space for political elites to reconstruct the state. The regulations and practices were shaped by a new system of registration that arose atop traditional mechanisms of social control. And in the face of threats, there emerged a transitivity between traditional and modern concepts, just as in the administrative system. This transitivity functionally facilitated the construction of the state's apparatuses of infrastructural power and pointed to a modern state apparatus that had yet to settle into place.

3

Antianarchism, Interimperial Security Collaborations, and the Ottoman Empire

The last half of the nineteenth century, including the Hamidian Era, was a period when political currents grew more varied, and state elites responded to the social demands giving shape to this political variation with suppression and containment. Alongside questions around the adequacy of political systems in responding to social demands, how the Ottoman government viewed and understood these demands is of critical importance. This was a period when deep social cleavages along ideological lines grew more visible and brought about ideological efforts at political mobilization through new means and methods. Such an environment created new possibilities for the Ottoman government to define new elements of threat and new conditions of danger.

There is a link immanent to everyday life between the "survival of the state" and systems of social control. This link rests on two foundations: there is, first, a need for institutionalized means of social control; second, the people must approve of—see as legitimate—the use of these means. One of the conditions ensuring such legitimacy is the state's pledge to provide security. Thus, the state gained great leeway in constructing and organizing the social order, pointing to security as the reason. This is why times of crisis in security were also times when the state enacted new security regulations with the greatest intensity. Security crises both reveal the limits of the state's capacity to govern and may lead to the state's use of new means to broaden its field of *penetration*. Several exemplary events in the second half of the nineteenth century reveal such transformations at work.

This chapter attempts to make sense of the assassinations carried out with increasing frequency in the second half of the nineteenth century, in line with the method of "propaganda by the deed," and to understand the efforts of governments working in interimperial/international collaboration and in the face of these assassinations to define anarchists and anarchist acts, particularly through the International Conference of Rome for the Social Defense against Anarchists in 1898. In any consideration of the antianarchist collaboration that formed the main axis of this conference, the St. Petersburg Protocol (1904), the Ottoman government's stance at both meetings is of central importance for what it reveals about new systems of registry and the place of the Ottoman government in the interimperial network of knowledge exchange. Positioning the Ottoman Empire in a Eurasian interimperial frame also enables us to explore the synchronizations of the various administrative systems of policing and surveillance developed in this period. This chapter looks at the administrative debates within the state apparatus, set in motion by cooperation between governments in the international system, on new rules and practices focused on security. This debate would in this long term bring about a series of institutional parallels.

Anarchists and Propaganda by the Deed

For Europe, the nineteenth century was a period in which the status quo was increasingly disrupted, the social order was reorganized, and the public increasingly demanded a part in the political process. Elites typically conceptualized these demands as forms of disorder, requiring police regulations to ensure the reconstruction—within certain confines—of the social order with reference to the concept of public safety. Pervasive in this period was an international fear related not so much to the working class itself but to its mobilization within rising socialist and nationalist movements. In particular, when the Concert of Europe, led by Klemens von Metternich, was threatened by the Revolutions of 1848, several new regulations related to the institutionalization of the police came about.

These types of regulations had already begun in France. In 1811, under Napoleon's chief of police, Joseph Fouché, a special unit was established with the aim of keeping an eye on society and monitoring the public. Political parties, mobilization at the borders, and booksellers were also monitored. In addition, among the duties of the railway police—established in 1846 and tasked with the security of railways and public order on trains—was political policing. Political policing was also included in the definition of the gendarmerie's duties. In particular, the Republican Guard of Paris, linked directly to the gendarmerie in 1849, was tasked with political policing for the capital. During the Third Republic, one of the basic duties of the Paris police was to keep the government abreast of everything. Especially after 1848, efforts were made to eradicate secret societies. The practice of exiling members of secret societies overseas was, within the framework of the by-laws and the new penal code of 1851, recognized as being within the scope of police authority. All of these duties should, of course, be considered alongside the ongoing censorship of the press.[1]

Like France, Austria-Hungary was an early example of the institutionalization of the police. The political police monitored both government opponents and the daily life of the people. Yet in the early nineteenth century, this function had not long been under the same umbrella as the institution of the public police. From 1791, people, publications, and theater plays, in particular those from France or that spread the influence of revolution, began to be approached in security terms. The state increasingly established a discursive link between the regime's security and individual security. By 1815, the Habsburg Empire had begun to centralize the police, and regulations were enacted to ensure that public police and political police were able to act in concert. One of the greatest concerns in this period was geographical mobility, which must be considered alongside the geographical spread of ideas. In the 1820s, for instance, Austria-Hungary shared information with the governments of Prussia and czarist Russia regarding foreign revolutionaries in its territory.[2] Moreover, the press, theaters, symbols, paintings, and books were subject to constant censorship.

The Orsini Affair in 1858 was an important turn for ideologically motivated acts of violence. While in England, Felice Orsini, an Italian nationalist, planned an attack at the Paris Opera with the aim of killing Napoleon III. The plot was ultimately unsuccessful, but the incident introduced new discussions of public order and internationalized problems of security. First, related to acts against the security of other states, it set off a debate on state legal regulations of all individuals residing within a state's borders and thus the situation of political refugees plotting assassinations of other states' leaders. Checks on foreigners, which had already grown more intense following the Revolutions of 1848, became even more frequent, particularly against workers and socialists. For instance, after this affair France issued a regulation to exile overseas political suspects without a trial.[3]

After 1848 in Russia, Czar Nicholas I gave the order to the Third Section, a political policing unit, to tighten censorship and monitoring. In the 1860s, the Russian state had recourse to such regulations as issuing emergency laws for the penal system and granting governors the authority to ban public gatherings and close all clubs or organizations they deemed contrary to the order of the state or the public or to morality.[4] One finds similar regulations in other European contexts. Following the unsuccessful assassination attempt against Czar Alexander II, the first security bureau was established in 1866. In 1875, rural administrators and the gendarmerie were tasked with monitoring teachings that attacked the state, society, or family life. In 1881, after an assassination attempt against Alexander II finally succeeded, the security bureau gained strength through a struggle with the political opposition and by the 1890s had assumed a central role in the state.[5]

In the process of the bureaucratic development and expansion of police units, even different administrative setups in different geographies shared certain broad aims. The operationalization of police units by states made international cooperation possible across police units. In the second half of the nineteenth century, there was increasing intergovernmental cooperation on matters of intelligence and the tasks of the secret police related to border regions. On the heels of this cooperation came common rules created for petty crimes. For instance, in 1869 Austria embarked with other governments on legal regulations related to preventing the international trafficking of white women.[6] In 1902, the Bureau on the Suppression of White Slave Trade was established, followed by the Paris Convention of 1910.[7] The creation of shared methods to trace criminals followed international cooperation. For example, European governments commonly used *portrait parlé*,[8] which made it possible to identify people through facial measurements, until the development in 1902 of the technique of finger-printing in Britain.[9] This period saw the beginning of the institutionalization of police organizations in states beyond Europe. These countries sent their own bureaucrats to Europe to learn new techniques and imported experts from Europe. As well as Japan, China, and the Ottoman Empire, the new Balkan states also took these steps after 1878.

By the 1880s, governments began to create alliances between policing organizations to take shared precautions against a "wave of terror" of bombings and assassinations that had emerged both inside and outside of anarchist movements, though they were generally identified with such movements.[10] The widespread public tendency to associate anarchists with bombings was also to be observed in the police and other organs of the state. That is, anarchism was identified in a pejorative fashion with acts of terror.

Certain factors facilitated this identification. In particular, the rallying cry of "propaganda by the deed," first proposed by Carlo Pisacane, was gaining ground within the anarchist movement. "Propaganda by the deed" rested on the idea that theoretical propaganda (that is, mass meetings, newspapers, declarations, and the like) is limited in effect and easily manipulated by the bourgeoisie, whereas propaganda by the deed can rouse the masses.[11] The notion was subsequently developed by the Italian anarchists Errico Malatesta and Carlo Cafiero as well as by the German radical democrat Karl Heinzen and the Russian Nikolai Chernyshevsky.[12] Chernyshevsky's writing first influenced nihilists in Russia and spread through the acts of the Zemlya i Volya (Land and Freedom) revolutionary party. After Mikhail Bakunin laid the theoretical groundwork for the idea, propaganda by the deed grew in popularity. However, following the suppression of the Paris Commune in 1871 and of village uprisings in Spain in 1873, efforts to mobilize villagers in Italy also ended in failure.

Propaganda by the deed was among the main subthemes of the International Anarchist Congress in 1881. Anarchist acts of violence with a propagandistic aim created a general atmosphere of fear, which in turn led to harsher preventive policing. The fact that violent acts took particular aim at members of royal families and high-ranking bureaucrats played no small part in inducing this fear. Certainly, with the atmosphere created by the Paris Commune of 1871, one observes policies aiming to resist organization by workers and to monitor and suppress even small-scale organization. Related to these events, legal and administrative changes took place in Italy, Spain, and Germany with the implementation of antisocialist and antianarchist laws.[13] In particular, the fact that geographical mobilization continued at high levels led to the increasing use of policing techniques.

Although there were unsuccessful assassination attempts before this period—including a sensational attempt on the life of Governor-General Fedor Trepov of St. Petersburg by Vera Zasulich in 1878—these attacks' popularity among anarchists can be said to begin with the shooting of Nikolai Mezentsev, head of the czarist political police in St. Petersburg, by Sergei Stepniak-Kravchinskii of the Zemlya i Volya that same year.[14] Indeed, 1878 was the year when violent anarchist acts began to occur across all of Europe. Following the St. Petersburg incident, attempts were made to assassinate the kaiser of Germany and the kings of Italy and Spain.[15] In 1881, Czar Alexander II was killed in the fifth attempt on his life. In France, anarchist acts of violence began with the bombing of the statue of Adolphe Thiers in Saint Germain in June 1881. Then an unemployed man named Émile Florian came to Paris to kill the republican leader Léon Gambetta but, when unable to reach his target, tried to murder the first bourgeois he came across. In the same year, President James Garfield of the United States was killed. In 1896, Shah Naser al-Din of Iran was killed, and in 1900 anarchists attempted to assassinate his successor, Mozaffar ad-Din Shah, in Paris.[16] Not all these acts were carried out by anarchists; other political movements also practiced propaganda by the deed. In the 1890s, sixty people died and two hundred were injured in such attacks. In Paris between March 1892 and June 1894, nine people died in eleven bombings. In 1893, the Paris police passed on to their counterparts in Berlin information on plans to assassinate Emperor Wilhelm II and his chancellor, Leo von Caprivi. The occurrence of these incidents one after another[17] convinced the police, the political elite, and the press that a grand international anarchist conspiracy existed. There was a widespread belief that a central committee was behind multiple events that were in fact not connected to one another.[18] Further, one of the greatest fears of this period was that French and Russian revolutionaries would work together and instigate international disarray.[19] The acts of the Russian revolutionary organization Narodnaya Volya (People's Will)—which split from Zemlya i Volya—were the most talked of during the 1880s because it was the first to use dynamite in an assassination attempt.

Antianarchist Collaboration: Alliances, Definitions, Methods

The attacks left their imprint on the period between 1880 and 1914, both through the methods employed by revolutionary movements and through the administrative and policing norms and practices that states developed when faced with these new methods. This period was one in which the police institutions of a number of countries worked together against revolutionaries in a manner determined by the international conjuncture.[20] As previously discussed, from 1850 police institutions began to use new techniques, and there were efforts to introduce Europe-wide standards for various practices.[21] In 1898, an antianarchist conference organized in Rome some three months after the killing of Empress Elizabeth (Sisi) of the Austro-Hungarian Empire[22] was central to the institutionalization of international cooperation.[23]

The Conference of Rome

Discussions about having an antianarchist conference began in the wake of bombings in Paris and Barcelona in 1893, but such a conference was not convened until 1898, following the killing of a royal, Empress Elizabeth, with a renewed determination to establish an international antianarchist police league. Socialist parliamentarians from France, Belgium, and Germany saw the International Conference of Rome for the Social Defense against Anarchists as a preparation of sorts for an attack on the left. A Swiss diplomat participating in the conference even noted that he wondered whether the initiative was meant as a blow against all revolutionary elements.[24] Because the perpetrator of the attack on the empress was Italian, anti-Italian uprisings and lynchings occurred in Germany and Austria-Hungary. In particular, Slavs on Austria's border with Italy invaded the homes of Italians and forced hundreds to leave the country. Intelligence from Russia and France suggested that this assassination was only the first in a series targeting heads of state and that the second would be the king of Italy. This conjecture, along with pressure from Germany and Austria-Hungary, left Italy little choice but to call for the conference.[25] The Ottoman government's participation in this conference coincided with a period when there was use of explosives and organized actions, including assassinations, within the empire, as discussed in the previous chapter. Particularly following the attempted assassination of Abdülhamid II by Armenian and Bulgarian revolutionaries, several actions in the empire were inspired by Narodnaya Volya, though many came after the Conference of Rome (see chapter 1). These sorts of actions mostly turned into ethnic conflict and were suppressed through the use of disproportionate state violence. Indeed, Abdülhamid II had come to be known in Europe as the "Red Sultan" because of the massacres of Armenians in 1894–96. The Ottoman Empire's participation in the Conference of Rome can thus be read as a means for it to take its place in Europe with the Great Powers and to renew its image within the context of the internationalization of policing techniques.[26] Further, these new techniques presented new possibilities for suppression and could be used against opposition groups in a way that would make the Ottoman Empire appear in a more positive light before the European public.

For the Ottoman government, the problems of learning the new policing techniques and creating a network to share classified intelligence information were significant in terms of state elites being able to create new bureaucratic processes related to the groups they saw as threats to the state. These processes rested not so much on the mechanisms of traditional social control employed by the Ottoman government in the past but on a bureaucratic identity registry based on the individual.

Matters Considered at the Conference
of Rome and the Conference Text

The Conference of Rome was convened to find solutions to five main problems: defining anarchist acts and anarchy; devising new practices to head off anarchist acts and publications; clarifying whether crimes and criminals related to anarchism entered into the scope of extradition treaties or not; reviewing regulations for keeping anarchists under constant police watch and, when necessary, for deporting or extraditing them; and making appropriate regulations to impede the circulation of printed materials that were perceived to spread anarchist ideas.[27] Preceding the conference, the governments of Belgium, France, Great Britain, and Switzerland clarified that they would add an addendum to the Protocol of Rome produced from the conference in the event that any decision taken at the conference did not accord with their own domestic laws.[28]

Governments were tasked with presenting their views and declarations related to this protocol to the Cabinet of the Conference Rome—an administrative body established to proceed with the decisions made by the participating governments as part of the conference—within three months. The recommendations were approved in Rome with a majority of votes after the declarations related to the protocol were endorsed.[29]

The most significant debate of the conference emerged around the definitions of *anarchist* and *anarchist act*. Russia argued that anarchism had to be defined independently of politics and that it could in no way be related to a political doctrine.[30] According to Russia, when anarchism is related to politics, anarchist acts could in some countries make use of regulations related to the protection of political rights and thus escape punishment. This definition, it was argued, gave anarchists a possible way out of being delivered to the state where they had committed a crime. Conference delegates approved Russia's recommendation to distinguish between anarchism and politics.[31]

Russia also recommended that all acts of violence carried out with the aim of destroying social order and all publications praising the methods and acts of criminal plans and carrying suggestions for related enterprises also be labeled as anarchism. Regardless of the name used, it was argued, those who carry out such acts or produced such publications should be defined as anarchists. Conversely, the representative of Monaco focused on the definition not of anarchism but of the anarchist act and recommended it be defined as an "act aiming at the destruction of all manner of social organization through the use of violence and violent means."[32]

Across these debates, the specific conditions of each country led to different interpretations. For instance, Switzerland argued that countries should define anarchist acts on a case-by-case basis. Great Britain felt that the right to political expression had to be protected and that any regulations must not stand in the way of this right.[33] Though Russia and Germany insisted on a more detailed definition, in the final document the Monaco representative's recommendation was approved.[34]

Following the assassination of the Empress Elizabeth on September 18, 1898, Minister of Foreign Affairs Count Agenor Gołuchowski of Austria used the recommendation of an international police union against anarchism to argue that strict measures could be adopted against anarchists without violating Switzerland's democratic principles. He based this argument on the claim that anarchists were not a political opposition but rather "wild animals without a country," constituting a threat not just to rulers but to everyone and to all private property. This expression was significant in that it rendered anarchism apolitical. Indeed, the general trend at the Conference of Rome was in line with this apoliticization. The debate on defining anarchism and anarchist acts attempted to conceptualize anarchism as a criminal fact, not a political fact. When anarchist acts were abstracted from their political meaning and transformed into a criminal matter, the governmental precautions or practices related to such acts became administratively more easily manageable by police organizations;[35] significantly, in announcing the conference, the Italian government had requested that administrative and technical personnel should participate. Anarchist acts, seen by elites as a threat to the state's survival, amounted to interrogations of the legitimacy of the state and of social inequalities. Attacks on state elites were considered attacks directly on the state's survival. This atmosphere created a space for elites to develop acts, rules, techniques, and practices in the name of state security. However, for these techniques and practices to be effective and developed within the administrative totality of the state, anarchist acts had to constitute a security threat that was defined apolitically. Apoliticization demonstrated the state's power in terms of the discursive construction of knowledge and how it could thereby render invisible those political demands it perceived as counter to its own aims.

By rendering security a technical matter of administration, police systems in different states—which at the international scale more or less resembled one another—became part of a more consistent and systematic structure. Rendering such matters technical further shed their political characteristics for the purposes of administration.

The problem of the return of criminals to states where they committed an illegal act, meanwhile, was regulated by bilateral extradition treaties and domestic laws, with meetings foreseen between the state where the crime was committed and the criminal's state of nationality. Here, too, Russia's recommendation made it into the final protocol even as objections were raised on the grounds that it included all political criminals. However, it was not put into practice. On the matter of the methods for the prosecution of criminals, the most important article on the agenda was all countries' approval of *portrait parlé*.[36] Articles forbidding the use of illegal explosive materials, the instigation of anarchist acts, the making of anarchist propaganda, membership in anarchist organizations, and the aiding and harboring of anarchists were also approved.

Participating governments approached the approval of the final text differently. Serbia approved the final conference document. Stating that some of the changes in penal codes related to anarchism were already present in its own legal system, it clarified that it would add to its laws what was not already present.[37] The Swiss government stressed that it was making a voluntary, not an obligatory, declaration: it thereby both supported the decisions taken and evaded the legal liability required of the protocol.

Like Serbia, France stated that many of the articles in the conference protocol were already part of its own laws. Yet in its law of July 28, 1894, France had defined anarchism not according to the act but according to the aim. In administrative structuring and organization related to regulations, France was more advanced than most of the other states. The French Directorate-General of Security, affiliated with the Ministry of Interior, was tasked with functions related to anarchists. Though the Ministry of Interior had for some time been sharing information with other states, at the conference France diplomatically made known its reservations regarding the practice of sharing because of the possibility that the greater cooperation defined at the conference could lead to negative outcomes.[38]

Romania found a contradiction in the fact that someone who killed an ordinary person would be included within the scope of the return of criminals, whereas those who organized the assassination of a member of the royal family or a head of government would not be returned as a political criminal.[39] The conference concluded on December 21, 1898, with the addition of several reservations to the final document. The Ottoman government signed the treaty on the condition that the treaty would not affect its own treaty with Russia on limitations around the return of Armenians to Ottoman lands. Romania and Switzerland signed on the condition that the right to decide whether someone within their own borders was or was not an anarchist would remain the right of that particular government. Great Britain announced its support without signing the protocol and thus avoided liability for making the necessary legal changes. France signed the protocol on the condition that its communication with the police organizations of other states would be kept confidential.[40]

The governments of Sweden, Norway, Denmark, Romania, Portugal, Holland, and Spain saw a need for precautions related to punishments of the press and to the delivery and return of anarchist criminals and had strong reservations about making clear pledges on these matters. The representatives of Russia, Prussia, Austria-Hungary, Spain, Italy, and Serbia were inclined to take strong precautions. The Ottoman government saw itself as part of this second group. Only some matters at the conference were approved unanimously, but because the right for participating states to partially approve the protocol or to approve with annotation or to reject certain articles was recognized, the conference document as a whole was approved by all states, if with annotations. The Ottoman representatives stated that their government would import only those precautions that were not in conflict with domestic law. As they stated at the fifth meeting of the Conference of Rome, "The delegates of the Ottoman government vote on the recommendations of the commission looking into the measures of the laws, and declare that its actions do not mean that it enters into a commitment or pledge on matters of changing or devolving, related to recommendations on the subject of Ottoman domestic law, and that there exist authorities of the Ottoman government on changes related to its own domestic law."[41]

Information Provided by Police Chiefs

One of the most important subjects of the Conference of Rome was the matter of how states would share organizational information related to police administrations.[42] The representatives of different police institutions presented their policing and filing methods and their operational techniques as part of the knowledge exchange at the conference. These practices and institutional structures were deeply connected to the different states' administrative systems. Although there were some systemic similarities in these modern states' security bureaucracies, the presentations also showed the differences between states in the means of policing.

Thus, Great Britain described how it did not deport foreigners it suspected of being anarchists but kept them under close surveillance. The London police accepted information and tips in any language regarding people who took refuge in England. This information had to be accompanied by a portrait of the person about whom information was being shared. When such a person was deemed to be harmful to the state, their portrait was distributed to all police units and to anyone in a relationship of any sort with the person. Thus, such a person had no chance of finding residence anywhere and in this way was compelled to leave the country.[43]

The police administration of the Netherlands was built upon local institutions. Every city had its police in the mayor's employ, but the central police was under the administration of the Ministry of Justice and governed by the attorneys general in major cities. The local city police were able to send away vagrants, but deportation could be carried out only by a royal decree issued by the Senate and the House of Representatives. If a police chief did not extend the residency permit of a foreigner after three months, the decision-making authority was transferred to a justice of the peace. The king had the authority to order the deportation of a foreigner who was found to be a threat to public safety. Following such a decision, the foreigner was given fifteen days to leave the country. If they did not follow this order, they would be sent to a place of their choosing. Instead of deportation, the king could also order that an individual be settled in a certain locale or forbid that person from residing in a certain place. Such orders were sent to the House of Representatives but were given quite rarely.[44]

Russia, meanwhile, had introduced passports to control and keep people under surveillance. A passport visa was valid for a specified duration. In addition, its police force was made up of people who had previously served in the army. There was about one police officer for every five hundred people and one police captain for every three thousand people. Every police officer received a salary of two hundred to three hundred rubles, and every police captain was paid three hundred to four hundred rubles (either per month or every three months). When a deportation was ordered, a police officer took care to purchase a train or boat ticket for the deportee. If the person to be sent away was dangerous, they were taken to the border by car.[45]

In Sweden, security and public safety were commonly assured using the Vagrancy Law. All foreign individuals who upset public order or public safety or who were found to be unable to secure their own livelihood were deported by a police escort if they hailed from a neighboring country. The government would carry out the necessary deportation measures on the king's order for foreigners who came from a nonneighboring country. The Swiss government deported individuals it deemed dangerous. Though there was a police office in every township, there was no unified police force. The execution of the law on anarchists, issued on April 12, 1894, was the attorney general's duty.[46]

The French system was the most advanced in its implementation of antianarchist policies.[47] To keep anarchists under surveillance, the Directorate-General of Security kept two files. The first had portraits of foreign anarchists expelled from France to prevent their reentry. The second had portraits of foreign anarchists who had not been expelled from France and who lived outside the country with the aim of keeping them under observation should they enter the country. These two files were distributed to all administrative officers and to police and the gendarmerie. France used *portrait parlé* to define and classify information from the images.[48] This method, if adopted by all states, could be used in particular to identify anarchists by their portraits. For this reason, France extended an open invitation to provide training in *portrait parlé* to all states.[49]

France also had a registry system intended to assure general control of anarchists. A private file was created on every reported anarchist, with the person's registry—a file with information about their identity and address—portrait, and criminal record registered in an appropriate fashion. In the unit where these documents were stored, the files were arranged alphabetically by last name. This collection of summaries—held in perpetuity, with erasures or additions made when needed—was held by the Directorate-General of Security and comprised investigations into anarchists. Continuous observation was to be carried out on people registered as anarchists.[50] A file with the names of anarchists found within a province was issued to the gendarmerie, special committee, and the police chief of that province. These units were required to monitor if anarchists worked in the local factories, stalls, and shops. In the event that anarchists changed locations, the gendarmerie and the chief were to report as accurately and quickly as possible their destinations and reasons for the move, along with all related information, by telegraph to the Directorate-General of Security as well as to the appropriate gendarmerie, special committee, and police chief. If anarchists changed location by train, the commissioners at primary points along the route had to be informed. The governors of both the province the person was leaving and the province they were going to were to be informed. If it was not known where an anarchist intended to go, the Directorate-General of Security was to be notified immediately. The directorate issued a telegram instructing a search be carried out everywhere for this person. It was rare that an anarchist whose destination was unclear was not deported by such means.[51]

When it came to deportations or expulsions of foreign anarchists who had settled in France, the rules were implemented with a degree of tolerance. Of foreigners, only those who publicized their ideas and who frequently and continuously attended anarchist meetings were deported or expelled. Those deported as anarchists were transferred to their own countries' borders in prisoner-transport vehicles. On arriving at the border, the French Ministry of Foreign Affairs informed the government to which the anarchists were subject.[52] Two sorts of difficulties in deportation were resolvable only through cooperation. First, countries sharing a border might refuse to allow entry to people who were not their own subjects. Transfer by prisoner-transport vehicles was possible only to countries sharing a border with France. A certain amount of time was required to ensure that anarchists from farther away left the country. In these cases, they were asked which border they wished to be sent to and were transferred to the jail closest to that border. They were released here and informed that they had to leave France within a short period or face criminal proceedings. Thus, when these anarchists were released, they were freed from all oversight. Some had to get permission to pass through countries between the one they were in and their own country. If difficulties occurred—if the expelled person was a subject of a country neighboring France, but their own country did not respond, or if a jailbreak occurred or if a criminal was being sought because of unclear laws or regulations in treaties related to return or to a political crime—then they could not be turned over to a foreign government.[53]

Belgium used two different practices for such foreigners, depending on whether they were in the country unwillingly or they resided there de facto or wished to reside there. If provisions related to passports were in force, the admission of foreigners to Belgium was not subject to dealings at the border. The use of passport checks and controls had been lifted in 1862, after European governments came to a consensus on the matter. However, during certain important political events—for instance, after the establishment of order following the suppression of the Paris Commune—passport controls were temporarily reinstated. Though a foreigner could enter Belgium without a passport, when necessary they had to prove their identity by showing a formal document. According to the Belgian Criminal Code, hoteliers and renters of furnished homes had to keep a registry of foreigners residing in their accommodations and provide it to the municipal administration every day. The municipal administration in turn had to immediately present a copy of the registry to the Directorate-General of Security, which was affiliated with the Ministry of Justice. Thus, the Belgian Directorate-General of Security knew at once of travelers arriving to the country's main areas. Further, foreigners staying for more than fifteen days at a hotel had to carry out an additional procedure: they had to inform local municipal officials where they were staying and provide a document containing information about their identity, such as their place and date of birth, the names of their parents, their place of residence, and where they had last stayed. This information was to be provided in the form of a tally and sent to the Directorate-General of Security. Foreigners who arrived with the intent of settling had to go through the same procedures. Using these tallies, the Directorate-General created a file for each foreigner. Aside from diplomatic officers, no foreigner was exempt from this rule, regardless of rank. For all foreigners in all circumstances, an investigation was conducted into their identity and criminal record. For this purpose, the Directorate-General applied to officials in the country of origin as well as in the country where the individual resided. When the investigation concluded, should the Directorate-General of Security deem it necessary, a request was made to the Ministry of Justice to deport the foreigner. Local officials and the gendarmerie were also required to inform the Directorate-General of any behavior by foreigners that they saw as contrary to peace and order.[54] When the Belgian government had to deport a malicious person, it did so without reservation: some twenty thousand people were deported annually, including vagrants. The gendarmerie conveyed each deportee to the border and then to their own country.[55]

The countries' individual policing techniques and filing methods show the infrastructures of policing in different European settings. These techniques and methods had significant importance for knowledge production and information gathering about foreigners, suspects, and anarchists. Although the details of process and lines of authority varied, methods of deportation and record keeping were broadly similar among the participants of the Conference of Rome. In particular, these shared methods related to the deportation of foreigners and record keeping about them were the first steps toward a form of international administrative cooperation on policing that would later come to be known as Interpol.[56]

Controls and Monitoring of Anarchists between States

The police officers present at the conference approved the methods related to supervision and surveillance implemented by France, Prussia, and Russia. A unanimous decision was taken to prepare a monthly tally of the anarchists deported from each country, including their population registry document, photograph, a description in line with *portrait parlé*, and the purpose and reason for their departure (even if by their own wishes). Each government's administrative police center was to send copies of all documents to the concerned offices of other governments. At the beginning of this exchange of information, many governments prepared charts with the names and addresses of administrative police centers.

In addition, representatives at the police meeting approved the use of *portrait parlé*, which France recommended as a technique for the identification of a person through their portrait, as a standard technic for international cooperation in policing and information sharing and generally used for bandits and anarchists. Although the first few pages of the passport contained some information used to verify a person's identity, as on an identity card, this information alone had come to be seen as insufficient. Instead, the *portrait parlé* method, a subtechnique of anthropometry, was developed: a measurement technique that focuses on the eyes to specify a person's identity and uses the angles and measurements of certain points on the body and face. Whereas anthropometry usually requires one to be close to one's subject, *portrait parlé* does not. This technique, which is used to find lost persons, requires one photograph taken from the front and one from the side. One police officer from every state was to be sent to Paris for training in *portrait parlé* in March after the conference.[57]

The Ottoman State, the Conference of Rome, and the St. Petersburg Protocol

Recommendations by the Ottoman Commission

Following the Conference of Rome, the Ottoman government set up a commission for the Ottoman response to the Rome Conference under the Ministry of Foreign Affairs to prepare its response to the Cabinet of Rome within the designated period. The commission included the chief of the Criminal Division of the Court of Appeals (Mahkeme-i Temyiz Ceza Dairesi Reisi), the correspondence officer on foreign affairs, the chief of the Court of Appeals, the legal counsel of the Sublime Porte, and the minister of foreign affairs.

The commission for the response to the Rome Conference initiated a study of conference decisions and proceedings and compared them to Ottoman domestic law, mainly the Ottoman Penal Code (OPC, Ceza Kanunname-i Hümayunu).[58] The commission's final report also considered how the OPC could be used for antianarchist legal practices. The commission examined the conference under five headings:[59] the first two related to its main rules, the third to administrative tasks, the fourth to the return of criminals, and the fifth to the issue of making new laws. The main rules rested on debates related to the definition of the terms *anarchist* and *anarchist act* and on the discussions of anarchism as not constituting a political view. Throughout this debate, Ottoman representatives held that in defining anarchism it was necessary to look not at the aims of the agent but at the nature of the act.

This position can be interpreted within the framework of the "principle of legality" in criminal law. According to the commission, administrative tasks focus on controlling and observing anarchists. Thus, the conference articles—which regulated the establishment of central administrations and the communication between them as well as the right to judge any deported anarchist based on past crimes—approved of sending an official to Paris to learn the *portrait parlé* technique to identify such people[60] and subsequently adopting its use. Related to Article 4, the commission endorsed the rules for the return of criminals as approved between governments and agreed to add acts of agitation and incitement to the accepted reasons for the return of criminals. It considered a decision on the delivery and return of those planning the assassinations of rulers, members of ruling families, and heads of state—no matter the circumstances—a major advance in banning propagandistic misrepresentation and seditious acts.

At the Conference of Rome, additions proposed by Ottoman representatives, though not approved by the majority, suggested that all manner of undertakings, alliance, enticement, instigation, and praise related to assassinations should be defined as acts requiring the return of the criminals in question.[61] The Ottoman delegation at the conference had also supported the German and Russian proposal on extradition procedures that was ultimately rejected. The main aim of that proposal was to eliminate the limits of extradition treaties and to gain wider legal ground for the deportation or extradition of so-called anarchists.[62] The Ottoman delegation had also proposed widening the procedures on extradition of perpetrators so that not only assassins of rulers, members of ruling families, and heads of states but also those involved in propaganda and agitation to promote assassination would be included within the extradition regulations. While preparing the Ottoman response to the Conference of Rome, the commission considered these rejected proposals, stating that if negotiations continued in the future, the Ottoman government would again take them up. The commission declared that the Ottoman government would act in accordance with the decisions of the Conference of Rome but was prepared to enter bilaterally into reciprocal agreements, negotiations, and conclusions with states holding positions similar to the Ottoman government's.[63]

On the issue of the making of new laws, the commission identified four main subjects.[64] First, it was necessary to import into the OPC the crime of anarchism. The commission recognized that a definition of this crime already existed in the criminal codes of certain states but clarified that adding such a crime to the OPC would ensure that heavier punishments were brought to bear in the event of crimes of an anarchist nature. It also stated that because anarchists could now not be identified as political criminals, having the specific crime of anarchism on the books would be important and necessary to prepare the legal reasons for their delivery and return. It was for this reason, the commission stated, that ever since such seditious ideas had begun to threaten public order and peace, for some seven or eight years, a number of European states had added articles related to anarchism to their criminal codes.[65] According to the commission, though such criminals were punished according to the degree of the crime committed in Ottoman lands, these punishments could in certain circumstances be rather mild relative to those given for anarchist acts. Because it was not possible to deport criminals when certain acts had features of political crimes, it recommended that a special section with a title invoking anarchist crimes be added to the OPC. The commission looked to the laws of such countries as France and Italy for how they identified such crimes and noted the necessity of designing appropriate punishments.[66]

For Conference of Rome clause 5.A, the commission recommended that, besides violent acts of an anarchist nature, certain acts that involve abetting such acts, up to and including participation, also be subjected to criminal penalties.[67] About such acts—five of the six concerning intentional injury or harm and one the intentional preparation and especially the production and storage of combustible or deadly materials known to have been used to carry out or intended to carry out an anarchist act as well as all materials used in their manufacturing—the commission referred to the appendix of OPC Article 58, which stated: "If anyone who produces or invents or transports or prepares or carries a firearms, ammunition, knives, bombs, or any other similar destructive, incendiary, or fatal device is found to be present in an act of murder or a matter of sedition, he is to be executed, and if he is not present in such an act but is found to have made such an attempt, he is to be sentenced to a minimum of fifteen years of hard labor."[68]

The second paragraph of the conference's clause 5.A was about those who carry out the same acts or create an enterprise to prepare such acts. It also concerned joining into an agreement or company created for such a purpose. Though OPC Article 58 specified the penalty to be given for "creating conditions or situations that involve a secret alliance between two or more people for the carrying out of a crime related to disrupting the internal and external security of the Ottoman Empire, or to assassination," applying the article to anarchist murders would be difficult, so the commission argued there was a need for a separate article on distinctions between anarchist crimes.[69]

Regarding paragraph 5.A.3 of the Conference of Rome recommendations, the commission stated that although OPC Article 63 articulated penalties "regarding those who carry out the performance of assistance in such a manner to bandit and brigand groups," and although Article 45 stated that "the collective agents of a crime are, in a circumstance where the law is unclear, to be punished as independent agents of the crime," it was not appropriate to use articles applied to bandits and brigands to deal with anarchists and to liken such groups to anarchists. The commission was of the opinion that so long as the crime of anarchism was not disentangled legally, delivering verdicts would not be possible.[70] Compared to the conference document, in the OPC the concept of anarchist remained an open one, and the commission thought that there was a need for a special article of law. With the clarification of penalties for crimes of praising a violent act of an anarchist nature and provoking or inciting such an act, openly or secretly (specified in OPC Article 66 as directed at "those who provoke and incite the people directly to carry out murder in violation of the internal security of the Exalted State"), the commission emphasized that such violations of internal security would be included within the scope of political crimes and so clarified the need for a special article of law even if the current article applied in some degree to such cases.[71]

The phrasing in paragraph 5.A.5 of the conference recommendations differed from the first line of the same clause, and because the phrasings were not close in meaning or intent, the appendix to OPC Article 58 clarified that the conference article's implementation would not be possible. In such a situation, through the application of the Gunpowder Regulation (Barut Nizamnamesi) of 1876, the seizure of materials produced was required, as was a monetary penalty of twice the value of the goods, such that the penalty in question was insufficient to explain the aims of the crime. Due to this discrepancy and because of the need to draw up a prison penalty, the Ottoman commission recommended that an article be added to this section related to anarchist crimes. Conference paragraph 5.A.6 saw that a new law was needed because no article in the penal code was capable of commenting in any way on the spread of anarchism among soldiers.[72]

Clause 5.B of the conference recommendations was related to laws within countries on deterring cooperation with anarchist acts. In general, what constituted cooperation was left up to a judge's discretion. Article 45 of the OPC included a general rule that needed to be reformed specifically for anarchist crimes because it currently mandated punishing collaborators as individual agents. Paragraph 5.E.2 of the conference recommendations mandated solitary confinement for anarchist acts, both for suspects in custody and during prison sentences. According to the commission, the third paragraph of the same section called for the revision of the OPC to attend to the matter of holding certain prisoners under observation following the completion of their sentences.[73]

Clause 5.F of the conference recommendations required a special legal provision related to execution as the punishment for the assassination of rulers, heads of states, and members of ruling families, while item G of the same article recommended that those sentenced to death for an anarchist murder should not be publicly executed. However, the Ottoman representatives considered the death penalty to have a deterrent function that was better preserved if the penalty were carried out publicly and did not believe that accepting this part of the document would be of use.[74]

Clause 5.H stated that all murders related to anarchism, regardless of their specific reasons, were to be seen as anarchist acts, and those responsible would be treated accordingly. The final document of the conference stated that those who endangered others while realizing their criminal aims and the presence of bad actors in a country were detrimental to public safety because they created an atmosphere in which the lives and property of all members of a society were in danger. Moreover, time would be spent, if not wasted, on discovering the motives of those who carry out anarchist acts. For these reasons, the commission considered it necessary to add an article to the OPC related to applying the punishment for conducting anarchist acts to any act having to do with anarchism, whatever the reason.[75]

Conference paragraphs 5.C.1, 5.C.2, and 5.D, on regulations related to the press, provided penalties in the appendix of OPC Article 66 related to the printing, publication, distribution, and storage of printed or unprinted harmful materials and reordered section 13 of the OPC on regulations related to the printing and distribution of dangerous documents. The Regulation on Printing Houses (Matbaalar Nizamnamesi) of 1885 set out penalties for those who transferred, distributed, and sold printed documents, pictures, and medals related to dissent. Yet with the addition to the OPC of an article related to anarchism, the need arose for specific regulations.[76]

Paragraph 5.C.2 of the Conference of Rome recommendations required criminal sentences for the publication and conveyance of legal proceedings and negotiations related to organized anarchist acts, particularly the publication of the suspects' declarations. It also required the creation of a new regulation granting the authority to legally forbid the statute of return when it was seen as endangering peace and public safety. The OPC had little clarity on this subject; though controls on the press existed, there was no specific order to prevent rulings from being printed. Under Conference clause 5.D, there were negative consequences for giving detailed accounts of anarchist acts in something published with the aim of delivering the daily news; thus, such a ban was considered appropriate, and, indeed, it was appropriate to ban all publication. Yet although pre-publication controls could to some degree prevent such news from appearing in the Ottoman Empire, rather than leaving this important matter to the personal discretion of press officers, it was decided that the matter should be incorporated into the OPC through the designation of an appropriate penalty.[77]

The Ottoman commission's proposals and responses to the final recommendations of the Conference of Rome were approved by the Council of Ministers (Meclis-i Mahsus-u Vükela) on May 27, 1899, and conveyed to the Cabinet of Rome.[78]

The Ottoman Antianarchist Draft

Following the Conference of Rome in 1898, the Regulations on Anarchist Crimes (Anarşist Ceraimi Hakkında Nizamname) were drafted as an addition to the OPC. These regulations defined anarchism and encompassed every act and effort carried out with the aim of destroying the social order. An individual involved in an act or attempt to damage the sovereign or to change the form of state administration was to be evaluated as an anarchist regardless of how they described themselves.[79] According to Article 2 of the regulations, the performance of or attempts to perform acts such as sedition, murder, killing, theft, intimidation or crimes such as opposing, disobeying, or insulting state officials to achieve anarchist aims was to be punished (per the first, second, and third clauses of the appendix and addendum of OPC Article 54; in Articles 55, 56, and 57; in the first and second clauses of Article 58; in Articles 58, 60, 61, 62, 64, and 66; in the appendix of Article 60; and in Article 136). Upon the completion of their punishment, the individuals would remain under police observation for a certain period.[80] Those who were present at an anarchist act, established an enterprise for such an aim regardless of its size, made such an agreement, or were involved lifelong in such an enterprise or agreement were sentenced to a minimum of ten years hard labor. According to Article 4 of the regulations, an individual who received an offer to join such an enterprise or agreement and did not join but also did not notify the government was to be sentenced to between one to two years. If they participated but informed the government, then after the required investigation, they were exempt from punishment and were placed under police observation for one to five years. According to Article 5, if it was established that individuals who were not a part of an enterprise or agreement but knowingly communicated with anarchists and abetted them by providing a meeting place were to be sentenced to at least five years of hard labor in the event that the crimes of those they aided were determined to be murder. If the crime did not result in murder, they were to be sentenced to a minimum of one year of imprisonment. In the same manner, if those who aided and abetted a crime were a part of an enterprise or agreement, they were to be sentenced to a minimum of one year of imprisonment. Those who perpetrated the act or attempt to print, overtly or covertly distribute, transport, sell, or display written, oral, printed, or unprinted provocative materials such as documents, booklets, newspapers, pictures, depictions, and portraits that were anarchistic of nature, seditious as described in Article 2, or criminal or that had the aim of carrying out crimes that violated the security of the state were considered an accessory to a crime. If the act in question did not take place or was planned but could not be carried out, then penalties of hard labor and imprisonment were to be imposed. These regulations make constant reference to the OPC section on crimes committed against the state, which emphasized and defined as crimes those acts considered with the concept of sedition (*fesad*).

The Regulations on Anarchist Crimes, though approved by the Ottoman Assembly, were not enacted. According to a document written by the Grand Vizierate, the anarchist scourge sweeping across America and Europe was seen in Ottoman lands only among Armenians and some Bulgarians. The vizierate saw the application of existing laws to the acts of such agents as sufficient. As such, with the Ottoman government's signing of the Protocol of Rome, it came to consider an anarchist act in the sense defined in that document as a crime against the state. Thus, although on the one hand making use of international cooperation and the new techniques that stemmed from it and on the other feeling no need for a distinct antianarchist law, the vizierate did not apoliticize the matter. Yet one must not forget that the antianarchist law in France, as discussed earlier in the chapter, took anarchism into the category of political crimes by looking not at anarchist *acts* but at the harboring of anarchist *aims*. Although the Ottoman government did not fully follow the decisions of the Conference of Rome, it was nevertheless in step with the most effective system in Europe.

The St. Petersburg Protocol

In 1904, following the Conference of Rome, the St. Petersburg Protocol was drawn up to regulate the return of anarchists to their home countries. On Russia's invitation, the states that participated in the protocol were Germany, Austria-Hungary, Denmark, Luxembourg, Holland, Portugal, Romania, Serbia, Sweden, Norway, Switzerland, the Ottoman Empire, Bulgaria, and Russia.

Prior to signing the St. Petersburg Protocol, Hakkı Beyefendi, legal counsel to the Sublime Porte, examined the recommendations made by Germany and Russia and wrote an opinion. In that document, the element seen as most important in terms of the problem of exchange had to do with the return to the Ottoman Empire of Ottoman Armenians who had previously immigrated to Russia.

A memo by the Ottoman Ministry of Foreign Affairs envoy to St. Petersburg—based on telegraph 42, dated February 29, 1904, and related to a notice sent to the Cabinet of Rome on September 6, 1899—relays the Ottoman government's explanation to Russia. The memo repeated the Ottoman government's declaration at the Cabinet of Rome but also its reservations around the reentry into Ottoman lands of Armenians in Russia. A copy of this declaration was presented in an appendix to the protocol to be signed. The declaration, dated September 6, 1899, and delivered by the Ottoman government to the Cabinet of the Conference of Rome, had voiced the condition that the Protocol of Rome not be contrary to concerted action by the Russian and Ottoman governments regarding Armenian émigrés in Russia.[81] Later, on the possibility that a phrase in a note sent to the government of Russia could create confusion, it was decided to rewrite the record to center not on the return of Armenians who had fled the Ottoman Empire for Russia but on their *not* returning.[82] In such a situation, the Ottoman representative in St. Petersburg, Hüsnü Bey, stated that all reservations already rested on an agreement related to preventing the return of Armenians to the Ottoman Empire and that reference to the earlier agreement would thus not lead to a mistake. It was again stated to the Russian state that the ruling on the return of anarchists would not include within its scope the return of Armenians who had gone to Russia from the Ottoman Empire.[83]

On the recommendation to establish a central police office with the aim of monitoring and providing information about anarchist movements, which was one of the main topics discussed at the St. Petersburg Conference, representatives from Sweden, Norway, and Denmark affixed an addendum requesting that this duty be left up to the police in their respective countries. Meanwhile, the governments of the Netherlands and Portugal did not grant their representatives the authority to sign the protocol, while the governments of Luxembourg and Switzerland did not have diplomats in St. Petersburg.[84]

According to Article 1 of the St. Petersburg Protocol, every anarchist deported from the signatory countries was to be transferred by the shortest possible road to the country to which they belonged. If the two concerned states did not share a border, the individual was to be returned by the shortest route—that is, sent to the border of the closest country sharing a border with their country and from there to their own country. Before the anarchist was delivered to the country where they held citizenship, the police of that state were to be informed within a certain period. If there were one or more countries between the deported person's own country and the country deporting them, then they were to be forwarded to the officials of those intermediate countries, and the officials were to be notified before they arrived. One of the governments could decide to allow the deported person to stay in that country. The deportee's citizenship state would thus be notified of the route by which the person was to be transferred. It was to be decided later by treaty states which officials would transfer anarchists and to which border points. In the absence of any regulation to the contrary, the deportee's transfer fees would be covered by the states through which they passed. According to Article 2 of the protocol, to collect information about anarchists and the deeds they committed, a centralized police department was to be established in every country. According to Article 3, it was up to each country to decide the manner in which necessary information on the country's officials, the anarchists in that country, and their propaganda and their harmful acts would be provided to the centralized police department.

Under Article 4, the central administrations of treaty states had to be, first, informed in writing of the circumstances of deportation and the anarchist's desire to leave; second, provided a written description of the anarchist's physical appearance, an official note on their criminal records, and, if possible, a photograph; and, third, informed of when and where the anarchist would enter a neighboring country so the latter could keep them under observation and take all necessary precautions. This communication was to be carried out immediately. Fourth, if an anarchist secretly left a country within the central administration's sphere of duty, and if their place of residence was known, then all central administrations were to be notified at the same time to facilitate the search for that person. Fifth, when an anarchist was deported or left a country of their own accord, if it was known beforehand which border they would cross, not only that country's central administration but also the relevant border officials had the authority to deal with the situation. The central administration of every country was charged with delivering to the central administration of the neighboring country a file compiled by border officials communicating this information.

According to Article 5 of the St. Petersburg Protocol, every central administration was required to provide the central administrations of all treaty governments with all information related to murder or a seditious crime of an anarchist nature. According to Article 6, every central administration was to share with its counterparts all information on any anarchist events within six months of their happening. In addition, central offices were required to answer without delay all questions related to anarchist acts posed to them by government offices.

These measures were to come into effect the day the protocol was signed, and states were to begin implementation without delay. States that were not present could participate in these rulings through a separate document. Every state was to notify the Russian government through diplomatic routes of its approval of the treaty and would in turn be notified by Russia which states had acceded to the document. Participation in the protocol required that all articles be duly approved with the aforementioned conditionalities.

All the representatives of participating states signed this protocol, which was intended to remain entirely confidential. The draft of the protocol and the signed protocol document were identical.[85] However, the Ottoman Empire, Denmark, Romania, Sweden, and Norway affixed addenda to the signed protocol. The Ottoman government clarified that, together with this protocol, the declaration it delivered to the Cabinet of Rome on September 6, 1899, remained valid. Thus, it once more asserted that this protocol did not affect the treaty between the Sublime Porte and the Russian government related to the return of Armenian émigrés in Russia. The Danish representative noted that the duties to be carried out by the administration of each country's police center (Articles 2–6) would in Denmark be administered by the city police of Copenhagen. Similarly, the representatives of Sweden and Norway stated that these duties would be administered by the Stockholm and Kristiania chiefs of police, respectively. The Romanian representative declared that the authority to determine for whom the term *anarchist* was to be used rested with its government and that whenever disagreement arose between two states as to whether a person was an anarchist, the authority to make the determination belonged to the government of the country where the suspect resided.[86]

Because the Flemish and Portuguese governments had not sent their final replies, and the governments of Luxembourg and Switzerland had not put forward their final reservations in written form, it was decided at the time of signing that all four would be withdrawn from the list of states on the protocol draft.[87] The protocol document came before the Ottoman Assembly, and—with the participation of the minister of interior, the minister of foreign affairs, the Chief Council of State, the undersecretary of the grand vizier, the minister of education, the minister of trade and public works, the minister of justice, the *sheyhülislam*, the minister of imperial religious foundations, the minister of finance, the director of the Imperial Arsenal, and the minister of the navy—it was decided on April 9, 1904, that the protocol would be implemented.[88]

Conclusion

The Conference of Rome and the St. Petersburg Protocol show how governments were beginning to use similar registry systems to make use of similar policing methods for similar crimes. In each meeting, one of the key problems had to do with strengthening the capacity of states' administrative infrastructural power in international cooperation against anarchists and anarchist acts framed as a security threat. Such state functions as punishment and deportation should be considered alongside their policies for recording and registering information. This process reveals how, in addition to the international system of diplomacy, the modern state's domestic organization and internal administrative systems also developed and took shape in international solidarity. Thus, there are clear resemblances among the policies, reactions, and discourses of various states toward raison d'état through the agency of elites.

The Ottoman Empire was also part of this new systemic collaboration. At the international level, there was a striking trend toward single or similar security-related administrative systems. While establishment of a common, centralized policing unit (the advanced stage of these developments) had yet to take place, these developments nevertheless offer important clues about modern state policies of self-protection. How the Ottoman government viewed the growing international antianarchist stance and cooperation also says much about its stance on security policies. The Conference of Rome and the St. Petersburg Protocol are important in terms of what they reveal about the administrative echoes of security debates that were very apparent within the political order of the Ottoman Empire.

The foundations of the interimperial knowledge exchange and administrative structures of policing also explores the Ottoman responses to issues related to public order and security. The Ottoman government's main legal framework for interimperial collaboration against anarchism was the OPC, in particular its section on "crimes against the state." The new interimperial collaboration gave the Ottoman government the opportunity to expand the practices outlined in this section. The Ottoman government also adapted the code as the main legal source of the government's definition of "anarchist acts" as political crimes. Russia, Germany, and Austria-Hungary had similar views on political violence. Moreover, the Ottoman responses to both the Conference of Rome and the St. Petersburg Protocol and their regulations on extradition reveal the Ottoman anxiety about the possible return of émigré Armenians to Ottoman land.

4

State Discourses of Threat from Ancient Concepts to New Narratives

Vagrant, Fesad, and Anarchist

This chapter explores the use of the terms *serseri* (vagrant) and *fesad* (sedition, seditious, conspirator, villain) as part of a historical process. They were often used in the Ottoman government's internal correspondence on matters of public order and security. The historical background of those state narratives and discourses on threat also points to the Ottoman mentality around public order and security. These discursive tropes were used in state correspondence as reference points in the matters of danger and threat, and their uses were easily adapted to the new legal framework of Ottoman modernization. During the Hamidian Era, the concepts of "anarchist" and "anarchism" were articulated mainly alongside those of "vagrant" and "sedition/seditious." This chapter thus aims to understand both what or whom the state saw as a threat and what it said about such elements.

To more clearly explicate the discursive link between the concepts of anarchist or seditious (*fesad*) and vagrant (*serseri*), the chapter draws heavily on a report presented by Minister of Police Hüseyin Nazım Paşa entitled *Ermeni Tarih-i Vukuatı* (The History of Armenian Incidents, January 3, 1897).[1] Though prepared by the minister of police, the document also includes correspondence between the Ministry of Police and other ministries and offices. It thus reveals the discourse established by various institutions within the state apparatus. At the same time, because the document also contains Hüseyin Nazım Paşa's own reports, it encompasses both the perspective of one high-ranking bureaucrat with the authority to make decisions on matters of security and the discourse of the state taking shape within this framework.

Old Concepts, New Meanings: *Serseri* and *Fesad*

Reinventing the Concept of Vagrant

The nineteenth century was for Europe marked by major problems around poverty and the state's struggle to control those who migrated to cities owing to rural poverty. In Great Britain, the Vagrancy Law of 1824 was issued to deal with the poor and veterans of the Napoleonic Wars who came to cities looking for work and were consistently considered a problem of public order for the administrative elite. Similarly, in the Ottoman Empire the arrival of seasonal workers (usually called *bekârs*, "bachelors") in cities, in particular Istanbul, can be considered within the same frame as elsewhere in Europe and America during the nineteenth and early twentieth centuries, when men ages fifteen to forty-five left their homes, jobs, and communities because of civil war, unemployment, economic depression, and other negative conditions. Men who were homeless or far from their homes were seen similarly across otherwise quite different geographies as threats to public order. These people created their own subcultures in their own urban localities.[2] While their subcultures ran somewhat contrary to the structure of cities organized around the settled core of the family, the seasonal laborers who created them were also instrumental to the sustainability of the urban economy.[3]

In the Ottoman Empire, one can draw a parallel between the Police Regulation (Zaptiye Nizamnamesi) of 1907 and the regulations and practices related to vagrants as well as controls related to seasonal workers. Here, the basic problem was the police's authority to control those who were residing temporarily in inns, hotels, apartments, and other rented spaces by means of identity cards or through a registry of such places. Even if such people were far from their usual places of residence for legitimate reasons, they could still be held in suspicion. In other words, administrators saw them as potential criminals. Because the places where they stayed were not family homes, the police saw them not as private places of residence but as public spaces that could be legally searched at any moment.[4]

The concept of vagrant constitutes a category of crime that rests not on acts but on a person's situation or form of existence. As a consequence, when vagrancy is defined as a crime, what truly matters is not to be present in an undesired act or to behave in the desired way but to be a person who corresponds to a certain definition. Vagrants were defined similarly in the registries of various states, usually by their names and places of origin. The point of similarity in these records is that of geographical mobility, which reveals the general characteristics of the category "vagrant." Mobility generally points to long-distance travel.[5] Vagrancy often amounts to being mobile, not being present in a specific locale, and not belonging to any particular group. Perceiving the geographical mobility of vagrants as something maleficent is not only about the ambiguity of the origins and destinations of their travels but also about what is perceived as the lack of a legitimate reason for their travels.[6] Vagrancy points not only to movement within a country but also to international movement, or it may involve long-term labor migration or traveling with the hope of finding subsistence work. In the historiography of migration history, migrants are generally classified according to their official status through such concepts as migrant laborer or refugee and not in terms of how they describe themselves. According to more recent studies, migration does not consist of movement in a single direction from a point of departure to another space. On the contrary, it occurs through a series of movements across several spaces. As such, it is difficult to talk about singular points of departure and arrival because of the uncertainty for the authorities regarding places of departure and arrival.[7] When this ambiguity is combined with characteristics such as poverty, youth, manhood, bachelorhood, and solitary travel, then in popular perceptions and for state elites there is little differentiation between poor migrants and vagrants.[8] If vagrants come from abroad, they are, for state elites, people who must not be let into the country. If they travel within the country, it is anticipated that they will cause problems in the public order of cities, so they should be prevented from doing so and made instead into efficient laborers. The definition of vagrancy as a crime facilitates state control over the poor and other marginal groups, who are seen as potential criminals even if they have never had a hand in any crime. Such supernumerary people, according to political elites, are threatening elements to the social order and public order.[9]

Vagrancy was initially taken up as a social problem in connection to labor and labor discipline. As such, the basic prejudice against vagrants had to do with their purported desire to lead an idle existence. A second issue was the link established between vagrancy and crime. Vagrancy was considered to be related to people who had made a habit of committing crimes or were characterized as professional criminals. Nineteenth-century elites generally perceived criminals as disruptive, homeless, rootless, drunken, and uneducated.[10] The *Report into the Prison and Reformatory System* issued in Canada in 1891 described people labeled as vagrants as those who were able to find work in the summer and when work was not to be found in the winter made plans to spend the season in prison.[11] Again, the basic problem was unemployment. People seen as vagrants generally worked as seasonal laborers and were jobless in seasons when there was no such work. Other important issues were the emergence of the problem created by sending to prison people who were unable to earn but had not committed any crime and the birth of state elite's desire to make a better classification of what they considered the criminal classes.[12] In the Hamidian Era, the state generally preferred to repatriate those who were vagrants yet who were neither suspects nor criminals. This traditional practice generally stemmed from the underdevelopment of state institutions.

In the research carried out in this framework over the past twenty years, vagrancy has been related to social policy, the history of migration, and labor history rather than being understood as a form of perversion, criminality, or marginality, as it was earlier. In discussions about vagrancy, state elites attempted to distinguish between the "deserving" and "undeserving" poor—between those who set out on the road to find work and vagrants or beggars with no intention of working—and to support and monitor them with an eye to their protection. In the nineteenth century in particular, vagrants were judged as amoral or as not possessing a work ethic not because they were external to the labor market but on the grounds that they did not even try to work or to earn an honest livelihood. Vagrancy thus represented the opposite of what was formally expected of people.[13]

Labor history generally focuses on working-class employment in modern industries. The *Lumpenproletariat* is approached as a separate phenomenon or else overlooked entirely. Unemployment should be considered alongside how the vagrant is defined. When unemployment is approached as spare or illegitimate time, then the concept of vagrancy should be considered alongside the struggle to formalize unemployment and to establish its place at the center of social policies. To constitute the administrative framework of social policies, it was necessary to have basic information about individuals' identities and to record this information. In this way, an office or administration that possessed various types of information about a person also possessed the ability to order that person's actions. Many documents exist related to the unregistered acts of vagrants. Thus, even if mechanisms to observe individuals' actions or to record such information were set up through the intermediation of the law, in practice such mechanisms did not always function with the desired or envisioned perfection.

People labeled as vagrants were in the eyes of state elites capable of easily joining in all manner of uprisings. As such, they were seen as a problem both of public order and of security. Another important point that consolidated how vagrants were perceived as a security problem relates to how the perception of threat varied based on situation or identity; for example, Italian vagrants might be considered to pose a greater threat after the assassination of Empress Elizabeth by an Italian in 1898. While vagrants were seen partly as a problem of subsistence in terms of the maintenance of public order in cities, people who belonged to social groups mobilized by modern ideologies such as nationalism, socialism, or anarchism were, precisely because of these articulations, defined through a double stigmatization in bureaucratic correspondence. In the definition of crimes or behaviors that upset public order, the decisive role played by state elites was to reflect the state's ways of imagining public order and security. For exactly this reason, when such definitions—which were highly political— were considered alongside the professionalization of the police, they were apoliticized and turned into technical matters, which resulted in the stigmatization of certain groups within society.[14] In the security and public-order practices of various states, one of the most common practices was to deport vagrants. Here, again, the perception of a threat from vagrants was compounded when used in conjunction with other perceived threats to security, such as anarchism or sedition, or with reference to such conditions as idleness, homelessness, and nomadism.

This entire way of understanding can be interpreted as a pattern from the past in the Ottoman administrative system. Sedition (*fesad*), anarchism (*anarşizm*), and vagrancy (*serseri*) are slippery and transitive concepts. If the concept of anarchism solidified when defined as a crime, generally it was not approached as such in low-level state correspondence, even if based on an action. Prejudices and identity played a more determining role. Through the Regulation on Vagrants and Suspicious Individuals (Serseri Mazannei Su'i Olan Eşhâs Hakkında Nizamname) of 1890, state elites defined vagrancy (*serseri*) as a type of marginality to be understood not as a result of being put aside by society but rather alongside the rationality of the state mindset. When political forms of imagination are considered alongside administrative or governmental tradition, this political thinking or political form of imagination brings about a series of apparatuses, processes of negotiation, and forms of articulation for the realization of the social order in the minds of high-level bureaucrats. The consequent problem of vagrancy, rather than being discussed alongside such phenomena as economic crisis, urbanization, and migration, took shape in the possible ruin of the city's imagined social order and through a new discourse of morality constituted largely in the written public sphere.[15] For this reason, establishing a link between unemployment and immorality simplified matters for elites. Elite perceptions of threat, meanwhile, constituted another dimension of this process. Instead of undertaking regulations to resolve social unrest by engaging in a constructive debate on the real reasons behind the conditions causing unrest, elites considered a range of ways of being or political identities as deserving of marginalization by narrowing the borders of the legitimate public sphere through policies and regulations in opposition to elements or situations seen as a threat. In this way, the political marginalization of the lower classes was also facilitated at the discursive level.

The Regulation on Vagrants and Suspicious Individuals of 1890 could be understood as a precaution against petty crimes. Yet when the law is read alongside other regulations, one is struck by how state elites established a link between public order and threats to the regime. While dangerous classes were defined or delimited according to their profession or lifestyle, ethnicity also strengthened or weakened the degree to which they were seen as threats or changed why they were seen as threats. According to the vagrancy regulation, people who had no job or clear and continuous residence, who could not prove that they led their lives in a legitimate manner, and who "wander here and there" were defined as vagrants and people of unknown circumstances (*meçhul'ül ahvâl*).[16] The important conditions here were not having a legitimate job and lack of clarity around where one stayed or went. If a person had an internal Ottoman passport (*mürur tezkeresi*), then their comings and goings were registered on the permit, which is to say their route was known. Traveling without an internal passport meant being potentially subject to punishment. To be stigmatized as a vagrant or to be perceived as a suspicious person was considered a natural result of traveling without an internal passport. Those defined as people of unknown circumstances were considered people who had previously committed such crimes as theft, pickpocketing, and charlatanry or who had abetted those committing such crimes.[17]

Because vagrancy, unlike acts forbidden by law or defined as crimes, was not defined based on actions but on a way of life, it was initially considered alongside the problem of public order. The police, who were tasked with assuring public order, also possessed great interpretational authority. Particularly when dealing with the vagrant, this authority became linked to the forms of stigmatization to which members of different social groups were subject. At the same time, the structure of the crime of vagrancy left the door open for different actors to offer different interpretations.[18] From the state's low-level civil servants to its administrative elite, the vagrancy issue had not only to do with assuring public order but also with ensuring the security of the state and its articulation of parts of the population perceived as a threat. The OPC had no regulations specific to people or situations seen as threats or potential threats. As such, with the Regulation on Vagrants, as also seen in Sweden and Belgium, anyone regarded as a potential threat could be easily banished or arrested. In this way, individuals were monitored by the state, and efforts were made to eliminate the possibility of individuals becoming risks with the intent of reducing so-called criminal tendencies in the vagrant population.[19]

One of the basic points here relates to the lack of clear definitions in the Regulation on Vagrants. Ferdan Ergut argues that this lack of clarity was of undeniable importance in increasing the state's infrastructural power and capacity to control society through administrative regulations and actors, while the police broadened their discretionary power.[20] Crimes of public order and the Regulation on Vagrants can be interpreted as apparatuses that facilitated the control of the population. Yet in the Hamidian Era such control was not only related to public order but also tied to deep worries around security. At the time, in addition to localized uprisings in the countryside and guerrilla-type bandit conflicts, the city centers and railroads were subject to bombings and assassination attempts (see chapter 2). As in western Europe, in the Ottoman Empire the concept of the vagrant presented the state with a broad interpretive space in which the vagrant could be linked to various forms of stigmatization. The discursive link established between seasonal laborers or vagrants and anarchism in Prussia was also established for Italian immigrants in many European countries. The Ottoman government used such links in its own formal correspondence. This opened up space for a discussion both of the state apparatus for record keeping and categorization in activities of classification and of the flexibility of the definitions made by the state.

The Survival of the State and the Concept of *Fesad*

The State's Discourse of Threat

There is no doubt that state elites of this period saw the survival of the state as being under threat. This perception of danger also affected the language used in state correspondence from the upper levels of government down to minor civil servants. The historical framework set out in the previous chapter demonstrates the historical and spatial stage established by this discourse.

Answering such questions as who used this discourse or how it was used and in which positions helps in understanding the actors who took part in the discourse constructed along the axis of danger or threat and in comprehending the mentality with which it was constituted. Thus, when attempting to understand the roles of those who used a discourse of danger and how they positioned themselves, we must also seek to understand the place of groups constructed as the objects of discourse within the state's perception of threat and its security mentality. This chapter also discusses the discourse of the center and the ways in which the state read the relations between fundamental actors.

Analyzing the state's mentality through the discourse of the people who represented its institutions reveals how certain meanings and representational forms in the institutional political field dominated over others[21] and how the state made use of the discursive field in question to achieve its security aims. In light of the fact that the discursive reflection of the state's mentality was built on an accumulation of knowledge, a key question we must ask is how the state classified and interpreted the information it held. One question of undeniable importance is whether through the discourse that the state constructed there existed a connection between the critical events of the era and the administrative political changes that took shape in these moments.

Tradition and the Concept of Fesad

The discursive field that the state constructed in relation to individuals or groups it saw as threats must be considered with an eye to historical continuity. The use of the concept of *fesad* points to this historical continuity. In Islamic thought, *fesad* refers to the disruption of order, of natural balance. This disruption may extend from the violation of settled legal and moral rules to the destruction of the political order constituted on such a foundation by acting in ways outside a manner of living that a religious understanding considers appropriate. As such, everything from theft to political revolt and rebellion are included within the definition of *fesad*.[22]

This is also how the concept of *fesad* is used in Ottoman government correspondence. In sixteenth-century documents, the terms *fesad* (sedition) and *fesatçı* (seditious) are used to characterize both insurrectionists, those who attempt to overturn the settled political powers, and those who break legal rules.[23] In that period, the behavior of irregular soldiers—usually dubbed "single men" (*levend*)—threatened the settled authorities because they had a high degree of geographical mobility without being subject to mechanisms of social control. Through such crimes ranging from theft and assault to rebellion, the problem of public order came to be perceived alongside the problem of the state's survival. The point is not that there was a quantitative rise in petty crimes but how state elites viewed any such rise. A wave of crime that grew with the Celali rebellions in the sixteenth and seventeenth centuries pointed, at its heart, to social unrest. For state elites, what changed these crimes into rebellion was that they created disorder and social tumult. As such, for elites, crime was never to be considered on its own but was to be interpreted as an indicator of potential rebellion.[24] With the classic understanding of the circle of justice (*daire-i adalet*), this connection among migrant men, the unemployed, and political rebellions persisted in the discourse of later years.[25]

In the time of Selim III (r. 1789–1807), most of the regulations made in relation to Istanbul focused on migrants to the city. The authorities saw unemployed single men and migrant laborers in particular as suspicious individuals and potential criminals. In prioritizing above all else policies related to public order in the city, Selim III operated along the axis of ancient traditions and new regulation. According to Betül Başaran, while the main axis was traced by ancient law (*kanun-u kadim*), public-order policies operated on two levels. The first was controlling entrance points to the city and blocking the entry of those without a valid reason for being there. The second was the strict surveillance of people who somehow evaded these controls.[26] Thus, these regulations can be interpreted in the sense that, in the eyes of political elites, the people who held primary responsibility for crime and uprisings were those who came to Istanbul from outside. This interpretation also demonstrates the population policy for Istanbul: to keep the city under control, it was necessary to expel drifters and those with no one in the city to vouch for them.

In Ottoman law, each suspect fell into one of three categories.[27] The first category comprised *kendi halinde*, "harmless," individuals who were known to not have previously committed a crime and who were known within their community for their honesty. Because such people had no previous criminal records, they were treated with the presumption of innocence. The second category was made up of those who were known to have previously committed a crime. Referred to as *mazanne* (suspicious persons) or *müttehem* (accused persons), these people did not benefit from the presumption of innocence. The burden of proof was on them to demonstrate they had not committed the crime in question, and they could be arrested the moment they were accused. The third category consisted of the *meçhul'ül ahvâl* (unknowns), those who had no one to vouch for them or about whom no one in the neighborhoods where they lived could say anything positive. Such people could be imprisoned until information was obtained about them.[28] Because they were people of unknown circumstances, authorities generally linked them to *fesad*. Thus, regulations and practices were realized to address Istanbul's problem of public order without taking into account the reasons that compelled individuals to abandon the place or community where they had previously lived.[29]

In Ottoman law, the sultan was responsible for the protection of the public order and all God's servants. Related to this responsibility, Selim III created, in addition to certain exemplary punishments, new categories of punishment within the scope of his own authority and beyond the Sharia to maintain order. Those who committed crimes corresponding to these categories were punished without a trial: doubt and possibility could take the place of evidence of a crime. Even if the suspect was in fact not guilty, the punishment would serve to dissuade others from breaking the law. The practice of punishment without trial was seen during the Celali rebellions.[30] The basic motivations for the practice were the fear of rebellion and worries about maintaining public order. The main reason for the breaking down of the public order was *fesad*, as opposed to *maslaha* (goodness, prosperity, public good, welfare). As seen in the work of Başaran on the late eighteenth century as well as of Mustafa Akdağ on the sixteenth century, those who (as Engin Deniz Akarlı puts it) persisted in behaving wrongly, did not pay heed to warnings, and had no one to vouch for them were generally categorized as *fesad*.[31] Akdağ writes of an edict forbidding public soup kitchens (*imaret*) from accepting people without someone to vouch for them.[32] Başaran's study looks at the regulations of the late eighteenth century and shows how for the Ottoman sultan those who came to Istanbul from the countryside as well as unemployed vagrants belonged to the category of *fesad*. These people were generally *meçhul'ül ahvâl*, and when they could find no one to vouch for them, they were met with suspicion.[33]

Political fear is not a notion that takes shape all by itself. It can be a political tool used by political elites to achieve a range of political aims and support their own moral or political beliefs. Internal rebellions create a wide space for state elites to create and implement new regulations. Of particular importance is the question of which social conflicts are fed by political fear as well as which groups' positions are bettered and which are worsened. The answer to this question also helps us understand which groups benefit from the political fear. Political elites' recognition of threats give rise to political fear, and the creation of a public related to this fear is at the same time deeply tied to processes of legitimacy.[34] The definition of political threat typically functions to the detriment of the powerless when inequalities prevail.[35]

The concept of *fesad* was, for these reasons, used broadly by the Ottoman state. Ranging from the OPC section on crimes against the state to lower-level government correspondence and all administrative documents generally, anything that upset the social order or had the potential to do so was characterized as *fesad*. As such, the concept of *fesad*, just like the concept of *serseri* (the vagrant), had a broad field of usage and could be easily linked to other social identities or stigmas. Thus, when defining such situations or facts or individuals as dangers and threats out of political fear, this concept was one of the central elements in the state's security discourse.

State Security Discourses in the Hamidian Era

Fesad, mostly referring to sedition, was the most frequently used concept in relation to security in state documents of the Hamidian Era. It was used with particular frequency to refer to Armenians, who, regardless of their association with the actual Armenian revolutionary movement, were suspected of being members of the resistance or were thought might become members at some future date. This usage was so widespread that it is found not only in administrative correspondence but in newspapers with the frequent appearance of terms such as *müfsid* (seditious) and *şaki* (bandit) in the penning of strong articles against Armenians. This discursive practice upset the Armenian community: in 1897, the community prepared a written statement requesting that the word *fesad* not be used in reference to Armenians and that an edict be penned to that effect.[36] An edict was passed but did not do away with the term's frequent use in connection to Armenians, even in state correspondence. Administrative documents' repeated use of the term for certain elements or groups can be interpreted as a type of propaganda. This administrative terminological repertoire, which amounted to a type of stigmatization, turned certain groups into *Others* and thus into *enemies* and, indeed, constructed a perception of the enemy as having inhuman characteristics. It created an us/them dichotomy and was socially constructed across religious, ethnic, racial, and cultural oppositions. As such, the groups defined as *fesad* became scapegoats upon whom all negative characteristics and behaviors could be foisted and who were held responsible for all problems in and disruptions of the imagined social order. In opposition to an "us" constructed as good was positioned a "them" visited by evil. Even without being present at any sort of antistate action, simply to be a member of a particular group involved being stereotyped, stigmatized, and blamed.[37]

The report by Minister of Police Hüseyin Nazım Paşa in 1897, *The History of Armenian Incidents*, shows how this issue was taken up in his documents and in other state correspondence.[38] Thanks to this report, it is possible to analyze in all its clarity the language that both the minister of police and officials in other state units used for the Armenian issue. In the report, the phrase most often used to explain or justify the Armenian massacres is *Ermeni fesadı* (Armenian sedition). In this sense, the entire report was constructed upon the concept of *fesad*. Nazım Paşa explained in his introduction why the report was needed and detailed how the primary means, forms of action, reasons for, and inside details of the "crimes of banditry known as Armenian sedition [Ermeni fesadı denilen âsâr-ı şekavet]" were known to no one, not even in the Armenian community. For those acts and situations that the author characterized as crimes of sedition, which emerged in different forms and included political crimes, propaganda, and violent acts, Nazım Paşa noted the existence of several incorrect and ill-intentioned interpretations. He stated that many writings had appeared in European and American newspapers that were contrary to the truth (i.e., what he and the Ottoman state perceived as the truth), and, indeed, some had been written by the very people responsible for seditious acts. Through such writings, he argued, those responsible for attempted sedition disguised their murderous intent, bloodshed, and cruelty. Nazım Paşa stated that this report was necessary to "shed light upon events." The report made two critical points: first, that the term *Armenian sedition* was not understood in the Ottoman Empire and, second, that it was not well understood in Europe, either. Nazım Paşa was thus attempting to show the "truth" to both a domestic and a foreign audience.[39]

In this attempt, the document took a certain discursive path wherein Nazım Paşa defined what he labeled as "Armenian seditions" (*Ermeni fesadiyyesi*): conflicts in Ottoman territories, at times between state powers and Armenian revolutionary movement members, at other times between Armenian revolutionary movement members and Kurdish tribes, and at yet other times between Armenian villagers and Kurdish tribes (the document shows such conflicts to be multilayered). "Armenian sedition" appears to be an umbrella concept containing such various senses as the Armenian issue, Armenian terror, the Armenian revolutionary movement, and the Armenian national movement. Within this usage, events, organizations, and people lumped into the category of "Armenian sedition" were portrayed as opposed to the state and as malicious. Here, the state defined those people it took to be opposed to it as evil or having evil qualities. People or groups characterized in this manner were abstracted from their human qualities and imprisoned in a sort of good/evil distinction.

Following the introduction, the report discussed several matters by way of other state reports: translations of documents from the Hunchak organization, in particular sections that explain the idea of anarchism, regulations detailing the duties of organization members, their plans for revolution, and planned assassinations of Ottoman government servants, especially Armenians; court decisions indicting members of the organization; writings on the matter in the foreign press; and related events in various places in the empire. The crucial point here is the absence of any discussion in the report about the reasons behind the Armenian revolutionary movement. When explaining the conflict, rather than to analyze all actors, their demands, and the issues they saw as problems, the report preferred to focus on the individual conflicts or events and to classify the parties involved as good or evil, constructive or destructive. This discursive construct shows the strength of the perception of a zero-sum game. In explaining events and as a consequence of a perception that pitted the state against those perceived as wishing to destroy it, it focused on *who* threw the first rock, not *why*. Rather than inquiring into the origins of the problem, the prevalent trend was to see the reason for the problem as opposition to the state. This framework transformed the whole matter into a problem of public order and security. In state correspondence detailing "local uprisings," some documents used the word *Ermeni* (Armenian) directly in place of *fesad* or *fesadcı*, thus stigmatizing every person or group in the discursive field as Armenian and every Armenian as *fesad*. The state approached the process solely as a security problem and, tied to this, perceived things through a good/evil opposition. The very adjectives Nazım Paşa used in explaining the problem serve to underscore this opposition. As discussed later, the sides or parties of the conflict were situated as polar opposites: the state on one side and Armenian members of the revolutionary movement on the other. In so doing, the state refused to see Armenians or their organizations as official political actors. The Armenian community was, according to the state, restricted to a single political actor: the Armenian Patriarchate.

Yet even if not everyone could be considered a political actor, there were certainly more than two actors. Each Armenian revolutionary organization was a different actor, as were Armenian villagers, the Armenians of Istanbul, Armenian migrant workers in Istanbul, the Armenian Patriarchate, Kurdish villagers, Kurdish tribes, the Hamidiye Cavalries, the gendarmerie, and the consulates of the Great Powers. Yet the correspondence was shaped by the Ottoman government's delimitation of the legitimate political actors in this particular case: the patriarchate, foreign governments, and the Ottoman government itself. According to state correspondence, because Armenian revolutionary organizations were not legitimate actors, they were not entities with whom the government could enter into direct negotiations with or reach an understanding with. The revolutionary organizations that wished to change the existing order of things and that were thus characterized by negatively loaded adjectives were thus passivized, rendered unable to enter the plane of legitimate politics. This was fundamentally in contradiction with the writings of the organizations, which certainly considered themselves legitimate actors. From the government's viewpoint, both how the opposing group explained violent events and, indeed, how it took up the entire issue were, according to Hüseyin Nazım Paşa, lies created by "Armenian sedition" (*Ermeni fesadı*).

Political Elite Discourses of the People

When describing the people involved in various political actions and assassination attempts, Hüseyin Nazım Paşa used the phrase "delinquents whom the committees employed in deceptive crimes [komitelerin bi'l-iğfâl cinayetlerde istihdam ettikleri mücrimin]." This phrasing suggested that those involved were there not in the name of a cause they believed in but because they had been deceived by revolutionary organizations. They had become careless, were cheated, and had thus carried out such acts and fallen into the state of criminality. As such, they were both responsible for these actions and fundamentally deceived. They were not aware of what they had done. In this way, these people and the acts they carried out were rendered apolitical.

Nazım Paşa based this discourse on the court statements of Armenians who were put on trial for crimes against the state. He explained that these statements were sufficient for disclosure and for the "assurance of conscience [temin-i vicdan]," asserting that the uprisings—or, in his words, "seditious acts [vukû'at-ı fesadiyye]"—had not come about through alliances between local people and an organization with the aim of banditry or out of a desire for an uprising. In other words, he underscored, these acts grew not out of local political visions but from the deception or manipulation of local populations.[40] As Selim Deringil discusses through another example, it was certainly advantageous for the state to explain the situation in this way: the state preferred not to negate its own subjects in official discourse. The state had gradually come to need its subjects, and if it were to see its subjects as always revolting or prepared to revolt, then it had to place itself in the position of a power prepared at any minute to suppress such uprisings. This stance required a military and police force perpetually at the ready. Yet there was no such force at the disposal of the Ottoman government.[41] And so, in places where uprisings existed, the responsibility and will were not that of the people but of organizations, according to the government.

In his report, Nazım Paşa drew a clear distinction between Armenians and Muslims. The millet system that the state employed to govern its subjects corresponds to this ideological categorization. However, the hierarchical order that Nazım Paşa, as minister of police, imagined was not accepted by the Armenian revolutionaries. He argued that within the just system of the Ottoman Empire, Armenians enjoyed security and religious freedoms and, indeed, had come to hold great wealth. Within the state, they reached high levels, occasionally critical positions of officialdom. Nazım Paşa's explanation of the state's attitude toward members of the Armenian community as the "Great Government's compassionate works [Hükümet-i Seniyyenin âsâr-ı şefkat-kârânesi]" can be interpreted as the state seeing Armenians as children to be shown compassion. Using such benevolent terms as *hüsn-i nazar* (trust), *emniyet* (reliability), *kemal-i safvet* (sincerity), *ihlas* (honesty), and *amiziş* (amenability) when speaking of Muslims both cast them in a positive light and emphasized that no problems existed between them and Armenians. Similar expressions were seen in correspondence after the Thessaloniki bombings in 1903. The minister of police, when attempting to explain massacres of Armenians (here he neutrally termed the massacres as "Armenian events"), primarily tried to show that Armenians experienced no problems under Ottoman government. Yet the language used by Nazım Paşa, one of the highest-ranking bureaucrats involved in such events, depicted Armenians as a social group that was tolerated by and even obliged to the state and in need of the Muslim people's goodwill. He wrote, "[Armenians] enjoyed a prosperous existence in the protection of the share of favor of his excellency the sultan [saye-i inayet-vaye-i hazreti padişahîde müreffeh içinde yaşamakta bulundukları halde]," and condemned even "the wise members of the Armenian community [Ermeni Cemaati ukalası]" as responsible for murders carried out in the name of "Armenian sedition [Ermeni fesadı]."[42] This narrative shows that the Armenian issue was seen as a security issue, for which the sole responsible parties were the revolutionary organizations.

This discourse, which demonstrates how state elites saw Armenians within Ottoman society, grew harsher. Following the massacre in Van in 1896, Saadeddin Paşa, who was in charge of Ottoman troops in Van, explained at length in a report written by İbrahim Edhem Bey and Cemal Bey how the history of the Muslim people in the region far predated that of Armenians.[43] As proof, he stressed that Armenians had come to Van at the invitation of Muslims, that their churches were built by Muslims, and that Muslim buildings were older than Armenian ones, and he cited population statistics to demonstrate that Armenians were a minority. He explained that Muslims saw it as a requirement of bravery to always protect Armenians and to look out for them. If even a minor wrong was done to the Armenians in the region by Muslims from another region, he argued, blood feuds occurred between the latter group and the local Muslims and lasted for months. No wonder, he wrote, "Kurds were offended by the ungratefulness of Armenians." The document listed the churches constructed or maintained by Kurdish *mirs* (rulers or princes) and stated that the gravestones and tombs that belonged to Muslims in the towns of Vestan and Ahtimar were far older than the church on Ahtimar Island, one of the oldest Armenian sites in the region.[44] The discourse used earlier by Nazım Paşa and others—that Armenians were tolerated by Muslims and the Ottoman government and that their religious freedoms were not limited—was made more aggressive by Saadeddin Paşa and reconstructed with the aim of proving which group was the more ancient and who was the true owner of these lands.

In fact, the basic problem had to do with determining who the "native" group was, and it was clear that the Ottoman political elites preferred the answer to be Muslims. According to this discursive construct, Armenians had been ungrateful in the face of the Muslim tolerance and protections afforded to them. Compared to Muslims, Armenians held more productive lands, evaded taxes, and complained about persecution by the Kurds but had thus far been protected from being attacked by the Kurds and had enjoyed peace. In explaining the violent events in Van, it was claimed that Armenians initiated them: through the declarations they printed, they had tried to provoke the mindless or unreasonable people of the region ("sebük-mağzân ahâlî-i kurâyı").[45] This characterization of people as unreasonable demonstrates that in the eyes of the state, the people were passive actors. They were positioned as open to deception and provocation and were unaware of their own interests or history. This sort of discourse is also observed in other administrative correspondence. Particularly following ethnic conflicts, information related to populations was collected and classified through the gathering of population statistics, and the truth was reconstructed in line with these official documents.

In Nazım Paşa's report, so-called anarchists were also depicted as evil individuals deceiving the people. Based on intelligence the Ministry of Police gathered, a Hunchak member named Minas Cheras had published a number of Armenian newspapers and "had come to poison the thinking of naive people by learning to be a mischief maker in imitating the acts of evil of criminal parties known by nihilist names in Russia and was involved in socialism, anarchism, and assassination in Europe."[46] In explaining the socialist and anarchist currents influencing Minas Cheras, the report identified them with the work of assassins and linked groups known as nihilists with crime and murder.[47] This characterization corresponded to general perceptions in Europe at the time. In following the malicious example of such groups, the report declared, Cheras had engaged in seditious activities capable of poisoning the minds of the naive.

The state defined the currents of thought that it saw as a threat to itself in terms of categories of crime. Not only that, it also declared such currents to be evil in the opposition of good and evil. It saw the spread of such currents among subjects (as in the example of Minas Cheras) as resistance movements that had poisoned the minds of naive or pure-hearted people ("sâde-dilân ahâlînin efkârı tesmim etmek").[48] There was no debate as to why such ideas were accepted by the people or even by a certain segment of the people. It was not the people who were responsible, but a few "evil" individuals who made use of their naivete. Even if people were active in rebellions, they were not active agents, according to the state. The people were a passive mass, ready to accept all ideas given to them.

The official correspondence in a report related to the Bab-ı Ali Demonstration in 1895 contains important clues about how bureaucrats saw both Armenians and Muslims. An official communication to the lieutenant governor stated that with "Armenians having grown so bold in this interim" since the Kumkapı Demonstration five years earlier, the "leading conspirators [erbab-ı fesad]" meant to stir up new problems and "attract the attention of European powers."[49] As a consequence, in order not to attract foreign attention, the armed forces were forbidden to open fire on crowds, and it was decided to bring a couple of people to the Sublime Porte (Bab-ı Ali) to hear out their woes.[50] What is striking in this and subsequent correspondence are the fears of Armenians "exceeding their limits" and of their acts "giv[ing] rise to European intervention." Foreign intervention, considered the most fundamental danger, had been brought within the realm of possibility by the actions of the state's own subjects, which constituted the basic grounds for placing Armenians within the category of internal enemy.

Another administrative letter sent to the lieutenant governor of Beyoğlu on the Bab-ı Ali Demonstration stated that in order to act in concert against Armenians, Muslims had used a code phrase of sorts: "Fire has broken out! [Yangın var!]."[51] Administrative authorities believed that a Muslim attack on Armenians would violate Istanbul's public order and give cause for foreign intervention: the biggest possible harm to state interests. For this reason, it was decided that an inquiry on potential Muslim attackers was to be carried out immediately. It was decided that there would be patrols in the areas in question and that undercover officers would be sent to placate Muslims gathered in these areas. Some Armenians were loyal subjects, and their being subjected to attacks by a segment of the Muslim population "was quite ugly and [may give] cause to foreign intervention, which was the biggest harm to state interests." In this situation, the authorities should take actions "in a manner that would calm rage and excitement of the Muslims, and the authorities should leave an impression . . . that no public-spirited Muslim [hamiyyetli Müslüman] would approve of any foreign intervention and that, by suggestion and causing to understand in a friendly manner, not even a shadow of the occurrence of inappropriateness would be allowed." If anyone used weapons or insisted on attacks, they were to be arrested. This correspondence has important clues about how an uprising in Istanbul was seen within the bureaucracy.[52] Attacks by some Muslims against all Armenians, regardless of whether the latter joined in the demonstration or not, were presented as against the state's interests. But bureaucrats also drew a distinction. Attacks against loyal Armenians were seen as a dreadful act and unbecoming of Muslims. Yet nothing was said on conflicts between Muslims and those Armenians who joined in such acts. In the same document, another important problem was maintaining the state's advantage. Because ethnic conflict in the streets of Istanbul could give rise to foreign intervention, it was understood as a central threat to the state's survival. This possibility was seen as more important than the loss of citizens' lives or than that ethnic conflict might make living together impossible.[53] Political elites perceived the state's interests as something abstracted from civil society. For every activity the government carried out, the basic point of reference was the problem of ensuring the state's survival.

Excitement (*heyecan*) and rage (*galeyan*) were put forth as the causes of Muslim attacks on Armenians. In Nazım Paşa's report and in other correspondence dealing with ethnic conflict, the two terms *excitement* and *rage* are of central importance and are repeatedly used to describe violence committed by Muslim individuals: for instance, "being moved to excitement and rage," "a person who is already engaged will be reduced by one level to excitement,"[54] "to bring the people to excitement,"[55] "the rage and terror resulting from the people,"[56] "shouts that 'Armenians are attacking the *medrese* [Islamic school]' as bringing Muslims to excitement,"[57] and "a number of people had gathered in the city, from people from nearby villages, because the minds of the public had been inflicted by excitement."[58] Another striking feature is the preponderance of phrases describing the need for self-defense by Muslims, such as "the reactions and defenses by people due to the need to protect self and life, through the sorrow created by injustices and acts of attack";[59] the incitement among Muslims and their armed self-protection;[60] the preparedness of Muslims (due to an absence of soldiers) to protect their lives and honor—they had tolerated their condition and patiently followed the government's advice but were now compelled to respond because they were unable to bear the attacks against Muslims by Armenian villagers allied with those responsible for sedition.[61] Muslims were perceived as a social group that could be easily excited to rage or who would take part in counterattacks with the aim of protecting themselves. Thus, the state saw Muslims as merely reactive or as a collective that acted on emotions without thinking of themselves. In explaining every event to emphasize the problem of protecting oneself, the most frequently underscored point was who started the event. The situation was thus perceived through a zero-sum logic. Yet when one looks at the number of dead in the reports sent, one can easily see that the Armenian losses were higher than the Muslim losses.

Another letter related to the Bab-ı Ali Demonstration, while relaying that certain members of the Muslim community had injured several Armenians, described Muslims as feeling sadness or hurt at such inappropriate actions ("hareket-i nâ-becâdan müte'essir olan"), implying that the basic reason for Muslim attacks on Armenians was their sadness in the face of the demonstrations. In government agents' discussions with Muslims to prevent such attacks, it was requested that speakers make clear that attacking Armenians and bringing about discord were not befitting of Islamic customs and did not serve the interests of the state ("şe'âir-i İslâmiyyet ve menâfi'-i devlet ile kâbil-i tatbîk olamayacağı"). It was ordered that it be communicated to these groups in an appropriate manner that attacks carried out in this way would not bring about positive results for either the state or themselves, that it was necessary to refrain from such attacks, and that, furthermore, those who acted contrary to these orders would be arrested. In this document, too, attacks against Armenians were taken up in terms of the state's survival. Here, among the main reference points were the rules of Islam.[62]

In another official message sent to the Istanbul chief of police, Muslims who attacked Armenians were described as a "number of turbaned and disorderly men." Important here, though, is that the term *fesad* was never used to describe Muslims neither for the Bab-ı Ali Demonstration nor for other uprisings and massacres. In the same document, it was ordered that because there were attempts to violate certain Christian homes and daggers had been thrust into their doors, because the situation was so "ugly [*çirkin*]," and because "excitement and rage [heyecan ve galeyan]" would again be aroused and a range of harms would come from this, disciplinary forces were to be more vigilant in not allowing any such attack on Christian and Armenian homes.[63] In another document about the Ottoman Bank incident in 1896, the authorities explained that the people had been worked up into a rage, several deaths had occurred, and some property damaged but that the police had taken the necessary precautions. The police had been able to pacify the people and arrest attackers, thereby forestalling attacks on Armenians.[64]

In correspondence about the Bab-ı Ali Demonstration, the arrest of Muslims who participated in assaults due to criminality or rage was explained as part of the measures to end the conflict between Armenians and Muslims. During the violent clashes, Armenians had taken refuge in churches out of fear of attacks. According to the same document, the police tried to convince the Armenians that there was no reason for loyal and obedient subjects of the state from each community to be in conflict and that the Armenians should come out.[65] In requesting that the Armenians in the church come out, the police were in one sense attempting to ensure a return to normal life by reestablishing public order and safety. Yet state elites were really more worried about how representatives of foreign states would evaluate the situation. Whatever the state's stance toward disturbances that transformed into ethnic conflicts and violence, it consistently had to attend to its image in the international arena. Acts of the state or how they were reflected could always be the subject of international intervention. For this reason, internal conflicts were discussed alongside the state's survival in terms of both domestic and foreign politics. This is why the problem of insecurity was perceived and imagined as the security of the state itself rather than the security of citizens.

Another significant point relates to the punishment of members of Armenian resistance movements. In another official document in the Nazım Paşa report, assassination attempts against police officers and the conflicts in Van were seen as preceding an attempt at revolution. The concern was expressed that if those held responsible for such acts, the so-called *Ermeni caniler* (Armenian killers), were not punished to deter others, revolts would continue to occur unchecked. In addition, it was thought that if no greater punishment than imprisonment was imposed, dissatisfaction among police officers would rise.[66]

Revolutionary Organizations, Anarchism, and Fesad

In discussing Armenian revolutionary organizations, Hüseyin Nazım Paşa's report overwhelmingly reflected an antianarchist perspective. It took this position undoubtedly because of European states' antianarchist stance as well as because of the international fear of an anarchist conspiracy. In examining the program of the Hunchak organization, Nazım Paşa attempted to understand its aims and particularly stressed that its plan was based on the idea of anarchism. The program stated that while some people held power, others were left without it under the former's oppression and that power needed to be turned over to the working class because wealth and happiness had come about thanks to them. Nazım Paşa's report interpreted this to mean that the Hunchak organization had "confessed" that its basic aim was anarchism;[67] indeed, from the government's perspective, anarchism was not openly claimed, only "confessed." The Armenian revolutionary movement was defined as a group of bandits characterized by "Armenian sedition" ("Ermeni fesadı nâmı verilen şekavetler"). As proof that Armenians lived in security, the report gave examples, such as that Armenians were no different from other non-Muslim groups in being allowed to follow their own laws and freedom of religion and that many were even employed in high positions in the state.[68] The report also noted that most Armenians had no complaints about the government and that they had no aim to establish a separate state.

These points were emphasized to show that Armenians living in Ottoman lands had no problems. Nazım Paşa was pushing the view that the Armenian revolutionary organizations were not aiming to achieve better living conditions for the Armenian community but simply to create social disorder and anarchy. In bringing about revolution, they wanted to ensure equality in wealth between the rich and poor through the sharing of public goods. By examining "Armenian sedition," argued Nazım Paşa and others like him, one could understand its basic aims and observe whether it was favorable to a rational civilization or not. They saw "Armenian sedition" as being far from the idea of civilization and, indeed, as being bent on its destruction. This phrasing shows how much of a danger Nazım Paşa saw in anarchism and demonstrates his fundamental approach to the issue: through oppositions. In official documents, anarchism was framed as something opposed to civilization. He also argued that the best way to understand the aims of anarchism was to leave it to the courts of conscience of the reasonable and merciful. This recommendation, to consider anarchism through feelings of pity and conscience, suggests that the situation was considered not only a concrete threat but also a form of emotional antagonism.

Underscoring the danger represented by Armenian anarchists in Britain and the United States, Nazım Paşa's report stated that they were professionally more advanced in committing seditious acts than their European counterparts. He gave as an example a speech in 1894 by the head of the Hunchak Committee of the United States, Nishan Karabetian, at a meeting celebrating the fourth anniversary of the Kumkapı Demonstration, in which he spoke of separating church and state, arguing that both were weights on human beings. Nazım Paşa contended that Karabetian's argument was also about revolutionary or anarchist ideas, which had nothing to do with the living conditions of Armenians. In his report, Nazım Paşa once more repeated how well and just were the lives of people in the Armenian community.[69] This point was repeated in other official documents and was meant to show that Armenian revolutionary organizations had not developed the ability to voice the needs or demands of Ottoman Armenians in general but rather were structures quite separate from the Armenian people and operated according to their own aims and demands. At the same time, this narrativization of the Armenian community reinforced the argument that the state's approach to the community was entirely positive. Thus, "Armenian sedition" was presented as serving the aims of anarchism, as irrational, and as opposed to the government, to religion, and even to marriage. It was contrary to rational civilization and more dangerous than examples of sedition in Europe.

This narrative and the arguments made repeatedly in different forms in Nazım Paşa's report aimed to show that Armenian organizations had no legitimacy at all even in the eyes of their own community. This narrative in part was directed at an international audience and in part demonstrated state elites' efforts to construct their own reality. This state discourse covered over the true dynamics of the Armenian issue, limited efforts to find a solution, and transformed the whole issue into a problem of security. In the same document, Nazım Paşa discussed a request to understand the situation and act accordingly, using words such as *insaf* (mercy), *vicdan* (conscience), and *adalet* (justice), suggesting how he, the minister of police, viewed the Armenian issue.[70] The report represented the Ottoman government as benevolent and Armenian resistance movements as malevolent. This narrativizing of one side as compassionate and the other side as tyrannical came out of seeing the issue as a struggle between good and evil. The state was presented as a good parent, showing compassion and justice to its subjects, whereas the Armenian committees were represented as nests of evil, whose lies and acts had the sole aim of provoking Armenian opposition to the Ottoman state in order to destroy it.

In a police investigative report included in Nazım Paşa's report, which contained extracts from Romanian newspapers on the arrest of two Armenians for being anarchists, what was at stake was proving once again that such Armenian conspirators (*Ermeni erbab-ı fesadı*) were focused on the idea of anarchism. This police document explained that these individuals had joined European anarchist organizations and had been directed by those organizations to the "true anarchists" and from there would be sent elsewhere. From the investigation, it emerged that several young people had been sent to an anarchist named Stoyanof and that in some cities there had been the wish to open "anarchist branches" of a sort. This was taken as proof that the ideas and actual aims of Armenian conspirators were anarchist in nature.[71] The state felt it had to address the issue that Armenian seditionists (*Ermeni fesadı*) were anarchists and were found to be working in cooperation with European anarchists. When one considers the serious fear of anarchists and the precautions taken against them in Europe at that time (as discussed in the previous chapter), one can perhaps understand why Armenian seditionists were given such weight in Ottoman state correspondence. Beneath this stance lay a suspicion that all anarchists could unite, and so for the Ottoman state to demonstrate to the international community the existence of a link between the Armenian movement and anarchism would damage the legitimacy of the movement in the eyes of the international public.

In another investigative report included in Nazım Paşa's report, Hunchak was blamed for violence and massacres in Sasun and Talori. Saying that the Hunchakist Hamparsum Boyacian had claimed that Armenians had won everywhere, intelligence information suggested that the organization had enticed Armenians to rebel under false pretenses.[72] To shed light on this case, it was seen as necessary to examine writings that mentioned rebellion in the organization's newspaper (in particular those related to the concerned regions). The report stated that it could be clearly understood from the Hunchak program that Armenian committees were working toward aims that were deserving of condemnation and that would create disorder in society and in the heart of contemporary civilization— for instance, by proposing everyone should be equal in material terms.[73] From the perspective of Ottoman bureaucrats, everyone being equal in financial terms would turn the social order upside down. One Hunchak letter discussed in an intelligence report drew attention to a complaint by the organization's base in London that there were not enough actions being carried out in Anatolia. The intelligence report stated that so-called müfsidin (seditious people) had demonstrated a willingness to unhesitatingly call for rebellion and attempt to spread anarchist ideas among Armenians. Based on such letters, state elites defined the Armenian movement as something that would profoundly upset the social order. Indeed, the movement did pursue the aim of establishing a new order and was therefore one of the biggest threats to the state's survival. The intelligence report also pointed out how a majority of the prisoners mentioned in the report had been pardoned out of the sultan's compassion and mercy or had had their punishments modified. Yet, the report noted, though the pardon, in a manner befitting the ruler, was a blessing to certain unreasonable Armenians who had temporarily deviated from the path of truth, leaders of the community had not appreciated it and had continued in their provocations and sedition.[74] The point made here was that Armenian organizations did not know their limits, were thankless, and continued in their acts despite the sultan's good intentions.

According to the Ottoman correspondence, the Hunchak Committee of London had two aims in the name of "Armenian sedition": one immediate and one longer term. The first was to establish an independent government by means of rebellion, bringing about unrest where Armenians lived. The second was to establish a government that would distribute wealth and land to individuals based on the principle of equality in a way that was not suited to any existing form of administration in Europe, and this would spread the idea of anarchy. To meet these aims, the "Armenian sedition" in London would broadcast malicious writings to the European public with the aim of inciting rage against the Ottoman government. According to the document, this London committee was indeed responsible for writings against the Ottoman government that had previously appeared in London newspapers. The committee was not based on the idea of reforms but rather on the aim of bringing about revolution and chaos in the East by taking Ottoman Armenians down the path of socialism, as the report attempted to demonstrate with reference to the committee's previous publications.[75] The basic crux of this document was the determination that the Hunchak organization had no intention of being satisfied by reforms but was in pursuit of a radical and destructive revolution. The state understood this destructiveness or subversion in terms of socialism and anarchism. The London Hunchak Committee, through its publications in London newspapers and through the assistance of the British, was seen as attempting to give courage to the conspirators (erbab-ı fesad) by making Ottoman Armenians come to hate their own government. The threatening ideas of the British Embassy and secret meetings between the embassy and the Armenian Patriarchate gave rise to negative interpretations and worked up the public.

Thus, according to Nazım Paşa, the biggest misunderstanding—caused by nihilism and socialism, which continued due to the "London Hunchak Committee's" provocations and were related to Armenian attempts at sedition—was that it was not possible to eradicate such attempts through reform. The gradual expansion of the seditious acts was in service of bringing about a government of the people that would stretch as far as the Caucasus, uniting Ottoman Armenians with Armenians in Russian, particularly in the Caucasian provinces. Nazım Paşa argued in response to this misunderstanding that there was no proof that the crimes carried out in the Ottoman Empire using the nihilist methods of conspirators (*erbab-ı fesad*) in Russia were in fact linked with Russian nihilists.

Yet Nazım Paşa also noted that among the Armenians were some from Georgia, then part of the Russian Empire, and so he called for an analysis of the committee that Armenian youth from Georgia had established in London against Russian interests as well of their writings. This problem, it was felt, merited investigation by the Russian state: Who was encouraging and supporting these Armenians from Georgia, and what were their relations with Armenian organizations?[76] By writing about the activities of Armenians from Georgia, Nazım Paşa was pointing to a possible cooperation between Ottoman and Russian revolutionary Armenians. Notably, the document discussing the London Hunchak Committee never directly blamed Great Britain. Indeed, it was emphasized that whatever Great Britain had done, it had been misunderstood by the "Armenian committee," and the misunderstanding had excited the committee.[77] As with the use of the phrase "simple folk" (*sade dilan ahali*), a picture was painted of the committee's bad intentions, without disparaging Britain. The document attempted to convey just how dangerous these organizations were by showing that, in fact, they had no truck with reform. Their calls for radical change rendered reforms nonfunctional. The constant emphasis on socialism and nihilism in the document were meant to show Britain and Russia that the situation presented a threat not just to the Ottomans but to all states. In the conflicts that emerged, violence among the state, Muslims, and Armenians always played a major role. Yet when explaining the violence, state reports used different descriptors for events with different actors. Expressions related to violence and accursedness ("vahşiyane ve mel'unane")[78] were often used in official reports to describe actions by Armenians, in particular those that resulted in death, as well as to describe their aims, encouragements, and agitations ("teşvîkât ve tahrîkât-ı mel'anet-kârânede").[79] Although the Armenians weren't the only ones to use violence, when they did employ violence, the use of such phrases in official documents rendered them monstrous, stressing their inhumane features.

The state also overlooked differences between Armenian organizations. In 1896, the administration of Van province announced that a conspiracy to organize a rebellion had been discovered involving Armenians who were part of the so-called Trushak organization (most probably referring to *Droshak*, the ARF's political newspaper, but described as an Armenian organization in Ottoman documents). An official document on this incident reported that in fact the previous information given by the Van administration on the "Trushak Committee," indicating it was *not* organizing a rebellion, was incorrect. This inaccuracy had emerged from interrogation of and house raids on Armenians arrested as part of the investigation of information on the planned rebellion in Van. The Ministry of Police stated that the "Trushak Committee" was as dangerous as the Hunchaks; indeed, there was not an ounce of difference in their desire to stir up rebellion, spill blood, use force and violence, and carry out assassinations. According to the ministry, the two organizations' aims were, first, to serve the ideas of socialism and, second, to establish an Armenian government based on the principle of the sharing of possessions.[80] According to Nazım Paşa, all such organizations ultimately had the same aim. The same ministry correspondence seems to suggest that though the Trushak organization was stronger in Van and its environs, it was supported by the Hunchaks. According to the minister of police, the basic motivation for the internal rebellions was to achieve an independent Armenia by establishing a link across organizations that were otherwise politically quite different. However, he did not address the questions of why and how such organizations were accepted by the locals (even partly) in such a large geography that spanned the provinces of Van, Erzurum, Adana, and Aleppo.

Another document written by the Ministry of Interior and included in Nazım Paşa's report evaluated rebellions by Armenian revolutionary organizations over a wide area—encompassing Samsun, Amasya, Sivas, and Trabzon—by looking at their programs. These programs, according to the document, rested on such anarchist aims as the equal sharing of public wealth and lands, a government of the people, and the annulment of religion and government. Though organizations published requests in the name of Armenia in their own newspapers, their short-term aim was to incite nationalist feelings and then to bring into being the ideals of anarchism. Furthermore, the document provided evidence that this goal was not targeted at the Ottoman government alone but aimed to increase adherence to the "diseased idea [fikr-i sakîmini]" of doing away with governing by all leaders and uniting all European nihilists and anarchists. According to the document, since the sedition (*fesad*) in question was being brought about by such illegitimate means as the threat of assassination and devastation, it was indisputable that the idea of anarchy was behind it.[81]

The document argued that rebellions brought about in the previous year by the Hunchak organization in Dersaadet (Istanbul), Van, and other areas had been unsuccessful thanks to the precautions taken by the government. The organizations, whose aims were one but whose forms of action differed, had entered into competition with one another because of the negative results they achieved and were attempting new uprisings. In this way, the Trushak Committee was helped by the Hunchak Committee in planning to bring about an uprising in Dersaadet.[82] In this narrative, again, state elites emphasized that the Armenian organizations' ultimate aim was not an independent Armenia but rather anarchy. Thus, by once again using antianarchist expressions to describe Armenian organizations' actions and aims, elites attempted to employ an international antianarchist stance. Although antianarchism was one of the bases of the report's discursive construct, all the events and phenomena it referred to were approached in terms of the state's survival.

The Armenian Patriarchate, Changing Stances, and Churches

The Ottoman government always saw the Armenian Patriarchate as the sole political actor representing the Armenian people. Yet as the organizations, actions, and rebellions of the Armenian movement began to become more visible, and as the Armenian problem began to become the subject of international politics, relations between the Ottoman government and the patriarchate began to change. When one looks at the Ottoman correspondence that ran parallel to the movement's actions, included in Nazım Paşa's report, this changing relationship becomes clearer.

In an official document dated September 28, 1895, based on intelligence about the Bab-ı Ali Demonstration, the grand vizier explained the

necessity of preventing the demonstration and taking the necessary precautions to prevent quarrels. In the event that the demonstration could
not be stopped, he proposed a new precaution: send the chief of police or
someone else of importance to the patriarch to ask whether he was aware
of the planned action and request him to immediately do whatever was
necessary to prevent it.[83]

According to a police report dated October 10, 1895, Armenian organizations had been emboldened by a succession of pardons for unsuccessful attempts to provoke foreign intervention and now was attempting to
reach this aim by carrying out "a major act of rebellion [vak'ayı ihtilaliye]"
in Istanbul. The report stated that, based on investigation, Armenian
revolutionary organizations were growing by the day. It proposed that,
though members of these organization had been arrested by the police,
their release following petitions to the Armenian patriarch had led many
Armenians to believe they would not be punished, regardless of what they
did. When intelligence was received of the Bab-ı Ali Demonstration, the
Istanbul chief of police, Hüsnü Bey, had gone to meet with the patriarch
the day before the planned action and request him to prohibit it. When
the patriarch refused to make such a call on the grounds that his word
would not be heeded, it was declared that he would be held responsible for
whatever happened.[84]

The state's basic aim was to try to solve or soften a security crisis
through the patriarchate's mediation. Yet, particularly with the Bab-ı Ali
Demonstration, the Ottoman state inserted the patriarchate into those
responsible for both demonstration and outcome. In this police report,
we observe that the Armenian patriarch's response to this event, which
was certain to happen and which he knew was being planned, was not to
prohibit it; instead, he apparently saw it as necessary and supported it. As
the demonstration dragged on, on its second night another representative was sent to ask the patriarch to issue a call for the dispersal of those
gathered. The police gave assurances that no charges would be pressed
and that those dispersed would be understood to have been deceived. The
Armenian patriarch warned that the supposed rebels would not listen to
his words, but he would nonetheless advise them to disperse. When the

crowd still remained at five in the evening, a formal communiqué was sent to the patriarch urging his dispersion of the crowd.

From the account in the police report, it is clear that the Ottoman government saw the patriarchate as acting in conjunction with Armenian revolutionary organizations. To explain the "degree to which the Patriarchate had acted favorably to the lowly ideas and aims of the revolutionaries [erbab-ı ihtilalin fikir ve maksad-ı denâ'et-kârânelerini ve Patrikhâne'nin onlara karşı ne derecelerde müsâ'ade-kârâne davrandığını]," the document described how Hunchak members entered the patriarchate church and pledged their aims in a ceremony.[85] Another doubt related to the patriarchate and other Armenian churches had to do with the number of "seditious people" present at the attacks who entered churches and were protected by priests and church staff. An official document written to the grand vizier noted that offering refuge in this way was inappropriate for church officials.[86]

What all this correspondence overlooked, however, was that the Armenian organizations themselves viewed the patriarchate as being on the side of the Ottoman government, so the patriarchate had no power to interfere: in the eyes of the organizations, it had no legitimacy to represent the entirety of the Armenian community. In short, the patriarchate was a suspicious political actor both for the Ottoman government and for Armenian revolutionary organizations.

Migrant Workers

As noted earlier, the state saw Istanbul's lower classes, specifically its migrant workers, as potential threats. The threat perceived from seasonal workers is particularly striking in formal correspondence. An official document dated July 28, 1895, and included in the Nazım Paşa's report explained how the police, in the face of assassination attempts directed against them, had to adopt more aggressive methods. Those who were caught by these methods included Armenian porters, laborers, and pumpers. The document stated that these individuals were not distressed by arrest; on the contrary, they wanted to be caught so their names would be written in Hunchak newspapers and their patriotism celebrated, and in the impending establishment of Armenia their arrests would be canceled, and they would be rewarded.[87] The Ministry of Police explained that so long as such provocations and publications continued, there was little use in arresting these people.

The official document saw as one of the major problems the spread of seditious ideas (*fikr-i fesad*) to the students of Armenian schools as well as changing attitudes toward the Armenian Patriarchate. Armenian officials in foreign consulates were of particular note because they were essentially untouchable; teachers in Armenian schools (seen as being under the patriarch's supervisory control) were considered, along with preachers, the primary means of "sedition" (*mefsedet*, from the same linguistic root as *fesad*). In addition, the patriarch was believed to have gathered together many "seditious people" (*erbab-ı fesad*). State elites believed that the patriarch not only publicized sedition (*fesad*) but had also sent to the British consulate and to London newspapers reports contrary to the Ottoman government's interests. According to the document, the Ministry of Police not only considered members of Armenian groups as threats but also believed that the Hunchaks had an audience among Armenians who supported an independent Armenia and that this idea had been accepted among Istanbul's lower classes and laborers who discounted disciplinary and police measures. Now, Istanbul's lower classes became seen as potentially dangerous groups who paid no heed to punitive measures. In addition, the patriarchate, once seen as a legitimate political actor, was now perceived as an internal enemy because of the relationship it was believed to have established with the British consulate. In particular, schools and churches were seen as institutions spreading the idea of an independent Armenia by the patriarchate's hand. The rest of the document was an investigatory report into the patriarch.[88] The fact that the state opened such a file on the patriarch is notable.

In describing the London Hunchak Committee's program as based on the principles and aims of nihilism, socialism, and anarchism, the document stated that this program, which encouraged foreign intervention and was based on greed that necessitated the principle of sharing property and thus appealed to the lowliest of people, had begun to implement its criminal articles.[89] Such remarks on the Hunchak program indicate how state elites viewed the lower classes. In avoiding any discussion of the economic or political problems the lower classes faced, the elites based their assumption of those classes' acceptance of the Hunchak organization on their greed and dismissed any objections to the existing social order and how it was negatively affecting the lower classes.

Another official document on the Bab-ı Ali Demonstration reported the belief that the Hunchak Committee had given rural Armenians the idea of petitioning. Also, although its members were known, there had been no results from their arrests or interrogations because they were sure that they would not be punished.[90] In a notice written to the lieutenant governor of Beyoğlu, even clearer statements were made about the Armenian lower classes. News had been received of Armenians who had come to Istanbul from the countryside and who had been indulged or spoiled by "widespread lies [erâcîf-i münteşire]." According to the notice, "a few had been hanging around, armed, in deserted spaces and had used shameless and inappropriate words and make threats in such places as taverns." Noting that the existing security practices had no impact on such "shameless behavior," the document reported that coal workers in Galata had begun a form of "inappropriateness [münasebetsizlik]." On this, a decision was made about "rounding up, through good plans, a number of Armenians who had come from the countryside and were found to be idling about, who had no work, and who merely aimed at bringing about evil, such Armenian scoundrels, and dispatching them to a police station."[91]

Where evidence of conspiracy was found, the Armenians concerned were handed over to the courts. Suspects about whom no evidence could be uncovered were repatriated under police supervision. Unemployed Armenians living in such places as inns and boarding rooms and thus seen as potential tools of seditious elements through the committees were also rounded up and sent back to their homelands, their traveling expenses covered, to prevent them from engaging in sedition or unseemliness. Security measures were put in place, including night and day patrols, as supplementary precautions against revolutionaries.[92] A large proportion of Armenians who arrived in Istanbul from the countryside came to carry out seasonal labor. As such, this decision made clear that the state viewed all Armenian seasonal workers as suspicious figures to be kept away from Istanbul.

According to another note, a majority of those who organized the so-called sedition at Dersaadet were Armenians from Tekfurdağı, some five thousand of whom were living in the households and bachelor quarters of Kumkapı, Gedikpaşa, and Samatya. The note claimed that many of the Tekfurdağı Armenians were deceived into becoming intermediaries for the Trushak Committee, which planned a new series of uprisings that would be more effective than those carried out the previous year by the Hunchaks and which was organizing the assassination of public servants and informants. Following attempts to return these suspects to their homelands by the police, inquiries and legal proceedings were transferred to the provincial governorate (*mutasarrıflık*)[93] so that they would not be able to return to Dersaadet by sea or road and thus could not organize any malicious acts.

Conclusion

To understand the structures of state elites' thinking, this chapter has explored the ways in which administrative–legal debates established a discursive field regarding social "elements" that state elites (in line with raison d'état) saw as a threat and the types of articulations that existed between concepts within this field. This discursive field was not based on brand-new concepts but on the concepts of vagrancy and sedition that were already central to state elites' threat perceptions and had historical roots in Ottoman imperial governance, especially for the capital. These historical concepts were useful for the imperial center to create ambiguity between public order and security. This ambiguity was also a reflection of the Ottoman state elites in how they used policing techniques and framed the implementation of legal codes, laws, acts, and orders. Thus, in the Hamidian Era an international antianarchist collaboration was reflected in the concepts employed by state elites in conjunction with pejorative references to "anarchists" and with administrative reforms of the period.

The state elite's use of the discursive tropes of vagrancy, sedition, and anarchism also points to the conceptualizations of the Armenian

Question during the violent events discussed in the reports of Minister of Police Hüseyin Nazım Nazım Paşa. The Ottoman bureaucracy's security discourse not only created an atmosphere of fear of a permanent political threat but also led to discrimination based on the suspicion that every Armenian could be associated with a revolutionary organization. The interpretation of the legal framework was established in relation with the security discourse and state narratives on the Armenian Question.

5

Controlling Geographical Mobility

From Early-Modern Practices to Modern Regulations

Across the extensive space of the empire, the Ottoman government tried to control all forms of geographical mobility, particularly in response to groups defined as threats in the late nineteenth century. Thus, the Hamidian Era was marked by regulations and administrative decisions designed to control travel. There was a consistent effort to regulate the geographical mobility of vagrants (*serseriler*) as well as of unknown and suspicious individuals (*meçhul'ül ahvâl eşhâs, mazanne-i su'i' eşhâs*).[1] These regulations and administrative decisions were mainly interwoven with the political perceptions of the Armenian and Macedonian Questions and with anti-anarchism in the late Ottoman Empire. Such practices of control, though they already had a deep history, began to be employed through modern techniques in the Hamidian Era through the reissuing of the Regulation Pursuant to the Regulation of Movement (Internal Passport Regulation, Men'-i Mürur Nizamnamesi) in 1841 and 1887, two Passport Regulations (Pasaport Nizamnamesi) in 1884 and 1894, and regulations related to hotels. However, legal regulations were not the only source of passport practices: decrees, orders, and even everyday administrative decisions by the bureaucracy's lower ranks also created a new regime of mobility.

The sociological literature on the modern state offers important analytical tools for making sense of the regulations and policies of control related to geographical mobility. As outlined in chapter 1, the modern state developed and put into place new definitions, classifications, and means of record keeping for its subjects. It also encoded and stored all this information and worked to standardize relevant phenomena or fields of action. This standardization ensured that all such fields were organized by the state. Strategies of governance, meanwhile, were built on these kinds of information and records. From the modern state's perspective, the foundations of administrative rule would be constituted through the proliferation, expansion, and detailing of statistical information—that is, through the intensification of technologies of surveillance.

The administrative structure of policies to control geographical mobility demonstrates a *network* of the state's intangible expansion into everyday life by means of both high-level political decisions—legislated via laws and decrees and communicated between administrative offices by notifications—and low-level administrative work. The legal framework was executed mainly through daily bureaucratic correspondence and ad hoc practices. Thus, not only administrative offices but also short-lived subject-oriented commissions, bureaucrats, and the communication between them via the circulation of documents created an "administrative network." Passport practices were not only about physical frontiers or geographical separations but also about jurisdiction and administration.[2]

The Ottoman infrastructure of international passports (subsequently referred to here as just "passports"), internal passports, and identity cards[3] was set up using both "old" and "new" administrative techniques, giving a rather eclectic character to attempts at state control over geographical mobility. Although the new regulations and institutions of the late nineteenth century brought a new legal framework, they did not create new institutional logics or governing techniques from scratch. They were instead generally practiced through "old" ways and benefited from the traditional local ways of confirming someone's identity. This way of stitching new techniques onto the old ways of collecting information on a person's identity using traditional social control mechanisms not only was about the lack of modern state infrastructure but was also a form of "institutional bricolage"—a "reworking of the institutional materials at hand."[4] Using the old ways also points to the empire's diversified and complicated power repertoire in its means of administration.

This chapter discusses how early-modern techniques of social control and surveillance to control mobility were institutionalized and practiced. It examines how old and new techniques were selected and combined. It points out how early-modern techniques of identification continued to be part of the empire's administrative practices, serving as the foundation for new types of identification practices.[5] Understanding how techniques and different types of social control mechanisms were selected and combined helps create a wider understanding of policies controlling geographical mobility during the late nineteenth century.

The Suretyship System, Migration, and Social Control

Passports, in particular internal passports, existed well before the modern period. The best-known reason for the use of internal passports was to prevent peasants from moving around the empire and thus assure the continuity of land-based forms of production. In the Ottoman Empire, the most commonly encountered reason for internal passports, besides land-based production, was to prevent migration to big cities, in particular Istanbul. Internal passports, or licenses of passage, were used to stave off potential problems in public order.[6] Efforts to control entry and exit in Istanbul were seen as important to prevent problems in sustaining the city's population, to thwart antisocial behavior by migrants (in particular seasonal workers, who were mostly young single men), and to control uprisings related to the city's status as a capital. The state's attempt to control geographical mobility consequently aimed to assure not only public order but also the stability of the political order.

In periods of crisis especially, we begin to see greater importance given to regulations and restrictions pertaining to migrants. During the sixteenth- and seventeenth-century Celali rebellions, for instance, which were prompted by economic and social woes, orders related to migration were passed down one after the other. Another period marked by crisis, the Patrona Halil Rebellion in the eighteenth century, saw a similar trend. Each of these periods was defined both by weaknesses in security and by migration to Istanbul from the countryside, largely owing to excessive taxation. Migration to Istanbul became attractive mainly because of insecurity in the countryside, the weakness of production in the face of rising taxes, and the benefits of life in the city, such as the exemption of the city's residents from some special taxes and assistance for the poor by religious institutions.[7]

Though it is unclear when the suretyship system aimed at preventing disorder began, it started in Istanbul, and its implementation gradually expanded. It was used to solve problems with settlement policies, public order, public safety, and the maintenance of the status quo in matters of taxation in the Ottoman Empire. Through the practice of surety, if someone were required to abandon their place of residence for an "acceptable reason," they would be allowed to travel if they could point to a guarantor who would ensure that the due taxes would be paid in their absence.[8] When authorities were searching for someone, often the first question they asked concerned the person's guarantor, which gave a useful means to locate individuals.[9] The suretyship system fell within oral traditions of record keeping.

Collective surety (*kefalet-i müteselsile*) was understood as a shared system of guarantee carried out on the principle that subjects in neighborhoods or villages would vouch for one another. For such a function, a judge (*kadı*), by the order of a police superintendent, would summon the men of a village or neighborhood to the court, where they would collectively vouch for one another, in particular elders for the young. The village magistrate would act as the guarantor of guarantors, and an imam or priest, as the religious representative, would act, together with the magistrate, as guarantor of all. On the matter of seasonal laborers, the concierge (*odabaşı*) of the bachelor lodgings where many stayed in the city or the local magistrate or chieftain (*kethüda*) was required to act as guarantor to those residing there. Most such bachelor lodgings were connected to foundations, and even if they were privately run, the state designated a chieftain and concierge for them.

For seasonal workers, the suretyship system was among the most important mechanisms of control. It was forbidden to employ a worker without a guarantor. The most important reason for this regulation was, without a doubt, the problem of public security. The suretyship system was seen as especially important for assuring public safety in big cities. For example, in 1579 one of the more significant issues of the time was

ensuring that men without a guarantor did not reside in Istanbul neighborhoods. When the state came to know of the presence of seditious people (*ehli fesad*) in Istanbul but was unclear who precisely was seditious,
it was announced that the people of Istanbul were to act as guarantors
for one another. This process was to be carried out by imams, muezzins,
chieftains, the concierges of foundation lodgings, and innkeepers. It was
ordered that those deemed suspicious (*mazanne, müttehem*) because they
lacked a guarantor were not to be protected. It was also announced that if
an individual acted in a seditious manner and had no guarantor, anyone
protecting them would be subject to hard labor. And if any seditious person (*ehli fesad*) was found in the drinking establishments (*meyhane* and
bozhane), those turning a blind eye were to be executed.[10]

In a document from 1596, it was ordered that all Greeks (Rum) and
Armenians in Galata and Tophane who were not locals and were not
married—that is to say, migrant laborers—were to provide the names of
their guarantors.[11] After the Tanzimat series of reforms in the early nineteenth century, the suretyship system was applied to the settlement of
migrants, and records were checked every six months. If a person with
a guarantor committed a crime and fled, the guarantor was responsible for locating them. If the guarantor could not locate the person they
had vouched for and present them to the courts, they themselves were
to be imprisoned until the guilty party was found. Before internal passports came into use, entry to Istanbul was governed by prohibiting anyone without a guarantor into neighborhoods. The task of inquiring into
the guarantor of a new arrival and, when necessary, informing the local
judge (*kadı*) was appointed to imams and was considered one of their
most important duties.[12]

As the number of those coming to Istanbul to escape taxation grew,
the problems of settlement and employment followed the problem of
provision. In 1567, when many people from Rumelia and Anatolia were
leaving their lands and settling in Istanbul, particularly in the Eyüp and
Kasımpaşa neighborhoods, an order was given, citing damage to public
property, to determine how many households existed in each neighborhood and who had lived there for less than five years. This order also
decreed that records would henceforth be kept of all those who resided in

a locale for less than five years. It was further decided that imams, muezzins, and magistrates were to prevent new arrivals from settling down and that those described as seditious, common criminals, or rogues, those without a guarantor, and prostitutes (whose places of operation were also to be determined) were to be imprisoned.[13]

Migration to Istanbul in the eighteenth century brought with it serious problems of provision and the city's food supply.[14] In 1724, during the reign of Ahmet III, an edict was issued to address this issue.[15] To prevent migration to Istanbul, measures would be in place to control entry and exit from the city. The homes of migrants without proof of continuous work would be raided, and they would be sent back to their homelands. A document dated 1724 forbade granting license of passage to those who wished to come to Istanbul from Anatolia or Rumelia. This ban was intended particularly to prevent the migration of entire households or families. It was ordered that those who arrived at Istanbul's checkpoints despite the ban were to be turned away.[16]

At this time, the Ottoman state saw Albanian migrants in particular as "dangerous" because many had participated in the Patrona Halil Rebellion in 1730.[17] In the attempts to control Istanbul and its environs, the entry of Albanian migrants was curtailed. To prevent migration and to return the unwanted, a decision was taken in 1734 to send so-called vagrants without guarantors back to their homelands, and any idle people who arrived at Istanbul by boat were to be returned via Kocaeli.[18] Yet migration continued, and orders on this matter remained on the agenda for quite some time. Indeed, an earlier edict in 1729 had already entirely forbidden attempts to migrate to Istanbul, and the ruling in 1734 simply included further efforts to control entries and exits in the city.[19] Underlying all such regulations was the fear that migrants might join an uprising. For this reason, one finds especially strict restrictions on Albanians and Kurds.

In 1740, a notice (*adaletname*) warned relevant institutions and offices to prevent household migration. It was requested that measures be taken so that those who came with permission to see to their provincial affairs would not come en masse. It was stipulated that those who arrived in the city to see to their own affairs had to have with them certain documents to prove their reasons for coming, such as an official warrant from a local military commander (*alaybeyi arzı/senedi*), a ruling from a judge (*kadı ilamı*), or any document showing they had come for work. For traders bringing provisions or goods to Istanbul, these procedures would be simplified. By 1764, though the security problem had more or less disappeared, preventing the continued migration was justified on the grounds that it had a negative effect on agricultural production, and a decision was taken to send back rural migrants. Strikingly, during this era the practices of taking a collective oath from the rural communities on not leaving their lands (*nezre bağlanma*) and obtaining collective surety were used to prevent migration to Istanbul, so no one from rural districts would be able to leave the countryside in an uncontrolled manner. An official bill (*hüccet-i şeriyye*) drawn up and registered by a senior accountant (*baş muhasebe*) was considered a precaution against unwanted influx to Istanbul. Those who abandoned their places of origin were to be sent back. All rural peoples were to make financial guarantees and vouch for one another. In this way, the imagined public order would be assured.[20] These attempts to administer control over geographical mobility used even more bureaucratized techniques in the eighteenth century.

Prohibitions on comings and goings from Istanbul were generally meant to prevent the immigration of entire households as well as to control the city's population. As such, the key issue here was to limit spatial mobility. A strategy of prohibition was pursued against all forms of geographical mobility to prevent migrant populations from settling in Istanbul. Yet this strategy changed as security came to be an important problem for central-state policies. In particular, following the reign of Mahmut II (1808–39), the state endeavored to develop effective systems of control and monitoring for all types of geographical mobility.

Migration, Public Order, and Administrative Changes in the Nineteenth Century

The regulation of modern bureaucratic information on personal identity, which started during the Tanzimat period, benefited from both traditional social control mechanisms and new registration methods. Alongside traditional mechanisms, modern documents such as identity cards, hotel registers, residence permits, documents of residence, and so on were used to control and surveil the poor and political suspects. The verification of identity information by cross-referencing different documents mostly drew on oral traditions of record keeping.[21] Ethnoreligious and local belonging made up the foundation of the imperial system of identification that emerged from the millet system. In this, the fundamental conditions of the Ottoman state's recognition of individuals were local—that is, belonging to a particular religion or a neighborhood directly affected by passport regulations.

In 1826, during the reign of Mahmut II, several administrative and legal changes were set in motion following the elimination of Janissary units, giving rise to changes in practices of public order. These administrative changes were, from the Ottoman government's perspective, the beginning of a period of intensifying security practices for Istanbul. The Ministry of the Superintendent of Guilds and Markets (İhtisap Nezareti), established in 1826, emerged at this time as an institution for ensuring public order in Istanbul. With the Janissary rebellion in 1826, a decision was taken to return corps members to their homelands. Yet the Janissaries had no desire to repatriate, and so they were deemed a threat to public order and security. The number of the unemployed in Istanbul was determined, and they, along with the Janissaries, were sent back to their homelands and ordered never to return.[22] In 1829, the institution of the *muhtarlık*, the office of the headman of a village or city neighborhood, was established. Musa Çadırcı ties this institution to the aims of eradicating migration to Istanbul and preventing security vulnerabilities. Çadırcı notes that the revisiting of rules regarding internal travel during this same period further supports this thesis.[23]

Also in the period of Mahmut II, the state began to collect knowledge of and keep records on the population under its rule. A census was conducted following the Russo-Ottoman War of 1828–29, and in Istanbul the Ministry of Census (Ceride Nezareti) was established to evaluate the results and see to population affairs, while census bureaus (*defter nazirliği*) were created in provincial centers under the Ministry of Interior. These bureaus resembled today's civil registry office. A unit was set up to store and encode the information collected by the Ministry of Census. To collect information on the population, the state made use of 1,831 agents across the empire, including guild chamberlains, religious leaders, and local registry officers. Thus, the state still had a need for local mediators or go-betweens to reach its population. Such mediators were important actors in traditional mechanisms of social control.

However, these two basic tools—controls on travel and the census to collect information on the population—were the beginning of a process that introduced direct intervention by the state, in lieu of intermediaries, to control the population. They led to the proliferation of written documents and the start of the collection of detailed data on the population. In this context, many forms of registration emerged, from birth certificates to residence documents and passports, and became a part of everyday life. It is here that we see surveillance becoming part of the processes of discipline.[24]

In the new *muhtarlık* system, a local headman's task was primarily to ensure the safety of a neighborhood or village. These officials were tasked with checking the internal passports of those arriving from other empire cities or villages and learning why or with what aims new arrivals came and how long they would stay. Internal passports served both to identify an individual and to document legitimate reasons why they had left their regular place of residence.[25] Local headmen were required to verify the authenticity of these passports and not to allow anyone into the neighborhood who arrived with a forged passport or with no passport at all. If someone came with the intent of staying, settling them in was also the local headman's task. Finally, the local headman had to appoint someone else or himself as the guarantor of the newly arrived person, record this in the neighborhood registry, and inform the head of the provincial census bureau (*defter nazırı*).[26] This entire process entailed connecting local people (who in the previous system had been connected to an imam or priest) to local headmen.[27] A collective system of surety was still in place, but now it existed through a regulation that put headmen in charge of local mechanisms of social control. Together with the establishment of the institution of the *muhtarlık*, registers known as *mahallat*, in which deaths and births were recorded, led to new practices of registration. These practices ensured that the state had access to numerical data on the population and remained abreast of population changes in cities. A similar practice was attempted in Russia, where local religious authorities kept private registers on marriages and deaths, and after 1831 there was an effort to standardize these registers. As in the Ottoman case, the aim in Russia was to ensure a constant flow of information about subjects to the czar and to ensure the official recognition of subjects.[28]

The establishment of the Ministry of the Superintendent of Guilds and Markets in 1826 was another important development. Much of this ministry's charter was devoted to regulating the comings and goings of new arrivals to Istanbul. Toward this end, it was stipulated that the number of tradespeople present in Istanbul was to be determined and that they were to be identified so as to make clear their names and likenesses as well as their guarantors. This system was designed so that the porters and boatmen at the landings of Galata, Üsküdar, and Boğaziçi in Istanbul as well as attendants in bathhouses and tradesmen and shopkeepers would be recorded. A copy of this registry was to be presented to the chief of the Office of Tax Collectors Related to Guilds and Markets (İhtisab Ağası). Internal passports were to be checked at the entries and exits to Istanbul, at Küçükçekmece, and at the bridge at Bostanbaşı, and entries were to be recorded in the same registry, with "To the Ministry of the Superintendent of Guilds and Markets" written on the internal passport. The newcomers had to submit these passports to the Office of Tax Collectors Related to Guilds and Markets, which would register this information. Names, reputations, lines of work, places of origin, and the reasons for and dates of arrival in Istanbul were to be recorded in two registries, one for each side of the city (the Anatolian and European parts). For seasonal migrants (*bekârs*, "bachelors") arriving in Istanbul, special inns were to be set aside, and those staying in such inns were to be linked to guarantors. According to the charter, such people were to be prevented from staying in Istanbul any longer than necessary. In an attempt to control this factor, it was to be noted in the registry of the chief of the Office of Tax Collectors Related to Guilds and Markets when they left the city. If an individual arriving from the countryside was said to be unemployed or a vagrant, this was to be indicated on their passport by noting, "To the Ministry of the Superintendent of Guilds and Markets, as is custom." If any impropriety was determined to have occurred when the individual in question arrived at the office to submit their internal passport, that person was to be deported from Istanbul.[29]

These changes were implemented through the sixteen articles in the Regulation Pursuant to the Regulation of Movement (Internal Passport Regulation, Men'-i Mürür Nizamnamesi) passed on February 10, 1841.[30] According to the regulation, anyone obtaining an internal passport was required to have it stamped by an imam and a *muhtar* and signed at the Neighborhood Secretarial Office at the Gate of the Serasker (Bab-ı Seraskeriye Mahallat Katibi Odası). After receiving the passport from the Court of Istanbul (*İstanbul Mahkemesi*), they were required to have it stamped again in the Office of Tax Collectors Related to Guilds and Markets if any impropriety was determined. If this process was carried out in the countryside, then a passport obtained from an imam or local headman (*muhtar*) was to be taken to an office of the Ministry of Population Affairs (Nüfus Nezareti) and signed. After being taken from the court, it also had to stamped by the police and registered by a clerk. In places where the Tanzimat reforms had yet to change local institutions, internal passports would continue to be issued as they had been previously, based on traditional mechanisms of social control. According to Article 16 of the Internal Passport Regulation, a record was to be kept of all internal passports issued, and this record was to be checked every three months.

In Article 3, we again encounter the suretyship system. Someone wishing to obtain an internal passport from somewhere other than the place of application needed two guarantors from the place of application. According to Article 10, an individual without a passport was to be detained if they could not point to their guarantor. Article 11 defined the period of detention as three days, after which the reason for the detention was to be recorded upon their return to their home region, and their internal passport was to be released. If this article was violated, then under Article 12 the individual was to be imprisoned and upon completion of the sentence escorted back to their homeland.

Article 6 laid out the information that had to be included in the internal passport: name, reputation, age, craft/profession, likeness (i.e., a written description of physical characteristics such as eye and hair color, height, and so on), province of residence, places to be visited, the place and date of issue, and the state to which they were subject. In this way, an individual's identity and places of travel could easily be ascertained. Article 8 described the procedure for monitoring those leaving Istanbul, who could obtain an internal passport by writing their names on a stamped note obtained from their neighborhood imam and *muhtar*. Shopkeepers and tradespeople could obtain a similar note from their chamberlain (*kethüda*), and seasonal workers (bachelors) staying in inns could get a note from the chamberlain (*kethüda*) of innkeepers, after which the names of such applicants were stricken from the records. Applicants were also to present to the Ministry of the Superintendent of Guilds and Markets a document from the High Council of Quarantine (Meclis-i Tahaffuz) showing that they were healthy. Exit from Istanbul by land was to be controlled by the inspection of internal passports at Büyükçekmece, Şamlar, Büyük Derbend, Yarımburgaz, Bulgurlu, and Beykoz. The exit of those departing by sea was controlled by the Port Chamber (Liman Odası).

The regulation (*talimatname*) of 1841 also aimed to control entries to the country because there was as yet no international passport regulation. Article 5 of this order stipulated that before going to another country, Ottoman subjects had to apply to the Ministry of Foreign Affairs for a passport, bringing with them a document that included identity information from the Ministry of the Superintendent of Guilds and Markets. Upon receiving approval from the Ministry of Foreign Affairs, they had to return to the Ministry of the Superintendent of Guilds and Markets and to the consulate of the place they intended to visit to get their document stamped. In the absence of a consulate, the regulation stipulated that the passport was to be stamped when the traveler arrived in the country they were visiting. Meanwhile, anyone entering the Ottoman Empire had to present their passports to the Ministry of the Superintendent of Guilds and Markets and have them signed. For passengers arriving by sea, the captain was to perform the first passport control, after which the passports were to be processed in the same way as others.

Through the regulation of 1841, an order was introduced for those coming to Istanbul to stay and for those wishing to move to a different neighborhood in the city. According to Article 16, those coming to the city had to go first to the Ministry of the Superintendent of Guilds and Markets to make known their profession, the name of the neighborhood in which they intended to settle, and the name of a person alongside whom they would work. This notification was possible through a certificate called an *ilmühaber*: a letter from an imam, priest, rabbi, local headman, magistrate of tradesmen, or caretaker of an inn or bachelor lodgings used as proof of the bearer's good behavior and also used for proof of identity. Those wishing to obtain an internal passport had to present a stamped *ilmühaber*[31] setting out their name, father's name, destination, where they were going and reasons for going, how long they would stay, and their likeness, all with the aim of controlling whether they had accurately declared their identity.

These regulations were soon followed by the establishment of the Ottoman police under the eighteen-article Police Law (Zaptiye Nizamnamesi) dated March 20, 1845.[32] The first two articles of the Police Law laid out the main duty of the police as being to ensure public safety and order. To this end, the police were vested with a considerable authority, including the authority to summon and employ regular soldiers at military posts. Articles 3 and 4 were on the control of travelers moving within the empire or arriving from other countries.[33] Internal-passport controls and international-passport controls for foreigners were important measures for regulating migration to Istanbul and making internal travel dependent on police permission. This responsibility follows from the outlined police duties of monitoring and inspecting such spaces as hotels, inns, and restaurants, as regulated by Article 10.

In 1867, the Passport Office Regulation (Pasaport Odası Nizamnamesi) was issued. According to this regulation, someone traveling to the empire from abroad had first to obtain a visa for their passport from the Ottoman consulate in their own country. The Passport Clerks Regulation Bill Draft (Pasaport Kalemleri Nizamname Layihası), dated May 2, 1869and the Passport and Internal Passport Regulation Bill Draft (Pasaport ve Mürür Tezkesi Nizamname Layihası), of the same date, had been prepared, yet these regulations, composed of six and seven articles, respectively, had yet to go into effect.[34] The Passport Office Regulation had been in use for some time. For foreigners, in addition to a passport, a visa and an internal passport were also necessary. According to Article 7 of the Passport Office Regulation, anyone could on arriving in the Ottoman Empire and obtaining a passport visa from his or her own consulate obtain an internal passport after presenting a written document allowing them to obtain such a passport to the Port Chamber or to officials tasked with such matters. One of the administrative changes carried out in this period was the introduction of a requirement that everyone who applied for an internal passport and a passport had to submit an identity certificate (*nüfus tezkeresi*). The processing and careful recording of certificates for passports and internal passports as a sort of incident report that included information on their family, previous residence, and travels also began at this time.[35]

Identification is among the most important elements for the administration of a system of control based on passports and internal passports. In the nineteenth century, obtaining information about the population was a critical matter for government. This task of obtaining and storing information, which began with censuses, continued with the regulation of identity documents. However, the taking of censuses remained quite disordered from the 1831 count until the Crimean War in 1853–56, aside from a few population reports. The economic bottleneck in which the state found itself with the Crimean War gave rise to the establishment of the Ministry of Registry of Property (Tahrir-i Emlak Nezareti), which, in registering properties liable for taxation and men who were liable to be taxed, issued tax population certificates and recorded identity information and tax burdens. Soon after that, in 1878, the Population Registration Regulation (Sicil-i Nüfus Nizamnamesi) was issued.

Thereafter, a signed and stamped population certificate, treated like a birth certificate or identity card, became a required document for all official matters. Through these documents, the state could both register the population and obtain all the necessary information about an individual in any situation with a single document. Not being registered or not providing population officers with the necessary document meant punishment. Such information as births, deaths, marriages, divorces, and changes of residence were registered locally and were reported regularly to the central government.

In this manner, the empire was able to develop a store of population information that was continuously updated. Certificates evolved away from their previous status as certificates of good standing. Local headmen or imams processed a document containing the identity information for every newborn child and were tasked with communicating it to population officers in the provinces. Certificates now amounted to the registration of standard identity information by the state; and in this manner, a population certificate was prepared for each newborn child.[36]

Conclusion

Administrative techniques to control geographical mobility were developed mainly to limit the internal travel of Ottoman subjects before 1826. The attempts to regulate all kinds of travel inside the Ottoman Empire were strongly connected to crises of security (especially in Istanbul), public order, continuity of agricultural production, and tax obligations. The tools that enabled such control were intrinsically based on surety and created a written form of oral testimonies to good behavior, mostly within the religious character of the localities. Although belonging to a group (millet) and belonging to a specific geographical unit (a village or a neighborhood) were fundamental markers in identifying individual identity, they also created the later techniques of information gathering to produce identity information as part of long-term imperial repertoires of power.

The bureaucratization of identity information using modern techniques came alongside a new system of surveillance in the nineteenth century. This new system was grounded mainly on local traditional practices of social control and created an administrative network not only with newly founded administrative offices but also with traditional local registration practices. Instead of operating while still lacking a modern bureaucratic infrastructure, the Ottoman Empire used this traditional/new hybrid structure to more efficiently control geographical mobility. This hybrid structure was based on both written records and oral practices of local social control mechanisms that ushered in the registration of individual identity. On the one hand, this structure recognized individual identities; on the other hand, it became the core of state surveillance, with permanent registration and modern documents on individual identity, which were significant tools of controlling geographical mobility in the form of travel permits.

6

Efforts to Control
Internal Geographical Mobility
under Abdülhamid II

Internal Passports

During the Hamidian Era (1876–1908), efforts to control geographical mobility were shaped largely by state elites' understandings of public order and perceptions of threat. Policies and practices for controlling internal and interimperial geographical mobility differed according to the political crisis. Through institutional and administrative changes related to the modern state apparatus, these policies and practices of control profoundly affected the daily lives of Ottoman citizens. The state's ways of controlling mobility, both within and at its borders, offer important clues to how it perceived its own subjects. This chapter explores the use of one of the methods it used: internal passports. It attempts to understand how the Ottoman government, in its efforts to control internal geographical mobility and establish the infrastructural means of the modern state, made use of traditional mechanisms of social control throughout the Hamidian Era. It also examines how such controls functioned in the field of legitimacy, concealed at times by raison d'état.

The Ottoman government's perception of threat from Bulgarians, Armenians, and anarchists paved the way for the use of identity documents, internal passports, and (international) passports as tools for labeling specific groups. The labeling process was based largely on three discursive tropes: *vagrant, anarchist,* and *sedition.* Especially during the Armenian massacres in 1894–96, and after the British Memorandum of

1895 regarding Article 61 of the Berlin Treaty (both discussed in chapter 2), limiting the mobility of Armenians and preventing the return of those who had left the empire for economic or security reasons became dominant concerns in Ottoman passport practices.

The Hamidian Era introduced new regulations both for internal passports and for passports more generally. On September 6, 1887,[1] the new Regulation Pursuant to the Regulation of Movement (Men'-i Mürür Nizamnamesi, hereafter Internal Passport Regulation), composed of twenty-five articles, revised the rules for internal passports. Internal passports were now required to be printed, counterfoiled, and officially stamped. According to Article 4 of the regulation, an individual was not required to submit an *ilmühaber* (see chapter 5) at their destination. Because it was already impossible to draw up an internal passport without an *ilmühaber*, submitting the internal passport alone was considered sufficient. Article 5 made it necessary to affix a revenue stamp to the printed document, attesting that the internal passport was not forged and that a fee had been received for the document. If the person requesting an internal passport was poor, another sort of stamp was applied that did not have a fee. According to Article 6, those who traveled frequently were to be registered not for every trip but once every six months.

Article 7 stated that internal passports would be issued by population administration transit offices in Istanbul and other localities and by population ministers and officials in the provinces. In this way, the bureaucratic structure was changed to require the submission of an *ilmühaber* along with the Ottoman identification document (*tezkere-i Osmaniyye*) when applying for an internal passport. Thus, the suretyship system began to act in conjunction with a system that was both more bureaucratic and defined by the individual. According to Article 9, state officials were to receive an *ilmühaber* from the heads or ministers of the office in which they worked; neighborhood residents from an imam or *muhtar*; madrasa students from their *müderris* (Islamic scholar, teacher); non-Muslims from the patriarchate, rabbinate, or church community or from rural metropolitans; monks from their abbots or village *kocabaşı* (elderly non-Muslim community leaders); inn residents from concierges, with the approval of the chamberlain of innkeepers; and foreign subjects from the representative of their own state or, for those from places without a representative in the empire, from the local government.

According to Article 10, internal passports were to include the bearer's job or craft, likeness, and destination, and the same information was to be provided for anyone traveling with the bearer. This article also decreed that internal passports would not be given to those unable to submit an *ilmüh-aber*, to those who presented *ilmühaber* that did not match their criminal record, and to those who were under police surveillance or banned from entry by the courts (*heyet-i adliye*). Internal passports could also be drawn up by subdistrict governors (*nahiye müdürü*) in villages. These internal passports were to be prepared by district population officers (*kaza nüfus memurları*) and dispatched directly to subdistrict administrators (*nahiyei müdürleri*). The internal passports were then turned over to the individuals in exchange for a fee. According to Article 15, subdistrict governors were to show their accounts noting fees received to a provincial population officer at the end of every month. Article 16 stipulated that everyone was required to produce an internal passport if requested by the police, and those without an internal passport or with a passport that did not have a visa would be fined. However, Article 18 added that they could again obtain permission to travel by indicating a guarantor and place of residence.

The Internal Passport Regulation is an example of a law carried out with the aim of what Anthony Giddens describes as the predictability of the everyday (see chapter 1), for which processes of surveillance are of central importance. It rested foremost on the bureaucratic definition and recognition of individuals. An individual had to verify their identity according to the criteria defined by the state's administrative mechanisms. By means of traditional social mechanisms of control, the state used its administrative apparatus to collect and control information that it saw as important to have on individuals in the empire. This information, stored and encoded by different state administrative units, regulated the behaviors of individuals. With the Internal Passport Regulation, which was an administrative regulation, it became possible for the state to exercise its authority over individuals' internal movement. All travelers in the empire had to obtain an internal passport, regardless of whether they were

Ottoman subjects or belonged to other states, and passports that Ottoman subjects coming from abroad had received from local population officers or consulates were insufficient for travel within the empire.[2] Thus, there were two levels of control on traveling within the Ottoman Empire. First, to enter the empire, passport controls were conducted, and then to travel within it an internal passport—a permit of sorts—was required. As such, the state collected information about the itineraries of both those from abroad and those traveling within the country. The relationship between surveillance and administrative power standardized everyday life practices through registration and encoding and ensured their coordination by the state.

The Verification of Individual Identity

The process of standardization and coordination was not without glitches. First, the state had to regulate the verification of individual identity. The fact that the new regulation did not immediately go into effect meant that previous practices continued for some time. Even as earlier practices continued, it was decided that internal passports and passports would not be issued to those who could not produce an Ottoman identification document (*tezkere-i Osmaniyye*) as an index of standardized identity.[3] However, in practice, problems remained, even in later years. A document written by the Ministry of the Interior to Mamüratilaziz province stated that traders and others like them would be designated as "unknown" if they could not produce an identity document. The Ministry of Interior also stated that the police or other administrative units should not issue internal passports or international passports without identity documents and that the officers issuing an internal or international passport to those without an identity document would be punished.[4] However, because most Ottoman subjects did not have an Ottoman identification document, an *ilmühaber* was considered sufficient for many purposes. Ship captains and their crews, who had to travel for work, for instance, were required to obtain an *ilmühaber* from port authorities and to be in possession of an internal passport.[5] If a traveler was accompanied by a spouse, children younger than twenty, relatives, or servants, these people would also be added to the traveler's certificate and internal passport, with information on their identity and itineraries. One of the striking elements here is that travelers were understood to be male. A man was defined as an agent; his wife was subjected to the same administrative treatment as a servant or a child younger than twenty. If married women traveled with their husbands, for administrative purposes they did not possess an individual identity. Travelers older than twenty other than wives and servants were required to have a separate certificate and internal passport.[6]

Presenting a certificate was one of the necessary conditions for obtaining an internal passport: the *ilmühaber* belonging to a Muslim or a non-Muslim had to be certified by, first, a local headman (*muhtar*) and elder council and then by the appropriate religious leader.[7] The correspondence of the Governmental Commission for Expediting Initiatives and Reforms noted the requirement for Ottoman Christian travelers that to get an internal passport they had to have an *ilmühaber* from their church or headman, and their sect had to be noted on that document. Furthermore, if those who left the countryside for Istanbul or elsewhere lost their internal passports or passports, they had to specify a guarantor or correspond with officials in their place of origin to arrange a new document.[8] For instance, a certain Armenian named Megerdech (written "Mıgırdiç" in the document) from Diyarbakır returned to Alexandria from the United States without a passport in 1895. In Alexandria, he, his brother Oseb, and his brother's wife (whose name is not listed on the document) obtained internal passports and used these documents to travel from Istanbul to Diyarbakır. Even though the trio did not have international passports, they were allowed to stay in Diyarbakır because they were able to list guarantors.[9] In another example, a group of Armenians wishing to enter Istanbul from Bulgaria and Eastern Rumelia were not granted internal passports by the authorities. These individuals, according to information provided by the Varna consulate (Varna Tüccar Vekaleti),[10] had been allowed into Istanbul without internal passports or passports. To resolve this situation, the Ministry of Police first notified those Armenians related to Istanbul—those who resided in the city and whose good standing was known—that the document could be drawn up.[11] Thus, the practice of suretyship was of critical importance to granting internal passports and passports[12] to Armenians from the provinces and creating a record of their connections.

To obtain an internal passport, the first condition was that one had to produce identification in a manner accepted by the state. The documents required still rested on traditional mechanisms of social control. In particular, as seen in the example of the *ilmühaber*, the infrastructural apparatuses depended on bureaucratization in the sense of the expansion of bureaucracy and the multiplication of its functions through the proliferation of administrative offices and procedures. In another way, they depended on the millet system of religious belonging, which can be seen as the very foundation of traditional mechanisms of social control. As discussed in the previous chapter, the *ilmühaber* was the proof of good behavior in the framework of traditional social control mechanisms. It was mainly a witness account by the local/religious authorities in the guarantorship system but became bureaucratized and standardized in the late nineteenth century. Even when internal passports and passports issued by population officers to non-Muslims listed their sect not as Christian but as Armenian or Greek (Rum) and were requested to alter this to read "Christian," the practice continued anyway,[13] demonstrating that practices rooted in the millet system could not easily be left behind. In fact, it is possible to interpret the millet system as central to ensuring the administrative system's viability. Traditional mechanisms of social control were part of the administrative network and allowed for the implementation of modern administrative orders.

In the Hamidian Era, mechanisms of social control and the administrative network had yet to be fully anonymized. Administrative anonymization as an ideal for the modern state refers to standardized bureaucratic procedures and practices for citizens as individuals, without exceptions based on religion, origin, or other differences. It also implies a direct relationship between the state and the individual. Administrative anonymization is equivalent to the modern state's formation (in the full sense) of modern apparatuses of infrastructural power. During the Hamidian period, the Ottoman state demonstrated a continued reliance on extensive power through the millet system, while strengthening its despotic power through the expansion of bureaucracy and its growing efficacy in daily life. Yet in the long term the insufficiency of extensive power in the state's new fields of action gave rise to the growing efficacy of policies related to the strengthening of infrastructural power and normative pacification.

The preparation of a bill governing the procedures for internal-passport checks at the Port of Istanbul is an example of this growing efficacy through policy. The Ministry of Interior decided to propose a bill about new procedures to check the passports and internal passports of arriving passengers.[14] A commission within the ministry was planned to reorganize procedures according to the guidelines of the Internal Passport Regulation and prepare new administrative documents to regulate the control of documents related to travel permission. For this, the Ottoman bureaucracy both employed people with the knowledge to regulate new fields of action and technicized a matter directly related to the problem of security. Owing to this technicization, administrative interventions into the everyday expanded.

The Monitoring and Regulation of Travel

The internal passport was the most basic means of monitoring the travels of citizens within the country. It also enabled the state to regulate travel in different ways. Especially during the Armenian massacres (1894–96) and after the British Memorandum of 1895, Ottoman attempts to limit Armenians' mobility intensified. Correspondence in 1896 related to the arrival of Armenians to Beirut gives clues regarding prohibitions coming from the center and how they were implemented locally, the use of internal passports, the conditions in which Armenians were seen as threats, and the fields of intervention maintained by the Commission for Expediting Initiatives and Reforms under the Ministry of Interior (Dâhiliye Nezâreti Tesrî-i Muamelât ve Islahat Komisyonu). Noting that the Armenian population of Beirut was quite small, the correspondence describes the lack of docks that could be used as routes on the provincial coasts where Armenians resided. Thus, the possibility that Armenians arriving from elsewhere might go to places where local Armenians lived in the city beyond the shore was quite low. Armenians arriving in Beirut without residence were described as "vagrants," and the correspondence noted that it had been decided that vagrant Armenians were to be sent to their homes, while those intending to go to Istanbul were to be kept in Beirut,[15] and thereafter, Armenians who were engaged in crafts and trade would be permitted to go anywhere, like members of other groups. The province of Beirut announced that those coming to Istanbul from elsewhere, even those holding internal passports to travel to other docks, would not be accepted and that there were Armenians who wished to remain in Beirut. Noting that Armenians held under guarantorship and surveillance had to be able to exercise their rights, the correspondence indicated that it would be out of order to send them back on the boats on which they arrived because there was nothing improper about the increase in the number of Armenians in Beirut. It was inquired of the Ottoman government as to whether it would be appropriate for these Armenians to be permitted to join their compatriots (*hemşerileri*) in Cyprus or Alexandria.[16]

The commission replied that because anyone engaged in crafts or trade was free to move about within the empire, if there was reason to believe that Armenians arriving in Beirut were engaged in such activities, they were not to be obstructed.[17] However, a decision requiring that those deemed vagrants (*serseriler*) or seditious (*müfsid*) were to be dealt with under special regulations and according to previous judgments points to the reality of the conditions in which Armenians were allowed to travel within the Ottoman Empire.[18] This incident in Beirut opened space for discussion on the conditions in which Armenians were seen as a threat and for interpretations of the commission's field of intervention and prohibition.

In another incident in 1894, Armenians living with their families in such places as Pazarcık, Bilecik, and Varna in Bulgaria and originally from communities in Muş, Bitlis, and elsewhere in Anatolia applied to the Ottoman consulate with the aim of returning to their homelands. These individuals' internal passports had expired, and they had not renewed them, so they requested new ones. According to an intelligence report, though, some of this group had ties to conspirators (*mefasidler*) where they lived, and for this reason they were not granted internal passports.

Upon this decision, these individuals applied to the police office and insisted on their request, presenting testimonials showing that they were in fact Ottoman subjects. The application by Priest Artin, son of Haruk, was rejected on the grounds that he had ties to "Armenian sedition" and that he had for eight years mixed with seditious people. It was also decided that these individuals would not be allowed entry into Istanbul if they did not have a visa issued by the Ottoman consulate in Varna on their passports because it was suspected that they would try to enter Ottoman lands by means of obtaining a passport from another state. The police would investigate, and, if required, the Varna consulate would also look into the situation. To avoid complaints, it was advised that merchants be treated kindly, and violence should be avoided throughout the process.[19] The emphasis on refraining from the use of violence begs the question regarding the regular use of violence by the Ottoman bureaucracy even in routine administrative procedures.

Regulations and Practices Related to Istanbul

It is striking that the regulations and practices concerning internal passports were generally conceived with a focus on Istanbul. They can be divided into two groups. The first concerned people aiming to come to Istanbul, and the second related to practices for deporting certain people from Istanbul.

The most common pattern in the implementation of internal passports was to introduce restrictions on entry to and exit from Istanbul. Rebellion following political activity was central to the state's perception of threat, and movement to and from the capital was considered one of the most significant problems. A salient point here relates to decisions regarding the deportation of seasonal laborers. Istanbul has always been a city that attracts labor,[20] and the state historically saw seasonal laborers as a group needing to be kept under constant control in governing the city, for two basic reasons. First, seasonal workers coming to Istanbul were perceived as "dangerous classes," in the same sense as they were seen in the European metropoles. When migration involved the movement of the lower classes, who were thought to be particularly apt to disrupt the public order, the migrants were subjected to special rules. As can be seen in police correspondence in 1903, it was not enough for such people to have an internal passport. This correspondence, which was on the subject of the necessity for carters and hirers of pack animals to possess an internal passport and be bound through suretyship, requested that passport rulings sent to the police commissariat be implemented and that these individuals be required to show their guarantors.[21] The Hamidian Era added to this perception a fear of bombings and assassinations as propaganda of the deed spread from Europe and a fear that nationalist sentiments would find acceptance among the city's lower classes. Thus, using internal passports for the control of comings and goings from Istanbul was considered a preventive measure against potential political activities and extended beyond the aim of securing public order. The restrictions and prohibitions introduced on entries to Istanbul are proof of this pattern.

In the years following the Thessaloniki bombings in 1903 (see chapter 2), security precautions around the entry of Bulgarians to Istanbul were kept in place, showing that internal passports were considered preventive practices in security policies. In 1905, it was determined that an experienced seditious Bulgarian group (*Bulgar erbab-ı fesadı*) was planning a new plot in Thessaloniki. The possibility that such individuals might come to Istanbul and commit similar acts there was to be prevented.[22] In 1906, information was received that the "Sofia Bulgarian Committee" (referring to the Bulgarian Revolutionary Committee) was sending a group of carters to provoke sedition (*fesad çıkaracakları*) in Istanbul. A decree was issued warning that no inappropriate acts should be permitted once these individuals entered Istanbul.[23] It was known that the opening of the Bulgarian Church in Istanbul in 1898 would bring a number of Bulgarians to the city, and an informant indicated that among them were experienced conspirators (*erbab-ı fesad*) aiming to stir up trouble. According to the Ottoman correspondence, though, "because among those coming to Istanbul were also a number of honorable and dignified individuals," it was thought inappropriate to forbid entry to everyone. For this reason, the police were tasked with preventing those who aimed to provoke inappropriate acts from entering the city, and if they were unable to stop them from coming in, they were to take all precautions to prevent any trouble from arising and to ensure that order was maintained.[24] These measures were, in effect, measures appropriate for an emergency situation: conditions had taken root in the everyday. In this way, emergency measures adopted with an eye to the problem of the survival were normalized.

Then there were practices related to individuals deported from Istanbul. Here, the most important criteria were whether they were "employed" or not and whether they were "seditious" or not. Examples of decisions to deport those considered to belong to the "idle" classes from Istanbul to their home regions include the following:[25] the return of vagrant Armenians in Istanbul to their homelands; the denial of entry to vagrants arriving from the countryside;[26] the denial of entry to Istanbul of anyone deemed to be of the idle, vagrant classes;[27] the decision to deport from Istanbul Armenians who were shown by two documents with different dates to be unemployed, without a craft, and with a criminal record; the expulsion and disciplining of vagrant Armenians who were thought to be suspicious and who had been expelled following the Ottoman Bank investigations in previous years (the attack on the bank and the pogrom of its aftermath were described as an "incident");[28] the decision to ban the entry of vagrants from the countryside by returning Armenians gathered in inns and hotels to their homelands;[29] the writing of "issued upon their nonreturn to Istanbul" on the internal passports and passports issued to unemployed and wageless individuals whose stay in Istanbul was deemed objectionable and the absence of such a phrase on the documents of those who left Istanbul for the purposes of trade or craft; the lack of measures to prevent them from traveling abroad or going anywhere within the empire aside from Istanbul;[30] and the sending to Chios, Lesbos, and Rhodes (not to return to Istanbul) of certain suspicious or convicted Armenian watermen found in the Port of Istanbul.[31]

The visit of Kaiser Wilhelm II of Germany to Istanbul in 1898 brought with it multiple warnings and conspiracy theories, and certain emergency measures were taken in the city. In Galata, several people were arrested on the grounds of being vagrants, and it was decided to repatriate them.[32] Intelligence brought about restrictions on entry to the city from elsewhere and led to the arrests of members of the urban lower classes: for instance, that the "Armenian Committee" would attempt to assassinate the German emperor in Istanbul;[33] that, according to information from the Washington embassy, an Armenian named Korbaşoğlu Minas had arrived in Istanbul dressed as a priest with the intent to plant a bomb in the path of the emperor;[34] and that, again from the Washington embassy, the "Armenian Committee" intended to present a petition to the German emperor and to cause incidents in Istanbul during his stay.[35]

The state widely employed the preventive function of internal passports, using its role in regulating travel to lay the groundwork for special practices toward groups labeled as seditious or conspirators (*fesad*) at this political conjuncture. For instance, a regulation was issued stating that Armenians living in Istanbul without an internal passport but who wished to travel elsewhere had to obtain an *ilmühaber* from their local police commissariat, explaining their reasons for travel.[36] For raison d'état, the priority was not the rule of law but the survival of the state. Whom state elites saw as a threat was demonstrated by whom the regulations were aimed at. Thus, regulations were created for Armenians arriving at Istanbul from Çatalca, Yalova, Karamürsel, Şile, Silivri, and Büyükçekmece. Similarly, the police deemed it unfitting for Armenians to travel from Istanbul to those regions without first obtaining an *ilmühaber*; such individuals, it was decided, must get that document from their local police commissariats. In these cases, such documents took on the function of internal passports. In addition to attesting to appropriate permission received from the district or lieutenant governorship, these documents had to record information on where the holder intended to go, how many days they would stay, why they went, and when they would return. Article 27, number 17, of the Official Stamp Law of 1873 (Resm-i Damga Nizamnamesi)[37] stated that *ilmühaber*s prepared for travel within a province could be used even without a printed stamp certifying payment.[38] This regulation points to an emergency situation related to security and indicates that administrative processes had become more refined compared to what they had been in the earlier Tanzimat period. In 1899, although Armenians who made a living through manual labor or as hired hands were allowed to come to Istanbul, it was suspected that such people aimed to organize in the city. All administrative units were notified that they should not grant permits to any Armenians wishing to come to Istanbul. Thus, state elites defined who was a threat based on their fears about the state's survival, and in response to such presumed threatening elements the administration deployed all its available apparatuses and introduced new practices. These practices laid out the field of action of administrative power, which in turn led to practices that marginalized and labeled the lower classes and Armenians in particular.

Disposing of Undesirable Individuals

Another function of internal passports was to dispose of unwanted groups. Following the bombings in Thessaloniki by Gemidzhi (an anarchist group also called the Boatmen of Thessaloniki; see chapter 2) on April 29, 1903, a memorandum was sent to the provinces of Edirne, Kosova, and Yanya on December 9 that year, imposing passport controls for Bulgarian conspirators (ethebab-ı fesad) arriving from elsewhere or leaving the empire for foreign countries.[39] An investigation revealed that members of a Bulgarian revolutionary group were operating with forged passports. The decision was taken to telegraph the lieutenant governors of Manastır, Kosova, Debre, and İpek with instructions to investigate when passports and internal passports had been granted for entry into Istanbul.[40]

Other correspondence in 1903 shows that upon receiving information that the Bulgarian revolutionaries were planning an action in Istanbul like the Thessaloniki bombings, security measures were again taken. First, it was requested that Bulgarians in Istanbul for whom the Bulgarian Exarchate could not provide surety and a declaration of safety were to be removed from the city. Those with a guarantor and who were deemed safe could stay. It was further requested that the Bulgarian Exarchate turn over the names of untrustworthy individuals to the government. Bulgarian sailors suspected of being part of the attempt and who were already known in Istanbul for supporting "seditious ideas [thefkâr-ı mefsedetkeranesi]" were to be admonished and sent back to their own homelands. In this way, there would be no one left in Istanbul who was both an Ottoman subject and a member of the "Bulgarian Committee." Despite these measures, rumors continued that some Bulgarian conspirators (erbab-ı fesadı) remained in Istanbul. For this reason, according to a representative of the

Exarchate, it was necessary to look into poor Bulgarians in Istanbul, who were mostly economically active laborers. It was also necessary to carry out investigations into Bulgarian traders and craftsmen who might be committee members.[41] From this correspondence, one understands that an internal passport was by itself not sufficient. When the internal passport is considered alongside the suretyship system, which was based on the millet system, one finds a broader space for interpretation related to the state's fields of penetration.

Ports and Checkpoints

Among the practices applied to those coming to Istanbul, controls at ports were particularly important. Much emphasis was placed on catching travelers leaving various locations inside and outside the empire without a passport and subjecting them to the appropriate measures of passport regulations.[42] For instance, upon the arrival in Trabzon of a number of people destined for Istanbul, including field hands and porters, the group was not allowed entry into Trabzon because it was considered possible that several of them were Armenians. The reason given for sending them back to their homelands and villages was that they were vagrants and thus had been prevented from going to Istanbul.[43] Another correspondence on the same event stated that the majority of those arriving at the port did not have internal passports and identity documents (*tezkere-i Osmaniyye*), which had raised suspicion. The decision was taken to prevent them from coming even into Trabzon and if they still managed to arrive in Istanbul to return them to their homelands. It was announced that if people were found without passports on boats, and if among them were vagrants, then the dock from which the boat entered would be identified, and the responsible officers would be punished. The provinces of Trabzon and Kastamonu, the lieutenant governor of Sinop, and the district governorships of İnebolu, Bartın, and Ereğli were to be telegraphed on the subject and advised that if vagrants arrived in Istanbul by such means, they would be sent back to their homelands or to Trabzon immediately.[44] For these individuals, most of whom were villagers attempting to migrate to find work due to their poor economic conditions, the state promised to set up a form of agricultural credit.[45] The decisions to implement precautions in provinces along the coast and not to issue internal passports to supposedly harmful and unidentified individuals should be considered within the context of a desire to prevent the unemployed, idle, vagrant classes from coming to Istanbul.[46] The prevention of "riffraff [ayak takımı] Armenians" from Samsun and other such vagrants from entering Istanbul represents a similar decision.[47]

Another similar incident took place at the Port of Mersin. The correspondence included a request that the Mersin Port Commission (Mersin Liman Komisyonu) go beyond internal passport checks to investigate suspicious-looking passengers and Armenians by asking local administrators about their identity and good behavior, demonstrating that merely checking internal passports was not considered enough to control geographical mobility in Ottoman geographies.[48] The Mersin Port Commission first collected information about passengers from local administrators and then informed the provincial government. Yet this process caused problems for the police. The commission was required to ask local governments to investigate not every passenger but suspicious Armenians and vagrants in particular.[49] In collecting and storing information, the port commissions and the central state solidified the state's infrastructural power through the administrative network thus created. The fact that the state's investigations rested on mechanisms of social control involving mediators or go-betweens also shows that the state still made use of extensive power—indeed, it had to do so. The central administrative units were still not numerous enough to spread across the empire's entire geography and thus to penetrate the lives of individual subjects. Thus, the state attempted to solve this problem of capacity in its infrastructural power through the networks created by extensive power.

In these examples, those who attempted to come to Istanbul, either for economic reasons or reasons of security, belonged to the lower classes. To keep Istanbul from taking in more people than needed and to prevent weaknesses in security (particularly with the intensification of security policies in the 1890s and especially after 1895), the state focused on preventing both seasonal and permanent migration. Policies preventing internal migration should be read alongside the population policies directed at Istanbul and prohibitions on household migration. In 1906, an Armenian woman named Arten, daughter of Nazeli, from a village near the town of Refahiye in Erzurum, asked the Ministry of Police, through the Armenian Patriarchate, for permission to come to Istanbul to see her husband, Markar, residing in Beşiktaş, Istanbul. The Ministry of Police wrote that it was found to be inappropriate for Arten to travel to Istanbul because people working in the capital could obtain permission to go to their homelands to reunite with family. The same response included a reminder that household migration to Istanbul was forbidden, with the aim of preventing certain groups of people from congregating in the city.[50]

To prevent security lapses, different administrative procedures were instituted. Practices such as the stamping of passports and internal passports by the port commission for passengers boarding at Samsun were approved by the Governmental Commission for Expediting Initiatives and Reforms because it showed that these documents had been seen by the port commission.[51] In this way, the stamp, as an administrative procedure, became a tool for ensuring communication across offices. Because stamps functioned as extensions of the central administration, port commissions were important units in this function. By taking action through passport regulations against passengers who arrived at the pier without an internal passport,[52] the police and the port commissions constituted the first ring of the administrative chain.

To control entries by sea, it was forbidden for ships to approach any port after the evening call to prayer. And though the Port Authority (Liman Başkanlığı) in Istanbul preferred that problems related to such matters be resolved through correspondence with provincial port authorities, this practice drew complaints from foreign consulates because officials at every pier in the empire operated with different procedures. Indeed, the governor of Trabzon sent a note to the Ministry of Interior requesting that this practice be clarified and made easier.[53]

Another important factor was that some of the traffic to and from Istanbul did not pass through official checkpoints. One of the preferred methods of entering the city for those without an internal passport was to arrive by sea on small, unregistered boats or at mooring points that were not official ports. The geography of the city's coastline made it easier for those without orderly documents to enter undetected. The apparatuses of infrastructural power were inadequate to cover the entire coastline. Because state power had not yet become penetrative, authoritative power was established by implementing regulations crafted in terms of orders and prohibitions. And when this was not enough, the focus was again on controls. A document on this matter describes a decision taken to provide the police with enough steamboats and small crafts to prevent "Armenian conspirators and shiftless vagrants" from entering Istanbul by sea.[54] Yet even if this decision were put into practice, it would have been difficult because of limitations in technology and staff.

Population Control and Statistics

When internal passports are approached as an apparatus of infrastructural power, they make it possible for the state to track its population and compile statistics. The function of monitoring the population and keeping statistics is an important tool for the state in governing a population and creates the most important database used to implement policies for crisis situations related to security. On July 12, 1902, the vizierate wrote to the Ministry of Interior on taking the necessary measures in light of rumors of actions among Armenians, information that many Armenians would be arriving to Istanbul as laborers, as well as intelligence received about a meeting to be held in Narlıkapı Church. The vizierate also requested in the same correspondence that the concerned administrative bodies give information to the vizierate and the Ministry of Interior on the types and aims of entries to Istanbul, the names and descriptions of those meeting in the church, and whether the number of Armenians who had come to Istanbul from the countryside to work as hired hands or in similar jobs exceeded the city's labor requirements. According to the vizierate, although both the Ministry of Police and the Municipality of Istanbul (Şehremaneti) had to know the proportion of Armenians who had come to Istanbul as seasonal laborers, neither had to date notified the vizierate of this figure. Without this information, it would not be possible to take immediate precautions. For this reason, the vizierate requested from the Ministry of Police and the Municipality of Istanbul the information and observations they had thus far collected as well as a list of those who would attend the meeting in question. The document reminded its readers that the requested information was not about an ongoing incident but about taking precautions. Before serious events occurred on matters related to public safety and the country's security, it was necessary to provide the Sublime Porte with this information. The vizierate also aimed at increasing the administration's operational capacity by using the information collected by means of techniques of surveillance.[55]

The encoding and storage of information were not by themselves sufficient for effective governance. The increase in bureaucratic capacity in the means of registering and filing the collected information based on surveillance was, in one sense, the grounds of the modern state's infrastructural power. The information collected by the police or the municipality or another administrative office had to be shared with different administrative bodies. This process of sharing information was deeply connected to knowledge production through new surveillance techniques, which also implies a new way of producing knowledge on population groups. For this knowledge production, the state needed new administrative bodies, personnel, and techniques to increase its infrastructural capacity to reach its citizens and their daily lives. To control everyday life, it was necessary to categorize these records by importance so that they could be easily accessed when it was deemed necessary. As such, the task of encoding occurred on multiple levels. Only in this manner would the strategies outlined for internal security become functional. Indeed, the very formation of the strategies for internal security depended on categorization and ease of access.

In the same correspondence, the vizierate noted that it was quite an ordinary thing for people to attend places of worship to carry out their religious obligations.[56] Yet the government also saw the transformation of churches into spaces of political debate as something detrimental to public safety (*asayiş*). To prevent breaches of public safety, the head of Religious Community Governments (Mezhep Müdürlüğü Mutasarrıfı, linked to the Ministry of Justice) was notified before the Narlıkapı Church meeting took place, and word about the meeting had been passed on by the Armenian Patriarchate.[57] The Ottoman administration was aware of the importance of the problem of coordinating encoded information and accordingly attempted to delimit a field of action. At the same time, this field of action showed the limits of the field of the public, as recognized by the state.

The vizierate and the Ministries of Interior and Foreign Affairs decided to do what was necessary by appointing able and honest civil servants within the church to gather information on the aims of the meeting and by having an informant or a spy placed outside the church to see to it that public safety was not endangered. Upon this decision, the Ministry of Police carried out an investigation into whether divisions within the Hunchaks (see chapter 2) had led to another alliance and created the possibility of new actions occurring within Ottoman territory. The police had little information to go on, aside from an incident involving an Armenian with a US passport who had gone to Izmir and distributed a threatening pamphlet (*tehditname*); he was taken into custody, but the arresting police officer was stabbed to death the next day by another Armenian. However, the police noted that although the propaganda and incitements of Armenian revolutionary organizations abroad were ongoing, their investigations led them to feel there was no reason to expect attempts at an Armenian uprising within Ottoman lands.[58]

Nevertheless, all precautions for any possible situation continued to be taken. Attention was paid to the rising number of lower-class Armenians in Istanbul and to their attempts to be freed of entrance controls and internal passports. According to the Ottoman government, because "lower-class Armenians were being used instrumentally in uprisings," their growing population was seen as harmful. Following the most recent incidents involving Armenians in Istanbul, the municipality (Şehremaneti) estimated there were some six thousand rural Armenians in Istanbul, apart from those engaged in trade and crafts.[59] This estimated number also pointed to the pull factors for migration to Istanbul.

The meeting in question had to do with a church assembly election, a process carried out every two to three years in Narlıkapı Church.[60] The participants in the election were the church's spiritual leaders. These individuals entered the church alone or in groups of two, indicated their votes on an official document, and deposited it into a box in the church. These documents were sealed with a stamp and were later opened to determine the election results. Nothing apart from the election was spoken about in these proceedings, as was confirmed by a report by the inspectors and civil servants present, who were familiar with the language used at the meeting. During the elections, the Ministry of Interior reported to the vizierate that the presence of any individuals who did not seem to belong to the expected style of proceedings would be noted.[61] The Ministry of Police requested the names of the seven people elected to the church assembly, and an investigation was ordered into whether there were any suspicious figures among them.[62] The vizierate stated that rumors about imminent acts by Armenians in Istanbul were baseless but that there nevertheless was a need for internal passports and limits to passage to prevent an increase in the population of Armenians in Istanbul.[63] All this correspondence demonstrates the perception that state elites held of lower-class Armenians as a potential tool for revolutionary purposes, and the main apparatus of infrastructural power employed to control this potential—beyond internal passports—was most certainly the police, who enjoyed broad discretionary powers and a wide sphere of influence.

Not only did the Ottoman government seek to distance from Istanbul those it labeled as vagrant (*serseri*), suspicious, or seditious (*fesad*), but it also kept careful records on such individuals.[64] In particular regarding seasonal laborers, the most striking example of such records is a file kept on Armenians arriving in Istanbul to work as porters, day laborers, and the like.[65] Under the assistant secretary of the Ministry of Interior, a Special Commission (Komisyon-u Mahsusa) was established to look into and record the condition of "vagrant Armenians" in Istanbul in a specific register. In time, this commission's duties were transferred to the Ministry of Police.[66]

Examples of the records maintained by the central state through the Special Commission include: a chart prepared by the police in December 1896 through the Special Commission's intercession, indicating those Armenians applying to travel to Ottoman lands or abroad (with the noted exception of Romania) for the purpose of trade, travel, medical care, or study;[67] another chart in 1896 showing the number of Armenians arriving by land and sea to Alexandria for the entire month of Teşrin-i Sani as well as their comings and goings;[68] the preparation and sending of a file by the

Special Commission with the names of Armenians who came to Istanbul and were working as porters, day laborers, and other similar positions;[69] in 1895, a list of those who received a passport or an internal passport by applying to the Special Commission to travel within Ottoman lands and abroad from January 20 to January 26;[70] the names of those coming and going in Istanbul;[71] a chart showing the relative numbers of Armenians, Armenian Catholics, and Protestants applying to come to Ottoman lands for the purpose of trade, travel, medical care, or study as well as a list of those who had come and gone for trade with a passport or internal passport;[72] records of vagrants in Istanbul and a file giving the names and reputations of Armenians sent from Istanbul to the countryside prepared by the police.[73] A request that names, reputations, trades, and misdeeds committed by those exiled can also be considered within this context.[74]

Controlling the Travel of Foreigners

One of the practices carried out at ports had to do with the requirements related to foreigners receiving internal passports, which enabled the state to control and regulate their travels within the country. Foreigners arriving at the Ottoman Empire from abroad were required to receive an internal passport in addition to holding a standard international passport. In an earlier proposal for the Regulation Bill on Passport Procedures (Pasaport Kalemleri Nizamname Lahiyası) in 1871, the issuing authority for the foreigners' internal passports was the Ministry of Police. Passport procedures, which were carried out in the name of the Ministry of Foreign Affairs but were administered by the Ministry of Police, applied to those traveling abroad and regulated internal passports for foreign subjects coming from abroad.[75] Through the proposal in question, a regulation was introduced that foreigners who came to the Ottoman Empire and wished to travel within the country had to bring a declaration/affidavit from their own consulates and carry it alongside the internal passport. At the base of this regulation were the aims of preventing acts seen as negative and stopping anarchists from crossing the border.[76]

The Internal Passport Regulation of 1887 required that internal passports for foreigners wishing to travel within Ottoman lands be granted by population ministers and officials: internal passports could not be issued to foreigners by passport officials.[77] It was deemed inappropriate to ask foreign subjects to obtain internal passports for journeys for which Ottoman subjects were not required to have internal passports. In such cases, Ottoman subjects proved their identity with an identification document (*tezkere-i Osmaniyye*). Similarly, rather than obtaining an internal passport from population officers, foreigners could prove their identities by presenting standard passports or an *ilmühaber* from their consulate giving their national status.[78]

In 1901, four foreigners en route to Istanbul (two English and two Flemish) had their passports processed for visas by the police in İskederun. But because they did not have internal passports, the procedures performed were deemed unlawful by the Ottoman government. Such people not only had to carry their international passports with them but also had to obtain internal passports.[79]

In order to obtain internal passports upon arriving in Istanbul, foreigners were required to bring an affidavit from their consulates specifying their identities, places of residence, reasons for coming, and duration of stay. Investigations by local officials and police into why they had come became part of regular procedures. The Commission for Expediting Initiatives and Reforms under the Ministry of Interior reminded the Ministry of Foreign Affairs that legal proceedings would ensue if antagonistic acts were observed among seditious (*mefsedet*) individuals. It emphasized that care was to be taken that travelers not become involved in politics and that the entry of "revolutionaries such as anarchists" be prevented. The commission also instructed the Ministry of Foreign Affairs that if such people did enter or pass through the empire, the necessary procedures would be carried out without problems being caused by embassies.[80]

Intelligence and Monitoring Practices

Internal passports were also used to gather intelligence and track individuals. For instance, in 1907 it was ascertained that a certain George (Jorj) Kolarasi, a Greek, who had set out with an internal passport for the purpose of going from Istanbul to Izmir did not in fact go to Izmir. This was considered a suspicious act. When he returned to Istanbul, the Ministry of Police wrote to the Istanbul Police Office to say that he had been taken under observation to gather information on his activities.[81] Other examples include precautions taken against the possibility that travelers departing from Adana and holding internal passports to come to Istanbul might stay in Izmir.[82] On another occasion, when French passengers arrived in Istanbul with internal passports and affidavits from their consulates to travel here from Beirut, the Ministry of Police communicated to Beirut that an investigation was being carried out into unknown Italian passengers on the same ship.[83] The Ottoman government saw it as necessary to carry out checks of the passports and internal passports of those entering the country by way of Egypt—which had become a "veiled" British protectorate after its occupation in 1882 but was under nominal Ottoman sovereignty—and Bulgaria and to request further information on such individuals with the aim of preventing individuals seen as troublesome from entering the empire from Europe and America. In particular, it was noted that internal passports could not be drawn up for travel to Egypt without first carrying out an inquiry into the applicant.[84] Egypt had both ports, such as Alexandria and Cairo, where ships bound for long-distance travel docked and cities where a range of political opinions circulated.[85] As such, those requesting internal passports for Egypt were, in the eyes of the center, possibly members of certain political groups. Yet the state did not carry out any intensive form of observation or inspection in Egypt both because of its distance from the center and because of limits to the state's capacity.

Illegally Issued Internal Passports and Forged Documents

One of the most significant problems the state faced in this area was the unlawful issuance of internal passports. When it was learned that population officers in Maraş, Siirt, and Çemişgezek had issued internal passports for travel to Istanbul to several people who did not meet the necessary requirements, the Commission for Expediting Initiatives and Reforms banned the entry into Istanbul of anyone, regardless of their status, from these areas, resulting in many complaints. It was then decided that the requests for internal passports would be met for anyone, including Armenians, except vagrants and seditious people.[86] It also emerged that internal passports to Istanbul bearing the stamp of a certain coffee shop proprietor had been sold to Armenians. It was ordered that the necessary measures be taken to prevent this.[87] However, checks did not always go smoothly in practice. On the grounds that "malicious acts" related to a certain group of experienced conspirators (erbab-ı mefsedet) had been allowed to occur, the Ministry of Police wrote to the provinces of Trabzon and Kastamonu to strongly emphasize that police and population officers were required to check the population documents and internal passports of those coming and going in the ports. The decision was taken to punish those officials found to be in violation.[88] Clearly, therefore, controls were not being carried out correctly. The decision to correct missing information or documents in the passports and internal passports of travelers passing through the Port of Iskenderun and to compensate officials issuing such documents points to something similar.[89]

Subalterns also developed their own strategies in the face of the regulations of observation and control introduced by the state. The Ottoman government learned, for instance, that some Armenians who had converted to Islam had reverted to their previous religion after receiving an internal passport to travel to Istanbul or elsewhere. The government decided that an exceptional rule be introduced to prevent such reversion because it was seen as "possible" that Armenians "might" use conversion as a route to carry out "seditious acts" and that similar occurrences had been observed among other Armenians who had converted.[90] This case demonstrates the Ottoman government's suspicion toward Armenian geographical mobility. Indeed, considering that most Armenians who converted to Islam chose to do so simply to protect themselves during the Armenian Massacres of 1894–96, their mobility was also a strategy for survival. In addition, there were exceptional regulations on Armenian mobility after the Treaty of Berlin. In an earlier example, people from Mount Lebanon went to Marseille via Egypt without passports, using internal passports with visas instead. This made it possible to change places at lower cost and with fewer controls. For this reason, the Ottoman state requested that Egyptian officials not issue visas for internal passports in the province of

Beirut owing to the public-order and security conditions.[91] Both incidents point to what Giddens describes as the dialectic of control (see chapter 1).[92]

According to document 723 (dated 1892) of the Department of Reforms (Tanzimat Dairesi) under the Council of State, it was announced to all lieutenant governors that files would be kept on population officers, and if an officer issued passports or internal passports in violation of regulations three times in one year, they would be dismissed or replaced.[93] When an internal passport was issued to someone from Bulgaria or Eastern Rumelia, these passports were not to be accepted in lieu of identification, and legal proceedings would follow for officers violating this rule.[94] Thus, the administration attempted to control its own personnel through these new regulations.

After the decision was taken to have the police return a group of forty laborers arriving in Yumurtalık (Adana) without internal passports, the laborers escaped after being released when a lieutenant at the port thought that the *ilmühaber*s they had gotten from their local headmen were sufficient. It was decided that henceforth this lieutenant could not be involved in civil affairs.[95] Whereas this official had continued to see traditional mechanisms of social control as adequate, the police, as an extension of the central administration, had moved on to other methods or apparatuses related to internal security. This incident demonstrates the problems that local administrative personnel had in conforming to the new system.

The case of people obtaining an internal passport to work in Istanbul and then using it to escape to the United States or to Europe[96] also shows the limits of extant controls or the existence of abuses and human smuggling. When the Ottoman government banned immigration to the United States in 1888, laborers and the poor began to use internal passports to reach port cities. In particular, Armenians from Eastern Anatolia took this route to reach foreign ships, using local boatmen and drawing on their networks. Those smugglers also gave them an opportunity to get to the United States via Liverpool or Marseille.[97]

Similarly, though it was forbidden for Armenians from the countryside who were not traders or who did not enjoy a good reputation to come to Istanbul, this policy was clearly not always strictly followed, and so it had to be announced that unless the Ministry of Police was informed,

permission was not to be granted to anyone but the exempted groups.[98]
Weaknesses in the administrative system opened up space for subalterns
to exploit them and weaponize them for their own interests. It is perhaps
through such examples that the dialectic of control becomes most visible.

Another incident emerges in the travel documents of individuals holding Ottoman citizenship who traveled between the empire and Bulgaria,
Serbia, and Romania for reasons of trade.[99] Certain individuals had lied
to Ottoman state officials in these countries to obtain passage documents
and had given these documents to members of a revolutionary group. They
had thus aided "conspirators" (müfsidin) to enter into Ottoman lands. To
ensure that such "treachery" did not recur, a consulate (vekalethane) had
to register the date and number of passports or internal passports issued
on each individual's identity document (tezkere-i Osmaniyye).[100] Yet some
who came to cities in the empire for the purpose of trade aided revolutionaries in entering into Ottoman lands by claiming that they had lost
their identity document, by getting an internal passport using an identity
document when their own passport had expired, and in some cases by
passing this internal passport on to revolutionaries described in the Ottoman documents as "conspirators" (fesad).[101]

People who manipulated the system in these ways were required to pay
a monetary fine in line with the Consulate Regulation (Şehbender Nizamnamesi) of 1881. Subsequently, when internal passports were declared
expired by population officers, a note of earlier registration was added to
the renewed internal passports.[102] When a guarantor was not listed who
could be held responsible for those claiming to have lost their documents,
the monetary fine for the misuse of internal passports, given in Article 4
of the Population Registration Regulation of 1878, was doubled.[103]

Though it was against the rules to record anything but a change in
location on an identity document, according to the provisions of the Population Registration Regulation related to identity documents, the holder's identity was processed in the same way, and the old document was
held by the Ottoman consulates for applications made outside the empire.
Because the number of passports and internal passports that could be
drawn up at consulates was limited, and because it was easy to ascertain
when the same document had been reissued by such units, it was deemed

unnecessary to append written records to these documents.[104] For those requesting an internal passport in place of a lost one, an identity document was to be arranged, with both a petition in line with the Population Registration Regulation (Article 8) and with their records in the main registry on an *ilmühaber* brought from their neighborhood. Any identity document presented for renewal on the grounds of wear and tear was to be examined, together with the individual's records, and the holder's circumstances were to be looked into. Those who submitted an incomplete or disorderly *ilmühaber* as well those using a passport, an internal passport, or a population document under a false name or a nickname would be subject to the necessary laws. The Public Administration of Population Records (Sicil-i Nüfus İdare-i Umumiyyesi) decreed in 1903 that in situations where it was not necessary to find a guarantor or to subject an applicant to any other forms of treatment, public officers and the police were to take care, for the protection of the law, not to allow such corruption.[105] From the state's perspective, the problem of confirming identity was among the most significant issues it faced. With modern security technologies yet to be developed, the state was compelled to carry out all its security controls through written documents. And, in this way, the state attempted to control its own personnel.

The ambiguity of such terms as *şüpheli* (suspect), *serseri* (vagrant), and *fesad* (seditious) applied particularly to Armenians, meaning that decisions attempting to control them affected a broad swath of the Armenian community. A document declaring that there was no problem with Armenians who were not thought to be vagrants or unemployed and who were traveling for trade to Istanbul or to other provinces seems to suggest that, in reality, restrictions were deployed in a manner that affected all Armenians, giving rise to a number of complaints.[106] Similarly, another document explained that it was not right to arbitrarily exile, without an inquiry, those vagrants whose stay in their homelands or in Istanbul was seen as problematic.[107] In particular, following the Ottoman Bank takeover and the pogrom against Armenians in Istanbul, many Armenians were sent away from the capital. In the wake of the takeover, those who were arrested but not charged were sent to their homelands. Among them were 166 Armenians sent to Samsun and 129 to Trabzon. They were put on a boat specific to this administrative task and accompanied by officers, and it was decided that local officials would prepare a short *ilmühaber* for each, testifying that they had arrived in their homelands.[108]

Travel restrictions following the occupation of the Ottoman Bank intensified by taking particular aim at Armenians. Because of the pogrom following the occupation, Istanbul ceased to be a safe city for Armenians. In such a context, in the manner requested by the British embassy and others, permission was granted for these institutions to issue passports or internal passports to Armenians who were in the service of foreign subjects in Istanbul and who had not become involved in any "incidents" so that they could go abroad or to their own homelands.[109]

Approximately one year after the occupation of the Ottoman Bank, a general pardon was issued to Armenians. Travel restrictions were lifted, and it was noted that Armenians who were not vagrants or unemployed could travel for reasons of trade to Istanbul or to other provinces without hindrance. Here, again, the basic criterion was being involved in trade. Two years after the Ottoman Bank incident, passports were once more on the agenda for rural Armenians who wished to return to their homelands—through the implementation of a suretyship system and the practice of issuing internal passport—as well as for those wishing to go abroad for trade.[110]

Conclusion

The Internal Passport Regulation of 1887 was the main legal document laying out the requirements for permits to travel inside the Ottoman Empire and represents the streamlining of administration and paperwork for such permits. However, it does not give the full picture of Ottoman policies controlling mobility inside the empire. Everyday administrative practices and their complicated organization reflected the different levels of state control or attempts at state control. Ottoman security anxieties deeply affected the new bureaucracy of surveillance and travel permits.

The combination of old and new techniques enabled the Ottoman government not only to track those it considered migrants, suspects, and criminals but also to expand the political effects of categories and the representational use of such categories with pejorative connotations in state correspondence. Internal passports had multifunctional uses that demonstrate the articulation of threat perceptions through the administration of geographical mobility inside the empire. The use of the discursive tropes "seditious," "vagrant," and "anarchist" in the correspondence relating to internal passports points at the marginalization of specific groups through policies to control geographical mobility. Internal passports became a tool for labeling and discriminating against seasonal workers, the mobile poor, anarchists (or so-called anarchists), Armenians, and Bulgarians as part of security policies.

7

Passport Regulations and Practices during the Hamidian Era

The modern passport emerged in revolutionary France in 1792, for political reasons.[1] Its use became more widespread as the need grew to control people traveling to certain strategic points or to prevent the entry of agents of foreign countries into France. Passports were also used to prevent vagrancy and related crimes,[2] and in time these practices came also to be based on the idea that it was necessary to keep migration under tight control.

In continental Europe, passports came to have many functions after the Congress of Vienna in 1815. According to Andreas Fahrmeir, these functions included demonstrating the holder's identity; making it possible for state officials to distinguish citizens from foreigners using a single document and, in particular, making it possible to conduct certain practices directed at foreigners; ensuring that the state could control travel and subject travelers to taxes or fees through the mediation of passports or visas; and helping officials to understand the political views of travelers by enabling communication between police officers through the coding of entries and exits.[3] According to Leo Lucassen, passports have two primary functions, one for the holder and one for the state. For its holder, a passport assures the right to travel freely, proof of nationality and identity, protection of the right to receive assistance from an embassy, and protection from deportation. For the state, a passport enables it to prevent its own citizens from traveling abroad, ensure controls for mandatory military service, keep under control regulations related to taxation and fees, arrest wanted criminals, protect the national economy, incentivize its own citizens to leave the country to reduce the population, be rid of unwanted elements of the population (the poor, the unemployed, criminals, and so on), control the entries and travels of foreigners, prevent unwanted foreigners from entering, deport unwanted foreigners, guarantee that foreigners leave when deemed necessary, monitor the population, monitor the travels of citizens (particularly through internal passports), and, through registration procedures specially created for foreigners, track foreigners' movements.[4]

In the Hamidian Era, passport and internal-passport regulations were remade to their modern sense, and controls of such documents were tightened. One of the basic reasons for this tightening was the perception of mobile groups as threats. This perception should be considered alongside the aim of regulating society on the basis of "peace and order."[5] The difference between the ideal society imagined by state elites and the conditions on the ground gave rise to a deep schism between these two elements, which led to constant reminders in everyday life of state authority and bureaucratic pressure, in the modern sense, manifesting in the shape of routine forms of control.

Passport regulations were based on two basic legal documents: the Passport Regulation of 1884 and the Passport Regulation of 1894.[6] When we consider implementation within the framework of these two basic documents, certain points become clearer: the aim of such regulations, whom they targeted, how the state positioned itself relative to the different elements composing its own subjects, and how the state viewed foreigners entering or trying to enter the Ottoman Empire.

These two legal documents were in fact quite similar. The 1884 regulation has fourteen articles, and its articles were expanded for the 1894 regulation. Articles 1-3 and 5-8 were identical. According to Article 1 of the 1884 regulation, anyone leaving the Ottoman Empire for another country was required to hold a passport. Because the passport also took the place of a person's identification, Article 2 regulated that it had to include information on the holder's dependents, residence, profession, father's name, and spouses and children when relevant. The passport was to be stamped with an official seal and was valid for one year. Such bureaucratic requirements amounted to the standardization of the definition of individual identity.

To define an individual—to understand who that individual is—was tied to rules previously established by the state.

According to Article 4 in both regulations, passports were to be issued both in Turkish and French. In addition, passports could be signed and authorized in Istanbul by the Ministry of Police or by the highest-ranking official of a province, shire, town, or township. According to Article 4 of the 1894 regulation, however, under certain conditions the subdistrict or county governors could issue passports with the permission of the Ministry of Interior. In addition, the passports of civil servants of Ottoman diplomatic missions were to be issued on behalf of the Ministry of Foreign Affairs. Identity was thereby approved by the state bureaucracy and gained validity, which both legalized the individual and amounted to rendering them legible in the eyes of the state.[7]

Under Article 6, Muslims were to obtain an *ilmühaber* (certificate of good behavior; see chapter 5) from an imam, the head of the village or neighborhood (*muhtar*), or teacher at an Islamic theological school (*müderris*). Non-Muslims, meanwhile, were to get this document from patriarchates, synagogues, or churches or, if not in Istanbul, from the metropolitan bishops or the office of the metropolite (*despothane*) or from their non-Muslim village elders (*kocabaşı*). If the person requesting a passport stayed in an inn, they were to obtain an *ilmühaber* from the concierge with the approval of the chamberlain of innkeepers. In this manner, the state tried to make use of traditional mechanisms of social control to verify identities, which was one of the biggest problems with modern passports. Because in most cases the official processing a passport did not know whether an applicant was in fact the person they declared themselves to be, such verification methods were applied as a practical solution of sorts.

The modern passport is one of the most important indications of the shift from the community to the individual. Seen through this lens, the Hamidian Era was a transitional period in the administrative mindset. In the passport practices of this period, individuals were still defined through traditional community relations. One of the most important reasons for this continued definition was the sheer size of the empire and the inadequacy of infrastructural power with respect to this geography.

The legitimate and effective control of mobility is possible only through a developed bureaucracy and technology.[8] Another important reason for the reliance on traditional methods was the fact that the empire still relied on the millet system to stay together. The millet system involved using collective definitions of identity for all bureaucratic processes of recording and registering. It involved a limited use of registry systems based on the individual, at least outside of Istanbul and a few important port cities. Clearly, these cities were spaces where not only people but also ideas moved about freely at high rates.[9] As a consequence, for the central state it was critical to control the comings and goings of people in port cities. We find a similar situation in continental Europe, particularly after 1848, in the controls exercised over railways and train stations.[10]

In both Passport Regulations, Articles 7 and 8 regulated the information that an *ilmühaber* must contain and to whom a passport could not be issued. According to Article 8, a passport could not be issued to someone without an *ilmühaber*, someone who was not abiding by a criminal judgment, or someone with an outstanding court case and thus a travel ban.

Differences between the two regulations again become apparent in Article 9. According to the 1884 regulation, those who obtained a passport but subsequently abandoned their travel plans were required to return the passport. In the 1894 regulation, this provision was expanded. Those who had applied for a passport for travel to a specific location but later opted out of it were still required to return their passports to the police, but, in addition, vagrants who were not wealthy or engaged in a trade or craft and who requested a passport to travel abroad were required to name a guarantor who would be able cover any costs that might emerge from sending them back to their home regions.

This expansion aligned with the new regulation of September 18, 1890, known as the Regulation on Vagrants and Suspicious Individuals (see also chapter 4), aimed at guaranteeing that the cost of repatriating vagrants (*serseri*) would be covered. A similar practice, though in reverse (that is, for those arriving from elsewhere) appeared in Holland and Germany after 1860. Thus, passports not only were tools of political control but also used as a method of control for the problem of who benefited from the welfare practices created to address the problem of poverty. When foreign workers arriving in Germany were in need of poverty assistance, they were required to have, in addition to a passport or a document showing their nationalities, proof of which state or municipality was responsible for them.[11] Even in a time when the passport regime was being liberalized,[12] the lower classes were required to carry with them a number of documents in addition to the passport.[13]

The Passport Regulations of 1884 and 1894 regulated not only Ottoman citizens intending to go to other countries but also foreigners entering the Ottoman Empire. Article 10 of the 1884 regulation and Article 11 of the 1894 regulation specified that anyone entering Ottoman lands had to obtain a passport from their own state and a visa from an Ottoman consulate or consular officer stationed in their country. For those coming from places without an Ottoman representative, it was enough to have a passport. According to Article 13 of the 1894 Regulation, an Ottoman visa was valid for a single journey only, but those who had to cross the border twice in a month could apply for a multiple-entry visa valid for six months. The same article stated that in situations threatening public safety, a visa giving the right to multiple entry could be canceled.[14] Article 14 in the 1884 regulation brought objections related to the requirement of a residence certificate (*ikamet pusulası*) from European states. Ultimately, the part stating that foreigners were required to hold a residence certificate was removed from the draft bill. Because the article related to the arrangement and distribution of residence permits was covered in the Nationality Regulation (Tabiiyet Nizamnamesi) of 1869, it was deemed unnecessary in the Passport Regulation of 1894.[15]

However, similar regulations on foreigners had been instituted in Europe after the Revolutions of 1830 and 1848. In 1883, authorities in Holland began for political reasons to ask for visas from French citizens. In France, the practice of following foreigners intensified in direct proportion to perceptions of threat. Foreigners coming to Prussia were required to have visas on their passports for every night of their stay. Yet just as the political situation within countries changed, so did these regulations. With an agreement on freedom of travel between German principalities in 1850, visa requirements were lifted; information related to travel cards and travel permission was standardized and simplified; and passport controls among these geographies came to an end.[16] In 1865, the North German Confederation established an agreement whereby passport requirements were lifted and the use of residence cards was ended for both foreigners and subjects of principalities.[17]

Articles 14, 15, and 16 of the 1894 Ottoman Passport Regulation listed the bureaucratic tasks required of those entering the Ottoman Empire. According to Article 17, someone without a passport and unable to prove their identity could not enter the Ottoman Empire. An individual with a passport but without a visa was to pay a fine that was twice the cost of the visa. If the individual entered the country without a passport, they were required to explain this situation to the Ministry of Police. Article 18 stated that the moment it was determined that a passport had been forged, Articles 156 and 157 of the criminal code would be activated. Indeed, the functionality of passports rested on their credibility. At a time when photographs or fingerprints were not widespread in Europe, physical characteristics and signatures were seen as distinctive features.[18]

With the French Revolution and particularly after 1815 in Europe, political developments, urbanization, industrialization, and geographical mobility tied to an unstable labor market had created a perception of threat particularly from the mobile poor. This perception led the state to define poor migrants as vagrants and stigmatize them as "pathological nomads."[19] To control the poor and perceived political threats, identity documents proliferated and included internal passports, passports, residence permits, certificates showing that foreigners had registered with the police, and residence documents.[20] Thus, one can say that rather than one document carrying the burden of identity, crosschecks were carried out between various documents.[21] In effect, passport regulations and practices should be considered alongside the problem of poverty, not just of security. Yet in the requirement of crosschecks the basic problem had to do with determining whether documents were forged. To reduce this risk for passports in particular, several different methods were experimented with.[22]

Modern passport practices should be considered primarily alongside systems of registry. Not only the fact that a person traveled but also where they went and where they stayed should be considered part of this system.

First of all, an individual's permanent residence had to be known to the state and its administrative officials. This information was, in a sense, part of the system of collective surety and made it easier to tap into local networks to collect information about individuals. The requirement that the police be notified of individuals' residence was an important part of the system in continental Europe.[23] For instance, the Austro-Hungarian Empire adopted this practice in 1782 with the aim of tracking politically suspicious or dangerous individuals.[24] In this way and particularly with an eye to ensuring Vienna's security, it became possible to track individuals seen as dangerous or foreigners suspected of being intelligence agents. The similarities between different state practices also points to the interimperial system of passports. Placing the Ottoman Empire in this system deepens our understanding of state formation in relation to controlling geographical mobility.

In the Hamidian Era, practices in passport controls related to growing perceptions of threat are particularly striking. Within the Ottoman Archives, a significant proportion of the documents related to passport controls have to do with the comings and goings of Armenians. In particular, many documents discuss controls along the Russian border and the problems related to those controls, and a large number of documents focus on foreign laborers and Balkan nationalists.

Who Could Obtain a Passport

One of the most important problems of the period had to do with determining to whom passports would be issued. Issuing passports to those who did not have the necessary qualifications and violating regulations when issuing passports were matters to which the government paid particular attention, and, clearly, several other problems were related to these matters.[25] It was forbidden for consulates to issue passports to anyone who had been barred from entering the Ottoman Empire.[26] On this matter, there exist many documents and practices, particularly related to Armenians. For example, when intelligence was received that several Armenians intended to pass into Anatolia by way of Russia in order to stir up "turmoil and sedition [suriş ve fesad]," Ottoman representatives were informed that such individuals were not to be given passports, and the decision was taken to send out a list of the names and occupations of twelve of the Armenians in question, along with a group photograph.[27] In this way, the state made use, for its own purposes and in a rational manner, of standard information defining these people's identities. Combined with this written information, photographs, which were then an important innovation, and the communication networks between administrative offices were used to prevent such individuals from obtaining Ottoman passports.

Ottoman subjects applying to Ottoman representatives abroad to receive a passport faced no particular difficulty when they could present the correct documents to verify their identities—that is, a certificate to prove Ottoman nationality (*tabiiyet şahadetnamesi*) provided by another Ottoman consulate or an old passports or an Ottoman identity document (*tezkere-i Osmaniyye*). If the applicant's identity could not be verified, however, a passport was issued only if trustworthy information on their identity was made available and by using an *ilmühaber* drawn up by local officials. Officials often did not grant passports to Armenians, which gave rise to complaints. In one such case, an order was sent to the Marseille consulate to grant passports to a group of Armenians. It was later ascertained that among those who had taken passports were some thirty to forty "revolutionary" Armenians from Europe and the United States, with ties to the Hunchaks, and these individuals were sent back to Marseille. A decision proclaimed that such people's aim was to bring turmoil to the Ottoman Empire and that such individuals were not to be granted passports.[28]

After the Armenian Massacres of 1894–96 led to the mass migration of Armenians, the Ottoman government ordered that they would not be allowed to return to Istanbul. However, permission to return was granted to Armenians who could present guarantors to testify that they had homes and family in Istanbul as well as to those whom the Armenian Patriarchate declared "trustworthy" or who were linked to collective surety (*kefalet-i müteselsile*). Many Armenians originally from other provinces came to Istanbul, and many tried to bring their families. Such individuals were sent, one by one, back to their homelands and were issued warnings with an eye to preventing any others from going to the city. The director of consular affairs opined that this situation had occurred not because consulates had issued passports in violation of regulation but because border officials had allowed these individuals to cross even without passports. The director announced that decisions related to the entrance of Armenians were to be implemented properly.[29] In this incident, one clearly sees that the state's methods for verifying identity still functioned partially through social structures and traditional local practices of confirming personal identity. It also shows how the state's border controls were still rather weak. As previous chapters have noted, this system, which operated through the networks of the surety and millet systems and was based on traditional mechanisms of social control, was a sign of "extensive power." The very fact that some Armenians had succeeded in arriving in Istanbul from abroad without the proper travel documents points to both the weakness of border controls and the lack of central-government regulation. In addition, as is evident in a previous ruling not to allow any Armenians (aside from certain known individuals) to travel to or from Russia even if they held passports, one sees that such documents as passports or visas were by themselves not considered sufficient to control comings and goings and, moreover, that such controls were shaped largely by fears of political revolt.[30] As such, holding a passport was not in itself enough for everyone to travel. Again, it was the political center that decided whether a passport bearer could leave the empire, whether they could return or not, and where they would be able to go.

Passports as Tools of Control

Passports as Tools for Determining Identity

On matters related to security, in addition to controlling travel and indicating who would come and go, passports were also employed to ensure political control and as a tool for determining identity. There are multiple examples of passports being used for intelligence purposes. For instance, when an Armenian named Nishan Artinov (Nişan Artinof) applied to a consulate for a visa for his passport to go to Istanbul, the application was not processed, and he was subsequently followed by police on the claim that his photograph resembled that of a socialist named Semavend.[31] It was seen as necessary to arrest Garabet (Karabet) Hartek, Yusuf Bachian (Baçyan), and Dikran Manok as "Armenian conspirators" (*fesadçılar*) while they were en route to Izmir on Ottoman and Bulgarian passports.[32] Or we see the order issued to arrest a Russian "Armenian evildoer" (*şerir*) named Hoseb upon his arrival in Istanbul based on the information that he would be coming there[33] or to arrest "Armenian anarchists" who came to Istanbul from the countryside on Iranian passports based on information that they would attempt the assassination of the Armenian Patriarchate district governor in Beyoğlu.[34] The sheer number of such cases makes it impossible to list them all.

When the people of Istanbul wished to go abroad, they had first to obtain a passport to prove their identities at their destination or to enter another country. For the lower classes, the cost of a passport was difficult to bear, and some would travel to Egypt on an internal passport and procure an international passport there to go to England.[35] The Ottoman state saw this practice as a problem in terms of proving a traveler's identity or determining their good standing, so it warned the Khedivate of Egypt to attend to the requirement that such individuals had to present a guarantor to obtain a passport.[36]

Passports as Tools to Prevent the Entry of Unwanted Foreigners

Another noteworthy type of practice one encounters in documents of the period has to do with preventing unwanted foreigners from entering the country. Determining which foreigners were undesirable was based on two main concerns. First, foreigners arriving in the country were not to cause any internal-security problems. Second, anyone who might disturb the internal public order was to be barred from entering.

The Ottoman state's security concerns were based foremost on the fear of secession or the partition of the empire. As such, the Ottoman government saw as a threat those elements that were involved in or seen to have the potential to support the Armenian movement or nationalist movements in the Balkans. In particular, the perception of threat from Armenians who were citizens of foreign states, in particular Russia, was very high. Here, the perception of threat from Bulgarians was related to transitivity at the borders, which had not yet become fixed even if Bulgaria had gained its independence.[37] This transitivity made it hard to define a "foreigner" and was a problem in itself, even without the threat of nationalist movements, for an empire trying to transform itself into a centralized modern state. A third group seen as a threat to security was made up of foreign anarchists. Alongside the international fear of anarchists, a possible alliance between the three groups—Armenians, Bulgarians, and foreign anarchists—was the stuff of nightmares for state elites. In terms of public order, the most unwanted were people belonging to the lower classes who generally entered the country with the aim of finding work and were defined as vagrants.

To prevent unwanted foreigners from entering the country, it was necessary to put in place practical plans for carrying out the state's central administrative apparatus through regulations—which is to say, plans for how border controls were to be carried out and how entries were to be prevented. Equally necessary were effective staff to implement the procedures. Passport officers with knowledge of the appropriate languages were stationed in the townships of Grebene and Alasonya and at six gates along the border with the aim of preventing banditry (*şekavet*), disorder, conspiracy, sedition (*mefâsidat*), and the entry of pernicious materials (*muzır eşya*) from Greece.[38] A request was made to increase the officers' pay, which can be seen as a preventive measure against bribes.[39] Thus, measures were taken to ensure that officials—who can be seen as a part of the infrastructural apparatuses of securing rule—would act in the manner stipulated.

A warning sent to all Ottoman representatives advised that they were to investigate all Armenians applying to them for visas on foreign passports and that they were not to issue visas to those whose entry had been prohibited.[40] Although it was made known that Armenians arriving from Russia without passports would not be let in,[41] in practice this restriction was not always possible to enforce. In fact, Armenians did arrive in the Ottoman Empire and in Istanbul specifically without passports or visas.[42] The entry of Armenians from Russia, even those holding an Ottoman passport, was entirely forbidden again in 1899. In response,

Russian Armenians requested permission to enter and leave the empire with a passport.[43] Subsequently, passports and visas were not issued to Armenians either to come from Russia or to go there—yet their exits and entries continued.[44]

The *administrative network* created by the state gained visibility through regulations, decisions, orders, and official documents such as identity cards and passports as well as through the mediation of registries and records related to these documents, through stored information, and through the personnel that the state employed. Thanks to this network structure, the state, when in need of intelligence, was able to make use of the information it had encoded and stored. Keeping these records and administrative processes directly affected the lives of ordinary people. After security and economic crises propelled migration among the lower classes, the difficult situation faced by those who wished to return to their homelands can be seen as the dark side of the administrative network.

One of the state's basic worries related to security was that those who came from the outside might engage in political activity. Thus, for instance, there was intelligence that a conspirator (*müfsid*), Ohannes Avadisian, was traveling from Filibe to Dersaadet to provide instruction and supplies to the "seditious" communities in Beşiktaş and Beyoğlu in Istanbul.[45] Or, in line with intelligence received from the emirate, the decision was taken to block members of a group of "bandits" who had escaped from the Ottoman Empire to Eastern Rumelia and who, as ordered by their committee, had returned to the empire to apply for passports in order to foment unrest.[46] Or there was a decree—based on intelligence that the Sofia Bulgarian Resistance Movement was planning to send a committee of coachmen to Istanbul to incite sedition—that these individuals should not be allowed entry.[47]

The potential of attacks by anarchists was high on the list of official security concerns. Practices similar to those directed at non-Ottoman Armenians were also carried out against lower-class foreigners and focused on political suspicions. In this period, incidents of propaganda by the deed were occurring across Europe and leading to new regulations related to migrant laborers. The Ottoman government in particular made use of new security measures against anarchists and socialists. The aim was to prevent such elements from entering the empire,[48] and to this end the state began to administer controls. The use of internal passports and individual declarations to be obtained by foreigners from the consulates of the states to which they belonged as well as denial of entry to those whose activities were seen as suspicious or to anarchists and similar revolutionaries clearly reflect the empire's stance on this matter.[49]

If someone from socialist or anarchist circles did happen to enter the Ottoman Empire and were taken into custody, they were photographed and a record created before they were deported.[50] In the 1890s, photography became part of the Ottoman surveillance system, along with other documentation of individual identity. Although the use of photography was not widespread because of the lack of technical personnel and budget, the Ottoman Empire was one of the first governments to practice new filing and storing technologies using photographs. This use of photography and the circulation of photographs in pursuit of anarchists were also part of the interimperial antianarchist cooperation in which the Ottoman Empire was involved (see figure 2). In one case, an investigation was launched into a Greek subject named Rano, who upon suspicion of being a socialist was deported from France, denied entry into Russia and Romania, and then attempted to come to Istanbul.[51] He was found to be without a job and always in pursuit of politics. It was ordered that "Rano the son of Rusi who had been expelled even from such a country as France, administered as a republic," and other socialists and anarchists like him be denied admission, photographed, and sent away.[52] A further instance of the use of this new technology was to send photographs of anarchists to the places where they were expected to arrive based on intelligence about their movements.[53]

A similar fear is evident in the banning of the entry of Italians who had been deported from France after an Italian anarchist killed the president of France or the banning of other Italians who had fled from France on their own volition, most of them without a passport.[54] These actions point to how Italians were widely seen as potential anarchists at the time and how the entry of great numbers of unemployed foreigners into the empire was considered highly undesirable from the perspective of public order. Similar governmental decisions include the perceived need to take

2. The Berlin Police Directorate sent Casimir Luigi Tavella's photographs to the Ottoman government when he was deported from Saxony by Leipzig Police on July 11, 1911. He was an Italian from Verona and was filed as being an anarchist. BOA, EUM. KADL., 11/1, 15 Rebüilevvel 1329 (Mar. 16, 1911), Başbakanlık Osmanlı Arşivi (Prime Ministry Ottoman Archives), Istanbul. Courtesy of Devlet Arşivleri Başkanlığı—Cumhurbaşkanlığı Osmanlı Arşivi (Presidency of State Archives—Presidential Ottoman Archives), Istanbul.

precautions against the possibility of anarchists being among the "mutinous" crew of the battleship *Potemkin* in 1905, who had surrendered to the Romanian government and come to Istanbul, most with Romanian passports,[55] and the order to prevent two passengers on a Bulgarian ship (Second Machinist Kristov and the cook Michailov, both determined to belong to a socialist party and to be mischievous and harmful) from disembarking, though the ship had landed, and to take police action in the event that they did disembark.[56]

In 1893, intelligence reached the Ministry of Interior, based on news in the Paris papers, that one Paul Raklos, an anarchist known to have been involved in a murder in the French Parliament, was coming to Istanbul. The ministry announced that when the individual in question arrived, he was to be taken into police custody.[57] Similar measures were taken to prohibit Italian anarchists deported from other countries from entering the Ottoman Empire.[58] Another instance had to do with sixteen European anarchists, among them three Armenians. According to an encoded telegram sent from the Ministry of Interior to the province of Aydın,[59] another document written to the ministers of interior and police stated that it had been announced by the Russian deputy of merchants that some among this group of sixteen individuals aimed to spread out to various locations in Europe, and some were coming to the Ottoman Empire.[60] In another example of intelligence, it was discovered that a group of vagrants affiliated with the Garibaldi Brigade in Italy had found an opportunity to enter the Ottoman Empire, and the Ottoman government decided to take all "proceedings and care [takibat ve takayyudat]" to prevent their entry.[61] In the hunt for anarchists, the efforts made by the chief interpreters at the Russian, French, German, and Austrian embassies to determine the identities of anarchists known to be bound for Istanbul are important indicators of the spirit of the time.[62]

Foreign laborers coming to the Ottoman Empire for work were also subjected to such practices. State representatives might not issue visas to workers or miners from Italy when their circumstances aroused suspicion;[63] there was a ruling that idle Italians were not to be granted visas to enter the Ottoman Empire without careful investigation in order to prevent disruptions to public order;[64] and orders were given that issuing visas to Italians in Romania who wished to go to Beirut to work on the Rayak–Hama railway should proceed only after investigations by the local consulates. Following the attempted assassination of King Leopold II of Belgium by the Italian anarchist Gennaro Rubino in November 1902, precautions and controls against Italians intensified further. Similarly, in 1894, two days after the killing of the President Sadi Carnot of France by the Italian anarchist Sante Geronimo Caserio, an order was issued that the entry of "vagrant Italians" from France into the Ottoman Empire was not be overlooked.

The active role played by Italians in the anarchist actions in Europe led the Ottoman Empire to carry out more investigations into people of this nationality. Anarchists who were understood to be Italian were photographed and immediately taken out of Istanbul.[65] Three Italian anarchists arriving in Istanbul were immediately arrested and sent back to their homelands.[66] Visas were not issued to Italian workers coming to Istanbul, citing the difficulty of sending them away if they had visas.[67] Such examples overlap with the aim of keeping Italians under constant control as a result of their being seen by the central state as politically suspect. The investigation into thirty Italian workers who, according to the Brindisi consulate, had set out for Istanbul on a ship named *Taormina* without visas[68] and, more generally, the denial of visas to Italian laborers or miners should be considered in this context.

The thirty laborers who left Italy for Istanbul on the *Taormina* did not receive visas even though they were bearers of legitimate passports.[69] The Italian embassy wrote to the Ottoman Ministry of Foreign Affairs that these individuals had set out for Istanbul without visas despite being told by the Italian government that they needed the visas. The embassy requested that the Ottoman government intervene as necessary.[70] Here, the Italian government's attitude should be considered alongside the diplomatic pressure that other European states exerted on Italy following the killing of the Empress Elizabeth of the Austro-Hungarian Empire by Luigi Lucheni on September 10, 1898. Italy's intent, as the country sending out the highest number of labor migrants, was probably to show that it did not politically support any citizens who played a central role in assassinations and bombings.

The use of passport controls to prevent people from entering the empire was exercised more strictly toward the lower classes. Practices in the Ottoman Empire also affected even Italians with less dubious antecedents. Following the arrest of several such Italians on the pretext of an inquiry into anarchists and their subsequent deportation, it was ordered that such practices not be repeated.[71]

To be sure, Italians were not the only foreigners subjected to such investigations. The antianarchist atmosphere in Europe also enveloped the Ottoman Empire. Investigations were carried out into laborers coming to the empire from foreign countries for work to determine if they were socialists or anarchists.[72] Records were kept of the names and origins of workers to look into whether there were anarchists and socialists working for foreign companies, and workers were controlled by means of their consulates.[73] Yet it is unclear whether these files were kept in the same way in every company or locale. We also find a practice like the suretyship system employed to control Greek workers. A decision not to bar the entry of Greek workers whose passport visas were complete and who were "determined by respected merchants" not to be harmful individuals shows that the Ottoman government still relied on traditional methods, even at the international scale.

In 1898, an investigation was launched into a group of laborers on the tip from the Washington embassy that there were anarchists among the workers at a quarry belonging to the Port of Istanbul.[74] A decision was taken to investigate if there were anarchists and socialists among the employees of foreign companies operating in the empire.[75] A memo from the Ministry of Foreign Affairs to the Viennese embassy requested that a file be created listing the places of origin of Austro-Hungarian laborers working on the Oriental Railway.[76] Faced with the possibility that laborers working for the company might be anarchists, the London embassy replied that investigations had been requested into "the state of their previous convictions and their political opinions [sevabıkı ahvâlleri ve efkârı siyasiyeleri]," but this was not possible, so an easier solution would be to carry out investigations into such people in their current locations.[77] A reply from the Paris embassy added that the French Ministry of Internal Affairs and the chief of police had been contacted regarding laborers whose names were recorded in the file: they were not socialists or anarchists, according to the embassy, so no criminal records for them had been found.[78] The Athens embassy stated that no information had been obtained from the police suggesting that those listed were anarchists.[79] A similar answer was received from the Geneva consul general regarding Swiss workers employed on the Oriental Railway.[80] This example demonstrates the level of international cooperation in the field of interimperial security. Control over mobility was formed around the issue of the political mobilization of the lower classes inside the anarchist movement. The fear of anarchism in conjunction with antianarchist regulations directly affected police investigations of migrant workers as part of background security checks.

In response to a request for information on one Mikara Raul, a worker on the Oriental Railway, the Swedish embassy stated that this name did not appear in the Swedish records of those working in the Ottoman Empire.[81] The Stockholm embassy noted that the person's name was not even Swedish. In the same document, the reply of the Spanish Ministry of Foreign Affairs on the results of an investigation by the Madrid embassy into one Abraham Laparna stated that no such person was among the Spanish subjects employed by the railway, and no such name could be found in the central records on anarchists. This correspondence with the various embassies regarding the information in the files of the Ottoman Ministry of Public Works and Trade was related in a document from the foreign minister to the Ministry of Interior, dated January 4, 1899, stating that no information could be obtained related to individuals named Mikara (Milikara) Raul or Abraham Laparna. The Ministry of Public Works and Trade's Railways Administration (Ticaret ve Nafia Nezareti Demiryolları İdaresi) informed the Ministry of Foreign Affairs on June 6, 1899, that it had collected the records in question from the companies. These records had included an informational note by the chief commissioner of Dedeağaç in Edirne that an official named "Abraham Sparta," not "Abraham Laparna," had been found and that although there was no one named "Mikara Raul," there was a "Melik Rupen" in the records. However, this person had left the job some sixteen years ago and had not been seen since. In the end, because the Railways Administration did not have a copy of the records in question and had little choice but to investigate according to the names in company records, it stated that this was not a suitable means of obtaining the needed information.[82] This example shows that suitable records were yet to be kept by the government and that the necessary administrative units did not have copies of workers' records. Nevertheless, through the records that were maintained, consulates carried out their investigations.

In another example of the hunt for anarchists, it was confirmed through intelligence that a certain "dangerous anarchist" who went by the name of "Paco" or various other pseudonyms was working in the quarry or in the railway office of an Istanbul dock company. This intelligence, based on the claims made by a spy and verified by the Ottoman consulate in New York, was announced by the Washington embassy.[83]

Companies and workplaces were seen as spaces where workers' activities could be monitored by the state—observed in the true sense of the word. The storage of information at companies was assured by keeping files on such matters, and plans were made for the state to be able to access this information when necessary. In this way, workers were both rendered legible to the state and made controllable through the keeping of records. Yet the fact that records were not always kept in an orderly fashion or that companies did not always wish to share such information negatively affected the state's aims.

Just as measures were taken to prevent anarchists from entering the country, measures were taken against organized movements in the Balkans, resulting from the application of methods of propaganda by the deed by nationalist and revolutionary movements in that region. For instance, in 1907 four anarchists—Iranian subjects who boarded a Russian-flagged ship from the Port of Varna—were arrested on the suspicion that they would organize attacks on foreign consulates in the name of the Bulgarian Committee. Subsequently, the Ottoman government decided to intensify its precautionary measures to prevent such people from entering the empire, specifically Istanbul.[84] After Bulgarian Committee members in Macedonia crossed borders with passports via Serbia and Montenegro, there was talk of taking measures against such incidents and even of arrests. Yet the word *derdestleri* (arrests) was subsequently stricken from this document.[85] In official correspondence, one frequently finds such warnings as those regarding the careful inspection of the passports and internal passports of "Bulgarian conspirators" (*erbab-ı fesad*) coming from or heading abroad.[86]

The relations constructed by Ottoman political elites among propaganda by the deed, rebellion, and foreign intervention are also evident in a note from the Rumeli Inspectorship stating that certain "Bulgarian sedition committees" had incited a battle in the region, specifically in the Manastır province. It claimed that these committees were involved in a number of activities in all major population centers, including an attempt to force European intervention through the destruction of foreign financial institutions and railway lines (in line with anarchist ways) and by provoking the massacre of Muslims. Such groups, the note stated, would begin "guerrilla warfare [çete muhaberesi]" in the third week of April and that they would in an anarchist fashion destroy railways and use dynamite and dumdum bullets. The Ministry of Foreign Affairs announced that the European press had uncovered such attempts and that meetings with the embassies of Russia and Austria had been held on the matter.[87]

As for many other issues in this era, one of the concerns related to foreigners had to do with public order; thus, a decision required the repatriation of foreign porters who unloaded ships in order to preemptively prevent them from committing theft, pickpocketing, or more serious crimes.[88] The decision, twice repeated, to repatriate vagrants and suspicious Greeks in the Ottoman Empire can be similarly interpreted.[89] Later it was learned that twenty-two Jewish Romanian nationals, men and women, holding Romanian passports and having been expelled from Russia, would be coming to the Ottoman Empire, followed by many more who intended to do the same. The view that these people were of the vagrant class and, as such, were not fit to come to the Ottoman Empire is related to how Ottoman bureaucrats saw such individuals as a threat to public order.[90] As has been evident throughout this chapter, the Ottoman government established a connection between dangerous classes and migration policies: those among the lower classes who were not bound to a job or a workplace constituted a potential threat particularly to the urban order. Such individuals were, according to state elites, prone to committing crimes such as theft and pickpocketing and thus to disrupting the order of the city. In addition, owing to their unhealthy living conditions, it was thought they would probably spread infectious diseases. Moreover, they might upset the city's population balance. All these reasons were sufficient, according to state elites, to prevent such people from entering the city.

Another means of preventing the entry of undesired foreigners was the use of visas. An announcement stated that when certain Iranians set out for the Ottoman Empire and Istanbul via Russia, they had come and gone without obtaining visas from the Ottoman consulate. The Ottoman state attempted to prevent such malpractice.[91]

A decision was taken to surreptitiously look into the conditions and identities of arriving foreigners who raised suspicion, even if no problems occurred during passport control. This decision underscores the inadequacy, for Ottoman state elites, of passport and visa controls by themselves in ensuring security. To carry out such an investigation, in addition to the available cadre of sixty police, thirty additional civil police were hired at a monthly wage of six hundred kuruş.[92]

Passports as Tools to Be Rid of Unwanted Parts of the Population

Another problem for the Ottoman government had to do with emigrating Armenians, and attempts were made to prohibit their return to the empire. Passport controls were thus used not only to be rid of unwanted parts of the population or to prohibit travel to undesirable countries but to prevent the return of unwanted peoples. Not allowing return also prevented people from leaving to find a better economic situation and thus kept the labor force inside the empire.

As previously mentioned, in 1888 the Ottoman government banned immigration to the United States.[93] The US government announced that it had little use for more labor migration, and the Ottoman government's decision to prevent those wishing to go to America was communicated to the provinces on March 21, 1888.[94] At this time, a group of seventy Armenians from Kharput had come to Istanbul with the aim of finding factory work in the United States, but their migration was prevented. They were returned to their homelands at the government's cost. The related document stated that after this point passports would not be issued to those with questionable aims wishing to go to the United States or another country to find work ("maksad-ı muzırraya hizmet etmek niyetiyle").[95] The notification from the United States that it no longer needed labor was not based on the perception of a political threat. Yet Ottoman state elites operated based primarily on their own security concerns and saw geographical mobility tied to labor migration as related to the revolutionary Armenians' illegitimate political aims.

Armenians continued to travel to North America, though, mainly via smuggling networks, and the Ottoman government tried to continue surveillance of "suspicious Armenians" simply because of the impossibility of performing routine controls over every Armenian aiming to travel on foreign ships.[96] Another factor in prohibiting immigration to the United States was the bilateral agreement between that country and the Ottoman Empire, which, in its English version, granted impunity to American citizens from arrest and Ottoman jurisdiction.[97] Interestingly, the Turkish version did not have this regulation, and this article eventually became an issue in an international legal conflict between the two governments. Because the Ottoman government's main concern here was the possibility of a conspiracy by revolutionary Armenian Americans who could travel back to the Ottoman Empire,[98] the prohibition remained in place until 1896.

According to the Ottoman Nationality Law (Tâbiiyet-i Osmaniye Kanunnamesi) of 1869, "only the central authorities can dispense the permission to expatriate (under Article 5) and order the banishment or expulsion of those who expatriate without permission" (Article 6).[99] Ottoman Armenians who gained US citizenship without permission from the Ottoman government were still Ottoman citizens under this law, and the Ottoman Empire claimed jurisdiction rights over them. On the advice of Minister of Police Hüseyin Nazım Paşa, the vizierate decided to use this law and the passport regulations, and Armenians who left for the United States without having their documents in order were labeled as "fugitives" (firari) in the Ottoman legal framework.[100] Even if these Armenians returned to the Ottoman Empire with orderly US passports, their entry would be strictly prohibited, and if they somehow entered anyway, they were considered fugitives. Moreover, if they traveled to the Ottoman Empire by ship, they were to be deported to the United States on the very same ship.[101]

The Ottoman government made another administrative regulation that added further complexity to passport practices toward Armenian emigrants: gaining US citizenship would deprive them of their property and inheritance rights in the Ottoman Empire. If Armenians wished to retain their rights, they would have to expatriate from the United States and reclaim their status as Ottoman citizens.[102] In 1896, the Ottoman government issued a letter of undertaking (taahhüd senedi) for Armenians who wanted to immigrate to the United States. Armenians who signed the document declared that they would "never return to the Empire" and filed two photographs with the document. In return, they were issued a travel document: usually an internal passport, not an Ottoman international passport.[103]

After the massacres of 1894–96, many Armenians applied to leave the empire for the United States. However, even if they had all the documents required, the passport officers in Kharput asked them "if they [had] rebelled [against the Ottoman state]," and this question was enough to frighten the applicants.[104] In addition to other documents, emigrating Armenians were also responsible for providing photographs, but the standards of these photographs were not regulated. Most of the ones in the Ottoman Archives are like family portraits of the time (see figure 3). Because of the limited number of photographers with equipment, obtaining photographs was not always easy. This was the case in Kharput, the place from which many Armenians migrated to North America. According to the British

3. An Armenian family migrating from Merzifon to the United States, 1906. BOA, FTG, 345, Başbakanlık Osmanlı Arşivi (Prime Ministry Ottoman Archives), Istanbul. Courtesy of Devlet Arşivleri Başkanlığı—Cumhurbaşkanlığı Osmanlı Arşivi (Presidency of State Archives—Presidential Ottoman Archives), Istanbul.

consul there, the only photographer in Kharput had no glasses and could not take photographs.[105] This problem was solved with the involvement of the British consulate.

The filing of those photographs was a new administrative procedure for the Ottoman bureaucracy. According to a later Ministry of Interior decision, twelve copies of each photograph—with payment for more than two photographs made from the ministry's budget—were supposed to be taken and held by the port commissions. Some administrative centers had freelance photographers, and in some police stations officers were trained to take photographs. Those photographs were supposed to be circulated to different Ottoman ports and police stations.[106] If the photographs did not arrive at the port commissions in time, Armenians who applied to leave for North America had to stay at the port under surveillance until the photos were delivered. This requirement created another form of victimization: in 1906, a group of twelve Armenian women and children had to wait more than six weeks in Trabzon until their photographs were delivered to the port administration. Although the governor of Trabzon and the British consul tried to solve the problem on their behalf, the regulation was strictly adhered to without exception.[107]

Restrictions on Armenian mobility were aimed not only at those seeking to immigrate to North America. For instance, a group of Armenians from Muş who had been in "Galoş" (probably referring to Cluj in Romania) for a number of years and who wished to return to their homelands without passing through Istanbul were refused passports on the grounds of a ban on the return of Armenians.[108] Because of a general pardon of Armenians after the Memorandum of 1895, the Ottoman government decided that visas would not be granted to returnees who were declared to be anarchists and seditious (anarşist ve müfsid), whereas the entry of all others was to be facilitated.[109]

Another document announced the decision, in response to the inquiries made by the Bulgarian Commissariat, to allow Armenians with homes and families in Istanbul as well as rural Armenians who wished to return to their homelands to return with an internal passport and registration through the surety system. It was also decided that passports would be available to those traveling abroad for trade. Russian Armenians who requested visas at the head consulate in Batumi to return to the Ottoman Empire would receive them unless they were known to be conspirators (*erbab-ı fesad*). If any among the arrivals aroused suspicion, the necessary places would be notified by telegraph as soon as they arrived there.[110]

To prevent the return of Armenians who had left the Ottoman Empire for foreign countries, under instructions never to return, their identity documents (*tezkere-i Osmaniyye*) were seized, and a note was added about this to their passports. The authority to do so rested with provinces and port commissions, who were obliged to share the information with the population registration office. The internal passports of emigrating Armenians were inscribed, "henceforth, not to return to the Ottoman Empire [ba'dema Memaliki Mahruse-i Şahane'ye avdet etmeyeceklerdir]." The port commission was to keep a file on such individuals, as was the Armenian Patriarchate.[111] Even Armenians who had left the country with orderly documents but who wished to return would not be granted passports. Meanwhile, the right to obtain passports was withdrawn from Armenians who had gone abroad without registering or through illegal means—as exiles or fugitives—even though they were Ottoman citizens.[112] The denial of passports to Armenians who wished to travel to Iran also points to how the empire determined where certain of its subjects could and could not go.[113] The phrasing of notations in formal documents ensured clear communication between bureaucratic offices (although notations in such documents also used phrases not found in any regulation), and the transformation of each of these documents into a source of intelligence rendered apparent the administrative network. The notations on passports stated such things as "henceforth, not to return to the Ottoman Empire"; in some instances, red ink was used, which meant the holder of the passport was a suspect; or codes were used to indicate the holder was considered seditious. These unusual administrative acts were formed within the security policies of the Ottoman government. Practices related to travel documents took shape in terms of the perception of threat, and, alongside the administrative network, they served to spread symbolic violence within society.

During and after the massacres of the mid-1890s, numerous Armenians left the country, mostly for Europe and Russia, and were prohibited from returning. With the Ottoman government's resistance to the reform program under the Berlin Treaty, France, Russia, and Great Britain sent the Memorandum of 1895 to the Ottoman government concerning the Armenian community in the Eastern Provinces. On October 20, 1895, the Ottoman government responded by saying it would prepare a reform scheme. Responding to international pressure, Sultan Abdülhamid II declared an amnesty that permitted Armenians to return between December 9 and 19, 1896. The Istanbul Police Directorate (İstanbul Polis Müdürlüğü) inquired first of the Ministry of Police and then of the vizierate on December 19 whether this decision also included Armenians who had obtained a passport and gone abroad for reasons of trade before and after the "incidents" in the empire. The day after the end of the amnesty period, the police prevented twenty-five Armenians who had come on a Georgian boat and had received a safe-conduct pass before the start of the amnesty period from leaving their boat. In the investigation into this group, some were found to be from Istanbul, and the rest from the countryside. A public officer was tasked with carrying out a deeper investigation and found that these Armenians had obtained internal passports before the end of the amnesty period or were not suspicious. The following day was a major Armenian festival, and so as not to cause any unwanted mutterings, they were allowed to leave the boat under supervision. On December 20, 1896, the police were asked whether they were to be handed over to their guarantors. It was decided that those whom the police understood to be in good standing would be released to their guarantors.[114]

According to a document written on December 21 by the minister of police to the vizierate, many more Armenians were expected to arrive by Russian and Georgian boats.[115] Because among them would be people who could not be admitted, the police were to take care not to allow such individuals to leave the boat. Despite this, the boat companies attempted to disembark all their passengers. For this reason, it was recommended that the Varna consulate, the Constanta consulate, and other units not grant passports or travel permits (pasavan) to Armenians deemed unfit to enter the Ottoman Empire. Another notification from the police to the vizierate stated that there were three Armenians on the Russian boat *Olga*, traveling from Odessa to the Port of Istanbul—"Mayans from Ekin" (who held an internal passport), his wife, and "Mardirus from Erzurum"; one Armenian named Migirdich on the Khedivate postal vessel *Tevfik-i Rabbani* from Alexandria; and two Armenians named Diyorgi Ohannes and Agop on the boat *Venüs* belonging to the Varna Nemçe Company, one of whom had boarded from Varna and one from Burgas.[116] To prevent these individuals from disembarking, the boats were brought under police supervision. The presence of up to ten Armenians on the French Company ship *Anadolu* passing through the Dardanelles, who had boarded in Marseille to come to Istanbul, was ascertained through a telegram sent by the inspector of explosive materials (*eczayı nariye müfettişi*) in Kale-yi Sultaniye. Exactly how to treat these people and others like them grew into a major concern on December 22, 1896.[117] In all such writings, the interesting part is how the Ministry of Police collected such detailed intelligence. Though it is possible that ship captains gave information about their passengers in advance, in fact the correspondence has little information on the sources of intelligence.

Another informational note from the police, written on December 24, 1896, relayed that fifty Armenians were present on a boat named *Joris* under a Bulgarian flag, while ten Armenian men and women were on a boat named *Sakız* belonging to the Georgian Company; none of them was to be allowed to disembark. It was noted that many more Armenians were en route, and permission to set foot on land had been granted within the pardon period.[118] On January 5, 1897, after the Ministry of Police inquired what to do now that the amnesty had expired, it was communicated to the Ministry of Foreign Affairs, the Ministry of Police, and the Ministry of Interior that a number of consulates had requested an extension to the period. Among the arrivals, those who belonged to "revolutionary committees [ihtilal komiteleri]" and the ones who had been involved in violent acts were to be separated out, and the remainder would benefit from the pardon.[119]

The Ottoman government's attention here was on preventing the return of certain Armenians to Ottoman lands—namely, those deemed evil or seditious persons and suspected evildoers (*su'i bilfesad ve mazanne-i su'i*)—not of those given permission to enter for certain circumstances. Thus, in the implementation of decisions, we find danger and suspicion as the basic reference points. The arrival of such people was seen as a danger for internal security. Because it was deemed easy for them to organize for sedition, agitation (*fesad*), or attack, it was necessary to investigate them. Yet because investigation was difficult, if not impossible, preparations were made to provide convincing answers to European consulates in Istanbul—which had initiated diplomatic meetings about the situation and had asked questions about the situation of the returnee Armenians arriving in Ottoman seas—and to extend the period of the pardon. The pardon was extended for another seventy-five days on the basis that the returnees would remain under police control, and an official report was prepared by the Special Assembly of Ministers (Encümen-i Mahsus-u Vükela) to be sent to the Ministry of Police. Those who arrived after the extension period ended were interned by the police, and those from Istanbul who were not under suspicion were released upon being linked to a guarantor affirmed by the patriarchate. Those from the countryside were sent to their homelands. Suspect individuals were punished under the law.

At this time, Armenians were arriving by the day from Edirne, and, according to the police, they would continue to come. The Royal Secretariat (Sadaret Mabeyin Başkitabet-i Celilesi) had established a special commission a couple of months before the amnesty to investigate the arrivals and prevent the return of experienced evildoers and conspirators (*erbab-ı şer ve mefsedet*). The Ministry of Police issued a missive dated August 28, 1897, in Istanbul and other locales where a number of local (here, "local," or *yerli*, was presumably used to characterize Istanbulites), rural, and foreign Armenian conspirators (*erbab-ı fesadı*) were present, ordering the police to carry out the necessary procedures to deport such individuals. A missive dated October 18, 1896, requested Undersecretary of the Interior Ahmet Refik Beyefendi that an investigation be conducted into the reasons for the migration of those Armenians wishing to relocate so as to ensure they would not return and that documents noting their guarantors be taken and entrusted to the patriarchate. Two commissions were to be established to collect further details. One, under the leadership of Hüseyin Hamid Beyefendi,[120] was to investigate the reasons why Armenians were traveling and to check their documents. This commission was also responsible for announcing migration rules and the documents required in the daily newspapers.[121] Several officials were assigned to the commission, yet it was understood that they would not be able to continue that work as required by the commission during the amnesty because of the significant obligations of their regular jobs as civil servants. The second commission, under the direction of Ahmet Refik Beyefendi, would be employed as the Ministry of Police's inquiry team had formerly been.[122]

The creation of these commissions exemplifies the state's stance toward those citizens it did not want in the empire or saw as a threat. The state, when presenting policies related to internal security, reviewed them in light of its own ambiguity around the separation of internal and external policy. This is one of the defining characteristics of the Hamidian Era. As a result, to actualize the practices the state had chosen or created, it obtained information in particular through the work of the police and designed new strategies according to this information. As the range and types of information obtained (or to be obtained) grew, further subunits were established to carry out these expanded functions. This period was one in which commissions were often used by administrations, and, in this way, the bureaucracy took its own decisions or, more accurately, employed initiative, expanded its scope, and at the same time further technicized decisions around security. While the administrative network thus functioned in a more practical way, particularly in the matter of security, it became a cloud of sorts that enveloped every aspect of life through its documents and commissions. Yet in the end the state could not carry out its planned duties because of a lack of qualified staff.

Through passport regulations, the state was able, to some extent, to ban travel to countries it did not want its citizens to go to or at least was able to prevent certain parts of the population from doing so. Besides North America, the Ottoman administration considered migration to Russia problematic. In one incident, some ten thousand laborers, all Ottoman subjects working in the environs of Batumi in Georgia, did not hold passports but rather Ottoman identity documents (*tezkere-i Osmaniyye*) or residence permits issued by the Ottoman consulate. Russia did not recognize these documents and announced that those who did not present a passport issued by the Ottoman government and with a visa from the Russian consulate would be deported. This requirement was also extended to

Iranian subjects. Upon this announcement, the Ottoman state declared that most of these individuals did not have Ottoman passports, that nearly all were Armenians, and that most were people from a "seditious class involved in unsavory events [hadiselere karışmış fesad takımından]" or had fled without permission after such events. Accordingly, such individuals would not be admitted to Ottoman territory; however, if there were any Muslims among these laborers, this prohibition did not apply to them.[123] Here, too, administrative functions were carried out with an eye to the state's survival and in line with perceived security concerns and were implemented differently for different groups of people.

In addition to the undocumented, there were also significant issues concerning the legal position of Armenians in the borderlands. After the Russo-Ottoman War (1877–78), the citizenship status of Ottoman Armenians in provinces annexed by Russia became problematic. There had always been mobility across the border, but after the war the subjecthood of Ottoman Armenians in the annexed provinces came into question. Soon after the war, it was decided that these communities could choose their subjecthood within six months. Shortly before this period ended, however, all these communities were naturalized or became Russian citizens to avoid dual subjecthood. This change created another layer of Armenian geographical mobility, with the return of some of these people to Anatolia now technically as foreigners.[124] To control geographical mobility in the borderlands, the Ottoman government forbade all Russian Armenians from entering the empire and Ottoman Armenians from traveling to Russia. Nonetheless, these regulations did not end traffic across the Ottoman–Russian border, even in 1900.[125] In 1897, the Ottoman government decided that Armenians who were forbidden entry would not be granted visas,[126] and in 1900 it ordered all its consulates to investigate Armenians holding foreign passports who applied for an Ottoman visa.[127]

Nor was the status of the Armenians of annexed provinces the only issue on this contentious border. After the Sasun massacre in 1894, nearly thirty thousand Armenians left Ottoman lands for Russia. This mass migration created a diplomatic crisis between the two states. The Ottoman Ministry of Foreign Affairs proposed a population exchange between

Ottoman Armenians and Russian Muslims who had been forced to leave their homelands in the Caucasus and made refugees by Russia. The Russian government did not accept this proposal, stating that the Armenian population would make it harder to manage Russian colonization in the Caucasus, especially in Kars (now in modern-day Turkey). In response, a memo from the Ottoman Ministry of Foreign Affairs reported that the return of these Armenians would fail established security measures and thus was considered a threat to state security, so a bilateral commission had to be established to check their identities.[128] The Ottoman Empire decided to open the border for the return of Armenians who had emigrated after the Sasun massacre, but only for a limited time and on the necessary condition that those returning were not vagrants, mischievous persons (*fesad*), or anarchists. However, implementing this decision needed proper bureaucratic infrastructure, which was absent on the border. According to the diplomatic correspondence, Russia declared that ten thousand Armenians would be deported to the Ottoman Empire in 1899, with additional groups of two hundred each in the following years, and so sent those ten thousand Armenians to the border.[129] Later, Russia negotiated for the railway concession in the Black Sea region of the Ottoman Empire in return for keeping Armenian migrants and committed not to deport them after the concession was granted.

Commander Mehmed Zeki Paşa of the Fourth Army wrote a report about the Armenians who left the Ottoman Empire for Russia before and after the Sasun massacre in 1894. According to his report, they numbered between twenty thousand and twenty-five thousand, although the exact figure was not available because they had no passports and did not leave the empire through ordinary bureaucratic procedures.[130] In the relevant Ottoman documents, the term *firari* (fugitive) was used to refer to Armenians who had left the empire for Russia without orderly travel documents.[131]

In 1901, Russia declared that migrant Armenians could obtain Russian citizenship and forced them to be naturalized. However, most Armenians did not wish to lose their Ottoman citizenship and tried to return to the Ottoman Empire. While the Ottoman government prohibited unregistered returns, it also put in place a new settlement policy under which returnees were sent to different provinces instead of to their home regions.[132] The correspondence from the Prime Minister's Office (Sadaret) to the Ministries of Interior, Foreign Affairs, and War emphasized that the return of these Armenians would change the population profile and that their return would create a security problem. Thus, the government perceived the very existence of Armenians who were also natives of the Ottoman Empire as a threat.[133]

Passports as Tools to Identify Suspects

Passports were used to find wanted criminals and political suspects. They were used for communication across administrative units through written notes or certain signs, such as the use of red ink. In 1899, it was learned, for example, that some vagrants were traveling through Romania, Serbia, and Bulgaria with the aim of fomenting revolt in the Ottoman Empire. They had obtained multiple passports from different locales using the same population document with the same name and had distributed them to the "good-for-nothings they had collected and organized among Serbian and Bulgarian subjects [Sırp ve Bulgar tebaasından cem ve tertip eyledikleri haşerate tevzi itdikleri]." This manipulation of the system propelled the practice of recording the dates and number of passports received on an individual's population documents. With the adoption of extraordinary measures for raison d'état and to prevent seditious (*fesad*) individuals from entering Ottoman lands, consulates placed a minuscule mark in the shape of the letter ف (F, signifying *fesad*) on the section of the passport that was busiest with stamps. These individuals were then arrested by the police.[134] Visas were issued in red ink to Armenians of foreign and Ottoman nationality in Batumi who wished to come to the Ottoman Empire,[135] and the passports of Armenians receiving passports from the Marseille chief consulate to come to the Ottoman Empire were also marked in a special way.[136]

The practice of inscribing passports of seditious individuals with ف/F for *fesad* continued in later years because it had several advantages for the police, and those whose passports had this mark were investigated and treated accordingly. In time, though, it became clear that the Bulgarian

Commissariat was not complying with this practice, and the Ottoman Ministry of Interior repeated to the Ministry of Foreign Affairs the relevant decision to serve notice to the commissariat.[137] This document, issued in 1903, also mentioned a similar case in which several vagrants in Romania, Serbia, and Bulgaria had received multiple passports from various locations using the same name and the same identity document with the aim of stirring up trouble in the Ottoman Empire. The same order was repeated, that the date and number of passports obtained under a single identity document should henceforth be indicated on that document. Thus, the state employed such methods of information storage to render society legible. Information was encoded not through filing and ordering documents but by marking them. These marked documents were increasingly subjected to administrative processing, and the encoding grew more functional.

The use of passports to prevent the entry of unwanted elements became an ordinary practice of government. Examples of how the government dealt with those whose entry could not be prevented include taking into police custody several individuals coming to Istanbul from Bulgaria who were thought of as vagrants or evildoers (*eşirras*) even though they held passports;[138] investigating and putting under police surveillance an Austrian machinist named Moris Forest, who arrived from Belgrade on a passport without a visa;[139] and investigating the behavior in the neighborhoods of a number of Armenians who had used Russian passports and Ottoman consulate visas to come to Istanbul.[140] Certainly, chief among these preventative measures was police detention.

Passports as Tools to Keep Statistics

Passports were an important apparatus for keeping statistics on entries and exits. Provinces kept lists of those who obtained passports to go abroad and sent them to the Ministry of Police.[141] There were also attempts to determine the number of passport-free exits and entries, particularly during extraordinary situations. After the Sasun massacre, the state attempted to determine the number of Armenians who had gone to Russia without a passport both before and after the incident.[142] In the police districts of

Beyoğlu, Istanbul, and Üsküdar, records were kept of the nationalities and information related to the comings and goings of foreigners in the capital.[143] Every month, a list of those who obtained passports in the provinces and went abroad was sent to the Ministry of Police.[144] Lists showing the number of Armenians receiving internal passports and passports were prepared.[145] Information was stored related to passport controls, with lists of the names of Armenians who came to Istanbul, the ships they arrived on (and which national agency ran the ships), and the travel documents they carried.[146] In addition, the Passport Commission (Pasaport Komisyonu), which was an administrative unit formed under the Police Ministry to file the necessary information about the arrivals and departures of the passengers, kept ten-day processing records for Armenians, Armenian Catholics, Protestants, and Ottoman Greeks.[147]

Passports as Tools to Enforce Obligations to the State

Passport fees were a source of income for the state. For instance, the state observed that some Syrians returning from America had obtained internal passports in Alexandria with an eye to paying less money before continuing on without an international passport stamped with a visa by an Ottoman authority, which was considered a violation of regulations that affected the Ottoman consulates' income.[148]

Passports were also seen as a means of controlling mandatory military service. Reserve soldiers were prevented from deserting overseas using their passports, and passports were denied to those who could not prove that they had carried out their mandatory duties.[149] Tax obligations and mandatory military service were carefully considered when granting passports. The Ministry of Foreign Affairs announced that passports and similar documents would not be drawn up for individuals who had not fulfilled their military or tax obligations to the state.[150]

Passport practices made manifest the institutionalization of certain practices of discrimination toward specific groups. These practices should be considered alongside the state's stigmatization through its use of terms such as *serseri* (vagrant), *fesad* (seditious, conspirator), and *anarşist* (anarchist).

Passports as Tools for Controlling the Seaways

Passports were used in another important mechanism related to spatial mobility: the control of ports and ships.[151] Within the framework of a decision in 1906 to keep under custody and observation any ships coming or going in the Port of Istanbul, not only on the day they entered or left the port but across the duration of their stay, such controls grew more intense.[152] In particular, where intelligence was already in hand, control measures led to ships being searched. For example, Austrian and Italian ships arriving in Thessaloniki and suspected of having Armenian anarchists were searched;[153] measures were taken to prevent certain Armenian anarchists arriving in Istanbul from disembarking in disguise or to prevent stowaways on foreign boats from entering Istanbul;[154] and shipping agents were told to take care that anarchists did not board Italian boats arriving at Ottoman ports.[155]

After the Italian government began to implement harsh measures against the Socialist Party, it was feared that Italian socialists might come to the Ottoman Empire, so precautionary measures were taken. The Ministry of Interior sent a decision to the Port Authority asking it to strictly implement the Passport Regulation for foreign nationals arriving to the Ottoman Empire, with the aim of preventing their entry. The Port Authority of Istanbul prepared a written statement with certain recommendations, including the setting up of a commission to implement the Passport Regulation. The Council of State approved these recommendations. The first of them was the warning to port officials to strictly implement the Passport Regulation. The state saw the activities of boat captains who obstructed this implementation as a major concern. In particular, attention was to be paid not to allow the entrance of people of unknown circumstances and professions, especially socialists who were "against the interests of whole of society and against the records of public law [hey'et-i ictimaiye aleyhinde ve kuyud-u kavânin-i umumiye hilafında]."[156]

The Council of State prepared a proposal to carry out investigations into people arriving at the Port of Istanbul by boat or by steamship.[157] For individuals coming by steamship and then attempting to leave on small crafts, investigations of those steering the latter were to be made.

Administrative processes regarding such individuals were transferred from the Municipality of Istanbul (Şehremaneti) to the port leadership. A Commission of Inspection and Supervision (Teftiş ve Nezaret Komisyonu) had to be established, with representation from the police, municipality, and the port. No one could be let off a ship without carrying out the necessary procedures, and a passengers' waiting room (*misafir dairesi*) had to be established for the passengers to wait in during the passport checks and administrative investigation. Passengers who set out for Istanbul by small craft were to be brought to either the Istanbul or the Galata customs office, where passport officers would carry out the necessary procedures. All manner of sea transport, in particular craft carrying articles of trade, were administratively within the municipality's purview, but dealings related to sea transport were carried out according to naval regulations. The written statement recommended that these duties be transferred to the port department tied to the Naval Ministry (Bahriye Nezareti). Small-craft operators who carried passengers who had not shown their passports to officials were to be penalized. Everyone wishing to enter or leave the country was required to hold a passport.

In another proposed regulation regarding passport controls, foreigners were required to obtain visas from both their own consulates and from Ottoman representatives in their countries. Those coming by land had to present their passports to officials at checkpoints, while those arriving by sea had to present them at the port. Anyone entering the country had to go in person to the port office (*liman dairesi*), an administrative unit under port authorities, in Kurşunlu Mahzen within twenty-four hours and present themselves to an officer on duty. If their intent was to resettle, they then had to go to the representative of their country for a residence record and inform the Ottoman government. A single document was to be prepared for every male person older than ten who entered the Ottoman Empire. If sailors or passengers who were registered as sailors in special books intended to stay on land, they had to go in person to the port chamber with a document showing that their names had been removed from the said books and had to register at that office. Those who first arrived in Istanbul and intended to travel within Ottoman territory had to obtain a special internal passport from the port chamber at Kurşunlu Mahzen. If they entered the Ottoman Empire from another port and wished to travel elsewhere within it, this document was to be obtained from an official stationed in their first place of arrival.

Their internal passports included a written description of their appearance and identity information and were endorsed by the consulates of their resident countries. Boat and steamship captains were tasked with carrying out passport and visa controls for all passengers, specifically with collecting and having a control officer check passport numbers and then returning them to the passengers. If one of the passengers did not have a passport, or if their passport did not meet requirements, the port chamber or an official on duty was to be notified. Such individuals without a passport or with an irregular passport had to personally obtain a surety bond issued by a representative of their country. If a passenger was unable to provide a reasonable explanation for their lack of documentation and could not obtain a surety bond from a state representative, they were to be deported. Passengers were required to provide the address of where they intended to go or to list a guarantor.[158] In another Council of State decision, again to prevent Italian socialists without passports from coming to the Ottoman Empire, it was decided to apply the Passport Regulation.[159]

At a later date, a notification sent from the consulate at Constanta in Romania to the Ottoman Ministry of Foreign Affairs stated that a number of "Armenians whose conditions were perpetually in doubt [ahvâlleri daima iştibah bazı Ermeniler]" intended to enter Istanbul without a passport and a visa. For this reason, the Ottoman government decided that boats coming from Romania were to be carefully inspected.[160]

A telegram sent from the high chief of the Port of Istanbul to various port authorities announced a prohibition on postal ships approaching the port after the evening call to prayer. However, according to later correspondence between authorities, it was decided to act according to the ships' "situation" in their approach to the ports during the evening. This qualification in practice created various ambiguities and was later withdrawn through a subsequent telegram. However, it is notable that the decision was made through the exchange of telegrams. Yet because different officers in different docks used different practices, consulates requested that a standard practice be introduced.[161]

Ship captains and small-craft operators (boatmen) who allowed their passengers to disembark outside places specified by the government as official ports faced the consequences laid out in Article 18 of the Passport Regulation of 1884. Another article in that regulation concerned operators of small crafts who picked up people in places other than official ports and bore them furtively to Russia. The Office of Reforms of the Council of State (Şûrâ-yı Devlet Tanzimat Dairesi) decided on these unregistered travels and the responsibility of the captains and small craft operators, too, would be processed according to Article 18 of the Passport Regulation.[162] When intelligence was received of a person working on a ship going between Varna and Istanbul—whom the Bulgarian Commissariat described as dark and tall, with a long dark mustache and no beard and as being intent on malice and sedition (*melanet ve mefsedet*)—the police were entirely responsible for dealing with him.[163] In another incident, when the Italian captain of a steamship bound for Drac, Angelo Piccapelo, presented to the authorities not an international passport but an internal passport, the situation was evaluated according to Article 12 of the Passport Regulation, and the necessary legal measures were carried out.[164]

In all such incidents, the law was formulated anew within the framework constructed by the administrative network and came to include more detailed regulations. Yet every time new rules were introduced, strategies such as smuggling, forgery, and bribery popped up to bypass them. The common people widely used such tactics to go around the regulations: they were strategies for staying alive, for keeping one's life going. Although it was not easy to access smuggling networks or pay bribes, the lack of better infrastructure in the Ottoman administration created a space for unregistered travel.

Problems in Administering Passports

Illegally Issued Passports and Forged Documents

From the state's perspective, one of the biggest problems in passport practices was illegally issued or forged passports. However strictly the state attempted to administer passports or safe-conduct procedures, it always met with circumstances that it could not forestall. For instance, it had been determined that passports had been issued to individuals of the vagrant (*serseri*) class who were moving around Romania, Bulgaria, and Serbia and wished to incite revolt in the Ottoman Empire. According to an intelligence report, the Ministry of Foreign Affairs and the Bulgarian Commissariat were warned and requested to take precautions.[165]

A document explained that two of five Armenians plotting attacks against Muslims had set out for Russia and had been apprehended. Iranian officials had issued passports to these "vagrants and fugitives of unknown identity." To prevent such cases, the Ottoman consulate in Tehran tightened the passport regulations in Iran, much as it had done before. It requested that for a passport to be issued in Iran, an *ilmühaber* from local authorities had to be submitted (as in the Ottoman Empire); moreover, a rule that Iranian passports could not be issued to foreigners who did not pay taxes to Iran had to be strictly enforced.[166] The Ottoman government requested that neighboring states implement similar security techniques in relation to unwanted border crossings. After all, if a control system related to passports were applied in only one country, it lost meaning.

When some Ottoman-subject Armenians in the provinces of Erzurum, Bitlis, and Van obtained Iranian passports in Russia and traveled in the Caucasus,[167] they requested visa endorsements from the Iranian consulate with the aim of coming to Istanbul using the Iranian passports. The Iranian government did not initiate any administrative investigation into the passport applications, and the authorities issued Iranian passports to these Ottoman subjects even if the Iranian passports should not have been issued to people who were not Iranian taxpayers. The Ottoman government thus identified these passports as forged passports. Yet a number of the forged passports, presented to the consulate through a middleman, were not endorsed. Based on this instance, the head consulate at Batumi was informed that officials were to proceed with caution regarding Armenians coming to the Ottoman Empire with Iranian passports. It was recommended to the Tehran consulate chargé d'affaires that Iranian officials not issue passports to such individuals. The Ministry of Foreign Affairs asked that the Iranian government instruct its officials in Russia, particularly at its head consulate in Tbilisi, but noted that officials driven to gain more income through the issuance of passports would probably not conform to the recommendation and would need to be supervised.[168] Controlling geographical mobility was possible only by developing similar rules and practices within a system of states.

The sale of forged passports was a lucrative black market within the Ottoman Empire. Ottoman subjects were caught in Yalta using forged passports. They were brought to the consulate at Sivastopol and found to have purchased three such passports from a forger for twenty-one kuruş and traveled with them from Rize to Yalta. It emerged that passport officers on the Black Sea coast of Trabzon were not sufficiently attentive during controls. They were warned, and an example of a forged passport was sent to the Ministry of Foreign Affairs.[169]

Another investigation revealed that members of the Bulgarian Committee had purchased forged passports, so it was decided that security investigations carried out when issuing passports would be intensified. The lieutenant governors of Manastır, Kosova, Debre, and İpek were notified by telegraph of the decision that they were not to issue internal passports to persons of unknown circumstances and to arrest people found to be suspicious.[170]

When some people wishing to disembark at the docks of Chios claimed, using forged passports, to be Greek subjects, though they were in fact Ottoman subjects, police and port authorities applied to the population registry to inquire into them. After their passports were stamped and noted as having been thoroughly inspected and found to be without problems, they were allowed to pass through the docks. After meetings with embassies, it was decided that, per the Passport Regulation, when a foreign subject passed to a foreign territory, their passport would be endorsed with a visa by the local government of the Ottoman province they were leaving from. This regulation would come into effect immediately.[171]

Another form of deception related to passports did not concern the use of a forged passport but the pretense of not having an international passport and so needing one to be issued to them. In one case, a large number of people, men and women, had applied to consulates to receive international passports, claiming that their documents had been lost.

Most presented an Ottoman identity document (*tezkere-i Osmaniyye*) to confirm their identities; some presented internal passports. On their internal passports were listed the places they intended to go: Ioanninia, Thessaloniki, and Izmir (Smyrna). It was determined that these people had concealed their original international passports because they really intended to go abroad on Georgian Company ships headed to Thessaloniki, which were carrying the passengers without checking their permits for international travel. Because those going from Istanbul to Greece were well aware of this route, police began checking the travel documents of passengers on these ships as they passed through Thessaloniki.[172]

Measures were taken to check whether passports and internal passports drawn up for Ottoman subjects in fact belonged to their holders. They included checking the personal description given on the document. A document presented to the Council of State by the Ministry of Foreign Affairs pointed out that people could resemble one another and that some made use of this fact to pass on an internal passport issued in their own name to someone else who resembled them. To prevent such mischievous people (*eşhâs-ı muzırra*) from entering and moving about in Ottoman lands on a forged internal passport, the Council of State deemed that the heights of applicants for passports or passage documents also be noted because, as correspondence between the Bulgarian Commissariat and the Ministry of Foreign Affairs pointed out, people may have similar features, skin tone, and body shape but different heights. These details were to be checked again at their destination.[173]

Information was received that some Armenians had registered their Ottoman passports to go abroad but given these passports to "certain revolutionaries [birtakım ihtilalcilere]." The Armenians had sent their passports from Russia to Van. A note on this subject was sent to the consulates of Vidin, Ruse (Rusçuk), and Varna and to the undersecretary in Plovdiv (Filibe), stating that the passports they already held were to be registered, and new passports were not to be issued to them. A note also stated that the Ministry of Foreign Affairs had sent the necessary orders to all consulates. According to a telegram from the Ruse consulate, certain unemployed Armenians had requested passports to go to Russia, and the Varna consulate had issued passports to "these sorts [bu gibiler]." The

Ruse consulate asked the central government whether passports had been issued. Because there was no doubt that Armenians wishing to go to Russia would pass through Anatolia, the response stated that the consulate should not issue passports to Armenians because doing so was not legal.[174]

Another problem for the Ottoman government related to people who traveled without passports. It was determined that individuals who came from Serbia into Ottoman lands were often poor, and so they crossed the border without obtaining passports.[175] These people most likely were laborers who got by on day labor. The same was true of laborers without passports headed to Tbilisi by road from Ottoman lands, particularly from Bitlis. The minister of foreign affairs wrote to the Ministry of Interior on January 16, 1893, that the province of Bitlis had been instructed to do what was necessary in this situation. A written response from Bitlis dated May 22, 1893, stated that while such crossings had occurred the previous year due to a drought, in the current year (1893) no one had gone to Tbilisi without a passport. That year, twenty-eight people had been granted passports. The minister of foreign affairs noted that based on information received from the head consulate of Tbilisi, twenty-seven people had gone from Bitlis to Tbilisi without documents, fifty-three with only identity documents (*hamidiye tezkeresi*), and thirty-nine with internal passports. These people had applied to the head consulate at Tbilisi for *ilmühaber*s to prove their identity because the Russian state had put the burden of proving identity and residence on foreigners as they entered the country. These "ignorant subjects [cühela-yı tebaa]" from the Ottoman Empire had applied to the head consulate in Tbilisi with a few "empty words [kıyl ü kal]." According to the Ottoman government, although it was clear that such people acted in violation of the Passport Regulation, it was also clear that they were in a quite difficult situation. To protect those traveling from Erzurum, Trabzon, Van, and Bitlis to the Russian provinces of Kafkasya, Kuban, Don, and Harkof from experiencing hardship, they were to be registered at Ottoman docks and borders as necessary, and a requirement would be introduced that such individuals had to obtain passports.[176]

Another example of the use of other documents to avoid having to obtain a passport involves laborers going to Romania. Local officials checked the passports carried by laborers returning from Romania to their homelands. These individuals were also required to obtain internal passports, but while they were en route to Romania, they were issued international passports rather than internal passports. Indeed, the Romanian police arrested those who wished to enter to any Romanian city with internal passports only. Such arrests led to complaints to the Ottoman consulate. Laborers preferred to receive internal passports from their own country rather than passports from the Ottoman consulate because this saved them money. Whereas, according to the regulation, Ottoman subjects who left the empire were required to obtain a passport and could use it for a year to come and go with the appropriate visa endorsements, subjects traveling within Ottoman borders were required to hold internal passports. Yet because the latter were not accepted in lieu of passports in foreign countries, they were required to carry passports when abroad, just as they were required to carry internal passports for travel within the Ottoman Empire.[177]

These incidents suggest that the lower classes often preferred not to obtain passports owing to the cost and tried to use other documents in their place. However, problems emerged from the international nature of the passport system. Even if the nineteenth century is often discussed as a period in which there was greater freedom in the use and control of passports, when it came to geopolitics, strict rules and controls took the place of freedom, especially for the lower classes.

Checkpoints and Passport Controls

Another problem had to do with certain malpractices in passport controls at the border. For instance, it was determined that the consulate at Bayezıd did not implement passport regulations for Iranians. Iranians crossing the border with passports lacking visas or without paying a fine was a problem.[178] Similarly, Russian "nihilists"—who were in fact barred from entering the Ottoman Empire—took advantage of the fact that passport officers at the border did not know Russian. It was decided that the necessary precautions were to be taken at the border gates, certain gates between Erzurum and Kars were to be closed, and officials who knew Russian would be sent to the border.[179]

Fields of Sovereignty

Passport regulations and practices also show the limits of the state's fields of sovereignty. In the process of constituting the modern centralized state, the crystallization of borders between states and the ability to penetrate a population within those borders grew into central problems. As frontiers began to give way to borders in this period, for the Ottoman state this process took shape through territorial losses. For example, a dispute emerged between Bulgaria and the Ottoman government related to the use of passports and internal passports in Eastern Rumelia, which further demonstrated just how important travel documents were in relation to the state's field of sovereignty.

In 1885, Eastern Rumelia was annexed by Bulgaria but remained de jure under Ottoman rule until 1908. Prior to the annexation, there were diplomatic conflicts in different areas between the Ottoman Empire and the Bulgarian Principality, including passports and internal passports. The Ottoman government drew up internal passports for people going to Eastern Rumelia, but Bulgaria did not recognize these documents.[180] In addition, the Bulgarian government stipulated that all documents prepared by the Ottoman state be authorized by the secretary of affairs of the Office of the Law of Composite at the Ministry of Foreign Affairs. The Ottoman government also stated that it held the authority within its borders to draw up and authorize documents and issue rulings about them and that these were matters of domestic law: the authority to specify how documents and vouchers were to be prepared in the Ottoman Empire did not belong to the Principality of Bulgaria. Under the Treaty of Berlin, which had established the autonomous Bulgarian Principality under Ottoman suzerainty, the Bulgarian request that the documents in question be drawn up by the Ministry of Foreign Affairs was not valid, but it was valid for these documents to be processed by the Notary of Istanbul (Dersaadet Noterliği) or the Authority of Contracts (Mukavelat Muharrirliği) and by the Ministry of Justice. The principality had already given up on its request that procedures of authorization be carried out by the secretary of affairs of the Office of the Law of Composite at the Ministry of Foreign Affairs, but the Ottoman government considered it more appropriate to follow the same procedures it used in Egypt and Tunisia, where documents were authorized by the vizier's private secretary after being sealed by the Ministry of Justice. Nevertheless, the Bulgarian government did not end its refusal to recognize Ottoman internal passports. According to the Ottoman state, responsibility in this matter—which had by now escalated into the subject of debate—lay with Bulgarian officials. They, in turn, simply did not accept Ottoman internal passports designed specifically (in order to ensure the continuation of the status quo) for foreigners headed to Bulgaria. Instead, they endorsed visas for the passports that foreigners carried with them. For the empire, this approach was equivalent to an assault on Ottoman law and the empire's field of authority.

According to the Ottoman Advisory Council's (İstişare Odası) legal opinion (mütaalaname),[181] Bulgaria avoided approving passports prepared by Ottoman officials for foreigners traveling to Bulgaria, as it had with documents and bills prepared in Istanbul or elsewhere in the empire and presented to the principality, if they had not been authorized by the legal secretary of the Ministry of Foreign Affairs. The Commissariat of Sofia had requested a meeting on this matter with the Legal Council of the Sublime Porte (Bab-ı Ali Hukuk Müşavirliği). In response, the Ottoman state explained the authorization of documents in official correspondence, which stressed that the Ottoman state's domestic law applied in this matter. On the matter of safe-conduct passes, travel from the Ottoman Empire to Bulgaria was considered as travel within Ottoman borders, and the legal measures that the empire saw as necessary were applied to foreign and Ottoman subjects alike. It was underscored that no complaints had been received on this matter.[182]

According to a note, the Bulgarian Principality had canceled the Ottoman internal passports of the Greek subjects Yanni and Atnabin (?), after which their Greek passports were endorsed with Bulgarian visas by the Bulgarian authorities. This drew complaints from the Ottoman consulate in Bulgaria. In response to verbal warnings from the Ottoman Ministry of Foreign Affairs and written ones from the Ministry of Interior, the Bulgarian government stated that it had no objection to Ottoman passage documents in both Turkish and French for foreigners traveling from the Ottoman Empire to Bulgaria. Yet if it were made optional for these documents to be authorized by the Bulgarian Principality, many people would obtain their passports fraudulently and claim that they were Greek subjects, with their foreign identification deemed authorized by the Royal Mint (Devlet-i Matbua) once they gained an Ottoman passage document. It was stated that this could be prevented by not issuing passage documents to those residing in Greece; these documents would be of use only in travel on passports with visas from the Bulgarian Principality. This answer showed the strategy of diplomatic diversion used by the Bulgarian Principality.[183]

Because there was no Ottoman notification (*tebligat*) in the communications on issuing the travel documents beyond the usual practice, the Ottoman Commissariat requested other documents from the Principality of Bulgaria as an explanation of the basis of the exceptions in following the usual procedure. It was noted that those who went from the Ottoman Empire to Bulgaria encountered difficulties. Those traveling from Istanbul to Bulgaria were subjected to a ten-franc toll. However, the passports of those who passed through Bulgaria and then returned there were seized, and they had no choice but to purchase a Bulgarian passport at the cost of five francs.[184] This practice was carried out only for Ottoman subjects. This file was important in terms of demonstrating how passport practices and the rules related to them were used in political power struggles.

Passports were in such incidents an important apparatus for tracing the field of state sovereignty. The geographical limits of the administrative power employed by the state were also shaped through such practices. Internal passports and passports were multifunctional documents. How these documents were used and the limitations to their fields of usage also point to the limitations in the modern state's capacity.

Conclusion

This chapter has analyzed Ottoman passport practices as part of the empire's security policies in the Hamidian Era. The Ottoman government's threat perceptions deeply affected how it sought to control interimperial geographical mobility. This chapter has aimed to explore how broad political issues became part of the everyday administration of geographical mobility. Analyzing the administration of passports at the micro level allows us to discuss the infrastructural and administrative power in which the state's organizational capacity was visible. Filing, encoding, and storing information on people and thus expanding administrative power were characteristic of Ottoman passport practices. Moreover, the administrative network—which included laws, bureaucratic offices from ministry offices to provincial port administration offices, legal regulations, orders, correspondence between offices, ad hoc commissions, local and traditional chains of social control, stamps on documents, and even freelance photographers—shows us the limits of this expansion (or of the state's capacity), the patterns of governing through the passports, and the ambiguity of the administrative actions. This ambiguity was created through multiple decrees, orders, and even ad hoc decisions. The ambiguous structure of administrative actions became the main characteristic of how passport laws were executed. Communication between different bureaus also benefited from this ambiguity, such as through the use of unstandardized signs or phrases (marking passports with an F or noting that the holder was "henceforth not to return to the Ottoman Empire").

The administration of passports also demonstrates the use of new technologies for surveillance. The Ottoman Empire was one of the few states that used photographs attached to passports to verify identity and for filing purposes in the late nineteenth century. The literature has discussed the expansion of the Ottoman police state during the Hamidian Era mostly by referring to censorship and political limitations in the public sphere, but the use of photography for policing also demonstrates the link among a security mentality, politics, and biopower in the late Ottoman Empire. This link adds a new layer to the discussion on labeling practices as symbolic violence toward marginalized groups, which was developed in synchronization with physical violence.

Physical frontiers, state sovereignty, and the legal belonging of citizens were important signifiers for passports; however, passport practices were also about legal orders meant to implement the law, but with lots of exceptions based mainly on ad hoc administrative decisions.

Conclusion

The periodization of the nineteenth century involves a wider field of meaning than simply explaining what happened during the historical interval between 1800 and 1900. The long nineteenth century, which covers (to follow Eric Hobsbawm) the years from 1789 to 1914, profoundly shaped our contemporary world through the revolutions and ideologies that emerged as a result of the transformations brought about by liberal capitalism, which came to dominate the entire world, and as a result of new social demands. Through this long nineteenth century, certain long-lasting institutional and functional transformations, which amounted to the state governmental apparatuses, became crystallized, leading to the emergence of today's modern state. The new techniques that emerged from these changes shifted the meaning of government to an entirely different plane. The state expanded and intensified its field of function and was transformed into a structure that held detailed information about the population within its borders. It was capable of infusing this population and in this way of establishing its power from within society. The transformation of the state took shape through differences as much as similarities across geographical contexts. In the Ottoman Empire, the last quarter of the nineteenth century can be interpreted within such a framework.

For the Ottoman Empire, the transformation that some writers source to the era of Selim III (r. 1789–1807) and others to the Tanzimat Edict (1839) is often read within the framework of modernization or westernization. This study has attempted to interpret modern state policies and related Ottoman state practices across the Hamidian Era. Rather than see these administrative transformations solely as progressivist modernization reforms, it has tried to understand the social and political bases of these transformations. In the consideration of the policies and practices that emerged in this way, making sense of the strategies of governance can also be said to be equivalent to making sense of the transformation of both the state's mentality and its governance.

Policies and practices related to the population in the Hamidian Era offer useful examples for us to make sense of this transformation. Following the Russo-Ottoman War of 1877–78, important demographic transformations occurred within the Ottoman Empire. According to Kemal Karpat, 1,015,015 Muslims migrated to the Ottoman Empire from Crimea, the Caucasus, and the Balkans during the nineteen years between 1877 and 1896.[1] By 1908, this figure had grown to 5 million. Following the Treaty of Berlin of 1878, the Ottoman state also lost, in addition to territory, some 4.5 million people, most of them Christians living in the lost territories. In such a situation, the central government's primary focus was on obtaining information about its human and natural resources. The settlement of Muslim migrants increased the proportion of Muslims in Anatolia. Islam was used as a melting pot of sorts to assimilate migrants to the political, economic, social, cultural, and geographical locales to which they came. The state was compelled to develop new techniques to control the new population structures emerging from such upending mobility. One would not be wrong to draw a direct connection between the state's administrative needs and its attempts to employ pan-Islamism.

On this point, the beginning of state attempts to collect statistical data is of considerable significance. In particular, the start of efforts to gather more detailed population statistics points to long-term change in the techniques of government. Following its territorial losses, the empire nevertheless remained geographically expansive and, in terms of population, remarkably heterogeneous. In this situation, the desire was to constitute strategies of government in accordance with information accessed about the population in the territories over which it ruled. In particular, one can say that there was an attempt to make use of information collected through new and old techniques of surveillance, not as a way to learn the proclivities of the people but as a way to steer or control them. Now, a more important matter than ruling the population within the empire's borders through traditional administrative apparatuses was to govern and administer the population.

Before the Hamidian Era, such structures as the Ministry of the Superintendent of Guilds and Markets, the institution of headmen of villages/neighborhoods (*muhtars*), and the Ministry of Census were established to administer population affairs, while census bureaus were set up in provincial centers to monitor the population and collect information about it. It is no coincidence that the Passport Regulations of 1884 and 1894, which governed internal travel, and the Passport Bureau Regulation (Pasaport Odası Nizamnamesi) of 1867, which governed international travel, were penned during the same period. Through the new Population Registration Regulation of 1878, which took effect following the renewal of such regulations in the Hamidian Era, the rules related to identity certificates (*nüfus tezkeresis*) grew even harsher. Information about people in the population registry grew more detailed. To be able to use such new technologies, new administrative units were established. Attempts were made to *penetrate society* through health and welfare policies, and reports were written about the population. In this way, the state, as an administrative apparatus, was "governmentalized." The first step taken to ensure the governmentalization of the state was to render society legible. The state took actions with the intent of possessing a detailed map of its subjects. A complex and inscrutable sociality, once rendered legible for the state, was standardized and rationalized for administration. The state, in a manner fitting such an aim, put into place new techniques of observation and developed policies according to the data it held.

In a second step, state subjects were expected to act according to certain codes of behavior. To this end, in the Hamidian Era violent interventions were developed based on distinguishing between the acceptable and the unacceptable, not so much to penetrate the people's behaviors as part of a governmental project but to delimit them. The basic reason for making these interventions was the problem of legitimacy, pointing to a crisis in hegemony. According to state elites, the crisis situation demonstrated that the state's security and survival were in danger. State elites decided that the state needed new mechanisms to ensure social control and new strategies related to the repressive apparatus until the hegemony of a new politics of legitimacy could be established. They introduced definitions of legitimate threat through an analysis of state interests and implemented strategies based on these definitions. In other words, they rebuilt the social order: the state had the opportunity to design that order as it wished because of the crisis situation.

With the Armenian revolutionary movement and nationalist struggles in the Balkans, the concept of sedition (*fesad*) came to dominate state discourses of security. As a result of modernization reforms and socio-economic transformations in major port cities such as Istanbul, the traditional strategies of government were no longer functional. Because the Ottoman state's capacity to directly penetrate its subjects was weak, such modernization amounted to the insolvency of power. And it is precisely because of this insolvency that administrative regulations and practices on security matters became so strict. The Hamidian Era was thus characterized by the struggles of a state elite facing an empire-wide crisis in legitimacy and seeking to regain that legitimacy through both consent and force. Abdülhamid II dismissed Parliament after the Russo-Ottoman War, and the Ottoman government continuously suppressed demands for political representation during his reign. While the government blocked legal channels for politics, violence directed at the Armenian community became a way of punishing demands for reform in the Eastern Provinces. The genocide of 1915 should be considered in light of the normalization of violence toward the Armenian community during the Hamidian Era.

We encounter here the Janus-faced nature of the search for legitimacy, which can be considered symbolic yet also relied on repressive policies—such as the security-related measures—that could be deployed at a moment's notice. Seasonal migrant laborers, whom the literature generally takes up within the context of public order, had since the era of Selim III been considered in terms of both public order and security. This trend continued in the Hamidian Era. Yet the beginning of the use of violent anarchist methods by the Armenian revolutionary movement and by Bulgarian nationalists, particularly after the 1890s, was among the reasons for the introduction of stricter controls on migrant laborers. Of crucial historical importance for the perception of threat among Ottoman state elites and for the security policies that took shape along these lines were the Bab-ı Ali Demonstration in Istanbul in 1895; the Kumkapı Demonstration in 1890; the Ottoman Bank raid in 1896, the bombing of the Ottoman Bank in Thessaloniki in 1903, and other bombings in urban spaces; railway sabotages; assassination attempts targeting police officers; and, finally, the failed assassination attempt on Abdülhamid II himself in 1905. But the reasons for these actions were never questioned. For the Ottoman government, the significant question was *who* threw the stone, not *why* the stone was thrown.

This situation brought about the Ottoman Empire's implementation of antianarchist practices that had come into their own in Europe. To make sense of this period, it is also important to consider, in addition to such measures, the ways in which state elites, acting in international concert, defined anarchists and anarchist activities. Following contemporary developments in Europe, the Ottoman state not only increased its precautions through such actions but also introduced new practices, particularly toward migrant laborers in Istanbul. Though it is unclear whether such practices were developed for any specific subject, it is clear that when they were applied to Armenians, the police kept records on such applications. In addition, massacres triggered the mass emigration of Armenians from Eastern Anatolia to foreign lands, and most of these native Anatolians could not get permission to reenter the Ottoman Empire later.

All these developments underscore the extent to which the state saw Armenians—in particular lower-class Armenians—as potential threats. To be sure, though, such measures were not limited to Armenians. The same security inquiries were carried out on Bulgarian nationalists and foreign laborers working in various locales throughout the empire. The security understanding of the period certainly contained class distinctions. Yet it would also be incorrect to claim that this connection was particular to the Ottoman Empire. One should not forget that in European governments, such as those of Germany, France, and Austro-Hungary, links were being established among vagrancy, anarchism, and seasonal laborers. We encounter a similar link at the discursive level in the Ottoman government's administrative correspondence. The constructed transitivity among the seditious person (*fesad*), the vagrant, and the anarchist helped to shape administrative practices around a series of stigmatizations.

When united with administrative practices, the discursive space that state elites established along the lines of raison d'état created broad room for them to maneuver. This expansion ironically both delimited the borders of the political and, through the construction of new forms of marginality, excluded certain elements, even giving way to symbolic violence. It also reformulated administrative practices according to different elements.

All foreign nationals arriving in the empire were also seen as potential threats. In addition to passport and customs controls, high-level security practices, such as the tracking of individuals and searches of hotel rooms after occupants had departed, became ordinary practices for European visitors in Istanbul, if not in every part of the empire.[2] The state's efforts in this arena can be interpreted as a reflection of its perceived stature within the international arena. This period—in which the "Eastern Question" was still very much current and the empire strove to have a place among the Great Powers—may give us some idea of the dimensions of insecurity.

By this period, the techniques of surveillance had been developed only to a limited degree. At the same time, one should not overlook the fact that priority was given to policing practices, which were conducted so as to avoid creating a rupture between subjects and the existing or imagined social order (as imagined, that is, by the central government) and to prevent subjects from opposing the social order. Thus, one can speak of a transformation in the techniques of government. Yet one should not overlook the fact that this transformation was rather limited, such that even with the political will for such aims, the state did not yet possess sufficient apparatus to implement them. The limits to *infrastructural power* demonstrate that in most regions across the empire forms of *indirect rule* still operated.

The last quarter of the nineteenth century was also a period of great human geographical mobility. Many academic works look into the reasons for this mobility, the routes people took, and the differences in types of geographical mobility. One exemplary instance through which the characteristics of this period have been explained is the historian Eric Hobsbawm's own family story, which he outlines in the introduction to *The Age of Empire* (1987), the third book in his trilogy on the nineteenth century.[3] At age nineteen, his mother went from Vienna to her uncle in

Trieste, who had established a chain of stores in Istanbul, Izmir (Smyrna), Aleppo, and Alexandria. His father hailed from a family that had migrated to London from Russian Poland, and he had settled in Egypt as a civil servant. The family adventure continued along a route linking Vienna, Berlin, and London. Such trajectories underscore how people were often able to change places for economic or political reasons (including war) and how normal this migration was considered at the time. Another example through which we can trace political and geographical mobility is the life of the Italian anarchist Errico Malatesta. Because of exile for his political views, his desire to publish his views, or his aim to support revolutionary actions, Malatesta moved across a broad geography between 1871 and 1921: Cairo, Geneva, London, Romania, Paris, Belgium, Buenos Aires, Spain, and Amsterdam. Following the assassination of King Umberto of Italy, when Malatesta tried to relocate to the Ottoman Empire, he was banned from entering the country and was not allowed to disembark from the ship on which he arrived.[4]

The last quarter of the nineteenth century in particular was for the Ottoman Empire a period of repeated attempts to control geographical mobility. Regulations at the time around internal passports, passports, and even hotels should be considered within this framework. The state attempted to render legible not only the movements within its own territories but also those out of and into its territories, employing modern techniques of observation and record keeping related to geographical mobility. Thanks to such records, it also rendered legible the people traveling with its own territories through standardized, detailed identification data. This aim should be considered alongside the state's efforts to regulate its own population. The premodern state possessed a limited degree of information about its own population, mostly to facilitate taxation. For the techniques of government it employed at the time and in terms of the foundations of its legitimacy, it had no need for more detailed and varied data. But the modern state's process of interpreting social dynamics and rationalization in the administrative sense brought about the standardization of society through subtle simplifications that separated society from its own complex world. Administrative power enveloped daily life like a web, which I conceptualize as an *administrative network.* Bureaucratic correspondence, offices, documents, photographs, bureaucrats themselves (from the higher ranks to lower ranks), and traditional social control mechanisms and their actors—all had their places in this wide administrative network. The Hamidian Era was part of a long process in developing the means of regulating, even enveloping, daily life. For example, in the state's controls on identity documents, passports, and internal passports (as in many other fields), its infrastructural power had yet to be fully established. These controls were still carried out through certain traditional mechanisms of social control. The problem of establishing infrastructural power made possible all sorts of discriminatory interventions, in the process rendering the state's population legible. While some of these interventions persisted—such as using gender to define identity—some were reformulated over the years and further detailed according to the perception of threat or in response to how state elites hoped to ensure the state's survival.

Passports have many functions for the state. In this study, the functions of passports have been considered through the conceptual lenses fashioned by Andreas Fahrmeir and Leo Lucassen. By examining passport regulations and practices in the Hamidian Era, this book has aimed to analyze the state's capacity for infrastructural power and its methods for rendering society legible. The richness of archival sources made this analysis possible. The documents accessed for this study show, through administrative correspondence, both the breadth and the limitations of the state's administrative apparatus. To control geographical mobility, the state was often not content only with passport controls; it also attempted to carry out crosschecks. For situations or people thought possibly to constitute a problem related to security, there was an attempt to administer passports and internal passports alongside the application of a system of suretyship. In the case of foreign workers, their records in the companies they worked for, their records in their current residences, and, indeed, their records in their own countries (obtained through consulates in those countries) and other places where they had lived were subjected to crosschecks. All of the correspondence on these records makes it possible for us to make sense of the structure and function of the administrative apparatus from the perspective of the sociology of the modern state.

Hotel regulations and practices, too, show a system of record keeping unique to the modern state. Forming the basis of this system of Ottoman records were, first, files that made known the locations, numbers, national status, and identification data of the owners of hotels and rented rooms across Istanbul; the owners of such public places as taverns, beer halls, and coffeehouses; and, finally, hospital administrations. Second, it involved recording the names of the local guarantors of residents of such places. If suspected individuals arrived at an inn or hotel, the owner was obliged to inform the police. Identification data and the travel routes of those staying in hotels were to be recorded in a file, and these files were subject to inspection. Such spaces were required to obtain licenses to operate, and the files containing data about who stayed at such places were to be inspected every twenty-four hours.[5]

Despite these practices, it was still difficult for the state to determine and track all those who entered the large, multiborder empire through clandestine means. As the techniques of control developed, so did methods for evading such controls: counterfeit passports, the use of different identities, entry through places aside from regular checkpoints (particularly for travel by sea), smuggling networks for migration, and even religious conversion made possible subaltern evasion of controls, particularly when combined with the inadequacies of the state's infrastructural apparatuses. The fact that subalterns had to search out such strategies gives some sense of the conflict-ridden nature of their daily life.

The strict passport regime implemented or attempted across the Hamidian Era as well as such security measures as the control of entries and exits in Istanbul in particular or the monitoring of suspected individuals can be interpreted as the results of a fear born of anarchist actions in Europe. For the Ottoman state of the Hamidian Era, the category of "internal enemy," in its modern sense, was constructed, and the limits of the political were shaped precisely through this basic reference.[6] In particular, security measures were put in place based on the effects of interimperial diplomacy and the Armenian revolutionary movement. They ensured a broad field of action for state security practices when citing internal threats. Interpreting the security understanding of this period solely in terms of Abdülhamid's personal characteristics runs the risk of rendering invisible the more complicated dynamics of the period.

For all the efforts made by contemporary state elites, however, technical and administrative inadequacies and insufficiently qualified personnel meant that it was not possible to fully control geographical mobility as desired. Nevertheless, this entire period should be considered one in which important administrative changes occurred in the legitimate control of geographical mobility by the modern state apparatus.

The state's attempt to control geographical mobility, acting particularly on the perception of threat, remains among the most important problems of state today. Following the attacks on the Twin Towers in New York City on September 11, 2001, a strengthened link was established among Islamophobia, Islam, and terrorism. The elaboration of passport and visa procedures in the United States, Great Britain, and the Schengen region as well as the development of new procedures for demonstrating identity after this point should be considered within the context of the relationship between geographical mobility and the perception of threat. Security practices for Muslim migrants, even when they are citizens of their state of residence, began to be differentiated from the practices applied to other groups. Thus, a link was established among migration, Islam, and terrorism at both the discursive level and the practical level. A new literature emerged related to how to prevent terrorism or how certain "elements" need to be controlled and monitored. Studies written around such a problematic have dated the beginning of international cooperation against anarchism to the Conference of Rome in 1898. New apparatuses or techniques such as fingerprints, retina scans, e-passports, and biometric photographs have over time come to be implemented at a global scale, similar to the globalization of record systems in the nineteenth century.

When we consider this process from the vantage point of contemporary Turkey, the picture changes. Of central importance to today's Turkish state is the Kurdish issue. For this reason, identity checks have been administered by the police since the 1990s; criminal record database technologies have been introduced; people are classified as suspect or not based on their place of birth, the place where their identities are registered,

or their names; Kurdish seasonal laborers have been stigmatized as terror-
ists wherever they go to work; Kurdish students are arrested on suspicion
of protests on university campuses: all these efforts define the Kurdish
issue in terms of the perception of threat. With the failed coup d'état in
Turkey on July 15, 2016, the label *enemies of the state* was applied more
widely, and passport cancellations, as an administrative act using national
police and Interpol databases, became easier, especially with the introduction of digital passports.

In the Hamidian Era and today, techniques developed in the attempt
to control geographical mobility and forms of delineating identity contain powerful data related to how the state defines its subjects and citizenship. Through such controls, categories seen as threats also show how the
state defines its desirable or ideal citizen. The picture that emerges is that
the state has continued to operate on a zero-sum game logic in aiming to
resolve political, social, and economic conflicts. Yet, rather than solving
conflict, this approach has brought about an increase in discriminatory
practices, the diversification and consolidation of forms of marginalization, and, ultimately, the growth of interventions based on brute violence.

Appendixes

Bibliographical Survey

Glossary

Notes

Bibliography

Index

Appendix 1

Protocol of Rome

Article 1 of the protocol document presented at the Conference of Rome stated that anarchism has nothing to do with politics and that in no way could one designate it as a political view. According to Article 2, every action that intends to destroy society through violent means is an anarchist action, and the people who carry out such acts are anarchists.

Article 3 lays out precautions to be taken (as summarized here):

3A. Every government is to keep under strict observation anarchists within its own territory.

3B. Every government is to establish a central administrative unit for this purpose.

3C. Every state is to share the information collected by this administrative unit that of other states.

3D. Anyone who had been deported as an anarchist is to be sent to the borders of their own country, so long as this is not against the laws of the country of deportation. If such a person is a citizen of a country not sharing a border with the deporting country, then he or she will have to be transferred, with each of the countries in between taking on transportation costs (presumably, those countries that see no problem with an anarchist staying there while in transit), and police officers will have to notify the police units of other states when an anarchist is transported.[1]

3E. If the foreigner to be sent has any ties, on account of past crimes, with court officers in their own country or in the countries they through, then agreement must be reached as to the results of the request for the transfer in a way that suits both the rules of treaties related to the restitution of criminals and the extant laws of the relevant states.

3F. To obtain information about the identity of anarchists, in line with recommendations by the police and public-safety chiefs of states participating in the conference, the method of *portrait parlé* is to be implemented.

Article 4 is made up of regulations related to the delivery and return of anarchists.

4A. In the event that an anarchist act constitutes a murder or a crime according to the laws of either the state requesting return or the returning state, then it should be subject to delivery and return.

4B. Under the same conditions, the rules of delivery and return will be applied to acts in future legal guarantees.[2]

4C. Anarchist acts are not to be interpretable as political crimes for the purposes of delivery and return.

4D. Assassinations organized against the life and liberty of a ruler or a head of government or against the life and liberties of members of the royal family should be excepted from the rules of delivery and return in all circumstances.[3]

Article 5 takes up new regulations and amendments that would need to be carried out in the laws of states participating in the conference.

5A. Aside from violent acts of an anarchist nature, punitive reforms must be made to prevent the following:

5A.1. The immediate preparation of such an act and in particular the production or storage of deadly or flammable devices, all manner of flammable materials, or materials used in conjunction with them, with the aim of carrying out an anarchist act or with the knowledge that they will be used in such a way.

5A.2. The existence of an attempt to set up a company, regardless of the number of partners, with the aim of carrying out or preparing the same sort of acts, as well as entering into an agreement or engaging with a company set up for such an aim.

5A.3. Whether through participation in the aforementioned companies or agreements or acting alone, soliciting and partially assisting anarchists by means of devices related to murder, means of communications, and the provision and preparation of a place of residence or gathering.

5A.4. Covert or overt instigation and encouragement of the carrying out of an act of violence of an anarchist nature, be it even through the praise of similar acts.

5A.5. The production and storage of all manner of explosive devices or materials to be used in the making of explosive devices, except for legitimate reasons.

5A.6. The encouragement among soldiers of disobedience related to rebellion (*fetretkerane*) as well as the printing and spread among soldiers of materials related to anarchism.

5B. The ratification in the laws of other countries of whatever is necessary to rattle those in league with anarchist acts.

5C. In the laws of other countries, the banning through criminal sentences of those acts mentioned elsewhere.

5C.1. The distribution, sale, display, and transfer of all manner of unprinted documents as well as booklets, newspapers, and similar printed documents, pictures, figures, and signs that are of an anarchist nature and that aid in the encouragement of a violent act.

5C.2. The printing and conveyance of legal proceedings related to an anarchist act, particularly the printing of a suspect's statement. (If nothing else, it is seen as appropriate that states possess the authority to legally ban such publications in the event that another decision is seen as posing a danger to peace and public order.)

5D. Examination by states as to whether it is appropriate to record to a degree the official reports published by newspapers related to anarchist acts.

5E. The approval in all countries of the following matters:

5E.1. The precautionary seizure of printed and unprinted documents and other materials whose distribution, sale, and display are forbidden.

5E.2. The implementation of solitary confinement for people deemed by the courts to require such treatment owing to anarchist actions.

5E.3. The granting of authority to judges, regarding people sentenced to punishments placed on all matter of anarchist crimes, along with murder and other crimes, to not allow such people to change their place of residence without informing administrative public officers and to call them to certain spaces (places of inspection).

5F. In the situation of assassination of a ruler, a head of government, or a member of the royal family, punishment by death is to be carried out in all countries.

5G. Those sentenced to death for anarchist murders are not to be executed in public.

5H. Whatever the reason for murders related to anarchism, they should be counted as anarchist acts, and those who dare to carry out such acts should be treated accordingly.

Appendix 2

The Ottoman Penal Code

Crimes against the State

Articles 48–54 of the Ottoman Penal Code (OPC) regulate crimes against the foreign security of the state, whereas Articles 55–62 relate to internal security. In 1899, the Ottoman Commission for the Response to the Rome Conference, in preparing an antianarchist act, referred in its proposals to Articles 55–62, 64, 66, and 136 of the OPC, which are summarized here.

Article 55 regulates punishments for those who incite rebellion against the sultanate, whether among Ottoman subjects or residents of the Ottoman Empire. If such acts result in a rebellion, the crime of incitement is punishable by death. Article 56 regulates punishments for inciting peoples of the Ottoman Empire to conflict with one another, looting in certain locales, acting to destroy the country, or carrying out murder. Article 57 notes, "If a group of bandits carry out or [are] a part of carrying out one of the crimes in Articles 55 and 56, then among the member of such bandits or banditry organizations, the heads and the centers of sedition are executed wherever they are taken into custody." These articles regulate that life sentences of hard labor are to be given to the remaining members, depending on their crimes and degrees of involvement. Article 58 lays out the punishments for involvement in forming a covert alliance made up of a number of people with the aim of carrying out one of the crimes mentioned in Articles 55 and 56, if the person has attempted to carry out certain actions and measures to prepare the causes for carrying out seditious acts (beyond speaking about such acts and deciding upon them), and if such acts have not yet reached the degree of factual occurrences. Punishments are also covered for circumstances in which only potential acts to be carried out were discussed within such an alliance or if there was discussion of establishing a covert alliance to carry out such acts. Article 59 covers punishments in the event that a civil servant, in the absence of a valid reason, takes command of a unit of soldiers, a military vessel, a castle, a

253

fortress, a port, or a city as well as what happens in the event that a civil servant, whoever they may be, does not obey the orders of the state to abandon military command and if commanders do not follow orders, in the absence of a valid reason, in granting permission for judicial process against soldiers in their retinue. Article 60 regulates punishment in the event that a soldier charged with the employment of the state's active-duty officials and police, whoever they may be, demands or orders actions against the military code or state order. Article 61 regulates punishment for acts that damage or destroy the state's ammunitions stockpile. Article 62 regulates the death penalty for those who seize or loot and raid the property and capital of the Ottoman Empire or its people. Moreover, those who act against the police forces or army fighting against such crimes and the leaders of or authorities in the bandit organizations formed in opposition to the Ottoman army are also sentenced to death. Members of such bandit organizations who do not have any authority are subjected to provisional hard labor if they are arrested in the places of seditious acts.

Article 64 concerns people in rebellious groups who are not in charge. Regarding their dispersal by government officials or the military, it stipulates that first-time offenders who conform to warnings and requests and who thus disperse or who are arrested, unarmed and without resistance, elsewhere than the scene of sedition will not be charged with sedition; moreover, if they have committed specific crimes, they will be punished based on these crimes and thus be subject to police monitoring.

According to Article 66, anyone who in places where people gather directly incites those people or residents to commit the crimes mentioned here, whether through speeches, posters, or publications, is to be punished in the same manner as those who commit the crimes; but if the incitements in question do not result in actions, they are to be punished by exile.

Article 136 concerns the punishment of those who commit destruction or damage of one or more telegraph lines during times of revolution or sedition and who in this manner interrupt communication.

Bibliographical Survey

One of the most controversial historical periods in Ottoman history is the reign of Abdülhamid II (1876–1908). Approaches to the period tend to fall into certain political-ideological polarizations. Although Abdülhamid II is seen as a great ruler from the perspective of political Islam, modernizationist writings often frame him in terms of the renunciation of westernization and modernization policies long thought to have begun with the Tanzimat reforms and in terms of Islamist reactionism. However, situating this period within the paradigm of modernization introduces a historical narrative dominated by orientalist discourse, conceptualized within the framework of the classic theses of modernization through Marx's "oriental despotism" or Weber's "patrimonial state." Historiography takes shape vis-à-vis the West in terms of what the West has and the Ottoman Empire does not—a state of deficiency or failure. As such, Ottoman history succumbs to an ambivalent reading of the "classical age": wounded by stagnation and fixity yet praised for a platonic state structure that worked wonders. This historiographical ambivalence reduces Ottoman history to the paradigm of stagnation and decline, attributed to such external factors as inflation and trade, and prevents a queering of history's totality that might otherwise allow for a glimpse of different points of rupture. At the same time, historical periods conceived through such labels as *decline* and *collapse*, taking an orientalist perspective that was shaped in the nineteenth century, are read as the reflection of a putative "Oriental" essence tied to Islam. Such a perspective further interprets the Ottoman classical period as an abnormality or exception and, labeling subsequent periods in terms of decline and collapse, analyzes the empire's final stretch as "inevitable" due to characteristics seen as tied to Islam. Because Islam was ideologically instrumentalized during the period of Abdülhamid II, this period is also approached as having halted or reversed innovations initiated during the Tanzimat period of reforms. Niyazi Berkes's commentaries on the reign of Abdülhamid II, part of his comprehensive work on secularism, may be offered as a base reference for scholarly analysis taking such a perspective.[1]

A turn in the historiography of the reign of Abdülhamid II, set in motion by the work of Stanford Shaw, situates Ottoman history within the paradigm of modernization, characterizing Abdülhamid II as the last monarch of the Tanzimat period.[2] Interpretations of the reign of Abdülhamid II in terms of administrative and political reforms became more common, with traces of this change seen in the work of Erik Jan Zürcher, who also draws strongly on the paradigm of modernization.[3] In addition, a number of studies examine such areas as education, railways, and the postal service in the same period. The shared characteristic of all these studies is an emphasis on the continuity of the modernization process, spanning from early Tanzimat initiatives into the republic. As such, the reign of Abdülhamid II is reframed as but one step in this process. Another important book on the period with this framework is François Georgeon's *Abdülhamid II* (2003), which cover a great many events in internal and foreign policy.[4] Through a detailed analysis of the period, Georgeon pursues a balanced account of the actors involved in foreign- and internal-policy events.

Chipping away at characterizations of this period in terms of Islamic reactionism, another significant part of the literature has taken shape in line with economic historiography. Even if the reign of Abdülhamid II has not been analyzed under a separate heading in economic historiography,[5] several works seeking to situate the Ottoman Empire within world history and with an eye to the long nineteenth century consider the period through the lens of the continuity thesis.[6] Engin Deniz Akarlı's doctoral dissertation (1979), following Şevket Pamuk's theses of dependence and growth, is a pioneering work on this subject.[7] Another groundbreaking study posing new questions and analyzing the period from the perspective of social history is Donald Quataert's collected volume *Osmanlı Devleti'nde Avrupa İktisadi Yayılımı ve Direniş (1881–1908)* (Social Disintegration and Popular Resistance in the Ottoman Empire, 1881–1908: Reactions to European Economic Penetration, 1987).[8] Quataert's articles in this book are also important in that each was a source of inspiration for master's theses, doctoral dissertations, and other books through the 2000s.[9]

Edward Said's critical work on orientalism[10] as well as variations of the modernization paradigm in the form of a range of critiques from within and without have also influenced how the history of the reign of Abdülhamid II has been written. Another important rupture here is, as Nadir Özbek emphasizes, a "consideration of the historical experiences of different geographies within a global temporality,"[11] set in motion by the works of Selim Deringil and Benjamin Fortna in the early 2000s.[12] Both writers explain the period's policies of legitimacy and education in terms of modern techniques of power employed more broadly by a range of states at the time. Deringil's works in particular draw on a broad conceptual array from Foucault to Habermas to analyze the discourses and actions of state elites in the administration of empire and to examine different facets of the imperial subject.

All of these works have made possible the formulation of new questions in the attempt to understand and interpret the administrative mindset of state elites during the Ottoman Empire. Particularly in line with recent debates on imperialism and colonialism, the works of Deringil, Ussama Makdisi, Christoph Herzog, Thomas Kühn, and Vangelis Kechriotis on the late Ottoman period are of undeniable importance to new debate on the Ottoman Empire.[13] In terms of the administration of empire, this debate started with Deringil's article "'They Live in a State of Nomadism and Savagery': The Late Ottoman Empire and the Post-colonial Debate" (2003) and Makdisi's book *The Culture of Sectarianism* (2000), which looks at the problem through the lens of internal colonization and expands this field of debate based on both Said's thesis of orientalism and Gramsci's concept of hegemony.[14] These studies point to a new tendency to explore the constitution and application of modern techniques of power and thus to expand the framework of investigation. Here, too, one must appreciate the significant contribution of critiques of the modernization paradigm over the past twenty years. This paradigm has grown more internally varied and, thanks to the reinvigoration of debates on a number of concepts specific to Western political culture, has benefited from the application of such concepts to Ottoman historical studies as well.

One of the most successful debates of this sort looks particularly at the concept of public space. Elizabeth Frierson's doctoral dissertation (1996) and a series of articles she penned within the same framework expand the concept's borders, through both geography and the introduction of a gender perspective. In addition, she shows that the concept's liberal democratic content is not subjective.[15] Another important source is Nadir Özbek, whose contributions have enabled a reinterpretation of this period through the concept of public space, situating the reign of Abdülhamid II within a framework emphasizing the mechanisms and practices of the social state.[16] In such studies, the prevailing internal conditions within the state's geography emerge as a critical determining factor.

In addition to these historiographical trends, one should not overlook a range of studies in Ottoman historiography—constituting a new field based largely on the nineteenth century—on policing, law, courts, prisons, and the gendarmerie, addressing a long-standing gap in work on such matters. The first studies on such matters were by retired public officials or workers in various security units related to these fields. However, these studies generally took up the development of security forces through the analysis of their institutions and through legal documents.[17]

For studies that, unlike the aforementioned work, carry out analyses based on sociology and political theory from a historical perspective, one can point to the doctoral work of Ferdan Ergut, later published as a book in Turkish.[18] This thesis brings the concepts of the sociology of the modern state, specifically in terms of debates on public safety, to bear on the reign of Abdülhamid II and the period up to the Republic of Turkey. Particularly through a detailed analysis of the Union and Progress period, Ergut's critical reading of the westernization thesis claims that the reign of Abdülhamid II has been approached almost exclusively in terms of police history and from the dominating perspective of the era's elites. For all its strengths, Ergut's analysis of the reign of Abdülhamid II is somewhat limited compared to his analysis of the Union and Progress period, probably because of the limited number and scope of studies on the former period at the time of Ergut's work at the turn of the twenty-first century. Nevertheless, Ergut's study paved the way for new debates and lines of inquiry into the history of policing and as such is pioneering. The sociology of the modern state presents a number of concepts that, in consideration of the historical period in question, facilitate our interpretation of the transformation of the state apparatus. The intellectual space opened by these concepts presents new possibilities for an analysis capable of interpreting changes to administrative institutions and practices in the Ottoman state in a way that does not get trapped in the impasses of the modernization paradigm.

The number of studies considering the Ottoman eighteenth and nineteenth centuries through Foucault's concepts of discipline, social control, and governmentality is steadily growing. These studies both show how public order and security have been constructed in other geographies beyond the West and expand the fields to which these concepts can be applied.[19] Two important collected volumes in this field, a relatively new field within Ottoman history writing, demonstrate how researchers have taken up the subject through different periods and theories: *Osmanlı'da Suç ve Ceza, 18.–20. Yüzyıllar* (Crime and Punishment in the Ottoman Empire: From the 18th to the 20th Century, 2007), and *Jandarma ve Polis: Fransız ve Osmanlı Tarihçiliğine Çapraz Bakışlar* (The Gendarmerie and the Police: Traverse Perspectives on French and Ottoman Historiography, 2009).[20] In these volumes, the contributions by Noémi Lévy in particular—who studies public order in the reign of Abdülhamid II—are important both for the period and for the history of policing. Lévy's research into the writing of history related to the concept of public order looks at the conjoining of the police (as an administrative apparatus) with local actors and within this context how the police, as among the most effective mechanisms of the modern administrative apparatuses of institutional social control, have worked with traditional mechanisms of social control.[21]

Security, public order, and the gendarmerie are still relatively new research themes. Looking beyond Istanbul to the provinces, Nadir Özbek attempts to make sense of social power struggles in terms of practices related to an administrative apparatus.[22] Also worth considering is Janet Klein's work. Analyzing the Hamidiye Light Cavalry, Klein perfectly shows how at the intersection of land problems, ethnic conflict, and local power relations, the state became involved in all such matters through forms of negotiation and power relations.[23]

In the historiography of the Hamidian Era, one of the most important discussions in the literature concerns the Armenian issue. The key event shaping this literature is the genocide of 1915, and various perspectives on this event have radically affected writing about the Armenian issue in Abdülhamid II's reign. Among these perspectives, Turkey's official historical thesis is essentially a denialist nationalist historical narrative. It denies the existence of the genocide and posits "Armenian uprisings" against the Ottoman state as the basic reason for the elimination of much of the Armenian presence in Anatolia. According to this perspective, the Armenian Revolutionary Federation provoked and misled the Armenian people and gave rise to Armenian uprisings against the state.

This nationalist literature, much of which was written after the 1980 military coup in Turkey, is devoted to proving the rebellious activities of Armenian revolutionaries and defines Armenians as disloyal internal enemies. There is thus, according to this thesis, a legitimate explanation for the violence directed toward Armenians, who, it asserts, had already shown themselves to be seditious. Works within this framework consequently refer to the massacres in 1894–96 as "Armenian rebellions."[24] This way of writing history—which selects a handful of historical events, ignores the rest, and does not situate violence in an analytical context—is devoted to the legitimization of state violence and can be characterized as the continuation within the academy of a state discourse of national security. While Bilal N. Şimşir, Stanford Shaw, and Justin McCarthy are among the best-known names to raise this scholarly issue with a nationalist view, in mainstream Ottoman studies silence has long prevailed on the massacres of 1894–96 and the genocide of 1915.

A second perspective, in contradistinction to denialist theses, has succeeded in creating a counterliterature on genocide. Chief among these works is Vahakn Dadrian's book *The History of the Armenian Genocide* (1995). Although this work has drawn criticism on account of its culturalist approach, which grounds the genocide in an "inherent resistance to change, rendering the specter of innovation threatening, and thus unacceptable to Muslim subjects," and in an "Ottoman culture of massacre," it is nonetheless important in terms of establishing a link between the genocide of 1915 and the massacres of the 1890s.[25] Raymond Kévorkian's detailed study is another pioneering work on the topic.[26] Taner Akçam's works also give the details of 1915, and in his recent volume, *Ermeni Soykırımının Kısa Bir Tarihi* (A Brief History of the Armenian Genocide, 2021), he uses a long-term perspective to discuss the Armenian Massacres in 1894–96 and the Armenian Genocide of 1915;[27] this perspective can also be seen in *The Thirty-Year Genocide* (2019) by Benny Morris and Dror Ze'evi.[28] However, the latter text is based mainly on culturalist arguments that mostly do not engage with recent debates on Armenian genocide.[29]

Changes in Ottoman studies in the past decade have contributed to the emergence of texts that make it possible to read the Armenian issue, alongside a separate genocide studies literature, as simply a part of the late Ottoman world. Deringil's work on conversion and self-orientalism, an edited volume on Diyarbakir prepared by Joost Jongerden and Jelle Verheij looking at the region's multiethnic structure from a spatial and socioeconomic perspective, and Sabri Ateş's work on the Ottoman border with Iran have linked historical sociology and historical anthropology to world history.[30] Another important book is Hans-Lukas Kieser's detailed study of the Eastern Provinces. In discussing the Armenian issue, it points to the sources of conflict between Armenians and Kurds and offers a useful framework for interpreting the central state's policies of entering into the Eastern Provinces in terms of local power relations and ethnoreligious disagreements.[31] The works of Edip Gölbaşi, Ali Sipahi, Owen Miller, Jelle Verheij, and Deborah Mayersen on the massacres in 1894–96 can be read as pioneering an important debate on the contexts of state and ethnoreligious violence.[32] Yaşar Tolga Cora's work on the social history of the Armenian community in the nineteenth century and Chris Gratian's recent book on the environmental transformation of the Ottoman countryside through migration and displacement in Çukurova (the region between Anatolia and Syria) open new areas of debate.[33]

İpek Yosmaoğlu's study of the Macedonian Question, violence, and ethnic conflict, *Blood Ties* (2014), takes a history-from-below approach and explores the process of constituting ethnic identities that match with territories by analyzing cartography, the educational system, statistics and censuses, and church rivalries.[34] Ramazan Hakkı Öztan's work on political violence and arms explores the tools of political violence during the Hamidian Era.[35]

Apart from these studies, one of the first works on passport regulations in relation to geographical mobility during this period was an article by Rona Aybay. This article approaches the Abdülhamid period as reactionary and autocratic and examines passport regulations largely within a legal framework.[36] Another of the first works to examine issues of security and public order alongside policies of controlling geographical mobility is Musa Çadırcı's article on prohibition of free passage (*men'-i mürur*) and passport regulations during the reign of Mahmud II (1785–1839).[37] Çadırcı reads the attempt to control geographical mobility in this period in terms of contemporary security problems. Florian Riedler and Christoph Herzog have taken up this matter more recently for the Hamidian Era in articles in the edited volume *The City in the Ottoman Empire: Migration and the Making of Urban Modernity* (2011),[38] building on a literature on migration. Herzog examines the reign of Abdülhamid II to explore passport regulations, looking primarily at the Union and Progress period. The relations among public order, security, forms of migration, and geographical mobility considered in another article by Riedler, "Public People: Seasonal Work Migrants in Nineteenth Century Istanbul," are important for making sense of this period. The author furthermore interprets all these matters alongside Armenian massacres at the time.[39] Will Hanley's book *Identifying with Nationality: Europeans, Ottomans, and Egyptians in Alexandria* (2017) offers insight into "nationality" as a legal concept between 1880 and 1914. Hanley analyzes a key issue in international private law as a category of legal affiliation and investigates this legal concept by setting the experience of ordinary people in the transimperial context.[40] Although his analysis is comprehensive, and the book has a part about identity papers that includes passports, his focus is on colonial legal history, and he does not analyze the migration policies in the political context of the Ottoman Empire.

David Gutman's book *Politics of Armenian Migration to America* (2019) focuses mainly on the migration of Armenians from the Kharput area in Eastern

Anatolia to the United States.[41] Nalan Turna's work on internal passports during the Hamidian Era is another important contribution to the field, especially on the controls of travels inside the empire.[42] Lale Can's work on pilgrims and the hajj also gives insights on travel practices and control of them during the late Ottoman period.[43]

Glossary

Armenian Patriarchate (Istanbul): One of two patriarchates of the Armenian Apostolic Church (the other is in Jerusalem), the Armenian Patriarchate of Istanbul was first established in 1461 in the aftermath of the Turkish conquest of Constantinople. Although it was originally responsible only for the city and its surrounding area, over the course of the seventeenth and eighteenth centuries it came to represent the entire Armenian Christian population and for a time even represented all non-Byzantine Christians within the Ottoman Empire. Following the Hamidian Armenian Massacres (1894–96), the Armenian patriarch was exiled to Jerusalem for condemning the violence and returned only following the Young Turk coup in 1908.

bekâr: Roughly translated as "bachelor," the term *bekâr* was used by the Ottoman government to describe male seasonal workers, in particular those who traveled to Istanbul. Regulations of the *bekâr* class reflected the changing understanding of "vagrancy" within the Ottoman Empire, wherein men who were far from their homes were considered threats to the state's security. Ottoman elites considered *bekâr*s dangerous because they often formed their own social circles, isolated from the rest of Ottoman society, and were thought to be particularly susceptible to revolutionary propaganda.

Bulgarian Exarchate (Istanbul): Established by a firman of Sultan Abdülaziz issued on March 12, 1872, after decades of tension between Bulgarian religious elites and the Greek Patriarchate of Constantinople. In line with their national reawakening, Bulgarians sought to establish Bulgarian schools and celebrate the liturgy in their native language. In accordance with the firman, the exarchate was granted autonomy like other Christian minorities. All dioceses within territorial Bulgaria were included. Any territory wherein a two-thirds majority of the Orthodox Christian population voted to be absorbed into the Bulgarian church

263

joined the exarchate. Voting resulted in Macedonia being ceded to the exarchate from the Greek Patriarchate.

Celali rebellions: A series of bandit uprisings in Anatolia beginning in 1519 and lasting until the defeat of Abaza Hasan Paşa in 1659. The term *celali* is derived from the name of a heretical priest, Sheikh Celal, who claimed to be the Mahdi—a descendant of the Prophet Muhammed come to vanquish injustice at the end times—and staged a revolt near Tokat in 1519. At the time, Ottoman bureaucrats referred to similar uprisings as *celali* as a way of discrediting them. The rebellions' purpose was not to overthrow the Ottoman Empire, though; rather, they were a response to dire economic conditions that had led to mass unemployment, currency devaluation, and corruption among tax officials. As such, their purpose was to extort resources for the peasant population. Many of the rebels were *sekbahn*s, musketeers who were out of work in times of peace and who were joined by Turkish and Kurdish nomads, vagabonds, and members of the Alevi denomination of Islam who had been subject to state oppression under Selim I.

circle of justice (*daire-i adalet*): The conceptual structure of the relationship between state and people within the Ottoman Empire in the centuries prior to the Tanzimat era. Sharia law and Islam were fundamental to the circle of justice: the sultan was the only person capable of interpreting the will of God and was considered His shadow on earth; therefore, the sultan was charged with implementing Sharia. In a simplified overview: the sultan must rule in order to implement Sharia on earth; in order to rule, the sultan needs an army; in order to have an army, resources must be created by peasants; in order to protect the peasants and their ability to produce, justice and order must be preserved by the state; in order to achieve true justice and order, Sharia must implemented on earth by the ruling sultan.

Cyprus Convention: The Cyprus Convention of June 4, 1878, was an agreement reached between Great Britain and the Ottoman Empire following secret negotiations. As a result of the agreement, the British were granted administrative control of Cyprus in exchange for representing Ottoman interests at the Berlin Congress. The British hoped that controlling Cyprus would help them prevent Russian expansion south and west toward Istanbul. The territory quickly became an important naval asset in protecting the Suez Canal and the route to British

India. Following the alliance between the Ottoman Empire and the Central Powers during the First World War, the British annexed Cyprus.

Dashnaktsutyun (Armenian Revolutionary Federation, ARF): A political party formed in Tiflis in 1890 from multiple extant Armenian revolutionary organizations. Within a year of its founding, internal disputes among ARF members—over what to include in the party's socialist program and whether to advocate for full Armenian independence or simply for reform within the Ottoman Empire—led some members to separate as the Hunchakian (Social Democrat) Party. ARF was greatly influenced by the Russian group Narodnaya Volya (People's Will) and adopted a similar decentralized structure as well as a program of armed rebellion, political violence, and propaganda by the deed. ARF was responsible, in whole or in collaboration with other revolutionary groups, for many large-scale demonstrations of resistance to the Ottoman Empire, including the Sasun Rebellion (or Resistance) of 1894, the Van Uprising of 1894, the Ottoman Bank takeover of 1896, the Khanasor Expedition of 1897, the Second Sasun Rebellion in 1904, and the failed assassination attempt on Sultan Abdülhamid II at Yıldız Mosque in 1905.

Delchev, Gotse: A prominent Macedonian Bulgarian revolutionary and one of the most important leaders of the Internal Macedonian Revolutionary Organization. Delchev believed that being Macedonian was tied to a sense of local patriotism within the multiethnic community; he adopted the slogan "Macedonia for the Macedonians" and applied it to the different nationalities in the region. He was killed by Ottoman forces on May 4, 1903, while helping to organize the Ilinden (Preobrazhenie) Uprising.

Entente Cordiale: An agreement signed between Great Britain and France on April 8, 1904. After negotiations to form an alliance with the German Empire failed in 1901, the British formed the Anglo-Japanese alliance. Aware of the French and Russian alliance, Great Britain wished to cool tensions with France stemming from the Japanese instigation of war against the Russian Empire in 1904. The main issue of contention between Great Britain and France related to their colonial interests in Africa. The agreement assured British control of Egypt and French control of Morocco and the free flow of trade through the Suez Canal and Straits of Gibraltar. This agreement formed the basis for the Triple Entente alliance of France, Great Britain, and the Russian Empire during the First World War.

External Macedonian Revolutionary Organization: An organization founded in Bulgaria soon after the founding of the Internal Macedonian Revolutionary Organization. The External Organization tried to court favor in Bulgaria for the Macedonian cause by participating in local politics and producing propaganda. Following the failed Melnik Rebellion of 1895, in which the External Organization joined the Bulgarian government in an attempt to spark an uprising in Macedonia, many Macedonians sought to distance themselves from the External Organization.

Garo, Armen: Born Karekin Pastermadjian, Armen Garos was an instrumental member of the Dashnaktsutyun (Armenian Revolutionary Federation, ARF) from the late Ottoman Empire until his death following the dissolution of the Armenian Republic in 1923. Garo was first introduced to ARF in 1894 while studying agriculture in France. He planned the takeover of the Ottoman Bank in 1896, along with Papken Siuni, who was killed during the operation. Following the bank takeover, Garo completed his doctoral studies in natural science at the University of Switzerland before returning to the Ottoman Empire and founding a chemical research lab in Tiflis. Garo helped organize the defense of Tiflis Armenians during the Armenian-Tatar Massacres (1905–7). During the Second Constitutional Era, Garo served as the representative of Erzurum to the Ottoman Parliament. Upon the founding of the First Republic of Armenia, he was elected ambassador to Washington, DC, a post he served in until the First Republic's absorption into the Soviet Union.

Gemidzhi group: Founded in 1898 in Switzerland by Bulgarian and Macedonian students who supported the cause of Macedonian independence. After failed plans for attacks in Istanbul and Adrianople, the Gemidzhi successfully carried out the Thessaloniki Assassinations, a multifront demonstration of political violence that lasted from April 28 until May 3, 1903, and included bomb attacks at multiple sites, such as the French passenger boat *Guadalquivir*, Thessaloniki's water and electric resources, and the Ottoman Bank.

Hamidiye Cavalry: A military organization named after Sultan Abdülhamid II, who established this military unit attached to the Fourth Army in 1891. The ranks of the Hamidiye were filled mostly with nomadic/seminomadic Kurdish tribes. By forming the Hamidiye Cavalry, the Ottoman Empire hoped to secure the eastern frontier against Russian aggression. The cavalry units were led by tribal chiefs who used their privileged position to harass the Armenian population of Eastern Anatolia as well as rival Kurdish tribes. The tribal chiefs with the Hamidiye affiliation played an integral role in the Armenian Massacres of 1894–96, wherein between eighty thousand and three hundred thousand people were killed, the vast majority Armenian Christians.

Hilmi Paşa: A civil servant who held multiple posts within the Ottoman Empire in the decades before its dissolution. Between 1902 and 1908, Hilmi Paşa served as inspector general of Rumelia. He worked alongside the Russian and Austro-Hungarian civil servants installed there under the terms of the Mürzsteg Reforms of 1903. Hilmi Paşa returned to Istanbul after the Young Turk Revolution in 1908 to serve as minister of interior, a position he held until 1909. From February 1909 until January 1910, he completed two terms as grand vizier, and in 1912 he was sent to Vienna as the Ottoman ambassador to Austria-Hungary, a position he would hold until the end of Ottoman involvement in the First World War.

Hunchak(ian) (Social Democratic) Party: An Armenian revolutionary political party founded by a group of Russian Armenian Marxist students in Geneva, Switzerland, in 1887. It was the first socialist political party to operate in either the Ottoman Empire or the Persian Empire. The Hunchaks held to a Marxist ideology, advocated for the creation of an independent socialist Armenian state, and endorsed a program of political violence. Although their measures to oppose the Ottoman Empire sometimes included peaceful demonstrations, such as the Kumkapı Demonstration of 1890 and the Sublime Porte Demonstration of 1895, they were also instrumental in leading Armenians in armed resistance against the Ottoman government, as in the Zeitun Uprising of 1896.

imam: An Arabic term for the religious-political head of an Islamic community. For Sunni Muslims, the imam is most closely comparable to a priest in Christianity; in this context, the imam leads worship at the mosque and provides religious guidance to the community.

Internal Macedonian Revolutionary Organization (IMRO): Established in Thessaloniki in 1893, IMRO was dedicated to the creation of an autonomous Macedonia within the framework of a larger Balkan federation. After helping to stage the failed Ilinden (Preobrazhenie) Uprising between August and October

1903, IMRO began utilizing political violence and terror tactics instead of overt political revolution to achieve its aims.

kadı: Used generally to refer to any magistrate or judge of a Sharia court with specific duties. Within the Ottoman context, *kadı* also refers to a specific bureaucratic role within the Ottoman administration. Each *kadı* was assigned a territory called a *kadıluk*, wherein they represented the sultan's legal authority. *Kadıs* operated with significant autonomy; they followed the sultan's orders but issued their own rulings on individual cases. *Kadı ilamı*, or "judicial verdicts," had no legal authority beyond individual cases. To carry out their rulings, the *kadıs* relied on the beys, their administrative counterpart who wielded the sultan's executive authority within a territory and had the power to punish individuals. Although the *kadı* courts were accessible to non-Muslims and foreigners, Muslim men were granted higher status within the judicial system.

London Protocol (1877): An agreement signed by representatives of Italy, France, Germany, the United Kingdom, Austria-Hungary, and Russia on March 31, 1877. The agreement called on the Ottoman Empire to institute immediate reforms to improve the situation of the empire's Christian population. The European powers reserved the right to observe Ottoman implementation of the reforms and, where they were inadequate, to "jointly pass resolutions" and take appropriate measures to ensure the Christians' welfare and maintain peace. The Ottoman Empire rejected the London Protocol by claiming it violated the empire's sovereignty and freedom from European intervention, as promised by the Paris Treaty of 1856.

millet system: The Ottoman system of governance by which non-Muslim minorities in the Ottoman Empire were granted autonomy within their communities. Individual millets, or religious communities, were headed by religious leaders who represented the communities' interests to the central government. The millet system enabled non-Muslim communities to maintain their own independent religious courts for managing their internal affairs; in return, the ruling elites of the millets performed state duties, such as collecting taxes and maintaining internal order.

muezzin: A member of a mosque's staff whose function is to call members of the Islamic faith to prayer. The muezzin is not a member of the clergy, and, depending on the circumstances, another Muslim can take their place to sound the call to prayer. The call to prayer is sounded five times a day, starting at sunrise. In addition to calling the faithful to daily prayer, the muezzin must also make an announcement when someone in the area surrounding the mosque has died.

Mürzsteg Reforms: The result of a memo issued by the Austro-Hungarian Empire and the Russian Empire in October 1903 in response to the Ilinden (Preobrazhenie) Uprising. Like the Vienna Program agreed to by the Russians, Hapsburgs, and Ottomans, the Mürzsteg Reforms resulted in the appointment of two civil servants—one each from the Russian and Austro-Hungarian Empires—to oversee the reform of the Ottoman bureaucratic administration, judiciary, and gendarmerie of the Macedonian vilayets, with a special emphasis on the inclusion of Christians within these institutions.

Narodnaya Volya (People's Will): A decentralized revolutionary political group in Russia that emerged in 1879 from the existing revolutionary group Zemlya i Volya (Land and Liberty) and that aimed to overthrow the autocratic system of czarist Russia. The split from Zemlya i Volya occurred over the value of political violence, with members of Narodnaya Volya taking up a program of propaganda by the deed—that is, acts of political violence to further their political cause. Narodnaya Volya is perhaps best known for the successful assassination of Czar Alexander II in 1881, after which the czarist regime was able largely to suppress the group's revolutionary activities. Narodnaya Volya was extremely influential on the structure and political programs of revolutionary groups that followed, chief among them Dashnaktsutyun in Armenia.

Ottoman Penal Code: Within the Ottoman Penal Code, Articles 55–62 deal with internal state security by identifying specific crimes against the state and codifying appropriate punishments. These articles deal with crimes such as insurrection and inciting rebellion and prescribe harsh punishments for those found guilty, including life imprisonment, exile, and death. Potential crimes are also dealt with in the penal code, wherein any discussion of committing a crime against the state or any plan to create an alliance to carry out such acts are punishable offenses.

Patrona Halil Rebellion: A rebellion of around twelve thousand Janissaries, mostly Albanians, in 1730 that resulted in the deposition of Sultan Ahmed III, who was replaced by Mahmud I. The rebellion began in response to a disastrous military defeat of the Ottomans by Persia. The Janissaries seized Istanbul and demanded the extradition of the grand vizier, whom they blamed for the Ottoman defeat. Although the sultan agreed to give up the grand vizier, who was subsequently killed along with his supporters and friends, he was nonetheless deposed. Horpeşteli Arnavut Halil, an Albanian Janissary who had fled to Istanbul after his involvement in two Janissary uprisings in 1720, was the leader of the rebellion. His Albanian comrades referred to Halil by the honorific *patrona*, or "vice admiral." During an uprising lasting nearly two months, many senior members of the Ottoman government were dismissed and replaced by the rebels. The rebellion ended when the khan of Crimea, the Ottoman grand vizier, the mufti, and the agha of the Janissaries united against the rebels. Patrona Halil was sentenced to death and executed, along with approximately seven thousand of his followers.

portrait parlé: A technique of measurement that focuses on the eyes to specify a person's identity and is a subtechnique of anthropometry, which functions through the use of angles and measurements, focusing on certain points on the body and face. Originally developed in the late nineteenth century by the French police officer Alphonse Bertillon, the "speaking portrait" used photographs taken from the front and the side. At the International Conference of Rome for the Social Defense against Anarchists in 1898, *portrait parlé* was standardized, and an international system of exchange and cooperation in identifying transnational criminals was established.

Zemlya i Volya (Land and Liberty): A clandestine Russian political organization with the goal of instigating a populist social movement of the working classes to overthrow the autocratic czarist regime. Zemlya i Volya promulgated the concept of propaganda by deed, or political violence, which was seen as directly reaching the masses, as opposed to theoretical propaganda, which could be easily manipulated and was limited in effect. A member of Zemlya i Volya was responsible for the assassination in 1878 of Sergei Stepniak-Kravchinskii, the head of the czarist political police in St. Petersburg—one of the first of a series of politically motivated assassination attempts globally in subsequent decades. The revolutionary organization Narodnaya Volya emerged from Zemlya i Volya in 1879 following an internal split over the value of political violence. Narodnaya Volya was more strongly in favor of political violence, and less than two years after the split it successfully assassinated Czar Alexander II.

Notes

Archive Abbreviations

A.MKT.MHM	Sadaret Mektûbî Mühimme Kalemi Evrakı
A.MTZ.(04)	Sadâret Eyâlât-ı Mümtâze Kalemi Belgeleri Bulgaristan
AYN.d	Ayniyât Defterleri
BEO	Bâbıâli Evrak Odası Evrakı
BOA	Başbakanlık Osmanlı Arşivi
DH.MKT	Dâhiliye Nezâreti Mektûbî Kalemi
DH.TMIK.M	Dâhiliye Nezâreti Tesrî-i Muamelât
FO	Foreign Office, London
HR.HMŞ.İŞO	Hariciye Nezareti Hukuk Müşavirliği İstişare Odası Evrakı
HR.SYS	Hariciye Nezareti Siyasi
HR.TO	Hariciye Nezareti Tercüme Odası Evrakı
İ.DH	İrade Dahiliye
İ.HR	İrade Hariciye
İ.HUS	İrade Hususi
İ.KAN	İrade Kanun ve Nizamat
İ.MTZ	İrade Eyalet-I Mümtaze Mısır
İ.ZB	İrade Zabtiye
MV	Meclis-I Vükelâ Mazbataları
ŞD	Şurayı Devlet
TFR.I.A	Rumeli Müfettişliği Sadâret ve Başkitâbet Evrakı
TFR.I.MN	Rumeli Müfettişliği Manastır Evrakı
TFR.I.SL	Rumeli Müfettişliği Selânik Evrakı
TFR.I.UM	Rumeli Müfettişliği Umum Evrak
Y.A.HUS	Yıldız Sadaret Hususî Mâruzat Evrakı
Y.A.RES	Yıldız Sadaret Resmi Mâruzat Evrakı
Y.EE	Yıldız Esas Evrakı
Y.EE.KP	Sadrıazam Kâmil Paşa Evrakı---Yıldız Esas Evrakı'na Ek
Y.MTV	Yıldız Mütenevvi Mâruzat
Y.PRK.ASK	Yıldız Perakende Evrakı---Askerî Maruzât

Y.PRK.BŞK	Yıldız Perakende Evrakı---Mabeyn Başkitâbeti
Y.PRK.DH	Yıldız Perakende Evrakı---Dâhiliye Nezâreti Maruzâtı
Y.PRK.EŞA	Yıldız Perakende Evrakı---Elçilik ve Şehbenderlik Maruzâtı
Y.PRK.HR	Yıldız Perakende Evrakı---Hariciye Nezâreti Maruzâtı
Y.PRK.KOM	Yıldız Perakende Evrakı---Komisyonlar Maruzâtı
Y.PRK.MK	Yıldız Perakende Evrakı---Müfettişlik ve Komiserlikler Tahrirâtı
Y.PRK.ŞH	Yıldız Perakende Evrakı---Şehremâneti Maruzâtı
Y.PRK.TKM	Yıldız Perakende Evrakı---Tahrirât-ı Ecnebiye ve Mâbeyn Mütercimliği
Y.PRK.UM	Yıldız Perakende Umumi Maruzat
Y.PRK.ZB	Yıldız Perakende Evrakı---Zabtiye Nezâreti Maruzâtı
ZB	Zabtiye Nezareti

Hijri and Rumi Calendar Month Abbreviations

A	Ağustos
B	Receb
C	Cemazeyilahir
Ca	Cemazeyilevvel
E	Eylül
H	Haziran
L	Şevval
M	Muharrem
Ma	Mart
My	Mayıs
N	Ramazan
Ni	Nisan
R	Rebiülahir
Ra	Rebiülevvel
S	Safer
Ş	Şaban
Su	Şubat
T	Temmuz
Te	Teşrin-i Evvel
Tş	Teşrin-i Sani
Z	Zilhicce
Za	Zilkade

Introduction

1. Başbakanlık Osmanlı Arşivi (BOA), Istanbul, Dâhiliye Nezâreti Tesrî-i Muamelât (DH.TMIK.M), 255/26, 22 Şaban (Ş) 1325 (Aug. 10, 1907).

2. BOA, Sadrıazam Kâmil Paşa Evrakı—Yıldız Esas Evrakı'na Ek (Y.EE.KP), 23/2294, 20 Zilhicce (Z) 1322 (Feb. 25, 1905).

3. For another discussion about the migration in a transottoman context, see Florian Riedler and Stefan Rohdewald, "Migration and Mobility in a Transottoman Context," *Radovi-Zavoda za hrvatsku povijest* 51, no. 1 (2019): 201–19.

4. Gerard Noiriel, *The French Melting Pot: Immigration, Citizenship, and National Identity*, trans. Geoffrey de Laforcade (Minneapolis: Univ. of Minnesota Press, 1996), xviii.

5. Jane Caplan and John Torpey, introduction to *Documenting Individual Identity: The Development of State Practices in the Modern World*, ed. Jane Caplan and John Torpey (Princeton, NJ: Princeton Univ. Press, 2001), 8.

6. John Torpey, "Revolution of Freedom of Movement: An Analysis of Passport Controls in the French, Russian and Chinese Revolutions," *Theory and Society* 26, no. 6 (1997): 839.

7. Andreas Fahrmeir, "Governments and Forgers: Passports in the 19th Century Europe," in *Documenting Individual Identity*, ed. Caplan and Torpey, 288–89.

8. John Torpey, *The Invention of the Passport: Surveillance, Citizenship and the State* (Cambridge: Cambridge Univ. Press, 2000), 22.

9. Leo Lucassen, "Eternal Vagrants? State Formation, Migration, and Travelling Groups in Western Europe, 1350–1914," in *Migration, Migration History, History: Old Paradigms and New Perspectives*, ed. Jan Lucassen and Leo Lucassen (Bern: Peter Lang, 1999), 239. France introduced the regulation of 1792 with the condition that everyone had to obtain a passport. If a person did not have a passport, they had to obtain one from the administrative unit at the border. Thus, the monitoring of individuals for the purposes of ensuring security became one of the period's important routines (Torpey, *The Invention of the Passport*, 42).

10. A regulation passed in the United States in 1882 was based on the racist exclusion of Chinese migrants and laborers. See "The Passport Question between the United States and Russia," editorial comment, *American Journal of International Law* 1 (1912): 189.

11. Elaine Glovka Spencer, *Police and the Social Order in German Cities: The Düsseldorf District, 1848–1914* (DeKalb: Northern Illinois Univ. Press, 1992), 76; Ulrich Herbert, *A History of Foreign Labor in Germany, 1880–1980* (Ann Arbor: Univ. of Michigan Press, 1990), 10–11.

12. Clive Emsley, *The English Police: A Political and Social History* (London: Longman, 1996), 158.

13. Lucassen, "Eternal Vagrants?," 235.

14. Torpey, *The Invention of the Passport*, 29–31, 52, 90, 92.

15. For local traditions of registration, see Keith Breckenridge and Simon Szeter, "Editors' Introduction: Recognition and Registration: The Infrastructure of Personhood in World History," in *Registration and Recognition, Documenting the Person in World History*, ed. Keith Breckenridge and Simon Szeter (London: British Academy, 2012), 1–36.

1. Theoretical Framework

1. Charles Tilly, *Coercion, Capital, and European States, AD 990–1990* (Cambridge: Blackwell, 1990).

2. Tilly, *Coercion, Capital, and European States.*

3. Anthony Giddens, *The Nation-State and Violence* (Berkeley: Univ. of California Press, 1987), 1–6.

4. Giddens, *The Nation-State and Violence*, 7–34.

5. Giddens, *The Nation-State and Violence*, 7–34.

6. Giddens, *The Nation-State and Violence*, 35–60.

7. Such is Gidden's interpretation of Bodin's discussion of sovereignty.

8. Giddens, *The Nation-State and Violence*, 83–121.

9. Giddens, *The Nation-State and Violence*, 172–97.

10. See Michael Mann, *The Sources of Social Power*, vol. 1: *A History of Power from the Beginning to A.D. 1760* (1986; reprint, Cambridge: Cambridge Univ. Press, 2003); and Michael Mann, *The Sources of Social Power*, vol. 2: *A Rise of Classes and Nation-States, 1760–1914* (1993; reprint, Cambridge: Cambridge Univ. Press, 1996).

11. The most important function of ideological power, one of the four sources of social power, is to give meaning to the world. Mann discusses two types of ideological power, transcendent and immanent. Transcendent ideological power points to a socio-spatial site. Ideological power is transcendent to the degree that it intersects or contains other networks of power. A religious cosmos is transcendent not because it breaks up secular space but because it intersects or combines (by conjoining) its own networks of power with such political and economic networks of power as empires and classes. Immanent ideological power is more sociological in that it refers to the morality or solidarity of a particular group. See Mann, *The Sources of Social Power*, 2:7.

12. See Mann, *The Sources of Social Power*, vols. 1 and 2.

13. Here, one should not overlook the fact that Mann considers this problem using the example of Britain. See Frank Trentmann, "The 'British' Sources of Social Power: Reflections on History, Sociology, and Intellectual Biography," in *An Anatomy of Power: The Social Theory of Michael Mann*, ed. John A. Hall and Ralph Schroeder (Cambridge: Cambridge Univ. Press, 2005), 285.

14. Mann, *The Sources of Social Power*, 1:1.

15. Philip S. Gorski, "Mann's Theory of Ideological Power: Sources, Applications and Elaborations," in *An Anatomy of Power*, ed. Hall and Schroeder, 103.

16. Parsons uses both of these concepts (Mann, *The Sources of Social Power*, 1:6).

17. Mann, *The Sources of Social Power*, 1:6–7; Robert Brenner, "From Theory to History: 'The European Dynamic' or Feudalism to Capitalism?," in *An Anatomy of Power*, ed. Hall and Schroeder, 192.

18. Mann, *The Sources of Social Power*, 1:7.

19. Brenner, "From Theory to History," 193.

20. Mann, *The Sources of Social Power*, 1:7.

21. Gorski, "Mann's Theory of Ideological Power," 102.

22. Mann, *The Sources of Social Power*, 1:8.

23. Gorski, "Mann's Theory of Ideological Power," 102.

24. Gorski, "Mann's Theory of Ideological Power," 103.

25. Michael Mann, "The Autonomous Power of the State: Its Origins, Mechanisms and Results," in *War and Capitalism: Studies in Political Sociology* (Oxford: Blackwell, 1988), 112, 113, 115; Mann, *The Sources of Social Power*, 2:59.

26. Even in one of the deepest discussions related to the relations established between geopolitics and state making (Gorski, "Mann's Theory of Ideological Power," 113), the place of religion is often overlooked despite its crucial place in early-modern states. Such an interest in religion in fact may bring a new perspective—based on religious institutions—to the problem of degrees of bureaucratization. The degree of bureaucratization is quite variable in early-modern states.

27. Mann, *The Sources of Social Power*, 1:477.

28. The concept of infrastructural power demonstrates that a highly centralized state can theoretically render ineffective a rival's networks of power. Yet the state may in some circumstances be weak in constructing its own networks. As a consequence, in the context of infrastructural power this generally means that if distributive power is at a high level, collective power may be at a low level.

29. Gorski, "Mann's Theory of Ideological Power," 111.

30. Mann, *The Sources of Social Power*, 2:460, 473, 479.

31. Through the concept of pacification, Mann establishes a relation between religion and capitalism similar to that of Weber (Gorski, "Mann's Theory of Ideological Power," 110).

32. Mann, *The Sources of Social Power*, 2:107–8.

33. Mann explains the transformation of power in terms of steps. See Ralph Schroeder, "Introduction: The IEMP Model and Its Critics," in *An Anatomy of Power*, ed. Hall and Schroeder, 3.

34. Mann, *The Sources of Social Power*, vol. 2; Schroeder, "Introduction," 3–6.

35. Michael Mann, "Ruling Class Strategies and Citizenship," *Sociology* 21 (1988): 339–54.

36. Schroeder, "Introduction," 8.

37. Mann, *The Sources of Social Power*, 2:505.

38. Mann, *The Sources of Social Power*, 2:56.

39. Rendal Collins, "Mann's Transformation of the Classic Sociological Traditions," in *An Anatomy of Power*, ed. Hall and Schroeder, 22.

40. See Trentmann, "The 'British' Sources of Social Power," 292; and Mann, *The Sources of Social Power*, 2:1–2.

41. Mann, *The Sources of Social Power*, 2:404–500.

42. Giddens, *The Nation-State and Violence*, 131–34, 238.

43. The characteristic institutional features of the modern state are taken up in a similar manner in Weberian and neo-Marxist concepts. See, for instance, Max Weber, *Economy and Society*, ed. Guenther Roth and Claus Wittich (Berkeley: Univ. of California Press, 2004).

44. On this debate, see Bob Jessop, *State Theory: Putting the Capitalist State in Its Place* (Cambridge: Polity, 1990), and Nicos Poulantzas, *State, Power, Socialism* (London: Verso, 2000).

45. Jessop, *State Theory*, 29.

46. See Zeynep Gambetti, "Foucault'da Disiplin Toplumu: Güvenlik Toplumu Ayrımı," *Mesele*, No. 20, (2008): 43–46.

47. Giddens, *The Nation-State and Violence*, 7–34. On this subject, Mann's definition of infrastructural power and his discussions of power established from within society are illuminating; see Mann, *The Sources of Social Power*, 2:7–9, 56–60.

48. See Michel Foucault, "Governmentality," in *The Foucault Effect: Studies in Governmentality*, ed. Graham Burchell, Colin Gordon, and Peter Miller (Chicago: Univ. of Chicago Press, 1991), 102–3.

49. Foucault, "Governmentality," 99–103.

50. Mitchell Dean, *Governmentality: Power and Rule in Modern Society* (London: Sage, 1999), 20.

51. Dean, *Governmentality*, 19–20.

52. See Michel Foucault, *Territory, Security: Lectures at the Collége de France 1977–1978*, trans. Graham Burchell, ed. Michel Senellart (Basingstoke, UK: Palgrave McMillan, 2007), 62–65.

53. Michael Dillon and Luis Lobo-Guerrero, "Biopolitics of Security in the 21st Century: An Introduction," *Review of International Studies* 34 (2008): 274.

54. Dillon and Lobo-Guerrero, "Biopolitics of Security," 275.

55. Mark Neocleous, *Imagining the State* (Maidenhead, UK: Open Univ. Press, 2003), 40.

56. Neocleous, *Imagining the State*, 41.

57. Neocleous, *Imagining the State*, 40–43.

58. Carl Schmidt, *Siyasal Kavramı*, trans. Ece Göztepe (Istanbul: Metis, 2006), 56–60.

59. Neocleous, *Imagining the State*, 45.

60. Neocleous, *Imagining the State*, 46.

61. Neocleous, *Imagining the State*, 49.

62. Michel Foucault, *Discipline and Punish: The Birth of the Prison*, trans. Alan Sheridan (New York: Random House, 1977).

63. Giddens, *The Nation-State and Violence*, 18.

64. Foucault, *Discipline and Punish*.

65. See Georg Rusche and Otto Kirchemmer, *Punishment and Social Structure* (New York: Colombia Univ. Press, 1939); Foucault, *Discipline and Punish*; and E. P. Thompson, *Customs in Common* (London: Merlin Press, 1991).

66. Pasquale Pasquino, "Theatrum Poiticum: The Geneology of Capital-Police and the State of Prosperity," in *The Foucault Effect*, ed. Burchell, Gordon, and Miller, 105–18.

67. Neocleous, *Imagining the State*, 50–51.

68. James C. Scott, *Seeing Like a State: How Certain Schemes to Improve the Human Condition Have Failed* (New Haven, CT: Yale Univ. Press, 1998), 9–84.

69. This process refers to the state's attempt to engineer society. Scott calls attention to the fact that social engineering's worst results occur when four factors come together: the administrative configuration of society and nature, high-modernist ideology, an authoritarian state that will use force in realizing high-modernist ideology, and, finally, a weak civil society (*Seeing Like a State*, 17–20).

70. Tilly, *Coercion, Capital, and European States*, 192; Giddens, *The Nation-State and Violence*, 69.

71. Tilly, *Coercion, Capital, and European States*, 401.

72. Foucault, *Discipline and Punish*, 147.

73. Stein Rokkan, *State Formation, Nation Building, and Mass Politics in Europe: The Theory of Stein Rokkan* (Oxford: Oxford Univ. Press, 1999).

74. Janifer Davis, "Urban Policing and Its Objects: Comparative Themes in England and France in the Second Half of the 19th Century," in *Policing Western Europe: Politics, Professionalism and Public Order 1850–1940*, ed. Clive Emsley and Barbara Weinberger (Westport, CT: Greenwood Press, 1991), 7; Barbara Weinberger, "Are the Police Professionals? An Historical Account of the British Police Institution," in *Policing Western Europe*, ed. Emsley and Weinberger, 77.

75. Davis, "Urban Policing," 8.

76. Clive Emsley and Barbara Weinberger, introduction to *Policing Western Europe*, ed. Emsley and Weinberger, xii.

77. Robert D. Storch, "The Policeman as Domestic Missionary: Urban Discipline and Popular Culture in Northern England, 1850–1880," *Journal of Social History* 9, no. 4 (1976): 487.

78. Storch, "The Policeman as Domestic Missionary," 487.

79. Spencer, *Police and the Social Order*. For more on the stereotyping of the poor as criminal, see Davis, "Urban Policing," 2–10, and Storch, "The Policeman as Domestic Missionary."

80. For a deeper discussion on the metaphor of the body related to this matter, see Neocleous, *Imagining the State*.

2. The Modern State, Power, and Security Policies in the Hamidian Era

1. For an example of this situation, see Cengiz Kırlı, "İrvanyalılar, Hüseyin Paşa ve Tasvir-i Zulüm," *Toplumsal Tarih* 195 (2010): 12–22.

2. Barbara Jelavich, *The History of the Balkans*, vol. 1: *Eighteenth and Nineteenth Centuries* (Cambridge: Cambridge Univ. Press, 1985), 192.

3. Jelavich, *The History of the Balkans*, 1:341–42. See also Antonis Anastasopolis, "Lighting the Flame of Disorder: Ayan Infighting and State Intervention in Ottoman Karaferye, 1758–59," *International Journal of Turkish Studies* 8, nos. 1–2 (2002): 73–88.

4. For a detailed discussion, see İpek Yosmaoğlu, *Blood Ties: Religion, Violence, and the Politics of Nationhood in Ottoman Macedonia* (Ithaca, NY: Cornell Univ. Press, 2014), introduction and chap. 6.

5. Fikret Adanır, *Die Makedonische Frage: Ihre Entstehung und Entwicklung bis 1908* (Wiesbaden, Germany: Steiner, 1979), 270–77.

6. For a discussion on Bosnia, see Hannes Grandits, *The End of Ottoman Rule in Bosnia: Conflicting Agencies and Imperial Appropriations* (London: Routledge, 2022).

7. See Cameron Ean Alfred Whitehead, "The Bulgarian Horrors: Culture and the International History of the Great Eastern Crisis, 1876–1878," PhD diss., Univ. of British Columbia, 2014.

8. See Jelavich, *The History of the Balkans*, 1:354–58.

9. See Mithat Aydın, "Osmanlı-Sırp, Karadağ Savaşlarında İngiltere'nin Balkan Politikası," *Ankara Üniversitesi Osmanlı Tarihi Araştırma ve Uygulama Dergisi* 15 (2004): 139–63, at https://dergipark.org.tr/en/download/article-file/114153.

10. M. S. Anderson, *The Eastern Question: A Study of International Relations* (London: Macmillan, 1983).

11. Anderson, *The Eastern Question*, 268. Because of the political discussion on the population numbers, different sources circulated information about those numbers. The numerical weights of different Macedonian groups are contradictory in the circulated information, each reflecting the political aims of the states carrying out the research. See Adanır, *Die Makedonische Frage*, 1–15.

12. Adanır, *Die Makedonische Frage*, 100–160.

13. Duncan M. Perry, *The Politics of Terror: The Macedonian Liberation Movements, 1893–1903* (Ann Arbor: Univ. of Michigan Press, 1988).

14. The so-called Melnik Rebellion was quashed, but it was successful in attracting the attention of the European public and Russia. Following the rebellion, there emerged in Macedonia discussions about the External Organization's relationship with Bulgaria, resulting in many Macedonians severing their ties with the organization (Adanır, *Die Makedonische Frage*, 109–15).

15. Adanır, *Die Makedonische Frage*, 116–33.

16. Perry, *The Politics of Terror*, 61–78.

17. Pancho Dorev, *Dokumenti za Bălgarskata Istoriya: Dokumenti iz Turkskitje Dărzhavni Arkhivi* (Sofia: Bălgarskata Akademija na Naukitje, 1940), n. 157.

18. For smuggling of arms, see Ramazan Hakkı Öztan, "Tools of Revolution: Global Military Surplus, Arms Dealers, and Smugglers in the Late Ottoman Balkans, 1878–1908," *Past & Present* 237, no. 1 (2017): 167–95.

19. Adanır, *Die Makedonische Frage*, 137–38, 145–47; Mahir Aydın, "Makedonya Meselesi ve Amerikalı Rahibenin Kaçırılması," *Osmanlı Araştırmaları* 13 (1998): 239–58.

20. For a discussion on violence as a tool for creating political belonging, see Yosma-oğlu, *Blood Ties*.

21. Adanır, *Die Makedonische Frage*, 160–65.

22. J. Bojkov, Michail Gerdjikov, Petar Mandjukov, Petar Sokolov, Slavi Merdjanov, Dimitar Ganchev, Konstantin Antonov, and others.

23. See BOA, Rumeli Müfettişliği Manastır Evrakı (TFR.I.MN), 8/775, 1 Safer (S) 1321 (Apr. 29, 1903); BOA, Yıldız Perakende Umumi Maruzat (Y.PRK.UM), 64/3, 1 S 1321 (Apr. 29, 1903); BOA, Y.PRK.UM, 64/2, 1 S 1321 (Apr. 29, 1903); BOA, Y.PRK.UM, 64/11, 4 S 1321 (May 2, 1903); BOA, Yıldız Perakende Evrakı—Askerî Maruzât (Y.PRK.ASK), 195/91, 20 S 1321 (May 18, 1903); and Mark Mazower, *Salonica, City of Ghosts: Christians, Muslims and Jews (1430–1950)* (New York: Knopf, 2005), 270–80.

24. Orhan Türker, "Selanik'te 28–29 Nisan 1903 Olayları," *Tarih ve Toplum* 182 (1999): 27–30.

25. Misha Glenny, *Balkans 1804–1999: Nationalism, War and the Great Powers* (London: Genta, 1999), 202.

26. Adanır, *Die Makedonische Frage*, 170–79.

27. BOA, Yıldız Sadaret Hususî Mâruzat Evrakı (Y.A.HUS), 447/132, 10 S 1321 (May 8, 1903).

28. Türker, "Selanik'te," 30.

29. Adanır, *Die Makedonische Frage*, 92–93.

30. Adanır, *Die Makedonische Frage*, 92–93; BOA, Y.A.HUS, 447/142, 12 S 1321 (May 10, 1903).

31. BOA, Y.A.HUS, 448/64, 20 S 1321 (May 18, 1903).

32. BOA, Y.A.HUS, 448/77, 21 S 1321 (May 19, 1903).

33. The notice in question came from a French citizen with the help of the French consulate. See BOA, Y.A.HUS, 448/99, 23 S 1321 (May 21, 1905), and Y.A.HUS, 448/135, 27 S 1321 (May 25, 1903).

34. BOA, Y.A.HUS, 448/111, 24 S 1321 (May 22, 1903).

35. BOA, Yıldız Perakende Evrakı—Mabeyn Başkitâbeti (Y.PRK.BŞK), 70/40, 23 Cemazeyilevvel (Ca) 1321 (Sept. 16, 1903).

36. BOA, Bâbıâli Evrak Odası Evrakı (BEO), 2073/155423, 23 S 1321 (May 21, 1903); BOA, Rumeli Müfettişliği Sadâret ve Başkitâbet Evrakı (TFR.I.A), 19/1814, 26 Şevval (L) 1322 (Dec. 31, 1904).

37. BOA, Sadaret Mektûbî Mühimme Kalemi Evrakı (A.MKT.MHM), 731/4, 3 S 1321 (May 1, 1903).

38. After such information was received, identity controls were tightened for those coming to the province. See BOA, Y.A.HUS, 465/10, 2 Zilkade (Za) 1321 (Jan. 20, 1904).

39. See BOA, Yıldız Perakende Evrakı—Müfettişlik ve Komiserlikler Tahrirâtı (Y.PRK.MK), 15/82, 16 Cemazeyilahir (C) 1321 (Sept. 9, 1903); Y.A.HUS, 457/129, 29 C 1321 (Sept. 22, 1903).

40. BOA, Yıldız Perakende Evrakı—Zabtiye Nezâreti Maruzâtı (Y.PRK.ZB), 33/57, 9 Receb (B) 1321 (Oct. 1, 1903); BOA, Dâhiliye Nezâreti Mektûbî Kalemi (DH.MKT), 776/18, 19 B 1321 (Oct. 11, 1903). On groups perceived as threats by both the public and the state based on conspiracy theories, such as those involving poisoning, see Ebru Aykut Türker, "Alternative Claims on Justice and Law: Rural Arson and Poison Murder in the 19th Century Ottoman Empire," PhD diss., Atatürk İlkeleri ve İnkılap Tarihi Enstitüsü, Boğaziçi Univ., 2011), 339–46.

41. BOA, Sadâret Eyâlât-ı Mümtâze Kalemi Belgeleri Bulgaristan (A.MTZ.(04)), 98/101, 10 Rebiülahir (R) 1321 (Nov. 30, 1903).

42. BOA, DH.MKT, 664/52, 8 Z 1320 (Mar. 7, 1903).

43. An office memo written on matters related to the interior to the office of the Vizirate I, dated 12 Z 1320 (Mar. 12, 1903), in BOA, DH.MKT, 664/52; and a telegraph from Çatalca to the Ministry of Interior, 23 Şubat (Su) 1318 (Mar. 8, 1903) is also placed in BOA, DH.MKT, 664/52.

44. "Dahiliye Mektûbî Kaleminden Huzur-ı Ali Hazret-i Sadaret-penahi'ye," 12 Z 1320 (Mar. 12, 1903), in BOA, DH.MKT, 664/52.

45. Encrypted telegraph from the Çatalca lieutenant governor, 29 Şubat 1318 (Mar. 29, 1903), in BOA, DH.MKT, 664/52.

46. "Zabtiye Nezareti Celilesi'ne Dahiliye Mektûbî Kaleminden," 20 Z 1320 (Mar. 20, 1903), in BOA, DH.MKT, 664/52.

47. "Dahiliye Mektûbî Kalemi'nden Ticaret ve Nafia Nezaret-i Celilesine," 17 Mart (Ma) 1319 (Mar. 30, 1903), in BOA, DH.MKT, 664/52; "Dahiliye Mektûbî Kalemi'nden Ticaret ve Nafia Nezaret-i Celilesine," 19 Ma 1319 (Apr. 1, 1903), in BOA, DH.MKT, 664/52.

48. "Dahiliye Mektûbî Kalemi'nden Edirne Vilayeti Vekalet ve Selanik Vilayet-i ce-lileriyle Kosova ve Manastır Vilayet-i behiyyeleriyle Çatalca Mutasarrıflığı'yla ve Zabtiye Nezaret-i Celilesine," 20 Ma 1319 (Apr. 2, 1903), in BOA, DH.MKT, 664/52.

49. Encrypted telegraph from the Çatalca lieutenant governor, 19 Ma 1319 (Apr. 1, 1903), in BOA, DH.MKT, 664/52; "Dahiliye Mektûbî Kalemi'nden Taraf-ı Vâlâ-yı Hazret-i Seraskerîye," 20 Ma 1319 (Apr. 2, 1903), in BOA, DH.MKT, 664/52.

50. "Dahiliye Mektûbî Kalemi'nden Taraf-ı Vâlâ-yı Hazret-i Seraskerîye," 30 Ma 1319 (Apr. 12, 1903), in BOA, DH.MKT, 664/52.

51. "Dahiliye Mektûbî Kalemi'nden Huzur-ı Âlî-i Hazret-i Sadaret-penâhîye," 1 Nisan (Ni) 1319 (Apr. 14, 1903), in BOA, DH.MKT, 664/52; official memorandum no. 298 (Apr. 6, 1903) is also in this file.

52. "Dahiliye Mektûbî Kalemi'nden Huzur-ı Âlî-i Hazret-i Sadâret-penâhîye," 3 Ni 1319 (Apr. 16, 1903), in BOA, DH.MKT, 664/52.

53. "Dahiliye Mektûbî Kalemi'nden Şehremânet-i Celîlesine," 7 Ni 1319 (Apr. 20, 1903), in BOA, DH.MKT, 664/52; "Umum Erkân-ı Harbiyye Dairesi Üçüncü Şubesi" no. 419, "Seraskerlikt'en Dâhiliye Nezaret-i Celilesi'ne," 3 Ni 1319 (Apr. 16, 1903), in BOA, DH.MKT, 664/52.

54. "Dahiliye Mektûbî Kalemi'nden Çatalca Sancağı Mutasarrıfiyet-i Aliyyesine," 13 Mayıs (My) 1319 (May 26, 1903), in BOA, DH.MKT, 664/52.

55. "Dahiliye Mektûbî Kalemi'nden Zabtiye Nezaret-i Celîlesine," 20 Ni 1319 (May 3, 1903), in BOA, DH.MKT, 664/52.

56. "Dahiliye Mektûbî Kalemi'nden Huzur-ı Âlî-i Hazret-i Sadaret-penahiye," 20 Ma 1319 (Apr. 2, 1903), in BOA, DH.MKT, 664/52.

57. BOA, Rumeli Müfettişliği Selânik Evrakı (TFR.I.SL), 45/4428, 27 R 1322 (Dec. 5, 1904).

58. Gül Tokay, *Makedonya Sorunu Jön Türk İhtilalinin Kökenleri (1903–1908)* (Istanbul: Afa, 1996), 47.

59. Enver Ziya Karal, *Osmanlı Tarihi*, vol. 8 (Ankara: Türk Tarih Kurumu Basımevi, 1983), 159.

60. On the reform of the gendarmerie, see Tokay, *Makedonya*.

61. This period is examined in detail from an international perspective in Anderson, *The Eastern Question*.

62. Selçuk Akşin Somel, "Osmanlı Ermenileri'nde Kültür Modernleşmesi, Cemaat Okulları ve Abdülhamid Rejimi," *Tarih ve Toplum: Yeni Yaklaşımlar* 5 (2007): 71.

63. Although protected by the same order as the Treaty of Berlin, the new guarantors were Britain, Russia, Austro-Hungary, and Germany.

64. On the internationalization of the Armenian issue from the denialist perspective, see Cevdet Küçük, *Osmanlı Diplomasisinde Ermeni Meselesinin Ortaya Çıkışı 1878–1897* (Istanbul: Türk Dünyası Araştırmaları Vakfı, 1985).

65. See Nadir Özbek, "Policing the Countryside: Gendarmes of the Late Nineteenth Century Ottoman Empire (1876–1908)," *International Journal of Middle East Studies* 40 (2008): 47–67; and Nadir Özbek, "Osmanlı İmparatorluğu'nda İç Güvenlik, Siyaset ve Devlet, 1876—1909," *Türklük Araştırmaları Dergisi* 1 (2004): 59–95.

66. Nadir Özbek, "Anadolu Islahatı, Ermeni Sorunu ve Vergi Tahsildarlığı, 1895–1908," *Tarih ve Toplum: Yeni Yaklaşımlar* 9 (2009): 59–85.

67. Mark Levene, "Creating a Modern 'Zone of Genocide': The Impact of Nation- and State-Formation on Eastern Anatolia, 1878—1923," *Holocaust and Genocide Studies* 12, no. 3 (Winter 1998): 393–433.

68. Özbek, "Anadolu Islahatı," 60. Further, for a wider perspective on the Anatolian reforms, see Ali Karaca, *Anadolu Islahatı ve Ahmet Şakir Paşa (1838–1899)* (Istanbul: Eren, 1993), and Musa Şaşmaz, *British Policy and the Application of Reforms for the Armenians in Eastern Anatolia* (Ankara: Türk Tarih Kurumu, 2000).

69. Esat Uras, *Tarihte Ermeniler ve Ermeni Meselesi* (Istanbul: Belge, 1987), 177–78.

70. See Özbek, "Anadolu Islahatı," 75–77.

71. On the Armenians and tax collection, one can say that the state adopted a stance like the one it adopted in the Balkans.

72. François Georgeon, *Abdulhamid II: Le sultan calife* (Paris: Fayard, 2003), 124.

73. Janet Klein, *The Margins of the Empire: Kurdish Militias in the Ottoman Tribal Zone* (Stanford, CA: Stanford Univ. Press, 2011).

74. The Sasun Rebellion of 1894 emerged as a tax uprising. The state saw it as a general Armenian uprising and violently suppressed it. See Hans-Lukas Kieser, *Der verpasste Friede: Mission, Ethnie und Staat in den Ostprovinzen der Türkei 1839–1938* (Zürich: Chronos, 2000), 211–12. For a detailed analyses of the Sasun massacre, see Owen Miller, "Sasun 1894: Mountains, Missionaries and Massacres at the End of the Ottoman Empire," PhD diss., Columbia Univ. 2015.

75. See Louise Nalbandian, *The Armenian Revolutionary Movement: The Development of Armenian Political Parties through the Nineteenth Century* (Berkeley: Univ. of California Press, 1963), 67–100.

76. Devey writes that local bureaucrats exaggerated the incident for a prize. Vice Consul Devey to Colonel Chermside, enclosure in National Archives, London, 2 No. 330, Turkey No. 1 (1890), 4-7, no. 4/2, Foreign Office (FO) 424/162, 66–69, no. 71/2; Sir W. White, British ambassador at Constantinople, to the Marquis of Salisbury, British Secretary of Foreign Affairs, No. 303, Confidential, July 30, 1889. Also compare the documents given in Bilal Şimşir, *British Documents on Ottoman Amenians*, vol. 2: *1880–1890* (Ankara: TTK, 1989), 645–49.

77. Nalbandian, *The Armenian Revolutionary Movement*, 100–101.

78. Nalbandian, *The Armenian Revolutionary Movement*, 107–17. See also Anahide Ter Minassian, "1876–1923 Döneminde Osmanlı İmparatorluğu'nda Sosyalist Hareketin Doğuşunda ve Gelişmesinde Ermeni Topluluğunun Rolü," in *Osmanlı İmparatorluğu'nda Sosyalizm ve Milliyetçilik* (Istanbul: İletişim, 1995), 163–288.

79. Whereas all the founders were Russian Armenians, Mariam Vardanian (Maro) was a member of a revolutionary organization in St. Petersburg and took part in an intellectual group within the organization. Further, founders had ties to the Russian Social Democrats. Both, in fact, were members of Zemlya I Volya (Land and Freedom) and Cherny Peredyel (Black-Earth Distribution) (Nalbandian, *The Armenian Revolutionary Movement*, 113–14).

80. The party united again in 1902 (Minassian, "1876–1923 Döneminde Osmanlı İmparatorluğu'nda Sosyalist Hareketin Doğuşunda," 177).

81. Gerard J. Libaridian, "Revolution and Liberation in the 1892 and 1907 Programs of the Dashnaktsoutiun," in *Transcaucasia, Nationalism, and Social Change*, ed. Ronald Grigor Suny (Ann Arbor: Univ. of Michigan Press, 1996), 187–98.

82. Libaridian, "Revolution and Liberation."

83. Nalbandian, *The Armenian Revolutionary Movement*, 161–68.

84. Nalbandian, *The Armenian Revolutionary Movement*, 152–60.

85. Miller, "Sasun 1894," 48–50.

86. Y.A.HUS, 237/45, in *Osmanlı Belgelerinde Ermeni İsyanları (1878–1895)*, vol. 1, Yayın no. 95 (Ankara: T.C. Başbakanlık Devlet Arşivleri Genel Müdürlüğü Osmanlı Arşivi Daire Başkaanlığı, 2008), 48.

87. Nalbandian, *The Armenian Revolutionary Movement*, 118.

88. BOA, Yıldız Perakende Evrakı—Tahrirât-ı Ecnebiye ve Mâbeyn Mütercimliği (Y.PRK.TKM), 18/33, 17 Z 1307 (Aug. 4, 1890); for a translation of the newspaper *Voltaire*'s news related to the Kumkapı Incident, see *Osmanlı Belgelerinde Ermeni İsyanları (1878–1895)*, 1:49–50.

89. See Akın Sefer, "The Docks of the Revolution: The Struggles of the Port Workers of Istanbul in the Late Nineteenth and Early Twentieth Century," MA thesis, Bosphorus Univ., 2009.

90. Nalbandian, *The Armenian Revolutionary Movement*, 119–20.

91. Habeus corpus is a judicial order tying the legality of arrest to a judge's decision as a means of doing away with processes that violate individual liberties.

92. On the petition, see Nalbandian, *The Armenian Revolutionary Movement*, 124.

93. "16 Eylül Sene 1311 Tarihiyle Hey'et-i Tahkikiyyeden Tanzim ve İ'ta Olunan Müzekkirenin Suretidir," in Hüseyin Nazım Paşa, *Ermeni Olayları Tarihi*, vol. 1, prepared by Necati Aktaş, Mustafa Oğuz, Mustafa Küçük, and T. C. Başbakanlık, Yayın no. 15 (Ankara: Devlet Arşivleri Genel Müdürlüğü Osmanlı Arşivi Daire Başkanlığı, 1994), 68.

94. To state elites, this phrase, *taşralı Ermeniler*, "Armenians of the countryside," meant seasonal workers in Istanbul.

95. "Makam-ı Celil-i Sadaret-i Uzmadan 16 Eylül Sene 1311 Tarih ve 311 Numara ile Cevaben Varid Olan Tezkere-i Samiyye Suretidir," in Hüseyin Nazım Paşa, *Ermeni Olayları Tarihi*, 1:68–70.

96. "Makam-ı Sami-i Sadaret-penahiden 16 Eylül Sene 1311 Tarih ve 317 Numara ile Varid Olan Tezkere-i Samiyyenin Suretidir," in Hüseyin Nazım Paşa, *Ermeni Olayları Tarihi*, 1:70–71.

97. "16 Eylül Sene 1311 Tarih ile Beyoğlu Mutasarrıflığı'na Yazılan Tezkere'nin Suretidir," in Hüseyin Nazım Paşa, *Ermeni Olayları Tarihi*, 1:74–75.

98. Georgeon, *Abdülhamid II*, 337.

99. BOA, Y.PRK.ZB, 16/51, 15 R 1313 (Oct. 5, 1895).

100. BOA, Y.PRK.ZB, 16/49, 15 R 1313 (Oct 5, 1895).

101. BOA, Yıldız Perakende Evrakı—Şehremâneti Maruzâtı (Y.PRK.ŞH), 7/35, 17 R 1313 (Oct. 7, 1895).

102. Nalbandian, *The Armenian Revolutionary Movement*, 123.

103. Hüseyin Nazım Paşa, *Hatıralarım: Ermeni Olaylarının İçyüzü*, ed. Tahsin Yıldırım (Istanbul: Selis Kitaplar, 2007), 21, also mentioning the *New York Times*.

104. "Üsküdar Mutasarrıflığı'na Keşide Olunan 19 Eylül Sene 1311 Tarihli Telgrafname Suretidir," in Hüseyin Nazım Paşa, *Ermeni Olayları Tarihi*, 1:76.

105. "Üsküdar Mutasarrıflığı'na Keşide Olunan," in Hüseyin Nazım Paşa, *Ermeni Olayları Tarihi*, 1:76–83.

106. "Beyoğlu Mutasarrıflığına Yazılan 19 Eylül Sene 1311 Tarih ve 714 Numaralı Tezkerenin Suretidir," in Hüseyin Nazım Paşa, *Ermeni Olayları Tarihi*, 1:78; Vahakn N. Dadrian, *The History of the Armenian Genocide: Ethnic Conflict from the Balkans to Anatolia to the Caucasus* (New York: Berghahn, 1997), 120.

107. Georgeon, *Abdülhamid II*, 337.

108. Hüseyin Nazım Paşa, *Hatıralarım*, 21.

109. Hüseyin Nazım Paşa, *Hatıralarım*, 26; Dadrian, *The History of the Armenian Genocide*, 120.

110. BOA, Yıldız Sadaret Resmi Mâruzat Evrakı (Y.A.RES), 76/56, 16 R 1313 (Oct. 6, 1895).

111. BOA, Y.A.RES, 76/61, 16 R 1313 (Oct. 6, 1895).

112. Georgeon, *Abdülhamid II*, 342.

113. Georgeon, *Abdülhamid II*, 337; Taner Akçam, *İnsan Hakları ve Ermeni Sorunu: İttihat ve Terakki'den Kurtuluş Savaşı'na* (Ankara: İmge Kitabevi, 1999), 81.

114. Georgeon, *Abdülhamid II*, 338; Akçam, *İnsan Hakları*, 81–82.

115. BOA, Yıldız Perakende Evrakı—Hariciye Nezâreti Maruzâtı (Y.PRK.HR), 22/22, 18 Rebiülevvel (Ra) 1314 (Aug. 27, 1894); BOA, Y.PRK.ŞH, 7/64, 23 Ra 1314 (Sept. 1, 1896).

116. Edhem Eldem, "26 Ağustos 1896 'Banka Vak'ası' ve 'Ermeni Olayları,'" *Tarih ve Toplum Yeni Yaklaşımlar_* 5 (2007): 114–15.

117. William Langer, *The Diplomacy of Imperialism 1890–1902* (Cambridge, MA: Harvard Univ. and Radcliffe College, 1935), 324.

118. "Taraf-ı Ali Seraskeri'den Ba Tezkere İrsal Olunan Talimat Sureti," 16 Ağustos (A) 1312 (Aug. 28, 1896), in Hüseyin Nazım Paşa, *Ermeni Olayları Tarihi*, 1:342.

119. Abdülhamid II's portraitist, Fausto Zonaro, describes how Istanbul's poor Armenians were killed in a massacre lasting days and how Christians' doors were marked with red paint. See Fausto Zonaro, *Abdülhamid'in Hükümdarlığında 20 Yıl: Fausto Zonaro'nun Hatıraları ve Eserleri*, trans. Turan Alptekin and Lotto Romano, ed. Cesare Mario Trevigne (Istanbul: Yapı Kredi, 2008), 158.

120. Eldem, "26 Ağustos 1896."

121. "Dâhiliye Nezâreti'ne Tezkere," 20 A 1312 (Sept. 1, 1896), in Hüseyin Nazım Paşa, *Ermeni Olayları Tarihi*, 1:354.

122. Eldem, "26 Ağustos 1896," 135–36; cf. Hüseyin Nazım Paşa, *Ermeni Olayları Tarihi*, 1:354.

123. Donald Quataert, *Social Disintegration and Popular Resistance in the Ottoman Empire, 1881–1908: Reactions to European Economic Penetration* (New York: New York Univ. Press, 1983), 96–103; Donald Quataert, "Osmanlı İmparatorluğu'nda İşgücü Politikası ve Siyaset: Hamallar ve Bab-ı Ali, 1826–1896," *Tarih ve Toplum* 33, no. 6 (1986): 46.

124. For a transliteration of the investigation report about the incident, see *Sultan İkinci Abdülhamid Han'a Yapılan Suikastın Tahkikat Raporu*, transliteration by Raşit Gündoğdu, ed. Ömer Faruk Yılmaz (Istanbul: Çamlıca Basım, 2007); and for a rendering of the document in modern Turkish, see Harun Tuncer, ed., *Sultan Abdülhamid Han'a Yapılan Suikastın Perde Arkası* (Istanbul: Çamlıca Basım, 2010).

125. See İlkay Yılmaz, "Propaganda by the Deed and Hotel Registration Regulations in the Late Ottoman Empire," *Journal of Ottoman and Turkish Studies Association* 4, no. 1 (May 2017): 137–56; and Houssine Alloul, Edhem Eldem, and Henk de Smaele, eds., *To Kill a Sultan* (London: Palgrave Macmillan, 2018).

126. BOA, A.MKT.MHM, 631/16, 25 Ca 1314 (Dec. 1, 1896). The research conducted consisted of internal passports, house searches, and hotel registries. See, further, BOA, DH.TMIK.M, 21/20, 25 Ca 1314 (Dec. 1, 1896).

127. For example, on intelligence that a Russian Armenian chemist under the alias "Artin Paltof" had provided materials to a "seditious sort," an inquiry was initiated. See BOA, DH.MKT, 2111/104, 12 Ca 1316 (Oct. 29, 1898).

128. See Taner Akçam, *A Shameful Act: The Armenian Genocide and The Question of Turkish Responsibility* (New York: Metropolitan Books, 2006), 72–95.

129. BOA, Yıldız Esas Evrakı (Y.EE), 31/1950 Mükerrer/45/83.22 Za 1299, 6 Ekim 1882 (Oct. 6, 1882). See also Selim Deringil, "2. Abdülhamid Dönemi Osmanlı İmparatorluğu'nda Simgesel ve Törensel Doku: Görünmeden Görünmek," in *Simgeden Millete 2: Abdülhamid'den Mustafa Kemal'e Devlet ve Millet* (Istanbul: İletişim, 2009), 62; and Selim Deringil, "The Turks and 'Europe': The Argument from History," *Middle Eastern Studies* 43, no. 5 (Sept. 2007): 716–17.

130. Stanford J. Shaw, "The Ottoman Census System and Population, 1831-1914," *International Journal of Middle East Studies* 9, no. 3 (1978): 325.

131. Kemal H. Karpat, *Ottoman Population 1830-1914* (Madison: Univ. of Wisconsin Press, 1985), 27.

132. Karpat, *Ottoman Population*, 28–29.

133. See Selim Deringil, "Geç Dönem Osmanlı İmparatorluğu'nda Ermeni Sorunu Çalışmak ya da Belgenin Gırtlağını Sıkmak," in *Simgeden Millete 2*, 228–29.

134. Karpat, *Ottoman Population*, 55–57. See also Isa Blumi, *Ottoman Refugees, 1878–1939: Migration in a Post-imperial World* (London: Bloomsbury, 2013).

135. Tarık Zafer Tunaya, "1876 Kanun-i Esasisi ve Türkiye'de Anayasa Geleneği," in *Tanzimattan Cumhuriyet'e Türkiye Ansiklopedisi*, vol. 1 (Istanbul: İletişim, 1985), 34–36.

136. Huri İslamoğlu-İnan, "Mukayeseli Tarih Yazımı İçin Bir Öneri: Hukuk, Mülkiyet, Meşruiyet," *Toplum ve Bilim* 62 (1993): 30.

137. Selim Deringil, "Osmanlı İmparatorluğu'nda Geleneğin İcadı, Muhayyel Cemaat (Tasarlanmış Topluluk) ve Pan-İslamizm," in *Simgeden Millete 2*, 29–30.

138. Selim Deringil, *The Well Protected Domains: Ideology and the Legitimation of Power in the Ottoman Empire 1876–1909* (London: I. B. Tauris, 2011).

139. Shaw, "The Ottoman Census System," 333–35.

140. See Nadir Özbek, *Osmanlı İmparatorluğu'nda Sosyal Devlet: Siyaset, İktidar ve Meşruiyet* (Istanbul: İletişim, 2002).

141. Jonathan W. Daly, *Autocracy under Siege: Security Police and Opposition in Russia 1866–1905* (DeKalb: Northern Illinois Univ. Press, 1998), 5.

142. Following the Ali Suavi incident, refugees in Istanbul were distanced from the capital, and security measures were tightened. See Georgeon, *Abdulhamid II*, 107–10.

143. See Fatmagül Demirel, *II. Abdülhamid Döneminde Sansür* (Istanbul: Bağlam, 2007).

144. Alf Lüdtke, *Police and State in Prussia, 1815–1850*, trans. Pete Burgess (New York: Cambridge Univ. Press, 1989).

145. Lüdtke, *Police and State in Prussia*, 1–6.

146. Jeff Goodwin, *No Other Way Out: States and Revolutionary Movements, 1945–1991* (Cambridge: Cambridge Univ. Press, 2001), 12.

147. See Neocleous, *Imagining the State*, 40.

148. Linda T. Darling, "'Do Justice, Do Justice, for That Is Paradise': Middle Eastern Advice for Indian Muslim Rulers," *Comparative Studies of South Asia, Africa and the Middle East* 1–2 (2003): 3; Linda T. Darling, "Islamic Empires, the Ottoman Empire and the Circle of Justice," *Comparative Studies in Society and History* 49 (2007): 329–57.

149. For a comparison of conceptions of citizenship across different empires in the nineteenth century, see Fikret Adanır, "Karşılaştırmalı Bir Değerlendirme: Çarlık Rusya'sı ve Habsburg İmparatorluğu Arasında Osmanlı'da Vatandaşlık," *Toplumsal Tarih Dergisi* 182 (2009): 54–63.

150. Foucault, "Governmentality," 93–94.

151. Pasquino, "Theatrum Poiticum," 111–12.

152. Apart from the public-debts issue, financial problems in Macedonia resulted in greater interference in Ottoman internal affairs by other major states. When Public Inspector Hilmi Paşa recommended an increase in customs duties, the Great Powers responded by establishing an international financial commission. Correspondence between the Sublime Porte and major states resulted in little progress on this issue,

though. Alongside the financial commission was the extension of the duty period of civil agents and foreign officers and an increase in Hilmi Paşa's authority. When the two sides could not reach an agreement, the Great Powers, with the exception of Germany, sent a threatening naval fleet, which came straight to the island of Limni in Çanakkale's waters and ensured that the Ottomans accepted all demands. The Great Powers were quite successful in increasing the authority of the financial commission in Macedonia on such matters as tax rates and judicial reforms. The commission increasingly became a tool to expand the Great Powers' influence in the provinces. See Tokay, *Makedonya*, 100–104.

153. See Deringil, "Osmanlı İmparatorluğu'nda Geleneğin İcadı," 29–30.

154. Betül Başaran, "III. Selim ve İstanbul Şehir Siyaseti, 1789–1792," in *Osmanlı'da Asayiş, Suç ve Ceza 18.-20. Yüzyıllar*, ed. Noémi Lévy and Alexandre Toumarkine (Istanbul: Tarih Vakfı Yurt, 2007), 116–34. For more on bachelor and migrant laborers, see Betül Başaran, *Selim III, Social Control and Policing in Istanbul at the End of the Eighteenth Century: Between Crisis and Order* (Leiden: Brill, 2014).

155. The Ministry of Police and the municipality of Altıncı were tasked with prohibiting the performance of a play on the death of Alexander II at the Verdi Theater in Beyoğlu. On this and other such examples, see Fatmagül Demirel, "II. Abdülhamid Dönemi Tiyatro Sansürü; . . . Ve Perdeler Sansürle Açıldı," *Toplumsal Tarih* 63 (1999): 38.

3. Antianarchism, Interimperial Security Collaborations, and the Ottoman Empire

1. Howard C. Payne, *The Police State of Louis Napoléon Bonaparte, 1851–1860* (Seattle: Univ. of Washington Press, 1966); Clive Emsley, "The French Police in the 19th Century," *History Today* 32 (1981): 23–24.

2. Donald Emerson, *Matternich and the Political Police: Security and Subversion in the Hapsburg Monarchy (1815–1830)* (Leiden: Martinus Nijhoff, 1968). For instance, Hungarian students were banned from receiving an education abroad, and a strict visa regime was applied to students coming to Austria (Emerson, *Matternich and the Political Police*, 47, 106, 114–15).

3. Hsi Huey Liang, *The Rise of Modern Police and the European State System from Matternich to the Second World War* (Cambridge: Cambridge Univ. Press, 1992), 57.

4. Daly, *Autocracy under Siege*, 18–19.

5. Richard J. Johnson, "Zagranihnaia Agentura: The Tzarist Political Police in Europe," in *Police Forces in History*, ed. George L. Mosse (London: Sage, 1975), 223–24; Daly, *Autocracy under Siege*, 4–6, 33–34.

6. Liang, *The Rise of Modern Police*, 151. Conferences on preventing trafficking in women included the Conferences of Amsterdam (1901), London (1902), and Paris (1902).

7. Liang, *The Rise of Modern Police*, 152.

8. See Peter Becker, "The Standardized Gaze: The Standardization of the Search Warrant in Nineteenth Century Germany," in *Documenting Individual Identity*, ed. Caplan and Torpey, 146–48, 151–53.

9. See Anne M. Joseph, "Anthropometry, the Police Expert, and the Deptford Murders: The Contested Introduction of Fingerprinting for the Identification of Criminals in Late Victorian and Edwardian Britain," in *Documenting Individual Identity*, ed. Caplan and Torpey, 168–71.

10. For more general information on anarchist terrorism, see Richard Bach Jensen, "Daggers, Rifles, and Dynamite: Anarchist Terrorism in Nineteenth Century Europe," *Terrorism and Political Violence* 16, no. 1 (2004): 116–53; Richard Bach Jensen, *The Battle against Anarchist Terrorism: An International History, 1878–1934* (Cambridge: Cambridge Univ. Press, 2014).

11. D. Novak, "Anarchism and Individual Terrorism," *Canadian Journal of Economics and Political Science* 20 (1954): 176–84.

12. Jensen, "Daggers, Rifles, and Dynamite," 117–18; Walter Laqueur, *A History of Terrorism* (1997; reprint, Piscataway, NJ: Transaction, 2001), 11, 14, 49–53; Liang, *The Rise of Modern Police*; Benjamin Grob-Fitzgibbon, "From the Dagger to the Bomb: Karl Heinzen and the Evolution of Political Terror," *Terrorism and Political Violence* 16, no. 1 (2004): 97–115.

13. For police cooperation in Germany, see Mathieu Daflem, "International Policing in 19th-Century Europe: The Police Union of German States, 1851–1866," *International Criminal Justice Review* 6 (1996): 36–57.

14. Laqueur, *A History of Terrorism*, 11; Lynn Ellen Patyk, "Remembering 'the Terrorism': Sergei Stepniak-Kravchinskii's 'Underground Russia,'" *Slavic Review* 68, no. 4 (2009): 758–81.

15. Jensen, "Daggers, Rifles, and Dynamite," 125.

16. Georgeon, *Abdülhamid II*.

17. For a list of these types of actions, see Barry Rubin and Judith Colp Rubin, *Chronologies of Modern Terrorism* (Armonk, NY: M.E. Sharpe, 2008), 6–24.

18. Laqueur, *A History of Terrorism*, 53. For detailed information on secret organizations, see Jap Kloosterman, "Hidden Centres: The Rise and Fall of the Secret Societies," paper presented at the conference "Zentren und Peripherien der europäischen Wissensordnung vom 15. bis zum 20. Jahrhundert' 3," German Historical Institute, Moscow, Sept. 24–26, 2009, at https://brewminate.com/a-history-of-secret-societies/.

19. Daly, *Autocracy under Siege*, 45.

20. Mathieu Daflem, "Wild Beasts without Nationality: The Uncertain Origins of Interpol, 1889–1910," in *Handbook of Transnational Crime and Justice*, ed. Philip Reichel (Thousand Oaks, CA: Sage, 2005), 275--85; Richard Bach Jensen, "The International Campaign against Anarchist Terrorism, 1880–1930s," *Terrorism and Political Violence* 21 (2009): 92; Jensen, *The Battle against Anarchist Terrorism*.

21. Mathieu Daflem, *Policing World Society: Historical Foundations of International Police Cooperation* (New York: Oxford Univ. Press, 2002), 12–34.

22. This assassination pushed Switzerland to change its national laws, to avoid foreign intervention, and to tighten police controls. The fact that Genoa hosted anarchists and refugees was met with doubt by other states. Yet another note that must not be overlooked is that since 1889 Switzerland had filed records containing the names, places of birth, addresses, and personal features of anarchists (see Liang, *The Rise of Modern Police*, 159–60). In terms of international cooperation, such information was relevant to the Ottoman state for use in monitoring anarchists.

23. Richard Bach Jensen, "The International Anti-anarchist Conference of 1898 and the Origins of Interpol," *Journal of Contemporary History* 16, no. 2 (Apr. 1981): 323–47.

24. Liang, *The Rise of Modern Police*, 161–62.

25. Jensen, "The International Anti-anarchist Conference of 1898," 325.

26. See Adil Baktıaya, "19. Yüzyıl Sonunda Anarşist Terör, 'Toplumun Anarşistlerden Korunması Konferansı (1898)' ve Osmanlı Devleti," *Bilgi ve Bellek* 8 (2007): 50–76.

27. See Jensen, "The International Anti-anarchist Conference of 1898"; BOA, Y.A.RES, 101/31, 12 S 1317 (June 22, 1899); and "From Rome Consulate to Foreign Affairs, Secret Correspondence of Formal Letter Number 2," 3 Kanunusani 1899, in BOA, Yıldız Perakende Evrakı—Elçilik ve Şehbenderlik Maruzâtı (Y.PRK.EŞA), 31/136, 20 Ş 1316 (Jan. 3, 1899). (This document includes the translation of the conference report by Reşıd Bey, Nurı Bey, and Hakkı Bey.)

28. "From Rome Consulate to Foreign Affairs, Secret Correspondence of Formal Letter Number 2."

29. BOA, Y.A.RES, 101/31, 12 S 1317 (June 22, 1899). For the recommendations, see appendix 1.

30. Liang, *The Rise of Modern Police*, 165.

31. "Hariciye Nezareti'ne 3 Kanunusani 1899 Tarihinde Roma Sefaret-i Seniyyesi'nden Varid Olan 2 Numaralı Mahremane Tahriratın Tercümesi Suretidir," Y.PRK.EŞA, 31/136, 20 Ş 1316 (Jan. 3, 1899).

32. Jensen, "The International Anti-anarchist Conference of 1898," 327–28.

33. Liang, *The Rise of Modern Police*, 162; Baktıaya, "19. Yüzyıl Sonunda Anarşist Terör," 66–67.

34. Jensen, "The International Anti-anarchist Conference of 1898," 327.

35. Liang, *The Rise of Modern Police*, 160; Daflem, "Wild Beasts without Nationality," 279.

36. Jensen, "The International Anti-anarchist Conference of 1898," 331–34.

37. Serbian government's statement sent from Serbia to the Italian Ministry of Foreign Affairs and added to the protocol on May 17, 1899, BOA, Y.A.RES, 101/31, 12 S 1317 (June 22, 1899).

38. French government's statement of April 20, 1899, BOA, Y.A.RES, 101/31, 12 S 1317 (June 22, 1899).

39. Romanian government's statement of April 10, 1899, BOA, Y.A.RES, 101/31, 12 S 1317 (June 22, 1899). This statement was added to the protocol on June 22, 1899; see Y.A.RES, 101/31, 12 S 1317 (June 22, 1899).

40. Liang, *The Rise of Modern Police*, 164.

41. "From Rome Consulate to Foreign Affairs, Secret Correspondence of the Formal Letter Number 2."

42. Jensen, *The Battle against Anarchist Terrorism*, 165–68.

43. See document number 2 in BOA, Y.PRK.EŞA, 31/136, 20 Ş 1316 (Jan. 1, 1899).

44. See document number 2 and attachment E in BOA, Y.PRK.EŞA, 31/136, 20 Ş 1316 (Jan. 3, 1899).

45. See document number 2 in BOA, Y.PRK.EŞA, 31/136, 20 Ş 1316 (Jan. 1, 1899).

46. "From Rome Consulate to Foreign Affairs, Secret Correspondence of the Formal Letter Number 2."

47. For detailed information on the police system in France, see Jean-Marc Berliére, "The Professionalization of the Police under the Third Republic in France 1875–1914," in *Policing Western Europe*, ed. Emsley and Weinberger, 36–54.

48. For *portrait parlé*, see Jensen, *The Battle against Anarchist Terrorism*, 166–67.

49. "From Rome Consulate to Foreign Affairs, Secret Correspondence of the Formal Letter Number 2."

50. "From Rome Consulate to Foreign Affairs, Secret Correspondence of the Formal Letter Number 2."

51. "From Rome Consulate to Foreign Affairs, Secret Correspondence of the Formal Letter Number 2."

52. "From Rome Consulate to Foreign Affairs, Secret Correspondence of the Formal Letter Number 2."

53. "From Rome Consulate to Foreign Affairs, Secret Correspondence of the Formal Letter Number 2."

54. "From Rome Consulate to Foreign Affairs, Secret Correspondence of the Formal Letter Number 2."

55. "From Rome Consulate to Foreign Affairs, Secret Correspondence of the Formal Letter Number 2."

56. Whatever the success of the Conference of Rome on this matter, in historical terms it was a first step. See Liang, *The Rise of Modern Police*; Jensen, "The International Anti-anarchist Conference of 1898," and "The International Campaign against Anarchist Terrorism;" Daflem, "Wild Beasts without Nationality"; and Mathieu Daflem, "International Police Cooperation in North America," in *International Police Cooperation: A World Perspective*, ed. D. J. Koenig and D. K. Das (Lanham, MD: Lexington, 2001), 71–98.

57. See attachment D in BOA, Y.PRK.EŞA, 31/136, 20 Ş 1316 (Jan. 3, 1899). For detailed information on the Prussian Police Force on the matter, see Lüdtke, *Police and State in Prussia*; and Herbert Reinke, "'Armed as If for a War': The State, the Military and the Professionalization of the Prussian Police in Imperial Germany," in *Policing Western Europe*, ed. Emsley and Weinberger, 55–73.

58. Ceza Kanunname-i Hümayunu (Criminal Code of Hümayun or Ottoman Penal Code), *Düstur*, Tertip 1, vol. 1 (Istanbul: Matbaa-i Amire, 1289 [1872–73]), 496–537.

59. The information under consideration in this section is based on Y.A.RES, 101/31, 12 S 1317 (June 22, 1899).

60. Baktıaya writes that the Ottoman State had made an agreement with a French expert before the conference ("19. Yüzyıl Sonunda Anarşist Terör," 71). See BOA, Zabtiye Nezareti (ZB), 45/27, 24 A 1898 (Aug. 24, 1898). For a detailed discussion, see İlkay Yılmaz, "The Ottoman State, Police Photographs and Anthropometry," *Journal of Photography*, no. 31 (2019): 90–100.

61. "From Rome Consulate to Foreign Affairs, Secret correspondence of the Formal Letter Number 2."

62. Jensen, *The Battle against Anarchist Terrorism*, 162.

63. "From Rome Consulate to Foreign Affairs, Secret Correspondence of the Formal Letter Number 2"; and see Jensen, *The Battle against Anarchist Terrorism*, 162.

64. BOA, Y.A.RES, 101/31, 12 S 1317 (June 22, 1899).

65. BOA, Y.A.RES, 101/31, 12 S 1317 (June 22, 1899).

66. BOA, Y.A.RES, 101/31, 12 S 1317 (June 22, 1899).

67. BOA, Y.A.RES, 101/31, 12 S 1317 (June 22, 1899).

68. Ceza Kanunname-i Hümayunu, *Düstur*, Tertip 1, vol. 1. See appendix 2.

69. Ceza Kanunname-i Hümayunu, *Düstur*, Tertip 1, vol. 1. See appendix 2.

70. Ceza Kanunname-i Hümayunu, *Düstur*, Tertip 1, vol. 1. See appendix 2.

71. Ceza Kanunname-i Hümayunu, *Düstur*, Tertip 1, vol. 1 (see appendix 2); Y.A.RES, 101/31, 12 S 1317 (June 22, 1899).

72. Ceza Kanunname-i Hümayunu, *Düstur*, Tertip 1, vol. 1. See appendix 2.

73. Ceza Kanunname-i Hümayunu, *Düstur*, Tertip 1, vol. 1. See appendix 2 and BOA, Y.A.RES, 101/31.

74. Ceza Kanunname-i Hümayunu, *Düstur*, Tertip 1, vol. 1. See appendix 2 and BOA, Y.A.RES, 101/31.

75. Ceza Kanunname-i Hümayunu, *Düstur*, Tertip 1, vol. 1. See appendix 2 and BOA, Y.A.RES, 101/31.

76. Ceza Kanunname-i Hümayunu, *Düstur*, Tertip 1, vol. 1. See appendix 2 and BOA, Y.A.RES, 101/31.

77. Ceza Kanunname-i Hümayunu, *Düstur*, Tertip 1, vol. 1. See appendix 2 and BOA, Y.A.RES, 101/31.

78. Meclis-i Mahsus, no. 454, 12 S 1317 (June 22, 1899), in BOA, Y.A.RES, 101/31. See also BOA, Y.PRK.HR, 27/31, 30 Z 1316 (May 10, 1899).

79. BOA, Y.A.RES, 116/23, 6 S 1320 (May 15, 1902). For the anarchism and antianarchism in the Ottoman Empire, see İlkay Yılmaz, "Anti-anarchism and Security Perceptions during the Hamidian Era," *Zapruder World* 1 (Spring 2014), at https://zapruderworld.org/journal/past-volumes/volume-1/anti-anarchism-and-security-perceptions-during-the-hamidian-era/; Axel Çorlu, "Anarchists and Anarchism in the Ottoman Empire, 1850–1917," in *History from Below: A Tribute in Memory of Donald Quataert*, ed. Selim Karahasanoğlu and Deniz C. Demir (Istanbul: Istanbul Bilgi Üniversitesi Yayınları, 2016), 551–83; Yılmaz, "Propaganda by the Deed"; Toygun Altıntaş, "The Ottoman War on 'Anarchism' and Revolutionary Violence," in *To Kill a Sultan*, ed. Alloul, Eldem, and de Smaele, 99–128; İlkay Yılmaz, "Conspiracy, International Police Cooperation and the Fight against Anarchism in the Late Ottoman Empire (1878–1908)," in *Age of Rogues: Rebels, Revolutionaries and Racketeers at the Frontiers of Empires*, ed. Alp Yenen and Ramazan Hakkı Öztan (Edinburgh: Edinburgh Univ. Press, 2021), 208–34.

80. See the summary of the OPC, Articles 55 to 62 in appendix 2.

81. BOA, Y.A.HUS, 469/36, 8 Muharrem (M) 1322 (Mar. 25, 1904).

82. İlkay Yılmaz, "Governing the Armenian Question through Passports in the Late Ottoman Empire (1876–1908)," *Journal of Historical Sociology* 32, no. 4 (2019): 388–403.

83. BOA, İrade Hususi (İ.HUS), 115/89, 24 M 1322 (Apr. 10, 1904).

84. BOA, İ.HUS, 115/89, 24 M 1322 (Apr. 10, 1904).

85. Cf. BOA, Y.A.HUS, 469/36, 8 M 1322 (Mar. 25, 1904); BOA, Y.A.HUS, 469/45, 10 M 1322 (Mar. 27, 1904).

86. BOA, Y.A.HUS, 469/45, 10 M 1322 (Mar. 27, 1904).

87. BOA, Y.A.HUS, 469/91, 16 M 1322 (Apr. 2, 1904).

88. BOA, İrade Hariciye (İ.HR), 388/14, 5 S 1322 (Apr. 21, 1904).

4. State Discourses of Threat from Ancient Concepts to New Narratives

1. *Ermeni Tarih-i Vukuatı* was published by the Ottoman Archives of the Prime Minister's Office as *Ermeni Olayları Tarihi* in 1994. See Hüseyin Nazım Paşa, *Ermeni Olayları Tarihi*, vol. 1, and Hüseyin Nazım Paşa, *Ermeni Olayları Tarihi*, vol. 2, prepared by Necati Aktaş, Mustafa Oğuz, and Mustafa Küçük, Yayın no. 15 (Ankara: T.C. Başbakanlık Devlet Arşivleri Genel Müdürlüğü Osmanlı Arşivi Daire Başkanlığı, 1994).

2. Eric H. Monkkonen, "A Disorderly People? Urban Order in the Nineteenth and Twentieth Centuries," *Journal of American History* 68 (1981): 545; Reşat Ekrem Koçu's book on the fire brigades demonstrates the existence of such a subculture in the brigade. See Reşat Ekrem Koçu, İstanbul Tulumbacıları: *Yangın Var* (Istanbul: Ana Yayınevi, 1981).

3. Most of the men traveling to the city left their wives and children behind in their homelands. It is unclear how women in their homelands got by and whether these men

sent money back. Though bachelors in Istanbul had permission to visit their homelands, it is another open question, one worth looking into, how many were actually able to do so.

4. Ferdan Ergut, "Policing the Poor in the Late Ottoman Empire," *Middle Eastern Studies* 38 (2002): 155. On regulations related to hotels, see Hikmet Tongur, *Türkiye'de Genel Kolluk* (Ankara: Kanaat Basımevi, 1946), 199.

5. Paul A. Slack, "Vagrants and Vagrancy in England, 1598–1664," *Economic History Review* 27 (1974): 365.

6. Sigrid Wadauer, "Establishing Distinctions: Unemployment versus Vagrancy in Austria from the Late Nineteenth Century to 1938," *International Review of Social History* 56 (2011): 34.

7. Wadauer, "Establishing Distinctions," 40–41. For a general evaluation of studies carried out on the history of migration, see Jan Lucassen and Leo Lucassen, introduction to *Migration, Migration History, History*, ed. Lucassen and Lucassen, 9–40.

8. In Slack's chart, most of the vagrants were single men (Slack, "Vagrants and Vagrancy," 366).

9. Ferdan Ergut, *Modern Devlet ve Polis, Osmanlı'dan Cumhuriyet'e Toplumsal Denetimin Diyalektiği* (Istanbul: İletişim, 2004), 244.

10. Harvey Graff, "Crime and Punishment in the Nineteenth Century: A New Look at the Criminal," *Journal of Interdisciplinary History* 3 (1977): 482.

11. *Report of the Commissioners Appointed to Enquire into the Prison and Reformatory System in Ontario, 1891* (Toronto: Warwick & Sons, 1891), 259, at https://babel.hathitrust.org/cgi/pt?id=aeu.ark:/13960/t53f5s583&view=1up&scq=272.

12. Prashan Ranasinghe, "Vagrancy as a Penal Problem: The Logistics of Administering Punishment in Late-Nineteenth-Century Canada," *Journal of Historical Sociology* 25, no. 4 (2012): 541.

13. Ranasinghe, "Vagrancy as a Penal Problem," 531–35.

14. Otwin Marenin, "Police Performance and State Rule Control and Autonomy in the Exercise of Coercion," *Comparative Politics* 18 (1985): 111–12.

15. For a similar perspective, see Jens Hanssen, "Public Morality and Marginality in Fin-de-Siécle Beirut," in *Outside In: Marginality in the Modern Middle East*, ed. Eugene Rogan (London: I. B. Tauris, 2002), 184; Nadir Özbek, "İkinci Meşrutiyet İstanbul'unda Serseriler ve Dilenciler," *Toplumsal Tarih* 11, no. 64 (1999): 34–43.

16. "Serseri ve Mazannei Su'i Olan Eşhas Hakkında Nizamname," 3 Sefer 1308, 6 Eylül 1306, and Sept. 18, 1890, in *Düstur*, Tertip 1, vol. 6: *1887–1890* (Ankara: Ankara Başvekalet Matbaası, 1939), 748.

17. For a conceptual discussion of real and artificial crimes, see Richard J. Evans, "Introduction: The 'Dangerous Classes' in Germany from the Middle Ages to the Twentieth Century," in *The German Underworld: Deviants and Outcasts in German History*, ed. Richard J. Evans (London: Routledge, 2015), 14.

18. Ergut, "Policing the Poor," 150.

19. See Foucault, *Discipline and Punish*, 76.

20. Ergut, "Policing the Poor," 151. As another dimension of this process, matters related in particular to vagrancy can be added to police regulations rather than to the criminal code.

21. Gordon C. Chang and Hugh B. Mehan, "Discourse in a Religious Mode: The Bush Administration's Discourse in the War on Terrorism and Its Challenges," *Pragmatics* 16 (2006): 2.

22. İlhan Kutluer, "Fesad," in *Türkiye Diyanet Vakfı İslam Ansiklopedisi*, vol. 12 (Istanbul: Türkiye Diyanet Vakfı, 1995), 421.

23. Mustafa Akdağ, *Türk Halkının Dirlik ve Düzenlik Kavgası Celali İsyanları* (Ankara: Bilgi Yayınevi, 1975), 163–78.

24. Both David Bayley and Ferdan Ergut tie the growth in the organization of the modern police not to any rise in the rates of petty crime in society but to the beginning of the perception of existing crimes as threats to the existing order. See David Bayley, *Patterns of Policing* (New Brunswick, NJ: Rutgers Univ. Press, 1985), 88, and Ergut, *Modern Devlet ve Polis*, 72.

25. In his study of crime and punishment in eighteenth-century Istanbul, Fariba Zarinebaf analyzes the relationship among migration to the city, public order, and uprisings. See Fariba Zarinebaf, *Crime and Punishment in Istanbul 1700–1800* (Berkeley: Univ. of California Press, 2010).

26. Başaran, *Selim III, Social Control and Policing in Istanbul*, 72–105.

27. Ahmet Akgündüz, *Osmanlı Kanunnameleri ve Hukuki Tahlilleri: Kanuni Sultan Süleyman Devri Kanunnameleri: I. Kısım Merkezi ve Umumi Kanunnameler*, vol. 4 (Istanbul: Fey Vakfı, 1992), 157; and see Mehmet Akman, *Osmanlı Devletinde Ceza Yargılaması* (Istanbul: Eren, 2004), 51.

28. Akman, *Osmanlı Devletinde Ceza Yargılaması*, 51–52. In *Discipline and Punish*, Foucault notes that vagrants were not seen as valid witnesses.

29. Başaran, *Selim III, Social Control and Policing in Istanbul*, 119.

30. Akdağ, *Türk Halkının Dirlik ve Düzenlik Kavgası*, 171–73.

31. Engin Deniz Akarlı, "Maslaha from 'Common Good' to 'Raison d'Etat' in the Experience of Istanbul Artisans, 1730–1840," in *Hoca, 'allame, puits de science: Essays in Honor of Kemal H. Karpat*, ed. Kaan Durukan, Robert W. Zens, and Akile Zorlu-Durukan (Istanbul: ISIS Press, 2010), 63–79.

32. Edict *Mühimme 5*, 159, in Akdağ, *Türk Halkının Dirlik ve Düzenlik Kavgası*, 173.

33. Başaran, *Selim III, Social Control and Policing in Istanbul*, 75–105. See also Akdağ, *Türk Halkının Dirlik ve Düzenlik Kavgası*, 171–79, 185, 208–13, 221–22, 226.

34. Robin Corey, *Fear: The History of a Political Idea* (Oxford: Oxford Univ. Press, 2004), 16.

35. Corey, *Fear*, 20.

36. BOA, DH.TMIK.M, 26/57, 15 Ş 1314 (Jan. 18, 1897); BOA, DH.TMIK.M 26/88, 20 Ş 1314 (Jan. 24, 1897). Each of these documents gives only the name, with no registration number or date for the written statement or edict.

37. For a more detailed discussion of this matter, see Debra Merskin, "The Construction of Arabs as Enemies: Post–September 11 Discourse of George W. Bush," *Mass Communication & Society* 7, no. 2 (2004): 157–60.

38. Hüseyin Nazım Paşa, *Ermeni Olayları Tarihi*, vols. 1 and 2.

39. Hüseyin Nazım Paşa, *Ermeni Olayları Tarihi*, 1:1.

40. Hüseyin Nazım Paşa, *Ermeni Olayları Tarihi*, 1:1.

41. Deringil, "2. Abdülhamid Dönemi Osmanlı İmparatorluğu'nda Simgesel ve Törensel Doku," 82.

42. Hüseyin Nazım Paşa, *Ermeni Olayları Tarihi*, 1:2.

43. "Dâhiliye Nezâret-i Celîlesi'nden Vârid Olan 8 Haziran Sene 1312 Târih ve 305 Numaralı Tezkerenin Sûretidir, Ferik Sa'deddîn Paşa ve Mahkeme-i Temyîz A'zâsından İbrahim Edhem ve Cemal Bey Taraflarından İ'tâ Olunan Takrîrin Sûretidir," in Hüseyin Nazım Paşa, *Ermeni Olayları Tarihi*, 2:248–54.

44. "Dâhiliye Nezâret-i Celîlesi'nden Vârid Olan 8 Haziran Sene 1312," in Hüseyin Nazım Paşa, *Ermeni Olayları Tarihi*, 2:248–54.

45. Hüseyin Nazım Paşa, *Ermeni Olayları Tarihi*, 2:57.

46. Hüseyin Nazım Paşa, *Ermeni Olayları Tarihi*, 1:3.

47. Hüseyin Nazım Paşa, *Ermeni Olayları Tarihi*, 1:3–4.

48. On the concept of *sade dilan ahali*, see also Deringil, "2. Abdülhamid Dönemi Osmanlı İmparatorluğu'nda Simgesel ve Törensel Doku."

49. Document written to Beyoğlu Governerate, Sept. 16, 1311, in Hüseyin Nazım Paşa, *Ermeni Olayları Tarihi*, 1:74–75.

50. Document written to Beyoğlu Governerate, Sept. 16, 1311, in Hüseyin Nazım Paşa, *Ermeni Olayları Tarihi*, 1:74–75.

51. Hüseyin Nazım Paşa, *Ermeni Olayları Tarihi*, 1:77–78.

52. Hüseyin Nazım Paşa, *Ermeni Olayları Tarihi*, 1:77–78.

53. Correspondence from Beyoğlu Governorate, no. 711 Numaralı, 19 Eylül 1311 (Oct. 1, 1895), in Hüseyin Nazım Paşa, *Ermeni Olayları Tarihi*, 1:77.

54. Hüseyin Nazım Paşa, *Ermeni Olayları Tarihi*, 1:87.

55. Hüseyin Nazım Paşa, *Ermeni Olayları Tarihi*, 1:90.

56. Hüseyin Nazım Paşa, *Ermeni Olayları Tarihi*, 1:90.

57. Telegram from Sivas Province Police Department, 5 Kânûn-ı Evvel 1311 (Dec. 17, 1895), in Hüseyin Nazım Paşa, *Ermeni Olayları Tarihi*, 1:133.

58. "Hey'et-i Teftîşiyye Tarafından Makâm-ı Sâmî-i Sadâret-penâhîye Takdîm Olunup Dâhiliye Nezâret-i Celîlesi'ne Bir Sûreti bâ-Tezkere İrsâl Buyurulan Lâyihadır, Trabzon Vilayet-i Aliyyesi Nefs-i Trabzon Vak'ası," in Hüseyin Nazım Paşa, *Ermeni Olayları Tarihi*, 1:165.

59. Hüseyin Nazım Paşa, *Ermeni Olayları Tarihi*, 1:90–91.

60. Correspondence from Mar'aş Police Department, 1 Teşrîn-i Sânî 1311 (Nov. 13, 1895), in Hüseyin Nazım Paşa, *Ermeni Olayları Tarihi*, 1:119–20.

61. "Hey'et-i Teftîşiyye... Trabzon Vak'ası," in Hüseyin Nazım Paşa, *Ermeni Olayları Tarihi*, 1:172.

62. "Beyoğlu ve Üsküdar Mutasarrıflıklarıyla Dersa'âdet Polis Müdîrliği'ne ve Jandarma Alayı Kumandanlığı'na Ta'mîmen Yazılan 19 Eylül Sene 1311 Târihli Tezkerenin Sûretidir," in Hüseyin Nazım Paşa, *Ermeni Olayları Tarihi*, 1:78.

63. "İstanbul Polis Müdîrliği'ne Yazılan 19 Eylül Sene 1311 Târihli Tezkere Sûretidir," in Hüseyin Nazım Paşa, *Ermeni Olayları Tarihi*, 1:79.

64. Correspondence from Interior Affairs, no. 564, 10 A 1312 (Sept. 1, 1896), in Hüseyin Nazım Paşa, *Ermeni Olayları Tarihi*, 2:346–57.

65. Correspondence to Beyoğlu and Üsküdar Governerates, Istanbul Police Department, and Desaadet Gandermary Regimental Command, 20 Eylül 1311 (Oct. 2, 1895), in Hüseyin Nazım Paşa, *Ermeni Olayları Tarihi*, 1:81–82.

66. "Kâtib-i Sânî-i Hazret-i Şehriyârî Atûfetlü Ahmed İzzet Beyefendi Hazretleri'ne Jurnal ve Huzûr-ı Me'âlî-Mevfûr-I Cenâb-ı Sadâret-penâhîye ve Adliye ve Mezâhib Nezâret ve Dâhiliye Nezâret-i Celîlelerine 25 Mayıs Sene 1312 Târihiyle Gönderilen Tezkerenin Sûretidir," in Hüseyin Nazım Paşa, *Ermeni Olayları Tarihi*, 2:235.

67. Hüseyin Nazım Paşa, *Ermeni Olayları Tarihi*, 1:9.

68. Hüseyin Nazım Paşa, *Ermeni Olayları Tarihi*, 1:45–46.

69. Repetitions in the state discourse create a pattern. See Chang and Mehan, "Discourse in a Religious Mode," 5.

70. Hüseyin Nazım Paşa, *Ermeni Olayları Tarihi*, 1:44–50

71. Hüseyin Nazım Paşa, *Ermeni Olayları Tarihi*, 1:44–45.

72. Hüseyin Nazım Paşa, *Ermeni Olayları Tarihi*, 1:55–64.

73. Hüseyin Nazım Paşa, *Ermeni Olayları Tarihi*, 1:59.

74. Hüseyin Nazım Paşa, *Ermeni Olayları Tarihi*, 1:60

75. Hüseyin Nazım Paşa, *Ermeni Olayları Tarihi*, 1:61.

76. Hüseyin Nazım Paşa, *Ermeni Olayları Tarihi*, 1:63.

77. Hüseyin Nazım Paşa, *Ermeni Olayları Tarihi*, 1:61.

78. "28 Eylül Sene 1311 Târihinde Tanzîm ve Takdîm Kılınan Fezleke Sûretidir," in Hüseyin Nazım Paşa, *Ermeni Olayları Tarihi*, 1:85.

79. "Dâhiliye Nezâret-i Celîlesi'ne Vârid Olan 30 Haziran Sene 1312 Târih ve 280 Numara ile Yazılan Tezkere Sûretidir," in Hüseyin Nazım Paşa, *Ermeni Olayları Tarihi*, 2:282–84.

80. "Dâhiliye Nezâret-i Celîlesi'ne Yazılan 23 Mayıs Sene 1312 Târihli Tezkere Sûretidir," in Hüseyin Nazım Paşa, *Ermeni Olayları Tarihi*, 2:244–45.

81. "Dâhiliye Nezâret-i Celîlesi'nden Vârid Olan 10 Ağustos Sene 1312 Târihli ve 564 Numaralı Tezkere Sûretidir," in Hüseyin Nazım Paşa, *Ermeni Olayları Tarihi*, 2:346–57.

82. "Dâhiliye Nezâret-i Celîlesi'nden Vârid Olan . . . Sûretidir," in Hüseyin Nazım Paşa, *Ermeni Olayları Tarihi*, 2:346–57.

83. "Makâm-ı Sâmî-i Sadâret-penâhîden 16 Eylül Sene 1311 Târih ve 317 Numara ile Vârid Olan Tezkere-i Sâmiyyenin Sûretidir," in Hüseyin Nazım Paşa, *Ermeni Olayları Tarihi*, 1:70–71.

84. "28 Eylül Sene 1311 Târihinde Tanzîm ve Takdîm Kılınan Fezleke Sûretidir," in Hüseyin Nazım Paşa, *Ermeni Olayları Tarihi*, 1:79–87.

85. "28 Eylül Sene 1311 Târihinde Tanzîm ve Takdîm Kılınan Fezleke Sûretidir," in Hüseyin Nazım Paşa, *Ermeni Olayları Tarihi*, 1:83.

86. "Makâm-ı Sâmî-i Sadâret-penâhîye Yazılan 17 Mayıs Sene 1312 Târihli Tezkerenin Sûretidir," in Hüseyin Nazım Paşa, *Ermeni Olayları Tarihi*, 2:232.

87. "Zabtiye Nezâreti'nden Makâm-ı Sadâret-penâhîye 16 Haziran Sene 1311 Târihiyle Yazılan Tezkerenin Sûretidir," in Hüseyin Nazım Paşa, *Ermeni Olayları Tarihi*, 2:64–67.

88. "Zabtiye Nezâreti'nden . . . Tezkerenin Sûretidir," in Hüseyin Nazım Paşa, *Ermeni Olayları Tarihi*, 1:66.

89. "Zabtiye Nezâreti'nden . . . Tezkerenin Sûretidir," in Hüseyin Nazım Paşa, *Ermeni Olayları Tarihi*, 1:66.

90. "Makâm-ı Sâmî-i Sadâret-penâhîye 17 Eylül Sene 1311 Târih ve 204 Numara ile Yazılan Tezkerenin Sûretidir," in Hüseyin Nazım Paşa, *Ermeni Olayları Tarihi*, 1:71–72.

91. "17 Haziran Sene 1311 Târih ve 223 Numara ile Beyoğlu Mutasarrıflığı'na Yazılan Müzekkirenin Sûretidir," in Hüseyin Nazım Paşa, *Ermeni Olayları Tarihi*, 1:74.

92. "Dâhiliye Nezâret-i Celîlesi'ne Vârid Olan 30 Haziran Sene 1312 Târih ve 280 Numara ile Yazılan Tezkere Sûretidir," in Hüseyin Nazım Paşa, *Ermeni Olayları Tarihi*, 2:282–83. For a similar case on a different date, see "Dâhiliye Nezâret-i Celîlesi'nden Vârid Olan . . . Sûretidir," in Hüseyin Nazım Paşa, *Ermeni Olayları Tarihi*, 2:346–57.

93. "28 Mayıs Sene 1312 Târihiyle Kâtib-i Sânî-i Hazret-i Şehriyârî Atûfetlü Ahmed İzzet Beyefendi Hazretleriyle Gönderilen Jurnal ve Dâhiliye Nezâret-i Celîlesi'ne Yazılan Tezkere Sûretidir," in Hüseyin Nazım Paşa, *Ermeni Olayları Tarihi*, 2:241.

5. Controlling Geographical Mobility

1. Christoph Herzog, "Migration and the State: On Ottoman Regulations Concerning Migration since the Age of Mahmud II," in *The City in the Ottoman Empire Migration and the Making of Urban Modernity*, ed. Ulrike Freitag, Malte Fuhrmann, Nora Lafia, and Florian Riedler (London: Routledge, 2011), 119–20. Herzog, in analyzing the Ottoman state's efforts to control geographical mobility, emphasizes historical continuity. As in this study, he attempts to read regulations regarding licenses of passage and passports alongside the Vagrancy Act and police regulations, but he focuses on the regulations of 1911 and 1914 rather than the regulation of 1884.

2. For an analysis of the passports in the frame of international system, see Mark B. Salter, *Rights of Passage: The Passport in International Relations* (Boulder, CO: Lynne Rienner, 2003), 11–12.

3. For more about the Ottoman identity cards and individual identification in the court records, see Vanessa Guéno, "S'identifier à l'aube de l'état civil (*nufûs*): Les justiciables devant le tribunal civil de Homs (Syrie Centrale) à la fin du XIXe siècle," *Revue des mondes musulmans et de la Méditerranée*, no. 127 (2010): 193–211.

4. David Stark and Laszlo Bruszt, *Post-socialist Pathways: Transforming Politics and Property in East Central Europe* (Cambridge: Cambridge Univ. Press, 1998), 103–4.

5. For a discussion about local orientation of identification practices, see Craig Robertson, "Four Documents, a Non-citizen, and a Diplomatic Controversy: The Documentation of Identity in the Mid–Nineteenth Century," *Journal of Historical Sociology* 22, no. 4 (2009): 476–96.

6. For more detailed information on migrants and public order in eighteenth-century Istanbul, see Betül Başaran, "Remaking the Gate of Felicity: Policing, Social Control, and Migration in Istanbul at the End of the Eighteenth Century, 1789–1793," PhD diss., Univ. of Chicago, 2006.

7. Halil İnalcık, "İstanbul," in *The Encyclopedia of Islam* (Leiden: Brill, 1978), 4:234, 239.

8. Abdullah Saydam, "Kamu Hizmeti Yaptırma ve Suçu Önleme Yöntemi Olarak Osmanlılarda Kefalet Usulü," *Tarih ve Toplum* 28, no. 164 (1997): 5.

9. Saydam, "Kamu Hizmeti Yaptırma."

10. Akdağ, *Türk Halkının Dirlik ve Düzenlik Kavgası*, 145–46.

11. Ahmet Refik Altınay, *Hicri On Birinci Asırda İstanbul Hayatı* (Istanbul: Devlet Matbaası, 1931), 21–22.

12. Saydam, "Kamu Hizmeti Yaptırma," 8–11; Akdağ, *Türk Halkının Dirlik ve Düzenlik Kavgası*, 272.

13. Ahmet Refik Altınay, *On Altıncı Asırda İstanbul Hayatı* (Istanbul: Devlet Basımevi, 1935), 139–40.

14. Yücel Özkaya, "XVIII. Yüzyılda Çıkarılan Adaletnamelere Göre Türkiye'nin İç Durumu," *Belleten* 38, no. 151 (1974): 459.

15. M. Münir Aktepe, "İstanbul'un Nüfus Meselesine Dair Bazı Vesikalar," *İstanbul Üniversitesi Edebiyat Fakültesi Tarih Dergisi* 9 (Sept. 1958): 6–7.

16. Ahmed Refik Altınay, *On İkinci Asr-ı Hicri'de İstanbul Hayatı (1689–1785)* (Istanbul: Enderun Kitabevi, 1988), 80–81, 105–6.

17. Başaran, *Remaking the Gate of Felicity*.

18. Altınay, *On İkinci Asr-ı Hicri'de*, 131–32, 199. The expulsion of unwanted "elements" in Istanbul to their homelands is something we encounter again later in the Hamidian era.

19. Aktepe, "İstanbul'un Nüfus Meselesine Dair Bazı Vesikalar," 9–13.

20. Özkaya, "XVIII. Yüzyılda Çıkarılan Adaletnamelere Göre Türkiye'nin İç Durumu," 460–61.

21. For global examples, see Breckenridge and Szeter, *Registration and Recognition*.

22. *Ankara Şer'iye Sicili*, no. 224, document no. 267, in Musa Çadırcı, "Tanzimat'ın İlanı Sırasında Anadolu'da İçgüvenlik," *Ankara Üniversitesi DTCF Tarih Araştırmaları Enstitüsü Tarih Araştırmaları Dergisi* 24 (1980): 54–55.

23. Musa Çadırcı, "Türkiye'de Muhtarlık Teşkilatının Kurulması Üzerine Bir Araştırma," *Belleten* 135 (1970): 415; Musa Çadırcı, "Anadolu Kentlerinde Mahalle (Osmanlı Dönemi)," in *Tarihten Günümüze Anadolu'da Konut ve Yerleşme* (Istanbul: Tarih Vakfı Yurt, 1996), 260.

24. Torpey, *The Invention of the Passport*, 16.

25. Charles Steinwedel, "Making Social Groups, One Person at a Time: The Identification of Individuals by Estate, Religious Confession, and Ethnicity in Late Imperial Russia," in *Documenting Individual Identity*, ed. Caplan and Torpey, 74. In Russia, no one could leave a place without official permission or a passport. For a study looking at the problem of rural-to-urban labor migration in Russia using internal passports, see Jeffrey Burds, "The Social Control of Peasant Labor in Russia: The Response of Village Communities to Labor Migration in the Central Industrial Region, 1861–1905," in *Peasant Economy, Culture and Politics of European Russia 1800–1921*, ed. Esther Kingston-Mann, Timothy Mixter, and Jeffrey Burds (Princeton, NJ: Princeton Univ. Press, 1991), 52–100.

26. Çadırcı, "Türkiye'de Muhtarlık Teşkilatının," 414.

27. Çadırcı, "Anadolu Kentlerinde Mahalle (Osmanlı Dönemi)," 259; Adalet Alada, *Osmanlı Şehrinde Mahalle* (Istanbul: Sümer Kitabevi, 2008), 185–86.

28. Steinwedel, "Making Social Groups, One Person at a Time," 69.

29. Osman Nuri Ergin, "İhtisab Ağalığı Nizamnamesi Evahir-i Muharrem 1242," in *Mecelle-i Umur-ı Belediye*, vol. 1 (Istanbul: İstanbul Büyükşehir Belediyesi Kültür İşleri Daire Başkanlığı, 1995), 330–33.

30. For a full transliteration of the regulation (*nizamname*), see Musa Çadırcı, "Tanzimat Döneminde Çıkarılan Men'-i Mürur ve Pasaport Nizamnameleri," *Belgeler* 19 (1993): 173–78.

31. Çadırcı, *Türkiye'de Muhtarlık Teşkilatının*, 414; Alada, *Osmanlı Şehrinde Mahalle*, 185.

32. For a full transliteration of the document, see Osman Nuri Ergin, "Polis Nizamı," in *Mecelle-i Umur-ı Belediye*, vol. 2 (Istanbul: İstanbul Büyükşehir Belediyesi Kültür İşleri Daire Başkanlığı, 1999), 875–78.

33. If we attempt to classify all the duties of the police according to the regulation, it is possible to say that the regulation had population control as its intent, that it served in the observation and supervision of public spaces, that it aimed to ban all manner of forms of behavior labeled as immoral and or as violating public safety through sedition, and that

it aimed to restrict publications, theater, and other forms of entertainment that might be of such a character. All of this was, in the end, the responsibility of what today would be called the *belediye zabıtası*, municipal police.

34. Şurayı Devlet (ŞD), 1278/19, 30 Ra 1288 (18 June 1871).

35. "Sicill-i Nüfus Vukuatları Hakkında Nüfus Nazır ve Memurları Tarafından İcra Olunacak Muamele ve İta Kılınacak Cetvellerin Sureti Tanzim ve İtasına Dair Talimat," *Düstur*, Tertip 1, vol. 5: *1883–1888* (Ankara: Ankara Başvekalet Matbaası, 1939), no. 47, 197–200 (specifically Article 5).

36. Shaw, "The Ottoman Census System and Population," 327–31.

6. Efforts to Control Internal Geographical Mobility under Abdülhamid II

1. 27 Temmuz 1303 (Rumi) or 18 Zilkade 1304 (Hijri).

2. BOA, DH.MKT, 1574/40, 9 R 1306 (Dec. 13, 1888).

3. BOA, DH.MKT, 1371/97, 14 M 1304 (Oct. 13, 1886).

4. BOA, DH.MKT, 2068/90, 6 R 1312 (Jan. 3, 1895).

5. BOA, ŞD, 2334/24, 12 B 1323 (Sept. 12, 1905).

6. BOA, DH.MKT, 2069/66, 2 Ramazan (N) 1312 (Apr. 14, 1896).

7. BOA, DH.MKT, 1476/115, 28 R 1305 (Jan. 12, 1888).

8. BOA, DH.TMIK.M, 6/87, 29 Z 1313 (June 11, 1896).

9. BOA, DH.MKT, 409/77, 17 S 1313 (Aug. 9, 1895).

10. The direct translation is "Varna Mercantile Authority."

11. BOA, DH.TMIK.M, 88/21, 18 S 1318 (June 17, 1900).

12. BOA, Meclis-i Vükelâ Mazbataları (MV), 95/31, 26 Z 1315 (May 18, 1898).

13. BOA, DH.MKT, 378/37, 1 Z 1312 (May 26, 1895).

14. BOA, İ.HUS, 45/10 Ş 1313 (Jan. 25, 1896).

15. A note written in red ink in the margins of the document stated, "Since it was publicly announced, it would be necessary to see to it that their provisions are protected, these *serseri*" (BOA, DH.TMIK.M, 14/33, 6 R 1314 [Sept. 14, 1896]).

16. BOA, DH.TMIK.M, 14/33, 6 R 1314 (Sept. 14, 1896).

17. BOA, DH.TMIK.M, 14/33, 6 R 1314 (Sept. 14, 1896).

18. BOA, DH.TMIK.M, 20/63, 19 Ca 1314 (Oct. 26, 1896).

19. BOA, DH.MKT, 249/36, 16 Z 1311 (June 20, 1894).

20. For a conceptualization of places that both pull and push labor power, see Jan Lucassen, *Migrant Labor in Europe, 1600–1900: The Drift to the North Sea* (London: Routledge, 1987), 5.

21. BOA, ZB, 466/75, 22 Teşrin-i Evvel (Te) 1319 (Aug. 4, 1903).

22. BOA, ZB, 31/5, 12 Ni 1321 (Apr. 25, 1905).

23. BOA, ZB, 31/15, 26 A 1322 (Sept. 8, 1906).

24. BOA, ZB, 30/12, 24 Ni 1314 (May 6, 1898).

25. For a source that takes up practices toward the unemployed and vagrants in terms of social policy in this period, see Özbek, *Osmanlı İmparatorluğu'nda Sosyal Devlet*. Also see chapter 1.

26. BOA, İ.HUS, 42/71313/R-85, 19 R 1313 (Oct. 4, 1895).

27. BOA, DH.TMIK.M, 5/14, 9 Z 1313 (May 22, 1896).

28. BOA, Y.A.RES, 88/41, 21 Ra 1315 (Aug. 20, 1897). In the decision to send this document, the most striking feature again is being bound to suretyship by the patriarchate. Alongside these three documents are many others with the same content and different dates.

29. BOA, İrade Dahiliye (İ.DH), 1327/1313/R-63, 19 R 1313 (Oct. 4, 1895).

30. BOA, BEO, 2249/168648, 19 L 1321 (Jan. 7, 1904).

31. BOA, ZB, 413/88, 4 Ma 1322 (17 Apr. 1906).

32. BOA, DH.MKT, 2136/32, 5 B 1316 (Nov. 20, 1898).

33. BOA, Hariciye Nezareti Siyasi (HR.SYS), 2862/24, Oct. 4, 1898.

34. BOA, HR.SYS, 2862/27, Oct. 3, 1898.

35. BOA, HR.SYS, 2862/26, Oct. 8, 1898.

36. BOA, ZB, 374/1, 25 Haziran (H) 1322 (July 8, 1906).

37. *Düstur*, Tertip 1, vol. 3 (Istanbul: Matbaa-ı Amire, n.d.), 302.

38. BOA, ZB, 71/82, 30 Temmuz (T) 1322 (Nov. 12, 1906).

39. BOA, BEO, 2232/167348, 30 N 1321 (Dec. 9, 1903).

40. BOA, Rumeli Müfettişliği Umum Evrak (TFR.I.UM), 4/349, 19 Za 1321 (Feb. 6, 1904).

41. BOA, Y.A.HUS, 448/77, 21 S 1321 (May 19, 1903).

42. BOA, ZB, 589/48, 27 Ma 1322 (Apr. 9, 1906).

43. BOA, İ.HUS, 29/1312/Ra 081, 25 Ra 1312 (Sept. 26, 1894).

44. BOA, BEO, 483/36200, 26 Ra 1312 (Sept. 16, 1894).

45. BOA, İ.HUS, 1312-Ra-25/81, 25 Ra 1312 (Oct. 26, 1896). See also Florian Riedler, "Armenian Labour Migration to Istanbul and the Migration Crisis of the 1890's," in *The City in the Ottoman Empire*, ed. Freitag et al., 165.

46. BOA, DH.TMIK.M, 4/41, 3 Z 1313 (May 16, 1896).

47. BOA, İ.HUS, 42/1313/R-13, 21 R 1313 (Oct. 10, 1895).

48. BOA, DH.TMIK.M, 23/42, 22 C 1314 (Nov. 28, 1896).

49. BOA, DH.TMIK.M, 23/42, 22 C 1314 (Nov. 28, 1896).

50. BOA, ZB, 20/26, 18 Eylül 1322 (Oct. 1, 1906).

51. BOA, DH.TMIK.M, 26/74, 17 Ş 1314 (Jan. 21, 1897).

52. BOA, ZB, 589/48, 27 Ma 1322 (Apr. 9, 1906).

53. BOA, DH.TMIK.M, 26/44, 12 Ş 1314 (Jan. 16, 1897).

54. BOA, DH.TMIK.M, 14/54, 7 R 1314 (Sept. 15, 1896).

55. Sadaret Mektûbî Kalemi to Dâhiliye Nezâreti, 6 R 1320 (July 13, 1902), in BOA, A.MKT.MHM, 634/15, 6 R 1320 (July 13, 1902).

56. Sadaret Mektûbî Kalemi to Dâhiliye Nezâreti, 6 R 1320 (July 13, 1902).

57. Sadaret Mektûbî Kalemi to Dâhiliye Nezâreti, 6 R 1320 (July 13, 1902).

58. Sadaret Mektûbî Kalemi to Dâhiliye Nezâreti, 6 R 1320 (July 13, 1902).

59. Bab-ı Ali Daire-i Umur-u Dahiliye Tesri-i Muamelat Komisyonu to Sadaret, 15 A 1318 (Aug. 28, 1902), in BOA, A.MKT.MHM, 634/15, 6 R 1320 (July 13, 1902).

60. Nazır-ı Umur-ı Dahiliye to Sadaret, 6 T 1318 (July 19, 1902), in BOA, A.MKT. MHM, 634/15, 6 R 1320 (July 13, 1902).

61. Nazır-ı Umur-ı Dahiliye to Sadaret, 6 T 1318 (July 19, 1902).

62. Zabtiye Nezareti to Dâhiliye Nezâreti, 30 H 1318 (July 13, 1902), in BOA, A.MKT. MHM, 634/15, 6 R 1320 (July 13, 1902).

63. Sadaret to Dahiliye, 15 A 1318 (Aug. 28, 1902), in BOA, A.MKT.MHM, 634/15, 6 R 1320 (July 13, 1902).

64. For a list of vagrant Armenians sent to their homelands by the police, see BOA, Y.PRK.ZB, 18/34, 25 Ra 1314 (Sept. 3, 1896).

65. BOA, ZB, 30/26, 21 My 1316 (June 3, 1900).

66. BOA, İrade Zabtiye (İ.ZB), 1/1314 B 1, 1 B 1314 (Dec. 6, 1896).

67. BOA, DH.TMIK.M, 26/58, 15 Ş 1314 (Jan. 19, 1897).

68. BOA, DH.TMIK.M, 26/4, 1 Ş 1314 (Jan. 5, 1897).

69. BOA, DH.MKT, 2355/57, 6 S 1318 (June 5, 1900).

70. BOA, DH.TMIK.M, 27/39, 29 Ş 1312 (Feb. 24, 1895).

71. BOA, Y.PRK.ZB, 24/30, 18 N 1317 (May 1, 1901).

72. BOA, Yıldız Perakende Evrakı—Komisyonlar Maruzâtı (Y.PRK.KOM), 9/22, 1 Ş 1314 (Jan. 5, 1897).

73. BOA, DH.TMIK.M, 70/43, 10 M 1317 (May 21, 1899).

74. BOA, DH.MKT, 2063/10, 27 Z 1310 (July 11, 1893).

75. BOA, ŞD, 1278/19, 30 Ra 1288 (June 18, 1871).

76. BOA, DH.MKT, 2131/14, 24 C 1316 (Oct. 10, 1898).

77. BOA, DH.MKT, 1557/39, 17 S 1306 (Oct. 23, 1888).

78. BOA, DH.MKT, 314/65, 6 C 1312 (Dec. 4, 1894).

79. BOA, ZB, 443/116, 17 Kanun-u Sani 1316 (Jan. 30, 1901).

80. BOA, DH.TMIK.M, 71/46, 3 S 1317 (June 11, 1899).

81. BOA, ZB, 381/135, 18 A 1323 (Aug. 31, 1907).

82. BOA, ZB, 402/21, 8 Teşrin-i Sani (Tş) 1321 (Nov. 21, 1905).

83. BOA, ZB, 408/14, 12 H 1320 (June 25, 1904).

84. BOA, DH.MKT, 2085/6, 30 Ca 1315 (Oct. 26, 1897).

85. On the political flows in the cities of Alexandria and Cairo, and on the relations between them, see Ilham Khuri-Makdisi, *The Eastern Mediterranean and the Making of Global Radicalism, 1860–1914* (Oakland: Univ. of California Press, 2013), chaps. 1 and 3.

86. BOA, DH.TMIK.M, 51/13, 15 Za 1315 (Apr. 6, 1898).

87. BOA, ZB, 20/76, 1 Aralık 1322 (Dec. 1906), BOA. The document was registered with a hijra year, but the month was written as "December" (Aralık) according to the Gregorian calendar, which makes it hard to give a proper Gregorian date.

88. BOA, DH.MKT, 2060/40, 20 Ş 1310 (Mar. 9, 1893).

89. BOA, DH.MKT, 1506/67, 24 Ş 1305 (May 6, 1888).

90. BOA, DH.TMIK.M, 145/49, 13 Ra 1321 (June 9, 1903).

91. BOA, DH.MKT, 1623/82, 17 N 1306 (Apr. 29, 1890).

92. Giddens, *The Nation-State and Violence*, 10–11.

93. BOA, BEO, 29/2110, 8 Z 1309 (July 4, 1892).

94. BOA, DH.MKT, 96/13, 18 Za 1312 (May 13, 1895).

95. BOA, DH.MKT, 239/12, 16 Za 1311 (May 21, 1894).

96. BOA, ZB, 588/1, 14 Te 1308 (Oct. 26, 1892).

97. BOA, İ.DH, 1075/84332, Mar. 14, 1888. For a detailed discussion of Armenian migration to North America, see David E. Gutman, *The Politics of Armenian Migration to North America, 1885–1915: Sojourners, Smugglers and Dubious Citizens* (Edinburgh: Edinburgh Univ. Press, 2019).

98. BOA, ZB, 588/46, 11 A 1317 (Aug. 24, 1901).

99. 3 Mart, Vidin Tüccar Vekaleti Tahrirat Sureti, in BOA, DH.MKT, 731/15, 4 R 1311 (Oct. 14, 1893).

100. 3 Mart, Vidin Tüccar Vekaleti Tahrirat Sureti.

101. 3 Mart, Vidin Tüccar Vekaleti Tahrirat Sureti.

102. 3 Mart, Vidin Tüccar Vekaleti Tahrirat Sureti.

103. Sicill-i Nüfus Nizamnamesi, 8 Şevval 1298 (Sept. 3, 1881), in *Düstur, Zeyl-i Sâni* (Istanbul: Mahmud Bey Matbaası, 1299 [1881–82]), 19–20.

104. Dahiliye Mektûbî Kalemi to Umum Vilayat, Elviye-i Gayr-i Mülhakaya Muharrerat Şehremaneti, Hariciye Nezareti, and Zabtiye Nezareti, Tezkere, BOA, DH.MKT, 731/15, 4 R 1321/17 H 1318 (Sept. 26, 1903).

105. Dahiliye Mektûbî Kalemi to Umum Vilayat, Elviye-i Gayr-i Mülhakaya Muharrerat Şehremaneti, Hariciye Nezareti, and Zabtiye Nezareti, Tezkere, 4 R 1321/17 H 1318 (Sept. 26, 1903).

106. BOA, DH.TMIK.M, 34/54, 14 M 1315 (June 14, 1897).

107. BOA, DH.MKT, 2078/40, 28 B 1314 (Jan. 2, 1897).

108. BOA, Y.PRK.ZB, 18/34, 25 Ra 1314 (Sept. 3, 1896).

109. BOA, A.MKT.MHM, 628/44, 27 Ra 1314 (Sept. 5, 1896).

110. BOA, MV, 95/31, 26 Z 1315 (May 17, 1898).

7. Passport Regulations and Practices during the Hamidian Era

1. Fahrmeir, "Governments and Forgers," 219.

2. See Philip John Stead, *The Police of Paris* (London: Stapless Press, 1957), 66–69.

3. Fahrmeir, "Governments and Forgers," 220.

4. Leo Lucassen, "A Many-Headed Monster: The Evolution of the Passport System in the Netherlands and Germany in the Long 19th Century," in *Documenting Individual Identity*, ed. Caplan and Torpey, 237.

5. Lüdtke, *Police and State in Prussia*, 21.

6. Respectively, *Düstur*, Tertip 1, addendum 4 (Dersaadet: Matbaa-I Amire, 1302 [1884–85]), no. 2055, 4–6; and *Düstur*, Tertip 1, vol. 6, no. 386, 1530–35. For an analysis of these documents from a legal perspective, see Rona Aybay, "Son Dönem Osmanlı, TBMM Hükümeti ve Erken Cumhuriyet Dönemlerinde Pasaportlar," *Tarih ve Toplum* 3 (1985): 46–53.

7. Scott, *Seeing Like a State*, 14.

8. John Torpey, "Coming and Going: On the State Monopolization of the Legitimate 'Means of Movement,'" *Sociological Theory* 16, no. 3 (1988): 242.

9. For the port cities, see Çağlar Keyder, Y. Eyüp Özveren, and Donald Quataert, eds., *Port-Cities of the Eastern Mediterranean, 1800–1914* (Binghamton, UK: Fernand Braudel Center, Binghamton Univ., 1993); Malte Fuhrmann and Vangelis Kechriotis, eds., "The Late Ottoman Port-Cities and Their Inhabitants: Subjectivity, Urbanity, and Conflicting Orders," special issue of *Mediterranean Historical Review* 24, no. 2 (2009); Edhem Eldem, Daniel Goffman, and Bruce Masters, eds., *Doğu ile Batı Arasında Osmanlı Kenti: Halep, İzmir ve İstanbul* (Istanbul: Tarih Vakfı Yurt, 2003); Malte Fuhrmann, *Port Cities of the Eastern Mediterranean: Urban Culture in the Late Ottoman Empire* (Cambridge: Cambridge Univ. Press, 2020).

10. Liang, *The Rise of Modern Police*, 30.

11. Lucassen, "A Many-Headed Monster," 249.

12. The period from the beginning of the nineteenth century to the First World War can be understood as one in which the passport regime was liberalized. For a counterargument to this thesis, see Lucassen, "A Many-Headed Monster."

13. In the period after 1860, though the requirement of having a passport had been lifted, foreign migrant workers still carried passports to be free from police harassment. See Lucassen, "A Many-Headed Monster," 246.

14. On passport and visa procedures by Ottoman representatives, see "Saltanat-ı Seniyye Şehbenderliklerine Gönderilecek Talimat," *Düstür*, Tertip 1, addendum 4, no. 2076.

15. BOA, İrade Kanun ve Nizamat (İ.KAN), 4/2, 7 C 1312 (Aug. 22, 1901).

16. Torpey, *The Invention of the Passport*, 76.

17. Torpey, *The Invention of the Passport*, 82.

18. Proving identity was among the most important issues of the era. For a detailed discussion of methods employed by the police, see Becker, "The Standardized Gaze"; Joseph, "Anthropometry, the Police Expert, and the Deptford Murders"; and Kristin Ruggiero, "Fingerprinting and the Argentine Plan for Universal Identification in the Late

Nineteenth and Early Twentieth Centuries," in *Documenting Individual Identity*, ed. Caplan and Torpey, 184–94.

19. Lucassen, "Eternal Vagrants?," 240.

20. Torpey, *The Invention of the Passport*, 47–60. For Holland, see Lucassen, "A Many-Headed Monster," 242. Those who had no discoverable registered residence in France were treated as vagrants and were sent to France's penal colonies. See Torpey, *The Invention of the Passport*, 51.

21. Lucassen, "Eternal Vagrants?," 235.

22. Fahrmeir, "Governments and Forgers," 227.

23. Lucassen, "A Many-Headed Monster," 250.

24. Emerson, *Matternich and the Political Police*, 10.

25. BOA, DH.MKT, 2081/20, 10 Za 1314 (Apr. 12, 1897).

26. BOA, DH.TMIK.M, 34/50, 13 M 1314 (June 24, 1896).

27. BOA, Y.A.HUS, 328/117, 28 Za 1312 (May 23, 1895). For the use of photography for policing in the Ottoman Empire, see Yılmaz, "The Ottoman State, Police Photographs and Anthropometry."

28. BOA, HR.SYS, 2790/35, Oct. 24, 1895.

29. BOA, Y.PRK.HR, 29/13, 30 Ca 1318 (Sept. 25, 1900).

30. BOA, DH.MKT, 1591/64, 4 C 1306 (Feb. 5, 1889).

31. BOA, HR.SYS, 2770/41, Oct. 15, 1894.

32. BOA, Y.EE.KP, 29/2896, 27 R 1324 (June 20, 1906).

33. BOA, DH.MKT, 1084/43, 3 R 1324 (May 27, 1906).

34. BOA, DH.TMIK.M, 20/54, 18 Ca 1314 (Oct. 25, 1896).

35. BOA, MV, 75/27, 14 Z 1310 (June 28, 1893).

36. BOA, MV, 75/27, 14 Z 1310 (June 28, 1893).

37. See Öztan, "Tools of Revolution."

38. BOA, BEO, 2118/158836, 22 R 1321 (Maliye'ye hitaben) (July 18, 1903).

39. BOA, BEO, 2118/158836, 22 R 1321 (Maliye'ye hitaben) (July 18, 1903).

40. BOA, DH.TMIK.M, 37/67, 19 Ra 1315 (Sept. 17, 1897).

41. BOA, MV, 98-1/7, 15 Ra 1317 (July 23, 1899).

42. BOA, Y.PRK.ASK, 157/6, 13 Ş 1317 (Dec. 16, 1899).

43. BOA, Y.PRK.HR, 28/35, 27 Ş 1317 (Feb. 28, 1900).

44. BOA, DH.TMIK.M, 94/18, 28 Ca 1318 (Oct. 23, 1900).

45. BOA, ZB, 31/83, 10 H 1324 (June 23, 1908), and BOA, ZB, 31/85, 15 H 1324 (June 28, 1908).

46. BOA, A.MTZ.(04), 154/11, 4 S 1325 (Apr. 19, 1907).

47. BOA, ZB, 31/15, 26 A 1322 (Sept. 8, 1906).

48. BOA, A.MKT.MHM, 541/20, 18 R 1315 (Sept. 15, 1897).

49. BOA, DH.MKT, 2131/14, 24 C 1316 (Nov. 9, 1898).

50. BOA, DH.MKT, 2068/45, 27 M 1312 (July 30, 1894).

51. BOA, DH.MKT, 267/30, 29 M 1312 (Aug. 1, 1894), and BOA, DH.MKT, 2068/45, 27 M 1312 (July 30, 1894).

52. Rano, son of Rusi, arrived in Istanbul without a passport on an Austrian postal ship. In Istanbul, he worked as a reporter for several foreign newspapers and had given a speech to a socialist organization. The information about his activities and the intelligence file circulated in the following places: Hejaz, Suria, Baghdad, Mosul, Aleppo, Tripoli, Yemen, Erzurum, Algeria, Diyarbekir, Bursa, Aydin, Thesaloniki, Adrianople, Angora, Konya, Sivas, Trebizond, Adana (Clicia), Kastamonu, Mamouret-ul-Aziz, Van, Bitlis, Izmir (Smyrna), Manastır (Bitola), Ishkodra, Ioannina, Kosovo, Chatalca, Benghazi, Basrah, Jerusalem, Der Zor, Biga, Crete, Lebanon, and Istanbul. See BOA, DH.MKT, 267/30, 29 M 1312 (Aug. 1, 1894), and BOA, DH.MKT, 2068/45, 27 M 1312 (July 30, 1894).

53. The photographs of two anarchists that came by a letter from Athens were sent to the central state: BOA, Y.PRK.ZB, 29/26, 3 Ca 1319 (Aug. 18, 1901).

54. BOA, İ.HUS, 25/1311 Z-102, 22 Z 1311 (June 26, 1894).

55. BOA, Y.PRK.ASK, 232/20, 18 C 1323 (Aug. 20, 1905).

56. BOA, ZB, 19/88, 1 A 1322 (Aug. 14, 1906).

57. BOA, DH.MKT, 186/25, 12 C 1311 (Dec. 21, 1893).

58. BOA, MV, 96/59, 23 B 1316 (Dec. 8, 1898).

59. BOA, Y.EE.KP, 14/1307, 10 Ca 1319 (Aug. 25, 1901).

60. BOA, A.MKT.MHM, 546/1, 24 S 1319 (June 11, 1901).

61. BOA, İ.HUS, 90/1319/C-72, 26 C 1319 (Oct. 10, 1901).

62. BOA, Y.PRK.HR, 30/54, 11 M 1319 (Apr. 30, 1901).

63. BOA, BEO, 1696/127178, 13 R 1319 (July 30, 1901).

64. BOA, DH.TMIK.M, 119/13, 15 Za 1319 (Feb. 24, 1902).

65. BOA, Y.PRK.ZB, 32/43, 26 M 1320 (May 5, 1902).

66. BOA, Y.PRK.ŞH, 12/2, 16 M 1320 (Apr. 25, 1902).

67. BOA, Y.PRK.ZB, 25/107, 16 R 1318 (Aug. 12, 1900).

68. BOA, DH.MKT, 1770/25, 29 S 1308 (Oct. 14, 1890); BOA, Hariciye Nezareti Tercüme Odası Evrakı (HR.TO), 345/48, Sept. 18, 1890. The passports of travelers entering the Ottoman Empire had to have visas. Italy accepted the requirement that Italian citizens bound for the Ottoman Empire had to obtain a visa from the Ottoman consulate before travel and informed its citizens of this requirement. Thirty Italian laborers entered Istanbul on an Italian boat without visas in their passports.

69. BOA, DH.MKT, 2512/109, 12 R 1319 (July 29, 1901).

70. BOA, HR.TO, 345/48, Sept. 18, 1898.

71. BOA, BEO, 1324/99243, 4 S 1317 (June 12, 1899).

72. BOA, DH.MKT, 45/4, 14 B 1315 (Dec. 8, 1897).

73. BOA, DH.TMIK.M, 63/40, 27 B 1316 (Dec. 1, 1899), and BOA, DH.TMIK.M, 68/60, 7 Z 1316 (Apr. 7, 1900). For investigations into Austrian and Greek workers, see BOA, DH.TMIK.M, 77/51, 9 B 1317 (Nov. 13, 1899).

74. BOA, DH.MKT, 2118/47, 30 Ca 1316 (Oct. 16, 1898).

75. BOA, DH.TMIK.M, 68/60, 7 Z 1316 (Apr. 17, 1899).

76. BOA, HR.SYS, 2862/34, Nov. 10, 1898.

77. BOA, HR.SYS, 2862/35, Nov. 12, 1898.

78. BOA, HR.SYS, 2862/37, Nov. 20, 1898.

79. BOA, HR.SYS, 2862/47, Feb. 10, 1899.

80. BOA, HR.TO, 355/94, Nov. 19, 1898.

81. BOA, HR.SYS, 2862/50, Mar. 8, 1899.

82. BOA, DH.TMIK.M, 68/60, 7 Z 1316 (Apr. 17, 1899).

83. BOA, A.MKT.MHM, 544/40, 8 Ca 1316 (Sept. 24, 1898); BOA, HR.SYS, 2862/17, Sept. 23, 1898.

84. BOA, DH.MKT, 1197/41, 2 Ş 1325 (Sept. 10, 1907).

85. BOA, A.MTZ.(04), 35/44, 12 S 1314 (July 23, 1896).

86. BOA, BEO, 2232/167348, 20 N 1321 (Dec. 9, 1903).

87. BOA, BEO, 2033/152437, 29 Z 1320 (Mar. 28, 1903). For the intelligence report and correspondence on the "Bulgarian sedition organization" that would use anarchist techniques, see BOA, Y.A.HUS, 444/104, 29 Z 1320 (Mar. 28, 1903). For the intelligence reports on Bulgarian revolutionary organizations that would use anarchist techniques, guerilla warfare techniques, and banditry, see BOA, Y.A.HUS, 444/125, 30 Z 1320 (Mar. 29, 1903).

88. BOA, DH.MKT, 1827/18, 29 Ş 1308 (Apr. 9, 1891).

89. BOA, İrade Eyalet-I Mümtaze Mısır (İ.MTZ), 20/888, 30 Za 1314 (May 2, 1897).

90. BOA, Hariciye Nezareti Hukuk Müşavirliği İstişare Odası Evrakı (HR.HMŞ. İŞO), 171/67, 29 N 1305 (June 9, 1888).

91. BOA, HR.TO, 347/120, June 14, 1892.

92. BOA, İ.ZB, 2/1317/M-1, 12 M 1317 (May 22, 1899).

93. BOA, İ.DH, 1075/84332, 18 B 1305 (Mar. 14, 1888).

94. BOA, DH.MKT, 1500/93, 1 Ş 1305 (Apr. 12, 1888), in *Osmanlı Belgelerinde Ermeni Amerikan İlişkileri (1839–1895)*, vol. 1, Yayın no. 85 (Ankara: T.C. Başbakanlık Devlet Arşivleri Genel Müdürlüğü Osmanlı Arşivi Daire Başkanlığı, 2007), 27–28.

95. BOA, DH.MKT, 1500/93, 1 Ş 1305 (Apr. 12, 1888), in *Osmanlı_Belgelerinde Ermeni Amerikan İlişkileri (1839–1895)*, 27–28.

96. BOA, BEO, 225/16809, 6 Z 1310 (June 21, 1893).

97. Sinan Kuneralp, "Ottoman Diplomacy and the Controversy over the Interpretation of Article 4 of the Turco-American Treaty of 1830," *Turkish Yearbook of International Relations* 31 (2002): 7–20.

98. For a memo from Police Minister Hüseyin Nazım Pasha about the issue, see BOA, Yıldız Mütenevvi Mâruzat (Y.MTV) 67/31, 19 S 1310 (Sept. 12, 1892).

99. Will Hanley, "What Ottoman Nationality Was and Was Not," *Journal of Ottoman and Turkish Studies Association* 3, no. 2 (2016): 287.

100. BOA, BEO, Ayniyât Defterleri (AYN.d), no. 1631, 567–75, 17 Za 1310 (Mar. 1, 1893).

101. BOA, BEO, AYN.d, no. 1633, 489, 27 Ra 1311 (Nov. 6, 1893).

102. BOA, HR.SYS, 2782/2, Aug. 16, 1893; and for the Ottoman report on the American president's view of solving the problem, see BOA, HR.SYS, 2736/30, Dec. 6, 1893.

103. BOA, DH.TMIK.M, 20/65, 19 Ca 1314 (Oct. 26, 1896).

104. BOA, DH.TMIK.M, 20/65, 19 Ca 1314 (Oct. 26, 1896).

105. National Archives, London, telegraph from Fontana, FO, 195/1944, p. 263, Nov. 19, 1896.

106. For an example for Kharput, see BOA, DH.TMIK.M, 174/13, 26 R 1322 (June 10, 1904); and for the circulation of a personal file belonging to a certain Agop from Tokat, see BOA, DH.TMIK.M, 230/7, 18 B 1324 (Sept. 7, 1906).

107. BOA, DH.TMIK.M, 233/58, 24 L 1324 (Dec. 25, 1906).

108. BOA, DH.TMIK.M, 75/10, 5 Ca 1317 (Sept. 11, 1899).

109. BOA, Y.PRK.BŞK, 49/34, 26 B 1314 (Dec. 31, 1899).

110. BOA, MV, 95/31, 26 Z 1315 (May 17, 1898).

111. BOA, DH.TMIK.M, 75/63, 20 Ca 1317 (Sept. 26, 1899).

112. BOA, DH.TMIK.M, 16/50, 21 R 1314 (Sept. 29, 1896).

113. BOA, MV, 112/8, 10 B 1323 (Sept. 10, 1905).

114. BOA, A.MKT.MHM, 632/3, 4 B 1314 (Dec. 9, 1896).

115. BOA, A.MKT.MHM, 632/3, 4 B 1314 (Dec. 9, 1896).

116. BOA, A.MKT.MHM, 632/3, 4 B 1314 (Dec. 9, 1896).

117. BOA, A.MKT.MHM, 632/3, 4 B 1314 (Dec. 9, 1896).

118. BOA, A.MKT.MHM, 632/3, 4 B 1314 (Dec. 9, 1896).

119. BOA, A.MKT.MHM, 632/3, 4 B 1314 (Dec. 9, 1896).

120. BOA, A.MKT.MHM, 632/3, 4 B 1314 (Dec. 9, 1896).

121. BOA, DH.TMIK.M, 20/59, 18 C 1314 (Oct. 25, 1896); BOA, Y.PRK.BŞK., 48/27, 5 C 1314 (Oct. 12, 1896).

122. BOA, A.MKT.MHM, 632/3, 4 B 1314 (Dec. 9, 1896).

123. BOA, MV, 109/17, 5 S 1322 (Apr. 21, 1904).

124. Eric Lohr, *Russian Citizenship: From Empire to Soviet Union* (Cambridge, MA: Harvard Univ. Press, 2012), 40–41.

125. BOA, Y.PRK.HR, 28/35, 27 Ş 1317 (Feb. 28, 1900).

126. BOA, DH.TMIK.M, 37/67, 19 Ra 1315 (Sept. 17, 1897).

127. BOA, DH.TMIK.M, 94/18, 28 Ca 1318 (Nov. 23, 1900).

128. BOA, Y.PRK.HR, 27/38, 4 M 1317 (May 15, 1899).

129. BOA, Y.PRK.BŞK. 58/104, 6 Za 1316 (Mar. 18, 1899); BOA, HR.SYS, 2840/22, Mar. 14, 1899.

130. BOA, Y.PRK.ASK, 151/15, 6 M 1317 (May 17, 1899). See also Raymond Kévorkian, "The Armenian Population of Sassoun and the Demographic Consequences of the

1894 Massacres," *Armenian Review* 47 (2001), at http://journals.openedition.org/eac/2789 and https://doi.org/10.4000/eac.2789. For a comparison between the different narratives on violence, see Miller, "Sasun 1894."

131. BOA, A.MKT.MHM, 642/20, 5 M 1318 (May 16, 1900).

132. For Russian citizenship of refugee Armenians, see BOA, HR.SYS, 2774/21, Jan. 17, 1901. For the decree about refugee Armenians and prohibition of their unregistered returns, see BOA, HR.SYS, 2840/37, Dec. 23, 1901; BOA, MV, 103/70, 29 Za 1319 (Mar. 9, 1902); and BOA, HR.SYS, 2863/66, Mar. 27, 1902.

133. BOA, A.MKT.MHM, 547/11, 5 C 1320 (Sept. 9. 1902).

134. BOA, DH.MKT, 2223/123, 12 R 1317 (Aug. 19, 1899); BOA, DH.TMIK.M, 75/19, 8 Ca 1317 (Sept. 14, 1899).

135. BOA, DH.TMIK.M, 18/59, 6 Ca 1314 (Oct. 13, 1896).

136. BOA, HR.SYS, 2748/6, Mar. 20, 1895.

137. BOA, DH.MKT, 662/10, 1 Z 1320 (Feb. 28, 1903).

138. BOA, DH.MKT, 2458/97, 16 Za 1318 (Mar. 7, 1901).

139. BOA, ZB, 391/3, 10 Ts 1323 (Nov. 23, 1907).

140. BOA, ZB, 23/22, 13 Te 1323 (Oct. 23, 1907).

141. BOA, DH.TMIK.M, 71/46, 3 S 1317 (June 21, 1899).

142. BOA, Y.PRK.ASK, 151/15, 6 M 1317 (May 16, 1899).

143. For one such fifteen-day file, see BOA, ZB, 703/46, 19 E 1307 (Oct. 1, 1891).

144. BOA, İ.HUS, 88/1319M-49, 3 M 1319 (Apr. 22, 1901).

145. For one such tally, see BOA, Y.PRK.KOM, 9/22, 1 Ş 1314 (Jan. 5, 1897).

146. BOA, Y.PRK.ASK, 100/73, 8 R 1312 (Oct. 7, 1894).

147. BOA, Yıldız Perakende Evrakı—Dâhiliye Nezâreti Maruzâtı (Y.PRK.DH), 11/56, 18 Ca 1318 (Sept. 13, 1900).

148. BOA, DH.MKT, 1680/143, 17 R 1307 (May 7, 1890).

149. BOA, DH.MKT, 1961/92, 19 Za 1309 (June 15, 1892).

150. BOA, DH.MKT, 1591/64, 4 C 1306 (Feb. 5, 1889).

151. For more information, see İdris Bostan, "İzn-i Sefine Defterleri ve Karadeniz'de Rusya ile Ticaret Yapan Devlet-i Aliyye Tüccarları 1780–1846," *Türklük Araştırmaları Dergisi* 6 (1990): 25–26; Necmettin Aygün, "XIX. Yüzyıl Başlarında İstanbul Merkezli Osmanlı Deniz Taşımacılığı," *Ankara Üniversitesi Osmanlı Tarihi Araştırma ve Uygulama Merkezi Dergisi* 23 (2010): 53–84.

152. BOA, ZB, 590/37, 20 My 1322 (Apr. 2, 1906).

153. BOA, Y.PRK.ASK, 14/76, 24 Ra 1314 (Oct. 2, 1896).

154. BOA, DH.TMIK.M, 21/44, 27 Ca 1314 (Dec. 3, 1896).

155. BOA, Y.A.HUS, 524/25, 4 B 1326 (Aug. 2, 1908).

156. BOA, ŞD 4/8, 26 Ra 1296 (Sept. 13, 1879).

157. BOA, ŞD 4/29, 13 M 1297 (Dec. 27, 1879).

158. BOA, ŞD, 4/8, 26 Ra 1296 (Sept. 13, 1879).

159. BOA, ŞD, 4/29, 13 M 1297 (Dec. 27, 1879).

160. BOA, A.MKT.MHM, 626/34, 22 R 1312 (Oct. 21, 1894).

161. BOA, DH.TMIK.M, 26/44, 12 Ş 1314 (Jan. 16, 1897).

162. BOA, DH.MKT, 1683/61, 25 R 1307 (Dec. 18, 1889).

163. BOA, ZB, 31/14, 26 T 1322 (Aug. 8, 1906).

164. BOA, DH.MKT, 799/54, 16 N 1321 (Dec. 5, 1903).

165. BOA, DH.MKT, 662/10, 1 Z 1320 (Feb. 28, 1903).

166. BOA, Y.A.HUS, 281/6, 17 Ra 1311 (Oct. 27, 1893).

167. For a detailed discussion on the mobility of the revolutionaries between empires, see Houri Berberian, *Roving Revolutionaries: Armenians and the Connected Revolutions in the Russian, Iranian, and Ottoman Worlds* (Oakland: Univ. of California Press, 2019).

168. BOA, DH.MKT, 327/53, 6 B 1312 (Jan. 2, 1895).

169. BOA, DH.MKT, 1413/41, 22 B 1304 (Apr. 16, 1887).

170. BOA, TFR.I.UM, 4/349, 19 Za 1321 (Feb. 6, 1904).

171. BOA, DH.MKT, 75/50, 7 Ra 1311 (Sept. 17, 1893).

172. BOA, DH.TMIK.M, 133/35, 12 B 1320 (Oct. 14, 1902).

173. BOA, A.MTZ.(04), 102/23, 14 Ca 1321 (Aug. 8, 1903).

174. BOA, A.MTZ.(04), 43/9, 3 Za 1314 (Apr. 5, 1897).

175. BOA, BEO, 2115/161358, 3 C 1321 (Aug. 26, 1903).

176. BOA, DH.MKT, 64/49, 2 S 1311 (Aug. 14, 1893).

177. BOA, DH.MKT, 1467/3, 15 Ra 1305 (Dec. 1, 1887).

178. BOA, DH.MKT, 125/9, 21 S 1311 (Sept. 2, 1893).

179. BOA, DH.MKT, 427/70, 24 Ra 1313 (Sept. 14, 1895).

180. BOA, A.MTZ.(04), 65/23, 19 L 1317 (Feb. 20, 1900).

181. Document No. 13199, dated Dec. 16, 1883, in BOA, A.MTZ.(04), 65/23.

182. Correspondence dated Oct. 28, 1883, in BOA, A.MTZ.(04), 65/23.

183. Document No. 1512, dated Jan. 31, 1889, in BOA, A.MTZ.(04), 65/23.

184. Document No. 1512, dated Jan. 31, 1889, in BOA, A.MTZ.(04), 65/23.

Conclusion

1. Karpat, *Ottoman Population*, 60–85.

2. BOA, ZB, 402/18, 22 Te 1321 (Nov. 4, 1905). A search carried out in the room where a German citizen had stayed in Istanbul turned up a banned book.

3. Eric Hobsbawm, *The Age of Empire 1875–1914* (London: Weidenfeld and Nicolson, 1987).

4. Errico Malatesta, *Errico Malatesta—His Life and Ideas*, ed. Vernon Richards (London: Freedom Press, 1965).

5. Yılmaz, "Propaganda by the Deed."

6. One can speak of discursive continuity in terms of the use of the category "enemy." See Biriz Gonca Berksoy, "The Policing of Social Discontent and the Construction of the Social Body: Mapping the Expansion and Militarization of the Police Organization in Turkey in the Post-1980 Period," PhD diss., Bosphorus Univ., 2007), chap. 5.

Appendix 1

1. The third article was crafted in the context of Prussia's recommendations. Even if the country from which an anarchist hailed did not designate the reasons for deportation within the framework of political crimes, Prussia recommended that such an individual be returned to their country of citizenship without looking into whether they were being sought for evading military service or not. Yet in this recommendation it was proposed that, related to the return of criminals under clause D of the article, if an anarchist was not being returned for criminal crimes in the country of their citizenship, and if they were not being searched for as military deserters, then they could be delivered over to their own countries. Despite opposition to this recommendation, it was requested that a final clause be added to the existing clause, stating: "An anarchist who is expelled and banished, if he is investigated in his country of origin due to a record of crimes, on the resolution reached by relevant states for the aforementioned matter of expulsion and banishment, in the treaty related to the return of the criminal and in accordance with laws and judgments, they are in agreement." In negotiations on this matter, members of the administrative commission recommended that it be transferred to the commission regulating the delivery and return of criminals, which was placed on the administrative commission's agenda. See "Rome Consulate to Foreign Affairs, Secret Correspondence of the Formal Letter Number 2," Jan. 3, 1899, in BOA, Y.PRK.EŞA, 31/136, 20 Ş 1316 (Jan. 3, 1899).

2. See art. 5, para. 1, 2, 4.

3. Representatives of the Ottoman state recommended that a phrase be added to the article yet were unable to get the required voted to do so: "and all manner of preparation, praise, or covert and overt agitation related to realizing such an aim." See "Rome Consulate to Foreign Affairs, Secret Correspondence of the Formal Letter Number 2," Jan. 3, 1899.

Bibliographic Survey

1. Niyazi Berkes, *The Development of Secularism in Turkey* (London: Hurst 1998); Niyazi Berkes, *Türkiye'de Çağdaşlaşma* (Ankara: Bilgi Yayınevi, 1973).

2. Stanford J. Shaw and Ezel Kural Shaw, *History of the Ottoman Empire and Modern Turkey*, vol. 2 (Cambridge: Cambridge Univ. Press, 1977), 172–71; Stanford Shaw, "Sultan

Abdülhamid II: Last Man of the Tanzimat," in *Tanzimat'ın 150: Yıldönümü Uluslararası Sempozyumu (Bildiriler)* (Ankara: Millî Kütüphane, 1989), 179–97.

3. Erik J. Zürcher, *Turkey: A Modern History* (London: I. B. Tauris, 1993).

4. Georgeon, *Abdulhamid II.*

5. Nadir Özbek, "Modernite, Tarih ve İdeoloji: II. Abdülhamid Dönemi Tarihçiliği Üzerine Bir Değerlendirme," *Türkiye Araştırmaları Literatür Dergisi* 2, no. 1 (2004): 71–90.

6. One of the most important works written from this perspective is İlber Ortaylı, *İmparatorluğun En Uzun Yüzyılı* (Istanbul: İletişim, 2003). Emphasizing historical continuity and from the perspective of the long nineteenth century, this work analyzes the Tanzimat period without touching much on the reign of Abdülhamid II.

7. Engin Deniz Akarlı, "The Problems of External Pressures, Power Struggles, and Budgetary Deficits in Ottoman Politics under Abdülhamid II (1876–1909): Origins and Solutions," PhD diss., Princeton Univ., 1976; Şevket Pamuk, "Foreign Trade and Foreign Capital in the Ottoman Empire, 1830–1913," PhD diss, Univ. of California, Berkeley, 1978.

8. Donald Quataert, *Osmanlı Devleti'nde Avrupa İktisadi Yayılımı ve Direniş (1881–1908)*, ed. Sabri Tekay (Ankara: Yurt, 1987).

9. E. Attila Aytekin, *Tarlalardan Ocaklara, Sefaletten Mücadeleye: Zonguldak-Ereğli Kömür Madenlerinde İşçiler, 1848–1922* (Istanbul: Yordam Kitap, 2007); Sefer, "The Docks of the Revolution."

10. Edward W. Said, *Orientalism* (New York: Pantheon, 1978).

11. Özbek, "Modernite, Tarih ve İdeoloji," 79.

12. See, for example, Deringil, *The Well Protected Domains*, and Benjamin C. Fortna, *Imperial Classroom: Islam, the State, and Education in the Late Ottoman Empire* (Oxford: Oxford Univ. Press, 2002).

13. Ussama Makdisi, "Rethinking Ottoman Imperialism: Modernity, Violence and the Cultural Logic of Ottoman Reform," in *The Empire in the City: Arab Provincial Cities in the Ottoman Empire*, ed. Jens Hanssen, Thomas Philipp, and Stefan Weber (Würzburg, Germany: Ergon, 2002), 29–48; Christoph Herzog, "Nineteenth-Century Baghdad through Ottoman Eyes," in *The Empire in the City*, ed. Hanssen, Philipp, and Weber, 311–28; Thomas Kühn, *Empire, Islam, and Politics of Difference: Ottoman Rule in Yemen, 1849–1919* (Leiden: Brill, 2011); Vangelis Kechriotis, "Postcolonial Criticism Encounters Late Ottoman Studies," *Historein* 13 (2013): 39–46.

14. Selim Deringil, "'They Live in a State of Nomadism and Savagery': The Late Ottoman Empire and the Post-colonial Debate," *Comparative Studies in Society and History* 43 (2003): 311–42; Ussama Makdisi, *The Culture of Sectarianism: Community, History, and Violence in Nineteenth Century Ottoman Lebanon* (Berkeley: Univ. of California Press, 2000). For another work by this same author that directly engages with Deringil, see Ussama Makdisi, "Ottoman Orientalism," *American Historical Review* 107, no. 3 (2002): 768–96.

15. Elizabeth B. Frierson, "Unimagined Communities: Women and Education in the Late Ottoman Empire, 1876–1909," *Critical Matrix* 9 (1995): 55–90; Elizabeth B. Frierson, "Unimagined Communities: State, Press, and Gender in the Hamidian Era," PhD diss., Princeton Univ., 1996; Elizabeth B. Frierson, "Mirrors Out, Mirrors In: Domestication and Rejection of the Foreign in Late-Ottoman Women's Magazines (1875–1908)," in *Women, Patronage, and Self-Representation in Islamic Societies*, ed. D. Fairchild Ruggles (Albany: State Univ. of New York Press, 2000), 177–204.

16. Özbek, *Osmanlı İmparatorluğu'nda Sosyal Devlet*; Nadir Özbek, "Osmanlı'dan Günümüze Türkiye'de Sosyal Devlet," *Toplum ve Bilim* 92 (2002): 7–33.

17. Halim Alyot, *Türkiye'de Zabıta* (Ankara: Kanaat Basımevi, 1947); Derviş Okçabol, *Meslek Tarihi* (Ankara: Ankara Polis Enstitüsü Neşriyatı, 1939); Tongur, *Türkiye'de Genel Kolluk*. In addition to these books, several articles and translations were published on these matters in the *İdare Dergisi* (Journal of Administration), particularly in the 1940s and 1950s.

18. Ferdan Ergut, "State and Social Control: The Police in the Late Ottoman Empire and the Early Republican Turkey, 1839–1939," PhD diss., New School for Social Research, 1999; Ergut, *Modern Devlet ve Polis*.

19. Cengiz Kırlı, "The Struggle over Space: Coffehouses of Ottoman Istanbul, 1780–1845," PhD diss., Binghamton Univ., 2000; Başaran, "Remaking the Gate of Felicity"; İlker Cörüt, "Social Rationality of Lower Class Criminal Practices in the Late Nineteenth Century İstanbul," MA thesis, Boğaziçi Univ., 2005; Hasan Şen, "The Transformation of Punishment and the Birth of Prison in the Ottoman Empire," MA thesis, Boğaziçi Univ., 2005; Zarinebaf, *Crime and Punishment in Istanbul*; Nurçin İleri, "Rule, Misconduct and Dysfunction: The Police Forces in Theory and Practice in Fin de Siècle Istanbul," *Comparative Studies of South Asia, Africa, and the Middle East* 34, no. 1 (Mar. 2014): 147–59.

20. Lévy and Toumarkine, *Osmanlı'da Suç ve Ceza, 18.–20. Yüzyıllar*; Noémi Lévy, Nadir Özbek, and Alexandre Toumarkine, eds., *Jandarma ve Polis: Fransız ve Osmanlı Tarihçiliğine Çapraz Bakışlar* (Istanbul: Tarih Vakfı Yurt, 2009).

21. Noémi Lévy, "19. Yüzyılda Osmanlı'da Kamu Düzeni Konusunda Çalışmak: Bibliyografya Üzerine Bir Değerlendirme," in *Osmanlı'da Suç ve Ceza*, ed. Lévy and Toumarkin, 55–67; Noémi Lévy, "Yakından Korunan Düzen: 2. Abdülhamid Devrinden 2. Meşruiyet Dönemine Bekçi Örneği," in *Osmanlı'da Suç ve Ceza*, ed. Lévy and Toumarkine, 135–45; Noémi Lévy, "Polislikle İlgili Bilgilerin Dolaşım Tarzları: Osmanlı Polisi İçin Fransız Modeli mi?," in *Jandarma ve Polis Fransız*, ed. Lévy, Özbek, and Toumarkine, 146–70.

22. Özbek, "Policing the Countryside"; Özbek, "Osmanlı İmparatorluğu'nda İç Güvenlik"; Özbek, "Anadolu Islahatı."

23. Janet Klein, "Power in the Periphery: The Hamidiye Light Cavalry and the Struggle over Ottoman Kurdistan, 1890–1914," PhD diss., Princeton Univ., 2002.

24. The *Ermeni Araştırmları Dergisi* (Journal of Armenian Studies), published by the Armenian Studies Institute since 2001, is filled with articles that consistently repeat

this perspective; see it at http://www.eraren.org/index.php?Lisan=tr&Page=DergiSayilar &DergiNo=1. Furthermore, see Justin McCarthy, Ömer Turan, and Cemalettin Taşkiran, *Sasun: The History of an 1890s Armenian Revolt* (Salt Lake City: Univ. of Utah Press, 2014).

25. Dadrian, *The History of the Armenian Genocide*, passim.

26. In *The Armenian Genocide: A Complete History* (London: I. B. Tauris, 2011), Raymond Kévorkian discusses the genocide within the framework of nationalist ideologies rather than from a culturalist perspective.

27. Taner Akçam, *Ermeni Soykırımının Kısa Bir Tarihi* (Istanbul: Aras, 2021).

28. Benny Morris and Dror Ze'evi, *The Thirty-Year Genocide: Turkey's Destruction of Its Christian Minorities, 1894–1924* (Cambridge, MA: Harvard Univ. Press, 2019).

29. See the debate on *The Thirty-Year Genocide* in "Book Forum: Benny Morris and Dror Ze'evi, *The Thirty-Year Genocide: Turkey's Destruction of Its Christian Minorities, 1894–1924*," *Journal of Genocide Research* 22, no. 4 (2020): 533–66.

30. Selim Deringil, *Conversion and Apostasy in the Late Ottoman Empire* (Cambridge: Cambridge Univ. Press, 2012); Joost Jongerden and Jelle Verheij, eds., *Social Relations in Ottoman Diyarbekir, 1870–1915* (Leiden: Brill, 2012); Sabri Ateş, *The Ottoman–Iranian Borderlands: Making a Boundary, 1843–1914* (New York: Cambridge Univ. Press, 2013).

31. Kieser, *Der verpasste Friede*.

32. Edip Gölbaşı, "The Official Conceptualization of the Anti-Armenian Riots of 1895–1897," *Études arméniennes contemporaines* 10 (2018): 33–62; Ali Sipahi, "Narrative Construction in the 1895 Massacres in Harput: The Coming and Disappearance of the Kurds," *Études arméniennes contemporaines* 10 (2018): 63–95; Miller, *Sasun 1894*; Owen Miller, "Rethinking the Violence in the Sasun Mountains (1893–1894)," *Études arméniennes contemporaines* 10 (2018): 97–123; Jelle Verheij, "'The Year of the Firman': The 1895 Massacres in Hizan and Şirvan (Bitlis Vilayet)," *Études arméniennes contemporaines* 10 (2018): 125–59; Deborah Mayersen, "The 1895–1896 Armenian Massacres in Harput: Eyewitness Account," *Études arméniennes contemporaines* 10 (2018): 161–83.

33. Yaşar Tolga Cora, "Transforming Erzurum/Karin: The Social and Economic History of a Multi-ethnic Ottoman City in the Nineteenth Century," PhD diss., Univ. of Chicago, 2016; Yaşar Tolga Cora, "The Market as a Means of Post-violence Recovery: Armenians and Oriental Carpets in the Late Ottoman Empire (c. 1890s–1910s)," *International Review of Social History* 66, no. 2 (2021): 217–41; Chris Gratian, *The Unsettled Plain: An Environmental History of the Late Ottoman Frontier* (Palo Alto, CA: Stanford Univ. Press, 2022).

34. Yosmaoğlu, *Blood Ties*.

35. Öztan, "Tools of Revolution."

36. Aybay, "Son Dönem Osmanlı."

37. Çadırcı, "Tanzimat Döneminde Çıkarılan."

38. Riedler, "Armenian Labour Migration to Istanbul"; Herzog, "Migration and the State," 119–20.

39. Florian Riedler, "Public People: Seasonal Work Migrants in Nineteenth Century Istanbul," in *Public Istanbul: Spaces and Spheres of the Urban*, ed. Frank Eckardt and Kathrin Wildner (Bielefeld, Germany: Transcript, 2008), 233–53.

40. Will Hanley, *Identifying with Nationality: Europeans, Ottomans, and Egyptians in Alexandria* (New York: Columbia Univ. Press, 2017).

41. Gutman, *The Politics of Armenian Migration*.

42. Nalan Turna, *19 yy dan ve 20 yy a Osmanlı Topraklarında Seyahat Göç ve Asayiş Belgeleri Mürûr Tezkereleri* (Istanbul: Kaknüs, 2013).

43. Lale Can, *Spiritual Subjects: Central Asian Pilgrims and the Ottoman Hajj at the End of Empire* (Stanford, CA: Stanford Univ. Press, 2020). For recent works on migration, see Z. D. Gürsel, "Looking Together as Method Encounters with Ottoman Armenian Expatriation Photographs," *Visual Anthropology Review* (2023) and Hazal Özdemir, "Osmanlı Ermenilerinin Göçünün Fotoğrafını Çekmek," *Toplumsal Tarih* 304 (2019): 82–90.

Bibliography

Archives

Başbakanlık Osmanlı Arşivi [Prime Ministry Ottoman Archives], Istanbul.
    Bâbıâli Evrak Odası Evrakı
        Ayniyât Defterleri
    Dahiliye Nezareti Mektûbî Kalemi
    Dahiliye Nezâreti Tesrî-i Muamelât
    Hariciye Nezareti Hukuk Müşavirliği İstişare Odası Evrakı
    Hariciye Nezareti Siyasi
    Hariciye Nezareti Tercüme Odası Evrakı
    İrade Dahiliye
    İrade Eyalet-i Mümtaze Mısır
    İrade Hariciye
    İrade Hususi
    İrade Kanun ve Nizamat
    İrade Meclis-i Mahsus
    İrade Zabtiye
    Meclis-i Vükelâ Mazbataları
    Rumeli Müfettişliği Manastır Evrakı
    Rumeli Müfettişliği Sadâret ve Başkitâbet Evrakı
    Rumeli Müfettişliği Selânik Evrakı
    Rumeli Müfettişliği Umum Evrak
    Sadâret Eyâlât-ı Mümtâze Kalemi Belgeleri Bulgaristan
    Sadaret Mektûbî Kalemi Evrakı
    Sadaret Mektûbî Mühimme Kalemi Evrakı
    Sadrıazam Kâmil Paşa Evrakı—Yıldız Esas Evrakı'na Ek
    Şurayı Devlet
    Yıldız Esas Evrakı

Yıldız Mütenevvi Mâruzat

Yıldız Perakende Evrakı—Askerî Maruzât

Yıldız Perakende Evrakı—Dahiliye Nezâreti Maruzâtı

Yıldız Perakende Evrakı—Elçilik ve Şehbenderlik Maruzâtı

Yıldız Perakende Evrakı—Hariciye Nezâreti Maruzâtı

Yıldız Perakende Evrakı—Komisyonlar Maruzâtı

Yıldız Perakende Evrakı—Mabeyn Başkitâbeti

Yıldız Perakende Evrakı—Müfettişlik ve Komiserlikler Tahrirâtı

Yıldız Perakende Evrakı—Şehremâneti Maruzâtı

Yıldız Perakende Evrakı—Tahrirât-ı Ecnebiye ve Mâbeyn Mütercimliği

Yıldız Perakende Evrakı—Zabtiye Nezâreti Maruzâtı

Yıldız Perakende Umumi Maruzat

Yıldız Sadaret Hususî Mâruzat Evrakı

Yıldız Sadaret Resmi Mâruzat Evrakı

Zabtiye Nezareti

National Archives, London.

Foreign Office

Published Works

Adanır, Fikret. "Karşılaştırmalı Bir Değerlendirme: Çarlık Rusya'sı ve Habsburg İmparatorluğu Arasında Osmanlı'da Vatandaşlık." *Toplumsal Tarih Dergisi* 182 (2009): 54–63.

———. *Die Makedonische Frage: Ihre Entstehung und Entwicklung bis 1908.* Wiesbaden, Germany: Steiner, 1979.

Akarlı, Engin Deniz. "'Maslaha from 'Common Good' to 'Raison d'Etat' in the Experience of Istanbul Artisans, 1730–1840." In *Hoca, 'allame, puits de science: Essays in Honor of Kemal H. Karpat,* edited by Kaan Durukan, Robert W. Zens, and Akile Zorlu-Durukan, 63–79. Istanbul: ISIS Press, 2010.

———. "The Problems of External Pressures, Power Struggles, and Budgetary Deficits in Ottoman Politics under Abdülhamid II (1876–1909): Origins and Solutions." PhD diss., Princeton Univ., 1976.

Akçam, Taner. *Ermeni Soykırımının Kısa Bir Tarihi.* Istanbul: Aras, 2021.

———. *İnsan Hakları ve Ermeni Sorunu: İttihat ve Terakki'den Kurtuluş Savaşı'na.* Ankara: İmge Kitabevi, 1999.

———. *A Shameful Act: The Armenian Genocide and The Question of Turkish Responsibility.* New York: Metropolitan Books, 2006.

Akdağ, Mustafa. *Türk Halkının Dirlik ve Düzenlik Kavgası Celali İsyanları.* Ankara: Bilgi Yayınevi, 1975.

Akgündüz, Ahmet. *Osmanlı Kanunnameleri ve Hukuki Tahlilleri: Kanuni Sultan Süleyman Devri Kanunnameleri: I. Kısım Merkezi ve Umumi Kanunnameler.* Vol. 4. Istanbul: Fey Vakfı, 1992.

Akman, Mehmet. *Osmanlı Devletinde Ceza Yargılaması.* Istanbul: Eren , 2004.

Aktepe, M. Münir. "İstanbul'un Nüfus Meselesine Dair Bazı Vesikalar." *İstanbul Üniversitesi Edebiyat Fakültesi Tarih Dergisi* 9 (Sept. 1958): 1–30.

Alada, Adalet. *Osmanlı Şehrinde Mahalle.* Istanbul: Sümer Kitabevi, 2008.

Alloul, Houssine, Edhem Eldem, and Henk de Smaele, eds. *To Kill a Sultan.* London: Palgrave Macmillan, 2018.

Altınay, Ahmet Refik. *Hicri On Birinci Asırda İstanbul Hayatı.* Istanbul: Devlet Matbaası, 1931.

———. *On Altıncı Asırda İstanbul Hayatı.* Istanbul: Devlet Basımevi, 1935.

———. *On İkinci Asr-ı Hicri'de İstanbul Hayatı (1689–1785).* Istanbul: Enderun Kitabevi, 1988.

Altıntaş, Toygun. "The Ottoman War on 'Anarchism' and Revolutionary Violence." In *To Kill a Sultan,* edited by Houssine Alloul, Edhem Eldem, and Henk de Smaele, 99–128. Basingstoke, UK: Palgrave Macmillan, 2018.

Alyot, Halim. *Türkiye'de Zabıta.* Ankara: Kanaat Basımevi, 1947.

American Journal of International Law. "The Passport Question between the United States and Russia." Editorial comment. 1 (1912): 186–91.

Anastasopolis, Antonis. "Lighting the Flame of Disorder: Ayan Infighting and State Intervention in Ottoman Karaferye, 1758–59." *International Journal of Turkish Studies* 8, nos. 1–2 (2002): 73–88.

Anderson, M. S. *The Eastern Question: A Study of International Relations.* London: Macmillan, 1983.

Ateş, Sabri. *The Ottoman–Iranian Borderlands: Making a Boundary, 1843–1914.* New York: Cambridge University Press, 2013.

Aybay, Rona. "Son Dönem Osmanlı, TBMM Hükümeti, Erken Cumhuriyet Dönemlerinde Pasaportlar." *Tarih ve Toplum* 3 (1985): 46–53.

Aydın, Mahir. "Makedonya Meselesi ve Amerikalı Rahibenin Kaçırılması." *Osmanlı Araştırmaları* 13 (1998): 239–58.

Aydın, Mithat. "Osmanlı-Sırp, Karadağ Savaşlarında İngiltere'nin Balkan Politikası." *Ankara Üniversitesi Osmanlı Tarihi Araştırma ve Uygulama Dergisi* 15 (2004): 139–63. At https://dergipark.org.tr/en/download/article-file /114153.

Aygün, Necmettin. "XIX. Yüzyıl Başlarında İstanbul Merkezli Osmanlı Deniz Taşımacılığı." *Ankara Üniversitesi Osmanlı Tarihi Araştırma ve Uygulama Merkezi Dergisi* 23 (2010): 53–84.

Aykut Türker, Ebru. "Alternative Claims on Justice and Law: Rural Arson and Poison Murder in the 19th Century Ottoman Empire." PhD diss., Atatürk İlkeleri ve İnkılap Tarihi Enstitüsü, Boğaziçi Univ., 2011.

Aytekin, E. Attila. *Tarlalardan Ocaklara, Sefaletten Mücadeleye: Zonguldak-Ereğli Kömür Madenlerinde İşçiler, 1848-1922.* Istanbul: Yordam Kitap, 2007.

Baktıaya, Adil. "19. Yüzyıl Sonunda Anarşist Terör, 'Toplumun Anarşistlerden Korunması Konferansı (1898)' ve Osmanlı Devleti." *Bilgi ve Bellek* 8 (2007): 50–76.

Başaran, Betül. "III. Selim ve İstanbul Şehir Siyaseti, 1789-1792." In *Osmanlı'da Asayiş, Suç ve Ceza 18.-20. Yüzyıllar,* edited by Noémi Lévy and Alexandre Toumarkine, 116–34. Istanbul: Tarih Vakfı Yurt, 2007.

———. "Remaking the Gate of Felicity: Policing, Social Control, and Migration in Istanbul at the End of the Eighteenth Century, 1789-1793." PhD diss., Univ. of Chicago, 2006.

———. *Selim III, Social Control and Policing in Istanbul at the End of the Eighteenth Century: Between Crisis and Order.* Leiden: Brill, 2014.

Bayley, David. *Patterns of Policing.* New Brunswick, NJ: Rutgers Univ. Press, 1985.

Becker, Peter. "The Standardized Gaze: The Standardization of the Search Warrant in Nineteenth Century Germany." In *Documenting Individual Identity: The Development of State Practices in the Modern World,* edited by Jane Caplan and John Torpey, 139–63. Princeton, NJ: Princeton Univ. Press, 2001.

Berberian, Houri. *Roving Revolutionaries: Armenians and the Connected Revolutions in the Russian, Iranian, and Ottoman Worlds.* Oakland: Univ. of California Press, 2019.

Berkes, Niyazi. *The Development of Secularism in Turkey.* London: Hurst, 1998.

———. *Türkiye'de Çağdaşlaşma.* Ankara: Bilgi Yayınevi, 1973.

Berksoy, Biriz Gonca. "The Policing of Social Discontent and the Construction of the Social Body: Mapping the Expansion and Militarization of the Police Organization in Turkey in the Post-1980 Period." PhD diss., Bosphorus Univ., 2007.

Berliére, Jean-Marc. "The Professionalization of the Police under the Third Republic in France 1875-1914." In *Policing Western Europe: Politics, Professionalism and Public Order 1850-1940,* edited by Clive Emsley and Barbara Weinberger, 36–54. Westport, CT: Greenwood Press, 1991.

Blumi, Isa. *Ottoman Refugees, 1878–1939: Migration in a Post-imperial World.* London: Bloomsbury, 2013.

Bostan, İdris. "İzn-i Sefine Defterleri ve Karadeniz'de Rusya ile Ticaret Yapan Devlet-i Aliyye Tüccarları 1780–1846." *Türklük Araştırmaları Dergisi* 6 (1990): 21–83.

Breckenridge, Keith, and Simon Szeter. "Recognition and Registration: The Infrastructure of Personhood in World History." In *Registration and Recognition: Documenting the Person in World History,* edited by Keith Breckenridge and Simon Szeter, 1–36. London: British Academy, 2012.

———, eds. *Registration and Recognition: Documenting the Person in World History.* London: British Academy, 2012.

Brenner, Robert. "From Theory to History: 'The European Dynamic' or Feudalism to Capitalism?" In *An Anatomy of Power: The Social Theory of Michael Mann,* edited by John A. Hall and Ralph Schroeder, 109–36. Cambridge: Cambridge Univ. Press, 2005.

Burds, Jeffrey. "The Social Control of Peasant Labor in Russia: The Response of Village Communities to Labor Migration in the Central Industrial Region, 1861–1905." In *Peasant Economy, Culture, and Politics of European Russia 1800–1921,* edited by Esther Kingston-Mann, Timothy Mixter, and Jeffrey Burds, 52–100. Princeton, NJ: Princeton Univ. Press, 1991.

Çadırcı, Musa. "Anadolu Kentlerinde Mahalle (Osmanlı Dönemi)." In *Tarihten Günümüze Anadolu'da Konut ve Yerleşme,* 257–63. Istanbul: Tarih Vakfı Yurt, 1996.

———. "Tanzimat Döneminde Çıkarılan Men'-i Mürur ve Pasaport Nizamnameleri." *Belgeler* 19 (1993): 173–78.

———. "Tanzimat'ın İlanı Sırasında Anadolu'da İçgüvenlik." *Ankara Üniversitesi DTCF Tarih Araştırmaları Enstitüsü Tarih Araştırmaları Dergisi* 24 (1980): 45–58.

———. "Türkiye'de Muhtarlık Teşkilatının Kurulması Üzerine Bir Araştırma." *Belleten* 135 (1970): 409–20.

Can, Lale. *Spiritual Subjects: Central Asian Pilgrims and the Ottoman Hajj at the End of Empire.* Stanford, CA: Stanford Univ. Press, 2020.

Caplan, Jane, and John Torpey, eds. *Documenting Individual Identity: The Development of State Practices in the Modern World.* Princeton, NJ: Princeton Univ. Press, 2001.

———. Introduction to *Documenting Individual Identity: The Development of State Practices in the Modern World,* edited by Jane Caplan and John Torpey, 1–12. Princeton, NJ: Princeton Univ. Press, 2001.

Chang, Gordon C., and Hugh B. Mehan. "Discourse in a Religious Mode: The Bush Administration's Discourse in the War on Terrorism and Its Challenges." *Pragmatics* 16 (2006): 1–23.

Collins, Randall. "Mann's Transformation of the Classic Sociological Traditions." In *An Anatomy of Power: The Social Theory of Michael Mann*, edited by John A. Hall and Ralph Schroeder, 19–32. Cambridge: Cambridge Univ. Press, 2006.

Cora, Yaşar Tolga. "The Market as a Means of Post-violence Recovery: Armenians and Oriental Carpets in the Late Ottoman Empire (c. 1890s–1910s)." *International Review of Social History* 66, no. 2 (2021): 217–41.

———. "Transforming Erzurum/Karin: The Social and Economic History of a Multi-ethnic Ottoman City in the Nineteenth Century." PhD diss., Univ. of Chicago, 2016.

Corey, Robin. *Fear: The History of a Political Idea*. Oxford: Oxford Univ. Press, 2004.

Çorlu, Axel. "Anarchists and Anarchism in the Ottoman Empire, 1850–1917." In *History from Below: A Tribute in Memory of Donald Quataert*, edited by Selim Karahasanoğlu and Deniz C. Demir, 551–83. Istanbul: Istanbul Bilgi ÜniversitesiYayınları, 2016.

Cörüt, İlker. "Social Rationality of Lower Class Criminal Practices in the Late Nineteenth Century İstanbul." MA thesis, Boğaziçi Univ., 2005.

Dadrian, Vahakn N. *The History of the Armenian Genocide: Ethnic Conflict from the Balkans to Anatolia to the Caucasus*. New York: Berghahn, 1997.

Daflem, Mathieu. "International Police Cooperation in North America." In *International Police Cooperation: A World Perspective*, edited by D. J. Koenig and D. K. Das, 71–98. Lanham, MD: Lexington, 2001.

———. "International Policing in 19th-Century Europe: The Police Union of German States, 1851–1866." *International Criminal Justice Review* 6 (1996): 36–57.

———. *Policing World Society: Historical Foundations of International Police Cooperation*. New York: Oxford Univ. Press, 2002.

———. "Wild Beasts without Nationality: The Uncertain Origins of Interpol, 1889–1910." In *Handbook of Transnational Crime and Justice*, edited by Philip Reichel, 275–85. Thousand Oaks, CA: Sage, 2005.

Daly, Jonathan W. *Autocracy under Siege: Security Police and Opposition in Russia 1866–1905*. DeKalb: Northern Illinois Univ. Press, 1998.

Darling, Linda T. "'Do Justice, Do Justice, for That Is Paradise': Middle Eastern Advice for Indian Muslim Rulers." *Comparative Studies of South Asia, Africa and the Middle East* 1–2 (2003): 3–19.

———. "Islamic Empires, the Ottoman Empire and the Circle of Justice." *Comparative Studies in Society and History* 49 (2007): 329–57.

Davis, Janifer. "Urban Policing and Its Objects: Comparative Themes in England and France in the Second Half of the 19th Century." In *Policing Western Europe: Politics, Professionalism and Public Order 1850–1940*, edited by Clive Emsley and Barbara Weinberger, 1–17. Westport, CT: Greenwood Press, 1991.

Dean, Mitchell. *Governmentality: Power and Rule in Modern Society*. London: Sage, 1999.

Demirel, Fatmagül. *II. Abdülhamid Döneminde Sansür*. Istanbul: Bağlam, 2007.

———. "II. Abdülhamid Dönemi Tiyatro Sansürü: . . . Ve Perdeler Sansürle Açıldı." *Toplumsal Tarih* 63 (1999): 36–43.

Deringil, Selim. "2. Abdülhamid Dönemi Osmanlı İmparatorluğu'nda Simgesel ve Törensel Doku: Görünmeden Görünmek." In *Simgeden Millete 2. Abdülhamid'den Mustafa Kemal'e Devlet ve Millet*, 53–94. Istanbul: İletişim, 2009.

———. *Conversion and Apostasy in the Late Ottoman Empire*. Cambridge: Cambridge Univ. Press, 2012.

———. "Geç Dönem Osmanlı İmparatorluğu'nda Ermeni Sorunu Çalışmak ya da Belgenin Gırtalığını Sıkmak." In *Simgeden Millete 2. Abdülhamid'den Mustafa Kemal'e Devlet ve Millet*, 219–48. Istanbul: İletişim, 2009.

———. "Osmanlı İmparatorluğu'nda Geleneğin İcadı, Muhayyel Cemaat (Tasarlanmış Topluluk) ve Pan-İslamizm." In *Simgeden Millete 2. Abdülhamid'den Mustafa Kemal'e Devlet ve Millet*, 19–52. Istanbul: İletişim, 2009.

———. *Simgeden Millete, 2. Abdülhamid'den Mustafa Kemal'e Devlet ve Millet*. Istanbul: İletişim, 2009.

———. "'They Live in a State of Nomadism and Savagery': The Late Ottoman Empire and the Post-colonial Debate." *Comparative Studies in Society and History* 43 (2003): 311–42.

———. "The Turks and 'Europe': The Argument from History." *Middle Eastern Studies* 43, no. 5 (Sept. 2007): 709–23.

———. *The Well Protected Domains: Ideology and the Legitimation of Power in the Ottoman Empire 1876–1909*. London: I. B. Tauris, 2011.

Dillon, Michael, and Luis Lobo-Guerrero. "Biopolitics of Security in the 21st Century: An Introduction." *Review of International Studies* 34 (2008): 265–92.

Dorev, Pancho. *Dokumenti za Bălgarskata Istoriya: Dokumenti iz Turkskitje Dărzhavni Arkhivi*. Sofia: Bălgarskata Akademija na Naukitje, 1940.

Düstur. Tertip 1, addendum 4. Dersaadet: Matbaa-ı Amire, 1302 (1884–85).

Düstur. Tertip 1, vol. 1. Istanbul: Matbaa-ı Amire, 1289 (1872–73).

Düstur. Tertip 1, vol. 3. Istanbul: Matbaa-ı Amire, n.d.

Düstur. Tertip 1, vol. 5: *1883–1888*. Ankara: Ankara Başvekalet Matbaası, 1939.

(4,7)*Düstur*. Tertip 1, vol. 6: *1887–1890*. Ankara: Ankara Başvekalet Matbaası, 1939.

Düstur, Zeyl-i Sâni. Istanbul: Mahmud Bey Matbaası, [1299] 1881–82.

Eldem, Edhem. "26 Ağustos 1896 'Banka Vak'ası' and 'Ermeni Olayları.'" *Tarih ve Toplum: Yeni Yaklaşımlar* 5 (2007): 114–214.

Eldem, Edhem, Daniel Goffman, and Bruce Masters, eds. *Doğu İle Batı Arasında Osmanlı Kenti: Halep, İzmir ve İstanbul*. Istanbul: Tarih Vakfı Yurt, 2003.

Emerson, Donald. *Matternich and the Political Police: Security and Subversion in the Habsburg Monarchy (1815–1830)*. Leiden: Martinus Nijhoff, 1968.

Emsley, Clive. *The English Police: A Political and Social History*. London: Longman, 1996.

———. "The French Police in the 19th Century." *History Today* 32 (1981): 23–24.

Emsley, Clive, and Barbara Weinberger. Introduction to *Policing Western Europe: Politics, Professionalism and Public Order 1850–1940*, edited by Clive Emsley and Barbara Weinberger, vi–xxv. Westport, CT: Greenwood Press, 1991.

———, eds. *Policing Western Europe: Politics, Professionalism and Public Order 1850–1940*. Westport, CT: Greenwood Press, 1991.

Ergin, Osman Nuri. "İhtisab Ağalığı Nizamnamesi Evahir-i Muharrem 1242." In *Mecelle-i Umur-i Belediye*, 1:328–49. Istanbul: İstanbul Büyükşehir Belediyesi Kültür İşleri Daire Başkanlığı, 1995.

———. "Polis Nizamı." In *Mecelle-i Umur-ı Belediye*, 2:875–78. Istanbul: İstanbul Büyükşehir Belediyesi Kültür İşleri Daire Başkanlığı, 1999.

Ergut, Ferdan. *Modern Devlet ve Polis, Osmanlı'dan Cumhuriyet'e Toplumsal Denetimin Diyalektiği*. Istanbul: İletişim, 2004.

———. "Policing the Poor in the Late Ottoman Empire." *Middle Eastern Studies* 38 (2002): 149–64.

———. "State and Social Control: The Police in the Late Ottoman Empire and the Early Republican Turkey, 1839–1939." PhD diss., New School for Social Research, 1999.

Evans, Richard J. "Introduction: The 'Dangerous Classes' in Germany from the Middle Ages to the Twentieth Century." In *The German Underworld: Deviants and Outcasts in German History*, edited by Richard J. Evans, 1–28. London: Routledge, 2015.

Fahrmeir, Andreas. "Governments and Forgers: Passports in the 19th Century Europe." In *Documenting Individual Identity: The Development of State Practices in the Modern World*, edited by Jane Caplan and John Torpey, 218–34. Princeton, NJ: Princeton Univ. Press, 2001.

Fortna, Benjamin C. *Imperial Classroom: Islam, the State, and Education in the Late Ottoman Empire*. Oxford: Oxford Univ. Press, 2002.

Foucault, Michel. *Discipline and Punish: The Birth of the Prison*. Translated by Alan Sheridan. New York: Random House, 1977.

———. "Governmentality." In *The Foucault Effect: Studies in Governmentality*, edited by Graham Burchell, Colin Gordon, and Peter Miller, 87–105. Chicago: Univ. of Chicago Press, 1991.

———. *Territory, Security: Lectures at the Collége de France 1977–1978*. Translated by Graham Burchell. Edited by Michel Senellart. Basingstoke, UK: Palgrave McMillan, 2007.

Freitag, Ulrike, Malte Fuhrmann, Nora Lafi, and Florian Riedler, eds. *The City in the Ottoman Empire: Migration and the Making of Urban Modernity*. London: Routledge, 2011.

Frierson, Elizabeth B. "Mirrors Out, Mirrors In: Domestication and Rejection of the Foreign in Late-Ottoman Women's Magazines (1875–1908)." In *Women, Patronage, and Self-Representation in Islamic Societies*, edited by D. Fairchild Ruggles, 177–204. Albany: State Univ. of New York Press, 2000.

———. "Unimagined Communities: State, Press, and Gender in the Hamidian Era." PhD diss., Princeton Univ., 1996.

———. "Unimagined Communities: Women and Education in the Late Ottoman Empire, 1876–1909." *Critical Matrix* 9 (1995): 55–90.

Fuhrmann, Malte. *Port Cities of the Eastern Mediterranean: Urban Culture in the Late Ottoman Empire*. Cambridge: Cambridge Univ. Press, 2020.

Fuhrmann, Malte, and Vangelis Kechriotis, eds. "The Late Ottoman Port-Cities and Their Inhabitants: Subjectivity, Urbanity, and Conflicting Orders." Special issue of *Mediterranean Historical Review* 24, no. 2 (2009).

Gambetti, Zeynep. "Foucault'da Disiplin Toplumu: Güvenlik Toplumu Ayrımı." *Mesele*, no. 20 (2008): 43–46.

Georgeon, François. *Abdulhamid II: Le sultan calife*. Paris: Fayard, 2003.

Giddens, Anthony. *The Nation-State and Violence*. Berkeley: Univ. of California Press, 1987.

Glenny, Misha. *Balkans 1804–1999: Nationalism, War and the Great Powers*. London: Genta, 1999.

Gölbaşı, Edip. "The Official Conceptualization of the Anti-Armenian Riots of 1895–1897." *Études arméniennes contemporaines* 10 (2018): 33–62.

Goodwin, Jeff. *No Other Way Out: States and Revolutionary Movements, 1945–1991*. Cambridge: Cambridge Univ. Press, 2001.

Gorski, Philip S. "Mann's Theory of Ideological Power: Sources, Applications and Elaborations." In *An Anatomy of Power: The Social Theory of Michael Mann*, edited by John A. Hall and Ralph Schroeder, 101–34. Cambridge: Cambridge Univ. Press, 2005.

Graff, Harvey. "Crime and Punishment in the Nineteenth Century: A New Look at the Criminal." *Journal of Interdisciplinary History* 3 (1977): 477–91.

Grandits, Hannes. *The End of Ottoman Rule in Bosnia: Conflicting Agencies and Imperial Appropriations*. London: Routledge, 2022.

Gratian, Chris. *The Unsettled Plain: An Environmental History of the Late Ottoman Frontier*. Palo Alto, CA: Stanford Univ. Press, 2022.

Grob-Fitzgibbon, Benjamin. "From the Dagger to the Bomb: Karl Heinzen and the Evolution of Political Terror." *Terrorism and Political Violence* 16, no. 1 (2004): 97–115.

Guéno, Vanessa. "S'identifier à l'aube de l'état civil (*nufûs*): Les justiciables devant le tribunal civil de Homs (Syrie Centrale) à la fin du XIXe siècle." *Revue des mondes musulmans et de la Méditerranée*, no. 127 (2010): 193–211.

Gürsel, Z. D. "Looking Together as Method Encounters with Ottoman Armenian Expatriation Photographs." *Visual Anthropology Review* (2023).

Gutman, David E. *The Politics of Armenian Migration to North America, 1885–1915: Sojourners, Smugglers and Dubious Citizens*. Edinburgh: Edinburgh Univ. Press, 2019.

Hall, John A., and Ralph Schroeder, eds. *An Anatomy of Power: The Social Theory of Michael Mann*. Cambridge: Cambridge Univ. Press, 2006.

Hanley, Will. *Identifying with Nationality: Europeans, Ottomans, and Egyptians in Alexandria*. New York: Columbia Univ. Press, 2017.

———. "What Ottoman Nationality Was and Was Not." *Journal of the Ottoman and Turkish Studies Association* 3, no. 2: 277–98.

Hanssen, Jens. "Public Morality and Marginality in Fin-de-Siécle Beirut." In *Outside In: Marginality in the Modern Middle East*, edited by Eugene Rogan, 183–90. London: I. B. Tauris, 2002.

Hanssen, Jens, Thomas Philipp, and Stefan Weber, eds. *The Empire in the City: Arab Provincial Cities in the Ottoman Empire*. Würzburg, Germany: Ergon, 2002.

Herbert, Ulrich. *A History of Foreign Labor in Germany, 1880–1980: Season Workers/Forced Laborers/Guest Workers*. Ann Arbor: Univ. of Michigan Press, 1990.

Herzog, Christoph. "Migration and the State: On Ottoman Regulations Concerning Migration since the Age of Mahmud II." In *The City in the Ottoman Empire: Migration and the Making of Urban Modernity*, edited by Ulrike Freitag, Malte Fuhrmann, Nora Lafi, and Florian Riedler, 117–35. London: Routledge, 2011.

———. "Nineteenth-Century Baghdad through Ottoman Eyes." In *The Empire in the City: Arab Provincial Cities in the Ottoman Empire*, edited by Jens Hanssen, Thomas Philipp, and Stefan Weber, 311–28. Würzburg, Germany: Ergon, 2002.

Hobsbawm, Eric. *The Age of Empire 1875–1914*. London: Weidenfeld and Nicolson, 1987.

Hüseyin Nazım Paşa. *Ermeni Olayları Tarihi*. Vol. 1. Prepared by Necati Aktaş, Mustafa Oğuz, and Mustafa Küçük. Yayın no. 15. Ankara: T.C. Başbakanlık, Devlet Arşivleri Genel Müdürlüğü Osmanlı Arşivi Daire Başkanlığı, 1994.

———. *Ermeni Olayları Tarihi*. Vol. 2. Prepared by Necati Aktaş, Mustafa Oğuz, and Mustafa Küçük. Yayın no. 15. Ankara: T.C. Başbakanlık, Devlet Arşivleri Genel Müdürlüğü Osmanlı Arşivi Daire Başkanlığı, 1994.

———. *Hatıralarım: Ermeni Olaylarının İçyüzü*. Edited by Tahsin Yıldırım. Istanbul: Selis Kitaplar, 2007.

İleri, Nurçin. "Rule, Misconduct and Dysfunction: The Police Forces in Theory and Practice in Fin de Siècle Istanbul." *Comparative Studies of South Asia, Africa, and the Middle East* 34, no. 1 (Mar. 2014): 147–59.

İnalcık, Halil. "İstanbul." In *The Encyclopedia of Islam*, 4:224–48. Leiden: Brill, 1978.

İslamoğlu-İnan, Huri. "Mukayeseli Tarih Yazımı İçin Bir Öneri: Hukuk, Mülkiyet, Meşruiyet." *Toplum ve Bilim* 62 (1993): 19–33.

Jelavich, Barbara. *The History of the Balkans*. Vol. 1: *Eighteenth and Nineteenth Centuries*. Cambridge: Cambridge Univ. Press, 1985.

Jensen, Richard Bach. *The Battle against Anarchist Terrorism: An International History, 1878–1934*. Cambridge: Cambridge Univ. Press, 2014.

————. "Daggers, Rifles, and Dynamite: Anarchist Terrorism in Nineteenth Century Europe." *Terrorism and Political Violence* 16, no. 1 (2004): 116–53.

————. "The International Anti-anarchist Conference of 1898 and the Origins of Interpol." *Journal of Contemporary History* 16, no. 2 (Apr. 1981): 323–47.

————. "The International Campaign against Anarchist Terrorism, 1880–1930s." *Terrorism and Political Violence* 21 (2009): 89–109.

Jessop, Bob. *State Theory: Putting the Capitalist State in Its Place.* Cambridge: Polity, 1990.

Johnson, Richard J. "Zagranihnaia Agentura: The Tzarist Political Police in Europe." In *Police Forces in History*, edited by George L. Mosse, 221–42. London: Sage, 1975.

Jongerden, Joost, and Jelle Verheij, eds. *Social Relations in Ottoman Diyarbekir, 1870–1915.* Leiden: Brill, 2012.

Joseph, Anne M. "Anthropometry, the Police Expert, and the Deptford Murders: The Contested Introduction of Fingerprinting for the Identification of Criminals in Late Victorian and Edwardian Britain." In *Documenting Individual Identity: The Development of State Practices in the Modern World*, edited by Jane Caplan and John Torpey, 164–83. Princeton, NJ: Princeton Univ. Press, 2001.

Journal of Genocide Research. "Book Forum: Benny Morris and Dror Ze'evi, *The Thirty-Year Genocide: Turkey's Destruction of Its Christian Minorities, 1894–1924.*" 22, no. 4 (2020): 533–66.

Karaca, Ali. *Anadolu Islahatı ve Ahmet Şakir Paşa (1838–1899).* Istanbul: Eren, 1993.

Karal, Enver Ziya. *Osmanlı Tarihi.* Vol. 8. Ankara: Türk Tarih Kurumu Basımevi, 1983.

Karpat, Kemal H. *Ottoman Population 1830–1914.* Madison: Univ. of Wisconsin Press, 1985.

Kechriotis, Vangelis. "Postcolonial Criticism Encounters Late Ottoman Studies." *Historein* 13 (2013): 39–46.

Kévorkian, Raymond. *The Armenian Genocide: A Complete History.* London: I. B. Tauris, 2011.

————. "The Armenian Population of Sassoun and the Demographic Consequences of the 1894 Massacres." *Armenian Review* 47 (2001). At http://journals.openedition.org/eac/2789 and https://doi.org/10.4000/eac.2789.

Keyder, Çağlar, Y. Eyüp Özveren, and Donald Quataert, eds. *Port-Cities of the Eastern Mediterranean, 1800–1914.* Binghamton, UK: Fernand Braudel Center, Binghamton Univ., 1993.

Khuri-Makdisi, Ilham. *The Eastern Mediterranean and the Making of Global Radicalism, 1860–1914.* Oakland: Univ. of California Press, 2013.

Kieser, Hans-Lukas. *Der verpasste Friede: Mission, Ethnie und Staat in den Ostprovinzen der Türkei 1839–1938.* Zürich: Chronos, 2000.

Kırlı, Cengiz. "İrvanyalılar, Hüseyin Paşa ve Tasvir-i Zulüm." *Toplumsal Tarih* 195 (2010): 12–22.

———. "The Struggle over Space: Coffeehouses of Ottoman Istanbul, 1780–1845." PhD diss., Binghamton Univ., 2000.

Klein, Janet. *The Margins of Empire: Kurdish Militias in the Ottoman Tribal Zone.* Stanford, CA: Stanford Univ. Press, 2011.

———. "Power in the Periphery: The Hamidiye Light Cavalry and the Struggle over Ottoman Kurdistan, 1890–1914." PhD diss., Princeton Univ., 2002.

Kloosterman, Jap. "Hidden Centres: The Rise and Fall of the Secret Societies." Paper presented at the conference "Zentren und Peripherien der europäischen Wissensordnung vom 15. bis zum 20. Jahrhundert," German Historical Institute, Moscow, Sept. 24–26, 2009. At https://brewminate.com/a-history-of-secret-societies/.

Koçu, Reşat Ekrem. *İstanbul Tulumbacıları: Yangın Var.* Istanbul: Ana Yayınevi, 1981.

Küçük, Cevdet. *Osmanlı Diplomasisinde Ermeni Meselesinin Ortaya Çıkışı 1878–1897.* Istanbul: Türk Dünyası Araştırmaları Vakfı, 1985.

Kühn, Thomas. *Empire, Islam, and Politics of Difference: Ottoman Rule in Yemen, 1849–1919.* Leiden: Brill, 2011.

Kuneralp, Sinan. "Ottoman Diplomacy and the Controversy over the Interpretation of Article 4 of the Turco-American Treaty of 1830." *Turkish Yearbook of International Relations* 31 (2002): 7–20.

Kutluer, İlhan. "Fesad." In *Türkiye Diyanet Vakfı İslam Ansiklopedisi*, 12:421–22. Istanbul: Türkiye Diyanet Vakfı, 1995.

Langer, William. *The Diplomacy of Imperialism 1890–1902.* Cambridge, MA: Harvard Univ. and Radcliffe College, 1935.

Laqueur, Walter. *A History of Terrorism.* 1997. Reprint. Piscataway, NJ: Transaction, 2001.

Levene, Mark. "Creating a Modern 'Zone of Genocide': The Impact of Nation- and State-Formation on Eastern Anatolia, 1878–1923." *Holocaust and Genocide Studies* 12, no. 3 (Winter 1998): 393–433.

Lévy, Noémi. "19. Yüzyılda Osmanlı'da Kamu Düzeni Konusunda Çalışmak: Bibliyografya Üzerine Bir Değerlendirme." In *Osmanlı'da Suç ve Ceza,*

18.–20. Yüzyıllar, edited by Noémi Lévy and Alexandre Toumarkine, 55–67. Istanbul: Tarih Vakfı Yurt, 2007.

———. "Polislikle İlgili Bilgilerin Dolaşım Tarzları: Osmanlı Polisi İçin Fransız Modeli mi?" In *Jandarma ve Polis: Fransız ve Osmanlı Tarihçiliğine Çapraz Bakışlar,* edited by Noémi Lévy, Nadir Özbek, and Alexandre Toumarkine, 146–70. Istanbul: Tarih Vakfı Yurt, 2009.

———. "Yakından Korunan Düzen: 2. Abdülhamid Devrinden 2. Meşruiyet Dönemine Bekçi Örneği." In *Osmanlı'da Suç ve Ceza, 18.–20. Yüzyıllar,* edited by Noémi Lévy and Alexandre Toumarkine, 135–45. Istanbul: Tarih Vakfı Yurt, 2007.

Lévy, Noémi, Nadir Özbek, and Alexandre Toumarkine, eds. *Jandarma ve Polis Fransız ve Osmanlı Tarihçiliğine Çapraz Bakışlar.* Istanbul: Tarih Vakfı Yurt, 2009.

Lévy, Noémi, and Alexandre Toumarkine, eds. *Osmanlı'da Suç ve Ceza, 18.–20. Yüzyıllar.* Istanbul: Tarih Vakfı Yurt, 2007.

Liang, Hsi Huey. *The Rise of Modern Police and the European State System from Matternich to the Second World War.* Cambridge: Cambridge Univ. Press, 1992.

Libaridian, Gerard J. "Revolution and Liberation in the 1892 and 1907 Programs of the Dashnaktsutiun." In *Transcaucasia, Nationalism, and Social Change,* edited by Ronald Grigor Suny, 187–98. Ann Arbor: Univ. of Michigan Press, 1996.

Lohr, Eric. *Russian Citizenship: From Empire to Soviet Union.* Cambridge, MA: Harvard Univ. Press, 2012.

Lucassen, Jan. *Migrant Labour in Europe, 1600–1900: The Drift to the North Sea.* London: Routledge, 1987.

Lucassen, Jan, and Leo Lucassen. Introduction to *Migration, Migration History, History: Old Paradigms and New Perspectives,* edited by Jan Lucassen and Leo Lucassen, 9–40. Bern: Peter Lang, 1999.

———, eds. *Migration, Migration History, History: Old Paradigms and New Perspectives.* Bern: Peter Lang, 1999.

Lucassen, Leo. "Eternal Vagrants? State Formation, Migration, and Travelling Groups in Western-Europe, 1350–1914." In *Migration, Migration History, History: Old Paradigms and New Perspectives,* edited by Jan Lucassen and Leo Lucassen, 225–52. Bern: Peter Lang, 1999.

———. "A Many-Headed Monster: The Evolution of the Passport System in the Netherlands and Germany in the Long 19th Century." In *Documenting Individual Identity: The Development of State Practices in the Modern World,* edited by Jane Caplan and John Torpey, 235–55. Princeton, NJ: Princeton Univ. Press, 2001.

Lüdtke, Alf. *Police and State in Prussia, 1815–1850.* Translated by Pete Burgess. New York: Cambridge Univ. Press, 1989.

Makdisi, Ussama. *The Culture of Sectarianism: Community, History, and Violence in Nineteenth Century Ottoman Lebanon.* Berkeley: Univ. of California Press, 2000.

———. "Ottoman Orientalism." *American Historical Review* 107, no. 3 (2002): 768–96.

———. "Rethinking Ottoman Imperialism: Modernity, Violence and the Cultural Logic of Ottoman Reform." In *The Empire in the City: Arab Provincial Cities in the Ottoman Empire,* edited by Jens Hanssen, Thomas Philipp, and Stefan Weber, 29–48. Würzburg, Germany: Ergon, 2002.

Malatesta, Errico. *Errico Malatesta—His Life and Ideas.* Edited by Vernon Richards. London: Freedom Press, 1965.

Mann, Michael. "The Autonomous Power of the State: Its Origins, Mechanisms and Results." In *War and Capitalism: Studies in Political Sociology,* 185–213. Oxford: Blackwell, 1988.

———. "Ruling Class Strategies and Citizenship." *Sociology* 21 (1988): 339–54.

———. *The Sources of Social Power.* Vol. 1: *A History of Power from the Beginning to A.D. 1760.* 1986. Reprint. Cambridge: Cambridge Univ. Press, 2003.

———. *The Sources of Social Power.* Vol. 2: *A Rise of Classes and Nation-States, 1760–1914.* 1993. Reprint. Cambridge: Cambridge Univ. Press, 1996.

Marenin, Otwin. "Police Performance and State Rule Control and Autonomy in the Exercise of Coercion." *Comparative Politics* 18 (1985): 101–22.

Mayersen, Deborah. "The 1895–1896 Armenian Massacres in Harput: Eyewitness Account." *Études arméniennes contemporaines* 10 (2018): 161–83.

Mazower, Mark. *Salonica, City of Ghosts: Christians, Muslims and Jews (1430–1950).* New York: Knopf, 2005.

McCarthy, Justin, Ömer Turan, and Cemalettin Taşkıran. *Sasun: The History of an 1890s Armenian Revolt.* Salt Lake City: Univ. of Utah Press, 2014.

Merskin, Debra. "The Construction of Arabs as Enemies: Post–September 11 Discourse of George W. Bush." *Mass Communication & Society* 7, no. 2 (2004): 157–79.

Miller, Owen. "Rethinking the Violence in the Sasun Mountains (1893–1894)." *Études arméniennes contemporaines* 10 (2018): 97–123.

———. "Sasun 1894: Mountains, Missionaries and Massacres at the End of the Ottoman Empire." PhD diss., Columbia Univ., 2015.

Minassian, Anahide Ter. "1876–1923 Döneminde Osmanlı İmparatorluğu'nda Sosyalist Hareketin Doğuşunda ve Gelişmesinde Ermeni Topluluğunun Rolü." In *Osmanlı İmparatorluğu'nda Sosyalizm ve Milliyetçilik*, 163–288. Istanbul: İletişim, 1995.

Monkkonen, Eric H. "A Disorderly People? Urban Order in the Nineteenth and Twentieth Centuries." *Journal of American History* 68 (1981): 539–59.

Morris, Benny, and Dror Ze'evi. *The Thirty-Year Genocide: Turkey's Destruction of Its Christian Minorities, 1894–1924*. Cambridge, MA: Harvard Univ. Press, 2019.

Nalbandian, Louise. *The Armenian Revolutionary Movement: The Development of Armenian Political Parties through the Nineteenth Century*. Berkeley: Univ. of California Press, 1963.

Neocleous, Mark. *Imagining the State*. Maidenhead, UK: Open Univ. Press, 2003.

Noiriel, Gerard. *The French Melting Pot: Immigration, Citizenship, and National Identity*. Translated by Geoffrey de Laforcade. Minneapolis: Univ. of Minnesota Press, 1996.

Novak, D. "Anarchism and Individual Terrorism." *Canadian Journal of Economics and Political Science* 20 (1954): 176–84.

Okçabol, Derviş. *Meslek Tarihi*. Ankara: Polis Enstitüsü Neşriyatı, 1939.

Ortaylı, İlber. *İmparatorluğun En Uzun Yüzyılı*. Istanbul: İletişim, 2003.

Osmanlı Belgelerinde Ermeni Amerikan İlişkileri (1839–1895). Vol. 1. Yayın no. 85. Ankara: T.C. Başbakanlık Devlet Arşivleri Genel Müdürlüğü Osmanlı Arşivi Daire Başkanlığı, 2007.

Osmanlı Belgelerinde Ermeni İsyanları (1878–1895). Vol. 1. Yayın no. 95. Ankara: T.C. Başbakanlık Devlet Arşivleri Genel Müdürlüğü Osmanlı Arşivi Daire Başkaanlığı, 2008.

Özbek, Nadir. "Anadolu Islahatı, Ermeni Sorunu ve Vergi Tahsildarlığı, 1895–1908." *Tarih ve Toplum: Yeni Yaklaşımlar* 9 (2009): 59–85.

———. "İkinci Meşrutiyet İstanbul'unda Serseriler ve Dilenciler." *Toplumsal Tarih* 11, no. 64 (1999): 34–43.

———. "Modernite, Tarih ve İdeoloji: II. Abdülhamid Dönemi Tarihçiliği Üzerine Bir Değerlendirme." *Türkiye Araştırmaları Literatür Dergisi* 2 (2004): 71–90.

———. "Osmanlı'dan Günümüze Türkiye'de Sosyal Devlet." *Toplum ve Bilim* 92 (2002): 7–33.

———. "Osmanlı İmparatorluğu'nda İç Güvenlik, Siyaset ve Devlet, 1876–1909." *Türklük Araştırmaları Dergisi* 1 (2004): 59–95.

————. *Osmanlı İmparatorluğu'nda Sosyal Devlet: Siyaset, İktidar ve Meşruiyet.* Istanbul: İletişim, 2002.

————. "Policing the Countryside: Gendarmes of the Late Nineteenth Century Ottoman Empire (1876–1908)." *International Journal of Middle East Studies* 40 (2008): 47–67.

Özdemir, Hazal. "Osmanlı Ermenilerinin Göçünün Fotoğrafını Çekmek." *Toplumsal Tarih* 304 (2019): 82–90.

Özkaya, Yücel. "XVIII. Yüzyılda Çıkarılan Adaletnamelere Göre Türkiye'nin İç Durumu." *Belleten* 38, no. 151 (1974): 445–91.

Öztan, Ramazan Hakkı. "Tools of Revolution: Global Military Surplus, Arms Dealers, and Smugglers in the Late Ottoman Balkans, 1878–1908." *Past & Present* 237, no. 1 (2017): 167–95.

Pamuk, Şevket. "Foreign Trade and Foreign Capital in the Ottoman Empire, 1830–1913." PhD diss., Univ. of California, Berkeley, 1978.

Pasquino, Pasquale. "Theatrum Poiticum: The Geneology of Capital-Police and the State of Prosperity." In *The Foucault Effect Studies in Governmentality*, edited by Graham Burchell, Colin Gordon, and Peter Miller, 105–18. Chicago: Univ. Chicago Press, 1991.

Patyk, Lynn Ellen. "Remembering 'the Terrorism': Sergei Stepniak-Kravchinskii's 'Underground Russia.'" *Slavic Review* 68, no. 4 (2009): 758–81.

Payne, Howard C. *The Police State of Louis Napoléon Bonaparte, 1851–1860.* Seattle: Univ. of Washington Press, 1966.

Perry, Duncan M. *The Politics of Terror: The Macedonian Liberation Movements, 1893–1903.* Ann Arbor: Univ. of Michigan Press, 1988.

Poulantzas, Nicos. *State, Power, Socialism.* London: Verso, 2000.

Quataert, Donald. *Osmanlı Devleti'nde Avrupa İktisadi Yayılımı ve Direniş (1881–1908).* Edited by Sabri Tekay. Ankara: Yurt, 1987.

————. "Osmanlı İmparatorluğu'nda İşgücü Politikası ve Siyaset: Hamallar ve Bab-ı Ali, 1826–1896." *Tarih ve Toplum* 33, no. 6 (1986): 42–47.

————. *Social Disintegraion and Popular Resistance in the Ottoman Empire, 1881–1908: Reactions to European Economic Penetration.* New York: New York Univ. Press, 1983.

Ranasinghe, Prashan. "Vagrancy as a Penal Problem: The Logistics of Administering Punishment in Late-Nineteenth-Century Canada." *Journal of Historical Sociology* 25, no. 4 (2012): 531–51.

Reinke, Herbert. "'Armed as If for a War': The State, the Military and the Professionalisation of the Prussian Police in Imperial Germany." In *Policing*

Western Europe: Politics, Professionalism and Public Order 1850–1940, edited by Clive Emsley and Barbara Weinberger, 55–73. Westport, CT: Greenwood Press, 1991.

Report of the Commissioners Appointed to Enquire into the Prison and Reformatory System of Ontario, 1891. Toronto: Warwick & Sons, 1891. At https://babel .hathitrust.org/cgi/pt?id=aeu.ark:/13960/t53f5s583&view=1up&seq=272.

Riedler, Florian. "Armenian Labour Migration to Istanbul and the Migration Crisis of the 1890's." In *The City in the Ottoman Empire: Migration and the Making of Urban Modernity*, edited by Ulrike Freitag, Malte Fuhrmann, Nora Lafi, and Florian Rielder, 160–76. London: Routledge, 2011.

————. "Public People: Seasonal Work Migrants in Nineteenth Century İstanbul." In *Public Istanbul: Spaces and Spheres of the Urban*, edited by Frank Eckardt and Kathrin Wildner, 233–53. Bielefeld, Germany: Transcript, 2008.

Riedler, Florian, and Stefan Rohdewald. "Migration and Mobility in a Transottoman Context." *Radovi-Zavoda za hrvatsku povijest* 51, no. 1(2019): 201–19.

Robertson, Craig. "Four Documents, a Non-citizen, and a Diplomatic Controversy: The Documentation of Identity in the Mid–Nineteenth Century." *Journal of Historical Sociology* 22, no. 4 (2009): 476–96.

Robin, Corey. *Fear: The History of a Political Idea*. Oxford: Oxford Univ. Press, 2004.

Rokkan, Stein. *State Formation, Nation Building, and Mass Politics in Europe: The Theory of Stein Rokkan*. Oxford: Oxford Univ. Press, 1999.

Rubin, Barry, and Judith Colp Rubin. *Chronologies of Modern Terrorism*. Armonk, NY: M.E. Sharpe, 2008.

Ruggiero, Kristin. "Fingerprinting and the Argentine Plan for Universal Identification in the Late Nineteenth and Early Twentieth Centuries." In *Documenting Individual Identity: The Development of State Practices in the Modern World*, edited by Jane Caplan and John Torpey, 184–94. Princeton, NJ: Princeton Univ. Press, 2001.

Rusche, Georg, and Otto Kirchemmer. *Punishment and Social Structure*. New York: Columbia Univ. Press, 1939.

Said, Edward W. *Orientalism*. New York: Pantheon, 1978.

Salter, Mark B. *Rights of Passage: The Passport in International Relations*. Boulder, CO: Lynne Rienner, 2003.

Saydam, Abdullah. "Kamu Hizmeti Yaptırma ve Suçu Önleme Yöntemi Olarak Osmanlılarda Kefalet Usulü." *Tarih ve Toplum* 28, no. 164 (1997): 4–12.

Şaşmaz, Musa. *British Policy and the Application of Reforms for the Armenians in Eastern Anatolia*. Ankara: Türk Tarih Kurumu, 2000.

Schmidt, Carl. *Siyasal Kavramı*. Translated by Ece Göztepe. Istanbul: Metis, 2006.

Schroeder, Ralph. "Introduction: The IEMP Model and Its Critics." In *An Anatomy of Power: The Social Theory of Michael Mann*, edited by John A. Hall and Ralph Schroeder, 1–17. Cambridge: Cambridge Univ. Press, 2005.

Scott, James C. *Seeing Like a State: How Certain Schemes to Improve the Human Condition Have Failed*. New Haven, CT: Yale Univ. Press, 1998.

Sefer, Akın. "The Docks of the Revolution: The Struggles of the Port Workers of Istanbul in the Late Nineteenth and Early Twentieth Century." MA thesis, Boğaziçi Univ., 2009.

Şen, Hasan. "The Transformation of Punishment and the Birth of Prison in the Ottoman Empire." MA thesis, Boğaziçi Univ., 2005.

Shaw, Stanford J. "The Ottoman Census System and Population, 1831–1914." *International Journal of Middle East Studies* 9, no. 3 (1978): 325–38.

———. "Sultan Abdülhamid II: Last Man of the Tanzimat." In *Tanzimat'ın 150: Yıldönümü Uluslarası Sempozyumu (Bildiriler)*, 179–97. Ankara: Millî Kütüphane, 1989.

Shaw, Stanford J., and Ezel Kural Shaw. *History of the Ottoman Empire and Modern Turkey*. Vol. 2. London: Cambridge Univ. Press, 1977.

Şimşir, Bilal, ed. *British Documents on Ottoman Armenians*. Vol. 2: *1880–1890*. Ankara: TTK, 1989.

Sipahi, Ali. "Narrative Construction in the 1895 Massacres in Harput: The Coming and Disappearance of the Kurds." *Études arméniennes contemporaines* 10 (2018): 63–95.

Slack, Paul A. "Vagrants and Vagrancy in England, 1598–1664." *Economic History Review* 27 (1974): 360–79.

Somel, Selçuk Akşin. "Osmanlı Ermenileri'nde Kültür Modernleşmesi, Cemaat Okulları ve Abdülhamid Rejimi." *Tarih ve Toplum: Yeni Yaklaşımlar* 5 (2007): 71–92.

Spencer, Elaine Glovka. *Police and the Social Order in German Cities: The Düsseldorf District 1848–1914*. DeKalb: Northern Illinois Univ. Press, 1992.

Stark, David, and Laszlo Bruszt. *Post-socialist Pathways: Transforming Politics and Property in East Central Europe*. Cambridge: Cambridge Univ. Press, 1998.

Stead, Philip John. *The Police of Paris*. London: Stapless Press, 1957.

Steinwedel, Charles. "Making Social Groups, One Person at a Time: The Identification of Individuals by Estate, Religious Confession, and Ethnicity in Late Imperial Russia." In *Documenting Individual Identity: The Development of*

State Practices in the Modern World, edited by Jane Caplan and John Torpey, 67–82. Princeton, NJ: Princeton Univ. Press, 2001.

Storch, Robert D. "The Policeman as Domestic Missionary: Urban Discipline and Popular Culture in Northern England, 1850–1880." *Journal of Social History* 9, no. 4 (1976): 481–502.

Sultan İkinci Abdülhamid Han'a Yapılan Suikastın Tahkikat Raporu. Transliteration by Raşit Gündoğdu. Edited by Ömer Faruk Yılmaz. Istanbul: Çamlıca Basım Yayın, 2007.

Thompson, E. P. *Customs in Common*. London: Merlin Press, 1991.

Tilly, Charles. *Coercion, Capital, and European States, AD 990–1990*. Cambridge: Blackwell, 1990.

Tokay, Gül. *Makedonya Sorunu Jön Türk İhtilalinin Kökenleri (1903–1908)*. Istanbul: Afa, 1996.

Tongur, Hikmet. *Türkiye'de Genel Kolluk*. Ankara: Kanaat Basımevi, 1946.

Torpey, John. "Coming and Going: On the State Monopolization of the Legitimate 'Means of Movement.'" *Sociological Theory* 16, no. 3 (1988): 239–59.

———. *The Invention of the Passport: Surveillance, Citizenship and the State*. Cambridge: Cambridge Univ. Press, 2000.

———. "Revolution of Freedom of Movement: An Analysis of Passport Controls in the French, Russian and Chinese Revolutions." *Theory and Society* 26, no. 6 (1997): 837–68.

Trentmann, Frank. "The 'British' Sources of Social Power: Reflections on History, Sociology, and Intellectual Biography." In *An Anatomy of Power: The Social Theory of Michael Mann*, edited by John A. Hall and Ralph Schroeder, 285–305. Cambridge: Cambridge Univ. Press, 2005.

Tunaya, Tarık Zafer. "1876 Kanun-i Esasisi ve Türkiye'de Anayasa Geleneği." In *Tanzimattan Cumhuriyet'e Türkiye Ansiklopedisi*, 1:27–39. Istanbul: İletişim, 1985.

Tuncer, Harun, ed. *Sultan Abdülhamid Han'a Yapılan Suikastın Perde Arkası*. Istanbul: Çamlıca Basım, 2010.

Türker, Orhan. "Selanik'te 28–29 Nisan 1903 Olayları." *Tarih ve Toplum* 182 (1999): 27–30.

Turna, Nalan. *19 yy dan ve 20 yy a Osmanlı Topraklarında Seyahat Göç ve Asayiş Belgeleri Mürûr Tezkereleri*. Istanbul: Kaknüs, 2013.

Uras, Esat. *Tarihte Ermeniler ve Ermeni Meselesi*. Istanbul: Belge, 1987.

Verheij, Jelle. "'The Year of the Firman': The 1895 Massacres in Hizan and Şirvan (Bitlis Vilayet)." *Études arméniennes contemporaines* 10 (2018): 125–59.

Wadauer, Sigrid. "Establishing Distinctions: Unemployment versus Vagrancy in Austria from the Late Nineteenth Century to 1938." *International Review of Social History* 56 (2011): 31–70.

Weber, Max. *Economy and Society*. Edited by Guenther Roth and Claus Wittich. Berkeley: Univ. of California Press, 2004.

Weinberger, Barbara. "Are the Police Professionals? An Historical Account of the British Police Institution." In *Policing Western Europe: Politics, Professionalism and Public Order 1850–1940*, edited by Clive Emsley and Barbara Weinberger, 74–89. Westport, CT: Greenwood Press, 1991.

Whitehead, Cameron Ean Alfred. "The Bulgarian Horrors: Culture and the International History of the Great Eastern Crisis, 1876–1878." PhD diss., Univ. of British Columbia, 2014.

Yılmaz, İlkay. "Anti-anarchism and Security Perceptions during the Hamidian Era." *Zapruder World* 1 (Spring 2014). At https://zapruderworld.org/journal/past-volumes/volume-1/anti-anarchism-and-security-perceptions-during-the-hamidian-era/.

———. "Conspiracy, International Police Cooperation and the Fight against Anarchism in the Late Ottoman Empire (1878–1908)." In *Age of Rogues:_ Rebels, Revolutionaries and Racketeers at the Frontiers of Empires*, edited by Alp Yenen and Ramazan Hakkı Öztan, 208–34. Edinburgh: Edinburgh Univ. Press, 2021.

———. "Governing the Armenian Question through Passports in the Late Ottoman Empire (1876–1908)." *Journal of Historical Sociology* 32, no. 4 (2019): 388–403.

———. "The Ottoman State, Police Photographs and Anthropometry." *Journal of Photography*, no. 31 (2019): 90–100.

———. "Propaganda by the Deed and Hotel Registration Regulations in the Late Ottoman Empire." *Journal of the Ottoman and Turkish Studies Association* 4, no. 1 (May 2017): 137–56.

Yosmaoğlu, İpek. *Blood Ties: Religion, Violence, and the Politics of Nationhood in Ottoman Macedonia*. Ithaca, NY: Cornell Univ. Press, 2014.

Zarinebaf, Fariba. *Crime and Punishment in Istanbul 1700–1800*. Berkeley: Univ. of California Press, 2010.

Zonaro, Fausto. *Abdülhamid'in Hükümdarlığında 20 Yıl: Fausto Zonaro'nun Hatıraları ve Eserleri*. Translated by Turan Alptekin and Lotto Romano. Edited by Cesare Mario Trevigne. Istanbul: Yapı Kredi, 2008.

Zürcher, Erik J. *Turkey. A Modern History*. London: I. B. Tauris, 1993.

Index

İlkay Yılmaz is currently a Deutsche Forschungsgemeinschaft-funded senior researcher in the Division of Modern History of the Friedrich-Meinecke-Institut at the Freie Universität Berlin. She was an Einstein Fellow in the Division of Modern History January 2020–March 2022 and a research fellow in the research program "Europe in the Middle East—The Middle East in Europe" (EUME) in 2020–21. She was a research fellow at the Leibniz-Zentrum Moderner Orient (Berlin) in 2014–15 and 2017–19. She worked as an assistant professor at Istanbul University from 2014 to 2016 and as a research assistant at Istanbul University in 2005–13 during her master and PhD studies. She was a visiting PhD candidate with a TUBITAK scholarship at Leiden University in 2009–10. She has conducted research on passport history, interimperial collaboration on policing, public order, state formation, security history, and history of violence in the Ottoman Empire during the nineteenth and twentieth centuries.

www.ingramcontent.com/pod-product-compliance
Lightning Source LLC
Chambersburg PA
CBHW021109270326
41929CB00009B/803